THE CAMBRIDGE COMPANION TO
AUGUSTINE'S *CONFESSIONS*

This *Cambridge Companion* serves as an authoritative guide to Augustine's *Confessions* – a literary classic and one of the most important theological/philosophical works of Late Antiquity. Bringing together new essays by leading scholars, the volume first examines the composition of the text, including its structure, genre, and intended audience. Subsequent essays explore a range of themes and concepts, such as God, creation, sin, grace, happiness, and interiority, among others. The final section of the *Companion* deals with its historical relevance. It provides sample essays on the reception history of the *Confessions*. These essays demonstrate how each generation reads the *Confessions* in light of current questions and circumstances, and how the text continues to remain relevant and raise new questions.

TARMO TOOM is Faculty Member of Georgetown University and a Fellow at John Leland Center for Theological Studies. Among other publications, he has edited *Patristic Theories of Biblical Interpretation* (Cambridge University Press, 2016) and *Augustine in Context* (Cambridge University Press, 2017).

D1457452

CAMBRIDGE COMPANIONS TO RELIGION

This is a series of companions to major topics and key figures in theology and religious studies. Each volume contains specially commissioned chapters by international scholars, which provide an accessible and stimulating introduction to the subject for new readers and nonspecialists.

(continued after Index)

THE CAMBRIDGE COMPANION TO

AUGUSTINE'S
CONFESSIONS

Edited by

Tarmo Toom
Georgetown University

CAMBRIDGE
UNIVERSITY PRESS

University Printing House, Cambridge CB2 8BS, United Kingdom

One Liberty Plaza, 20th Floor, New York, NY 10006, USA

477 Williamstown Road, Port Melbourne, VIC 3207, Australia

314–321, 3rd Floor, Plot 3, Splendor Forum, Jasola District Centre,
New Delhi – 110025, India

79 Anson Road, #06–04/06, Singapore 079906

Cambridge University Press is part of the University of Cambridge.

It furthers the University's mission by disseminating knowledge in the pursuit of
education, learning, and research at the highest international levels of excellence.

www.cambridge.org
Information on this title: www.cambridge.org/9781108491860
DOI: 10.1017/9781108672405

First published 2020

Printed in the United Kingdom by TJ International Ltd. Padstow, Cornwall

A catalogue record for this publication is available from the British Library.

ISBN 978-1-108-49186-0 Hardback
ISBN 978-1-108-44981-6 Paperback

Contents

Contributors

Notker Baumann is Visiting Professor of Early Church History, Patristics, and Studies of the Eastern Church, University of Erfurt, Germany

Jason David BeDuhn is Professor of the Comparative Study of Religions, Northern Arizona University, USA

Anne-Isabelle Bouton-Touboulic is Professor of Latin Language and Literature, University of Lille, France

Sarah Catherine Byers is Associate Professor of Philosophy, Boston College, MA, USA

Phillip Cary is Professor of Philosophy and Scholar in Residence at the Templeton Honors College, Eastern University, PA, USA

Giovanni Catapano is Associate Professor of Medieval Philosophy in the Department of Philosophy, Sociology, Pedagogy, and Applied Psychology at the University of Padua, Italy

Volker Henning Drecoll is Professor of Church History, University of Tübingen, Germany

Matthew Drever is Associate Professor of Religion, University of Tulsa, OK, USA

Katrin Ettenhuber is Fellow and Director of Studies in English, Pembroke College, University of Cambridge, UK

Paul van Geest is Professor of Church History and History of Theology, Tilburg University, the Netherlands

Carolyn Hammond is Dean and Director of Studies in Theology, Gonville & Caius, University of Cambridge, UK

Lenka Karfíková is Professor of Philosophy, Charles University, Czech Republic

Annemaré Kotzé is Associate Professor in the Department of Ancient Studies, Stellenbosch University, South Africa

Johannes van Oort is Extraordinary Professor of Patristics, University of Pretoria, South Africa; Professor Emeritus, University of Utrecht and Radboud University Nijmegen, the Netherlands

Gert Partoens is Professor of Latin Literature, University of Leuven, Belgium

Patrick Riley is Associate Professor of French, Colgate University, NY, USA

Eric Leland Saak is Professor of History, Indiana University, USA

Tarmo Toom is Faculty Member of Georgetown University, Washington, DC, and a Fellow at John Leland Center for Theological Studies, Arlington. VA, USA

Marie-Anne Vannier is Professor of Theology at Lorraine University, France; Member of the Institut Universitaire de France

Mark Vessey is Principal of Green College, University of British Columbia, Canada; Professor of English Literature, University of British Columbia, Canada

Acknowledgments

It has been a tremendous privilege to work with outstanding scholars, men and women from Great Britain, the United States, Germany, France, Italy, Canada, the Netherlands, Belgium, South Africa, and the Czech Republic, and to collect their expert essays into a volume called the *Cambridge Companion to Augustine's* Confessions. I would like to express my gratitude to all of contributors, who have been, like Nebridius, "most acute investigators of very difficult questions" (Augustine, *conf.* 6.10.17). Our collective special gratitude is due to our editor Beatrice Rehl and the Cambridge University Press.

Abbreviations

xii List of Abbreviations

Hex.	Ambrose, *Hexaemeron*
Hort.	Cicero, *Hortensius*
Hypot.	Sextus Empiricus, *Pyrrhoniae Hypotyposes*
L'EPHE	*L'École Pratique des Hautes Études*
LCC	Library of Christian Classics
LCL	Loeb Classical Library
LDAB	Leuven Database of Ancient Books
Leg.	Cicero, *De legibus*
Marc.	Porphyry, *Ad Marcellam*
MS	Manuscript
Myst.	Ambrose, *De mysteriis*
Nat. deor.	Cicero, *De natura deorum*
NE	Aristotle, *Nicomachean Ethics*
NPNF	The Nicene and Post-Nicene Fathers
Off.	Cicero, *De officiis*; Ambrose, *De officiis*
OGHRA	*The Oxford Guide to the Historical Reception of Augustine*
Or.	*Oratio*
Otio rel.	Petrarca, *De otio religioso*
Parm.	Plato, *Parmenides*
PG	*Patrologia Graeca*
Phd.	Plato, *Phaedo*
Phrd.	Plato, *Phaedrus*
Phys.	Aristotle, *Physics*
PL	*Patrologia Latina*
PMLA	Publications of the Modern Language Association of America
Rep.	Plato, *Republic*
Rer. nat.	Lucretius, *De rerum natura*
REtAug	*Revue des Études Augustiniennes*
Secr.	Petrarca, *Secretum*
Sent.	Porphyry, *Sententia*
S.l.	*Sine loco*
SMRT	Studies in Medieval and Reformation Thought
S.n.	*Sine nomine*
Symp.	Plato, *Symposium*
Tim.	Plato, *Timaeus*
Top. diff.	Boethius, *De topicis differentiis*
USTC	Universal Short Title Catalogue
V. Aug.	*Vita Augustini*

V. phil.	Diogenes Laertius, *Vitae philosophorum*
Vg	Vulgate
VL	*Vetus Latina*
WSA	Works of Saint Augustine: A Translation for the 21st Century

AUGUSTINE'S WORKS

b. conjug.	*De bono conjugali*
b. vita	*De beata vita*
c. Acad.	*Contra Academicos*
c. Adim.	*Contra Adimantum*
c. ep. Man.	*Contra epistulam Manichaei*
c. Faust.	*Contra Faustum Manicheum*
c. litt. Pet.	*Contra litteras Petiliani*
c. Sec.	*Contra Secundinum Manicheum*
cat. rud.	*De catechizandis rudibus*
civ. Dei	*De civitate Dei*
conf.	*Confessiones*
cons. Ev.	*De consensu Evangelistarum*
Cresc.	*Ad Cresconium*
div. qu.	*De diversis quaestionibus octoginta tribus*
doc. Chr.	*De doctrina Christiana*
ench.	*Enchiridion*
en. Ps.	*Enarrationes in Psalmos*
ep.	*Epistulae*
f. et symb.	*De fide et symbolo*
Gesta coll. Carth.	*Gesta Collationis Carthagiensis*
Gn. adv. Man.	*De Genesi adversus Manicheos*
Gn. litt.	*De Genesi ad litteram*
Gn. litt. imp.	*De Genesi ad litteram imperfectus liber*
gramm.	*Ars grammatica breviata*
imm. an.	*De immortalitate animae*
Jo. ev. tr.	*In Joannis euagelium tractatus*
lib. arb.	*De libero arbitrio*
loc. in Hept.	*Locutionum in Heptateuchum*
mag.	*De magistro*
mor.	*De moribus*
mus.	*De musica*
nat. b.	*De natura boni*

ord.	*De ordine*
persev.	*De dono perseverantiae*
praed. sanct.	*De praedestinatione sancorum*
retr.	*Retractationes*
s.	*Sermones*
s. Dolbeau	*Sermones Dolbeau*
s. Dom. mon.	*De sermone Domini in monte*
Simpl.	*Ad Simplicianum*
sol.	*Soliloquia*
spir. et litt.	*De spiritu et littera*
Trin.	*De Trinitate*
util. cred.	*De utilitate credendi*
vera rel.	*De vera religione*

Introduction: What Is the Cambridge Companion to Augustine's *Confessions*?

TARMO TOOM

To introduce an introduction, first a few words about the subject of this Companion, about Augustine's *Confessions*.

Augustine's *Confessions* is undoubtedly among the most renowned works of Christian literature ever. In fact, it's a classic of world literature that keeps generating editions,[1] translations,[2] commentaries, and monographs.[3] In the *Confessions*, readers have enjoyed Augustine's rhetoric and his beautiful Latin. Some have pondered about the phenomenon called "autobiography," others have qualified such genre designation, and still others have wondered about the very possibility of it. Some have admired the *Confessions* as a pearl of Western literary culture. Wittgenstein called it "the most serious book ever written."[4] Many readers have also studied the *Confessions* for its brilliant theological and/or philosophical insight. On the other hand, there are also those who have been disturbed by Augustine's alleged narcissism and infantile megalomania, or those who have been deeply puzzled by Augustine's suspiciously selective memory and, consequently, have

---

[1] The Latin critical texts can be found in *Augustine, Confessions: Books 1–8 and 9–13*, trans. C. J.-B. Hammond, LCL 26/27 (Cambridge, MA: Harvard University Press, 2014 and 2016), which uses the text of J. J. O'Donnell, *Augustine* Confessions (Oxford: Oxford University Press, 2012 [original 1992]), vol. 1. This is also available online www.stoa.org/hippo/frame_entry.html. An earlier critical edition was prepared by L. Verheijen, *CCL* 27 (Turnhout: Brepols, 1990). For premodern editions, see *PL* 47, 134–138.

[2] For available translations in major languages, see a bit dated A. Keller, *Translationes Patristicae Graecae et Latinae* (Stuttgart: Anton Hiersemann, 1997–2004), vol. 1, 99–102, as well as www.augustinus.de/einfuehrung/uebersetzungen-im-www.

[3] For a comprehensive bibliography for Augustine's *Confessions*, see www.augustinus.de/literatur/literaturdatenbank/recherche.

[4] R. Rhees (ed.), *Ludwig Wittgenstein: Personal Recollections* (London: Blackwell, 1981), 105.

doubted the author's credibility, as well as the truthfulness and historicity of his (meta)narrative.[5]

Perhaps it should not be hastily presupposed that every potential reader of the *Cambridge Companion to Augustine's* Confessions has, in fact, read the classic itself; that is, Augustine's *Confessions*. Mark Twain reported someone's (Professor Winchester's) definition of a classic as "something that everybody wants to have read and nobody wants to read."[6] More seriously, Gadamer has explicated that to consider a text a classic, one thinks of something permanent and always relevant. The "classical" speaks in such a way that it is not merely a statement about what happened in the past, but it also addresses the present. In fact, it has the ability to speak directly to the situation of a reader in any time.[7]

> When we call something classical, there is a consciousness of something enduring, of significance that cannot be lost and that is independent of all the circumstances of time – a kind of timeless present that is contemporaneous with every other present.[8]

Consequently, the possible meanings of Augustine's *Confessions*,[9] a classic, are far from having been exhausted during the seventeen centuries of its interpretation.[10] Each generation reads it in the light of its own questions and circumstances and, therefore, reads it very differently. There will never be a definitive reading of the *Confessions* and maybe because of that, it continues to be ever so fascinating. Accordingly, if the *Companion* manages to make people read the *Confessions*,

---

[5]   In a letter to Darius, a Roman general, Augustine assured the addressee that his *Confessions* gave a complete picture of what he was. "In them [i.e., in the *Confessions*] pay attention to me and see through me what I was in myself" (*ep.* 231.6 [*CSEL* 57:509], trans. R. Teske, WSA II/4 [Hyde Park, NY: New City Press, 2005], 122). This is precisely what rhetoricians do – they ask their readers to believe that what they say is really the case.

[6]   M. Twain, *Speeches* (New York: Oxford University Press, 1910), 194.

[7]   H.-G. Gadamer, *Truth and Method*, second ed., trans. J. Weinsheimer and D. G. Marshall (New York: Crossroad, 1989, reprint, New York: Continuum, 1995), 289–290; M.-A. Vannier, *Les* Confessions *de Saint Augustin* (Paris: Cerf, 2007), 10–11.

[8]   Gadamer, *Truth and Method*, 288.

[9]   That the meanings of texts are never exhausted is obviously true about any ancient text, or any text *per se*.

[10] Arguably, the *Confessions* have gained a greater prominence since the twelfth century (J. J. O'Donnell, *Augustine: A New Biography* [New York: HarperCollins, 2005], 63). For an overview of modern studies (*wissenschaftskritische Erforschung*) of the *Confession*, see E. Feldmann, "*Confessiones*," in *Augustinus-Lexikon*, ed. C. Mayer (Basel: Schwabe, 1986–), vol. 1, 1134–1193, at 1135–1139.

or to facilitate their ongoing reading of this book of Augustine in any way, it is fulfilling its purpose.

Next, a few words about the *Cambridge Companion to Augustine's* Confessions. Why such a book and why in this moment of time?

Recently, there have been several methodological paradigm shifts that have influenced one's perception of texts, classics or not. There has been a move from historical-critical approaches to sociological, literary-rhetorical, and various reader-response approaches. This means that attention has shifted from approaches focusing on authors and their worlds, to the approaches focusing on texts and their worlds, and then again to the approaches focusing on the readers and their worlds.[11] In addition, reception studies have affected the study of antiquity in general, and patristics in particular (including Augustine's writings). Because of such methodological shifts and plurality of methods, the authors of the chapters in this volume are not asked to constrain themselves strictly to a particular approach, but are granted freedom to adopt the one(s) they deem fitting. At the same time, with increasing awareness it is realized that any methodology is not merely a matter of choosing an "objective" procedure, but likewise a matter of attitude or disposition with which this choice is made and with which the inquirer approaches a text.[12] In short, it is important to both acknowledge and assess how some new(er) ways of reading have affected the current perception of the *Confessions*. In its own way, *Cambridge Companion* attempts to do just that.

Additionally, Augustine's *Confessions* is a particularly relevant text for today's college students. Having taught the *Confessions* from undergraduates through to doctoral students, I have realized this very acutely. Unfortunately, for an average college student, life often tends to be a downhill spiral pretty much until his/her third year. Approximately at that time most people start putting their lives together again and look for the meaning of life. Some also (re)discover God/religion. When students read Augustine's *Confessions* in their senior year or so, they relate extremely well to the *Confessions* – as if it were their own story. This is true even in the case of students of religions other than Christianity, for Augustine's *Confessions* is marvelously inclusive by

[11] G. Castle, *The Literary Theory Handbook*, Blackwell Literature Handbooks (Oxford: Wiley-Blackwell, 2013), 11–47; M. A. R. Habib, *A History of Literary Criticism: From Plato to the Present* (Malden: Blackwell, 2005), 560–569.
[12] P. Hart, "Theory, Method, and Madness in Religious Studies," *Method and Theory in the Study of Religion* 28/1 (2016), 3–25, at 15–16.

using, almost exclusively, the designation "God." All those who have discovered the relevance Augustine's *Confessions* for themselves could certainly use an authoritative guide into this text. Hopefully, *Cambridge Companion* will serve this purpose in a trustworthy manner.

To set up certain parameters for the *Cambridge Companion*, the first thing to say is that it does not attempt to provide its readers the "total" Augustine. In this respect it is rather different from the magisterial two editions of the *Cambridge Companion to Augustine* (2001 and 2014). Instead, it focuses on a single, yet one of the most outstanding, work of Augustine – the *Confessions* – and largely limits itself to what the author contends in it. Obviously, it is quite impossible not to invoke everything that one happens to know about Augustine and his literary corpus while writing essays about his *Confessions*. Nevertheless, the *Companion*'s specific focus on just one text of Augustine has some ramifications for what one might expect to find in it about the author and his thought.

In addition, this volume does not strive to be comprehensive and offer a running commentary on every section and chapter in the thirteen books of the *Confessions* in its narrative order.[13] Such commentaries, more and less elaborate, are readily available in various languages.[14] Instead and in addition to various introductory issues, the *Companion*

---

[13] E.g., O'Donnell, *Augustine:* Confessions, vols. 2 and 3; and M. Simonetti et al. (eds.), *Sant'Agostino:* Confessioni, five vols. Scrittori greci e latini (Milano: Fondazione Lorenzo Valla, A. Mondadori, 1993–2000), where, in addition to a general ca. 130-page introduction, as well as the text in Latin and Italian, every book has its own introduction, bibliography, and commentary.

[14] In addition to the titles already mentioned, there are wonderful collective commentaries on the *Confessions*, such as K. Paffenroth and R. P. Kennedy (eds.), *A Reader's Companion to Augustine's* Confessions (Philadelphia: Westminster John Knox, 2003), which takes every book as an interpretative key for the whole *Confessions*. Another study, which analyzes each book of the *Confessions* and summarizes the state of research on this book, is N. Fischer and C. Mayer (eds.), *Die* Confessiones *des Augustinus von Hippo: Einführung und Interpretationen zu den dreizehn Büchern* (Freiburg: Herder, 1998). A multilingual, four-volume example should be mentioned as well: L. F. Pizzolato et al. (eds.) *"Le Confessioni" di Agostino d'Ippona*, Lectio Augustini 1–4 (Palermo: Augustinus, 1984–1987). There are also numerous single-author guides or commentaries/analyses of the *Confessions* in various languages; e.g., J. M. Quinn, *A Companion to the* Confessions *of St. Augustine* (New York: Peter Lang, 2002); J. Brachtendorf, *Augustins* "Confessiones" (Darmstadt: Wissenschaftliche Buchgesellschaft, 2005); T. Toom, *Sest Sinu silmale pole suletud süda kättesaamatu (conf. 5.1.1): Saateks Augustinuse Pihtimustele [The Closed Heart Does Not Shut Out Your Eye (conf. 5.1.1): A Companion to Augustine's Confessions]* (Tallinn: Allika, 2011); C. Conybeare, *The Routledge Guidebook to Augustine's* Confessions (London: Routledge, 2016).

focuses on carefully selected key themes, investigates what Augustine says about them, and how they might be important for understanding the *Confessions*. "To hammer those few big nails deeper into our minds is much more memorable that to tap gently at every page [of the *Confessions*]."[15]

The *Cambridge Companion to Augustine's Confessions* also does not attempt to present any kind of new consensus on Augustine's *Confessions*. Predictably, the opinions of the contributors will vary, if not contradict each other. Yet, resisting any urge to harmonize the expressed opinions will hopefully result in demonstrating how differently, in fact, the *Confessions* can be read and understood. To enhance the potential variety of interpretations, an international team of leading Augustinian scholars has been asked to to write essays specifically for this volume. Indeed, "of making many books there is no end" (Eccl 12:12), even if "the many books" are just about another book – Augustine's *Confessions*. Accordingly, the aim of the *Cambridge Companion* is not only to present the best scholarship on the *Confessions*, but also to generate many more fresh readings and rereadings of this masterpiece.

The aforementioned disclaimers help to clarify what the *Cambridge Companion to Augustine's* Confessions is envisioned to be.[16] To begin with, a "companion" should shed light, with reasonable detail, on the questions of the provenance of the text. Thus, Part I is about the becoming of the *Confessions*; about some important introductory matters, such as the composition of the *Confessions*, its structure, genre, and intended audience.

Part II focuses on the selected themes, or key concepts, of the *Confessions*.[17] According to rhetorical analysis, the preface of Book 1 (chapters 1–5) functions as a table of contents for the entire work. Several of the keywords, which are selected for the *Companion* and that find further elaboration in the twelve remaining books of the

[15] P. Kreeft, *I Burned for Your Peace: Augustine's* Confessions *Unpacked* (San Francisco: Ignatius, 2016), 7.
[16] Plotinus used a negative methodology of elimination (*Enn.* I.6.9) that was intended to gain some positive results.
[17] *Catalogus verborum VI: Confessionum Libri XIII, CC* 27, *Thesaurus linguae Augustinianae* (Eindhoven: Pays-Pas, 1982); and R. H. Cooper et al. (eds.), *Concordantia in libros XIII confessionum S. Aurelii Augustini*, two vols. (Hildesheim: Olms/Weidmann, 1991). The latter is a concordance to the Skutella (1969 [1934]) critical edition of the *Confessions*.

Confessions, are found in this section. The judiciously chosen themes[18] focus on what Augustine says about a given topic (or topics) in the *Confessions*, how it functions in the whole, and how it illuminates the whole.[19]

An approach that highlights certain strategic themes presumably distinguishes a reference work (i.e., the *Cambridge Companion*) from a running commentary. Contributors have been asked to give some idea of the location of particular themes in the larger corpus of Augustine's writings as well. After all, and to paraphrase Bruce Gordon, "Augustine was no one-book wonder."[20] The *Confessions* belong to a larger body of Augustine's writings and early Christian literature. Thus, invoking the larger intertextual context of Augustine's other writings may help to illuminate the particular themes in the *Confessions*.

Part III assesses the impact and the afterlife of the *Confessions*. Already Augustine's friends and foes mentioned this treatise and the author himself admitted with satisfaction, "I know those books have given great pleasure to many and continue to do so" (*retr.* 2.6).[21] Today, the *Confessions* has been translated into many languages – including Korean, Arabic, and Finnish – and studied for a very long time. A fuller reception history of Augustine's *Confessions* would merit a separate volume, if not two or three. However, in order to make the reception history of Augustine's *Confessions* manageable and fitting for a single volume as its third part, merely a sampling of the reception of Augustine's *Confession* in three periods of history is provided. This should give the reader at least a sufficient idea of the impact, popularity, and historical relevance of the brilliant *Confessions*.[22]

In addition, since manuscripts and translations come about after a text already exists, Part III begins with these topics. Because most

---

[18] Partially for practical reasons and after much deliberation and debate, the following topics have been omitted: body, Christ, Church, death, ethics, evil, friendship, Mon(n)ica, rhetoric, rest, and temptation. Some of these (e.g., rhetoric) are not topics that are pursued either for their own sake or for the sake of any of the alleged main themes of the *Confessions*. Rather, they are formal features of the text. Furthermore, and unfortunately, essays on some topics were never submitted.

[19] What is presumed here is that the *Confessions* is also and often readers' point of initial access to the ideas in the other works of Augustine.

[20] B. Gordon, *John Calvin's* Institutes of the Christian Religion*: A Biography*, Lives of Great Religious Books (Princeton, NJ: Princeton University Press, 2016), 2.

[21] *CCL* 57:94; trans. B. Ramsey, WSA I/2 (Hyde Park, NY: New City, 2010), 114.

[22] See D. Weber, "*Confessiones*," in *The Oxford Guide to the Historical Reception of Augustine*, ed. K. Pollmann and W. Otten (Oxford: Oxford University Press, 2013), vol. 1, 167a–174a.

people read the *Confessions* in translations, it seems proper that the *Cambridge Companion* introduces at least the most important English translations, the first of which was evidently published in 1620.[23] Although all essays in this volume in a sense guide one's reading of the *Confessions*, Part III ends with a specific essay suggesting reading strategies for this work – "Reading (in) the *Confessions*" – for there are texts, which do not open by merely opening the book.

The targeted readership of the *Cambridge Companion to Augustine's* Confessions is the academically inclined wider public, scholars, and especially teachers and students, as many colleges and universities (departments of literature, history, theology, philosophy, and psychology) have either a separate course on Augustine's *Confessions*, or include it as one of the items to be studied for a different course. *The Cambridge Companion to Augustine's* Confessions is written in a style that is at once erudite and accessible.

[23] M. Murray, "Matthew, Sir Tobie," in *OGHRA*, vol. 3, 1383a–1385b, at 1384a–1384b.

Part I

Circumstances of Composition

1 Title, Time, and Circumstances of Composition: The Genesis of the *Confessions*

CAROLYN HAMMOND

Augustine lived through two imperial dynasties, the Valentinian (364–392) and the Theodosian (392–455), and eleven emperors (counting both east and west). The *Confessions* describes events from the year 354 when he was born in North Africa, until 386 when he was baptized, shortly before the death of his mother Monnica. It was completed and published a decade or more after the events it described; but nothing is known for certain about the process of its composition. This prompts questions about the relationship between history and memory – the writer as recorder of events, and the author as protagonist, in the text – which complicate the task of interpretation.

THE AUTHOR OF THE *CONFESSIONS*

The originality of the work is difficult to overstate. Augustine's modern biographer, Peter Brown, describes the *Confessions* as an "astounding novelty" written by a man who "felt compelled to reveal himself."[1] His conversion to Catholic Christianity in 386, which led to the composition of this *sui generis* work, was – so Augustine claims – partly prompted by the story of another conversion, that of Antony of Egypt a century before (*conf.* 8.6.14). That story was written in the third person (supposedly by the fourth-century Greek bishop and theologian, Athanasius). The gulf between such third-person biographical writing and the *Confessions* is wide, while earlier texts narrated in the first person focused on iconic deaths, not human self-discovery. No literary forebear comes close, in terms of genre, to Augustine's story of his birth and growth into Christianity. Although the text is written in the first person, as (for the most part) a dialogue between the author and God, the *Confessions* is not an autobiography. It is not even a *bios*, a birth-to-

---

[1] P. Brown, *Augustine of Hippo: A Biography*, a new ed. (Berkeley: University of California Press, 2013), 153.

death story of a distinguished or inspiring individual. In terms of narrative scope it is more akin to the *Iliad* than to the *Odyssey*; a diagnostic slice through a whole, not a comprehensive narrative.

Understanding what the *Confessions* is begins with how Augustine himself described it (not only in the years that followed its composition, but also toward the end of his life); and what he may have meant when he chose to call it by that name. The text's range carries readers beyond any stated or presumed "authorial intention" into disciplines not even invented in the author's own time, such as psychology. Yet, authorial intention, although only one aspect of the meaning of any work of art, remains a vital one. The aim, therefore, is to orientate readers of the *Confessions* as to what Augustine's careful linguistic choices (he was, after all, a professor of rhetoric) were meant to evoke in them. This will clarify why he wrote what he did when he did – the timing and circumstances of the *Confessions* composition, intended influence, and dissemination. Referring to the *Confessions* as a "book" (*liber, uolumen* – a book in scroll form, not a *codex*) that has been "published" could be misleading: in the ancient world, "publication" meant that an author's composition had been recorded in writing, and read aloud and/or copied for others to read, and was therefore *editus*, "in the public realm," without further authorial rights over the work. Its chances of survival depended on its being copied and so disseminated further.[2]

The author of the *Confessions* is famous enough to be known by the single name "Augustine" (abbreviated in English antique theological writings to "Austin"). While a *praenomen* "Decimus" (often attached to premodern editions) can be dismissed as a corruption of *doctor* or *dominus*, the *nomen*, "Aurelius," which attaches to his name in many of the best manuscripts, is not so easily disposed of. If he did have a *praenomen*, no convincing record of it survives. There is good reason to suppose, however, that the *nomen* "Aurelius" is as authentic as it is unimportant. Salway refers to the "edict known as the *Constitutio Antoniniana*, by which the emperor Caracalla granted all free subjects Roman citizenship in A.D. 212"; it bestowed the name "Aurelius" on all persons thus enfranchised, and their descendants.[3] By Augustine's time it would have been invisible by reason of its very ubiquity. Other writers were content to refer to him only by the name "Augustinus," which – insofar as the Roman system of *tria nomina* is relevant at this date – would have been his *cognomen*. De la Bonnardière's attempt to dismiss the *nomen* "Aurelius" as a corruption based on a misreading leaps from a persuasive case that a text of Orosius has been mispunctuated[4] to a less convincing thesis that the *nomen* has, by fallacious attribution, infected the texts of other works.[5]

The names of Augustine's closest relations also attract interest: they point to a more polyglot hinterland than the thoroughly Roman text of the *Confessions* seems to indicate. Although his father's name "Patricius" has a grand Roman resonance, his mother's, "Monnica," points to a Punic origin; as does the name Augustine chose for his own son – Adeodatus. Adams explains it as a calque of a Punic name, either Iatanba'al or Mutunba'al ("Baal-has-given," or "Gift-of-Baal"), "Baal" being the Punic word for "Lord," a divine descriptor.[6]

CONTEXT AND CIRCUMSTANCES OF COMPOSITION

Toward the end of his life, in 427, Augustine declared his intention of surveying all his writings to date, and commenting on flaws or weaknesses in them:

> (1) I should not put off reviewing my modest output [*opuscula mea*], whether books, letters or theses, with a kind of forensic rigor [*iudiciaria seueritate*], marking down whatever I now dissent from, as with a censor's pen ... (3) I will even include what I wrote when I was still a catechumen ... still puffed up in the way of secular writings [*saecularium litterarum inflatus consuetudine*] ... Perhaps the reader will discover how my writing has progressed [*quomodo scribendo profecerim*], if they read this modest output in the order in which it was written [*ordine quo scripta sunt*]. (Augustine, *retr.* Prol. 1 and 3)

---

[4] "The fathers ... who are now at rest: Cyprian, Hilary, and Ambrose ... and those still living: Aurelius[,] Augustine, and Jerome" (Orosius, *Liber Apologeticus* 1).

[5] Cf. M. M. Gorman, "Aurelius Augustinus: The Testimony of the Oldest Manuscripts of Saint Augustine's Works," *Journal of Theological Studies* 35 (1984), 475–480.

[6] Punic was a language of migrants from the eastern end of the Mediterranean (Phoenicia) who had colonized western areas like the northern coast of Africa centuries before (see J. N. Adams, *Bilingualism and the Latin Language* [Cambridge: Cambridge University Press, 2008], 238–240). He notes that Augustine's friend Quodvultdeus has a similarly calqued name.

This work, *Retractationes*,[7] has its own claim to be *sui generis* along-side the *Confessions*, not least for its novel thesis that there is some-thing to be learned from tracing the chronological unfolding of an author's oeuvre. What he says in *Retractationes* about the *Confessions* not only helps to date that work, but also makes explicit some of its aims and even achievements. It was the sixth book he wrote after his consecration as a bishop, an event that probably took place in 395. In *retr.* 2.6, before explaining two passages that he now finds unsatisfactory, he states:

> The thirteen books of my own confessions/*Confessions*,[8] and about my evil and good deeds [*de malis et de bonis meis*], praise God as righteous and good; and they enthuse the human mind and emotion [*humanum intellectum et affectum*] towards God. At any rate, so far as I am concerned, this was how they operated in me when I was writing them [*hoc in me egerunt cum scriberentur*] and how they affect the people who read them [*et agunt cum leguntur*]. What others may feel about them, is their business; but I do know that they have delighted many of my brothers, and continue to delight them. From book one to book ten they are about me [*de me scripti sunt*]; the other three books are about the holy Scriptures, from where it is written "In the beginning God made heaven and earth" [Gen 1:1] up to "rest on the seventh day" [Gen 2:2].

That first sentence gives a content-based descriptor for the work: thir-teen books of "confessions." Augustine also provided a more traditional kind of title, an incipit, as he did for every book referred to in *Retracta-tiones*: "This work begins, 'Great are you, O Lord' [*Hoc opus sic incipit: magnus es, domine*]." So we know that he himself had two ways of referring to his *paruum opus*; either by its incipit, or as "the books of my confessions." It is noteworthy that he remarks on the effect reading his confessions/*Confessions* has, not only on other readers, but also on himself: whether he is referring to the work in its final form, or to the divine praises it contains (and so his original experience of uttering them, rather than the later one of recording them), is not clear.

The position of the *Confessions* within *Retractationes*, then, gives a narrow window for relative dating. The *terminus ante quem* is set by

---

[7] It should be translated not as *Retractions*, but as *Revisions* or *Recensions*.
[8] Because there is no distinction between upper- and lower-case letters in early manuscripts, only context can show whether Augustine has the title (*Confessions*) or contents ("confessions") in mind.

Retractationes' following item, a reference to Augustine's thirty-three books against Faustus the Manichaean written between 397 and 401.[9] The relative importance of that work in Augustine's early output is signaled by its length, and by references to the dangerous teachings of the Manichaean bishop and teacher in the *Confessions* (*conf.* 5.3.3; cf. 6.11.18; 7.9.13). The *terminus post quem* is set first by a work no longer extant, and before that by the first three of his four books *De doctrina Christiana* (*On Teaching Christianity*).[10] These were composed in 395–396. It is at least possible that the incomplete state of *De doctrina Christiana*[11] and the beginning of composing the *Confessions* are interrelated. The detached, analytical approach to Scripture of the former made way for a spiritual, emotional, intellectual, and – above all – *personal* approach in the latter.

The *Confessions* could, therefore, have been composed as late as 400–401. But if the relationship between Augustine's breaking off from writing *De doctrina Christiana* and his starting on the *Confessions* is given weight, it pushes the probable date back to 396 or 397. The fact of his having been baptized ten years before 396 might add a little weight to the earlier dating. More persuasive is the case O'Donnell makes in his commentary for 397, on the grounds that, at the time of writing the *Confessions*, Augustine seems to have been unaware that Ambrose had died, and Simplicianus had succeeded him as bishop of Milan, in April 397. Not so compelling is O'Donnell's suggestion that on rhetorical and stylistic grounds the whole text "must" have been composed as a single unit at a single time.

The question of dating is complicated because limited external evidence encourages conclusions based also on theories about what the text is intended to be, and how it is intended to be read; as well as conjectures about the genesis of the text in its final form. So working from the theory that parts of the text have a separate origin in a history centered on Augustine's friend Alypius;[12] or that Books 1–10 and 11–13 (or 1–9 and 10–13; or 1–9, 10, and 11–13) were originally separate, can lead to different views of when the act of writing began; and how the

---

[9] Augustine's *Contra Faustum* was written between 398 and 400 (*retr.* 2.7).

[10] *Retr.* 2.4. The first phase of composition broke off before the end of Book 3, which was then completed together with Book 4, in 426.

[11] It is not the incompleteness that is atypical of Augustine's writings, but the decision to go back decades later and finish what he had earlier set aside.

[12] P. Courcelle, *Recherches sur les Confessions de Saint Augustin* (Paris: Boccard, 1968), 31–36; cf. J. J. O'Donnell, *Augustine:* Confessions (Oxford: Clarendon, 1992), vol. 2, 360–362.

text is interpreted. Augustine himself suggested a 1–10/11–13 book division (*retr.* 2.6); but for a modern reader the text reaches a more natural cadence at the end of Book 9, when the story of his growth into Christianity ends. It is marked by a *sphragis*,[13] and by its subject-matter – the death of Monnica – which brought the period of the author's Christian adolescence to an end as he left behind his mentor to grow up into mature Christian independence. Book 10 then effects the transition from microcosm to macrocosm. This can still be under-stood as following Augustine's own division of the *Confessions*: for in Book 10 he lays bare his thinking at the actual time of writing. As he lets go of what lies behind and reaches forward to what lies ahead, he furnishes readers with a cluster of confession-terminology, such as is scattered throughout the text (as a unifying explanatory factor), but never in greater density than here:

> I want to accomplish [truth] in my heart, in making my confession openly before you [God] [*in corde meo coram te in confessione*]; but with my pen I want to do so before many witnesses [*coram multis testibus*]. (conf. 10.1.1)

> I have already declared the benefits which have brought about my confession to you ... When I am bad, confessing to you is nothing more than dissatisfaction with myself: whereas when I am devout, confessing to you is nothing more than not giving myself the credit for it ... So my confession to you, O my God, is made silently in your sight, and yet not silently [*tacite ... et non tacite*]: it is a silence without uproar, but it resounds with affection [*tacet enim strepitu, clamat affect*]. (10.2.2)

> What have I to do with other people, that they hear my confessions [*audiant confessiones meas*], as if they are going to cure all my weaknesses? (10.3.3)

> I too, Lord, will therefore go on confessing to you so that others can hear [*ut audiant homines*]. (10.3.3)

> When the confessions of my past misdeeds [*confessiones praeteritorum malorum meorum*] – which you have forgiven and covered to make me glad in you, changing my soul through faith and your sacrament – are read about and heard [*cum leguntur et*

---

[13] Or "seal" – a device familiar from Classical poetry, a brief element of self-revelation at the end of a work or, as here, a section of a work.

audiuntur], they animate the heart, to stop it sleeping in despair and saying, "I can't!" [*ne dormiat in desperatione et dicat, non possum*].
(10.4.4)

This torrent of confessing culminates in statements that confirm that Augustine is, albeit obliquely, telling readers why he is writing; and what he is writing – reflections that are taking place at the same time as they are being composed:

> What good is it, my Lord (when each day my conscience makes confession to you [*cotidie confitetur conscientia mea*], more certain in its hope of your mercy than in its own lack of guilt), what good is it, I wonder, that in these writings I also make confession to other people in your presence [*hominibus coram te confiteor per has litteras*], not of what I have been, but of what I am now? ... As for who I am now, at this time of [composing] my confessions [*in ipso tempore confessionum mearum*], look! There are plenty of people who want to know that ... but their ear is not attuned to my heart, where I truly am whoever I am. They want, therefore, to listen to me confessing what I am deep within [*confitente me quid ipse intus sim*], in that place where neither eye nor ear nor mind can penetrate. (*conf.* 10.4.4)

Just a few lines later, he makes his most definite statement about the genesis of the work – "this is the harvest of my confessions [*fructus confessionum mearum*]"; and about its imagined audience – "I make this confession not only before you, but also in the hearing of those sons of men who are believers, companions in my joy and sharers in the transience of my humanity [*confitear non tantum coram te ... sed etiam in auribus credentium filiorum hominum*]" (*conf.* 10.4.6). The opening of Book 10, then, is a reminder of the need to be sensitive to how the text is focalized: by distinguishing Augustine-the-narrator (within the text) and Augustine-the-historical-individual (composing the text). Beyond the meager external materials, and this complex internal material, there remains plenty of room for theorizing and conjecture, but none for certainty.

RESONANCES: TITLE AND CONTENT

Perhaps the most difficult of the introductory questions faced by the reader of the *Confessions* is the range of meanings of this firmly attested title – "thirteen books of [my] confessions/*Confessions*." That range covers both the internals of the text (content, themes, and ideas) and also external referents – how to understand the terminology – *confiteor* and *confessio* and cognates – by comparison with other writings. Augustine had two types of literary model for his writing.

First, there were the Latin Classics, which influenced him in terms of style, diction, and genre; and which made up the whole of his formal education. His overall debt to Latin Classical[14] literature has been comprehensively analyzed by Hagendahl.[15] Going by frequency of reference, his chief influences for the *Confessions* are Virgil and Cicero: but they appear there as hooks on which to hang explorations of wisdom, and of the power of mythic narrative, so the debt is thematic rather than linguistic or literary.

Second, there were the holy writings of Christianity, both the canonical Scripture and early Christian writers conventionally known collectively as "the fathers." These he encountered in church worship and in private reading.[16] At that early period, before his encounter with Ambrose, bishop of Milan, he approached Scripture in the same way as he would have approached Classical writers of Latin prose, and judged them by the same standards:

> Scripture seemed to me unworthy of comparison with the merit of Cicero's writings. My pomposity was repelled by its restraint, while my powers of perception could not penetrate its depths [*tumor ... meus refugiebat modum eius et acies mea non penetrabat interiora eius*]. (*conf.* 3.5.9)

He was certainly sensitized by his education in rhetoric to stylistic and figurative features in the Latin Bible,[17] and sometimes commented on them in that light.[18] But, later on, for him Scripture came to stand apart, in a separate category from what we might call "literature,"[19] as being of divine origin, and open to different interpretative criteria from other writings.

---

[14] The conventional umbrella term for non-Christian literature of this period, "pagan," is pejorative and misleading. No non-Christians of the late imperial period thought of themselves as "pagans."

[15] H. Hagendahl, *Augustine and the Latin Classics*, two vols., Studia Graeca et Latina Gothoburgensia 20 (Göteborg: Universitatis Gothoburgensis, 1967).

[16] Augustine, *conf.* 3.3.5 and 3.5.9.

[17] The Bible version Augustine knew best was that known as the *Vetus Latina* (*VL*). He was unenthusiastic about Jerome's Vulgate (Vg).

[18] E.g., Augustine, *doc. Chr.* 4.7.11, referring to Rm 5:3–5.

[19] A term for which there is no precise equivalent in antiquity.

Both these types of writing influenced his use of the term *confessio* and its cognates in the composition of the *Confessions*. It is generally clear from the context which resonance is uppermost in the text. The language of the *Confessions* is rich in features that would not be found in Ciceronian prose, but this should not be taken as evidence that Augustine's Latin was of a debased or vulgar type. Rather, the content (an intimate conversation) drives his choice of style and diction.[20]

As for the title itself, Ratzinger observed long since that in Classical sources the noun *confessio* has a predominantly negative flavor, indicating an admission of guilt, not praise.[21] The positive sense of "declaration of praise," on the other hand, is "innate in the word's biblical usage."[22] Verheijen produced an invaluable analysis of the language of the *Confessions*,[23] in which he drew attention to the equivalent Greek term within Scripture, *exhomologēsis*; a Greek text attributed to Origen points to the praise/sin range of meaning, "'Confession' means thanksgiving (*eucharistia*) and praising (*doxologia*). It also occurs in the sense of admitting sins."[24]

A predominantly positive resonance, then, is the default in Scripture, with a clear equivalence between Latin *confessio* and Greek *exhomologēsis*. Augustine's contemporary, and sometimes correspondent, Jerome also drew attention to this lexical range:

> "Who will confess [*confitetur*] you in hell?" In this verse "confession" is used not in the sense of repentance, but of glorification and praise [*non pro poenitentia sed pro gloria et laude accipitur*], such as we also read in the gospel, "I confess to you, Lord of heaven and earth." (Ps 6:6; Mt 11:25)[25]

This double-meaning, *confessio*-positive and *confessio*-negative, provided Augustine with material for preaching on more than one occasion. In a sermon (c. 412), he took the same gospel text as Jerome to reflect on

[20] M. R. Arts, "The Syntax of the Confessions of Saint Augustine." PhD dissertation, Catholic University of America, 1927, 126–127.

[21] J. Ratzinger, "Originalität und Überlieferung in Augustins Begriff der *confessio*," *REtAug* 3 (1957), 375–392, at 377. Unlike the compound verb *confiteor* ("I confess"), the simple verb form *fateor* retains the predominantly negative resonance of guilt (e.g., "I admit it, I know it [*fateor et scio*]" [*conf.* 1.5.6]).

[22] O'Donnell, *Augustine* Confessions, vol. 2, 3; citing Verheijen's *Eloquentia Pedisequa* (see fn. 23).

[23] M. Verheijen, *Eloquentia Pedisequa: Observations sur le style des Confessions de Saint Augustin* (Nijmegen: Dekker & Van de Vegt, 1949), 69.

[24] Origen(?), *Selecta in Psalmos* (*PG* 1653D–6A).

[25] Jerome, *Comm. in Is.* 11.38.16 (*PL* 24:394.16).

the meaning of confession. It is a passage worth quoting at length not only for that reflection, but also as a reminder that not everyone in his congregation was awake to the subtle distinctions in which he, and his fellow language-professionals, took delight, and detected meaning.

> We find that when we read the word "confession" [*legimus confessionem*] in the Scriptures, we must not always understand it as a word for sinners [*peccatoris*] ... Once, when the reader spoke the word, there followed the sound of you beating your breasts, though what you had actually heard was the Lord saying, "I confess [*confiteor*] to you, Father." At that precise word, "I confess," when it was uttered, you beat your breasts. But what does beating the breast mean, if not to make clear what is hidden in the breast, and by openly striking it to admonish the concealed sin? Why have you done this, if not because you heard "I confess to you, Father"? You certainly heard "I confess," but you did not pay attention to who is confessing [*qui confitetur, non attendistis*]! So pay attention now. If Christ said, "I confess," and Christ is completely free from every kind of sin, then [confession] is not an act of sinners only, but sometimes also of those who praise God. So whether we praise God, or admonish ourselves, we are "confessing." Both kinds of confession are devout [*pia est utraque confessio*], whether you censure yourself because you are not sinless; or whether you praise God, who has nothing to do with sin. (Augustine, *s.* 67.1)

Augustine's concern with verbal precision here is theological rather than lexical. Both here and elsewhere he stressed that if the noun *confessio* or the verb *confiteor* attach to Christ, who was without sin, the only meaning possible must be praise. For the reader of the *Confessions*, then, the question at issue is whether he would have chosen the title of his extraordinary book to evoke primarily the sense of Classical *confessio*, in which admission of sin predominates; or Christian *confessio*, in which laudatory acknowledgment of God predominates. There is a further usage of *confessio* in a Christian context, also positive, linked to confessions specifically of faith, declarations of belief, even creedal formulations.[26] That adds to the multivalence of the title, while drawing it further into the realm of the positive. Against this must be set the intratextual criterion of the emphasis within the *Confessions* on

[26] In this sense a Christian who maintains faith under torture or threat of death is called a "confessor."

Augustine-the-protagonist's wrongdoing and rejections of God. Together with the fact that "publication" of the *Confessions* took place around the time when he began to formulate his radical views on divine grace and human sin, this can be taken to point toward the more negative reading. But the presence of both senses, within the text of so subtle a writer, neither obliterating the other (although the positive predominates), makes the likeliest conclusion that he saw them as multiple faces of the same object. In other words, for Augustine, recognition of God's goodness and recognition of human unworthiness were inseparable in the life of a Christian.

Without straying too far into matters of genre, it needs stating that Augustine was not writing the *Confessions* only for himself; nor is the *Confessions* only a historical record of what was, at the time, a spontaneous overflow of powerful religious feeling. The form is conversational (with the style of Latin to match), the addressee from the beginning, frequently evoked, is "God" or "the Lord."[27] The author is writing for others, as well as for himself; and for God, and his text demands an audience: there has to be someone he is confessing *to*. That role of listener was played by God: but Augustine also had a human audience, consisting of readers and hearers of the text. Of them too he had expectations. This is explicit from Book 2, when he follows a dialogue with God – in which allusions and quotations from Scripture do duty for the voice of his divine interlocutor – by showing awareness of a wider audience:

> Who am I telling this [*cui narro haec*]? Certainly not you, my God! But I am narrating this story in your presence to my kind, to the whole human race [*apud te narro haec generi meo, generi humano*] ... so that I, and whoever reads this [*quisquis haec legit*], may ponder the depths from which we must cry out to you. What is closer to your ears than a heart that makes its confession [*cor confitens*] to you and a life that is faithful? (*conf.* 2.3.5)

Thus, Augustine's narration was directed to a double end: to draw attention to how far his readers are from God at the moment when they become ready to invoke him; and to reassure them that, paradoxically, God is close to every "confessing heart." From this point, theme and purpose are inextricable. It is possible to imagine the text as a monologue in performance, with a divine interlocutor whose thoughts and

---

[27] In Latin, *deus* and *dominus*. The terms can refer to the first or second persons of the Christian Trinity, according to context.

responses are imagined, understood, and supplied by the protagonist, but whose own voice, in book after book, is not heard, until a climax is reached right in the center of the text (*conf.* 7.10.16). A clustering of Scriptural references leads to the climactic moment when God steps out of his "silent role [*kophon prosōpon*]" role to address Augustine directly, "You called from far off, 'truly I am who I am' [*clamasti de longinquo, 'immo uero ego sum qui sum'*]" (Ex 3:14).

At the end of Book 9 of the *Confessions*, there is a similar shift: Augustine the narrator steps out of his character as Augustine the protagonist, to make a demand of his audience:

> Inspire, O my Lord, my God, your servants my brothers, and your sons who are my masters – for I serve them with my heart and voice and writings – inspire them, whenever they read this, to remember at your altar your servant Monnica and her sometime husband Patricius ... Let them also remember with dutiful love those who ... were my brothers and my fellow citizens in the everlasting Jerusalem ... So may [Monnica's] last request to me be fulfilled for her more abundantly through many people's prayers – prompted by these confessions/*Confessions* – than by my prayers alone. (*conf.* 9.13.37)

Here is another innovation: to address the reader at the end of a piece of writing is not in itself novel; to address readers and ask them to do something in return for what they have received is, to say the least, distinctive.

None of this complexity makes the *Confessions* an opaque composition. Plenty of readers treat it as a straightforward source of biographical information. Augustine's friend, biographer, and fellow bishop Possidius was one such. He produced a thematic catalog of Augustine's works, called *Indiculus*, in which he grouped the *Confessions* with other works aimed at interested general readers (*omnes studiosi*) rather than specialized theologians.[28] In his *Life of Augustine*, written only a couple of years after the bishop of Hippo's death in 430, Possidius referred to the *Confessions* as a biographical narrative:

> I shall not attempt to work in all the details about himself – what he was like before his realization of grace, and what he was like after receiving that grace – as the blessed Augustine [*beatissimus*

---

[28] Possidius, *Indiculus* 106.3.

Augustinus] described them in his books of *Confessions* [in suis confessionum libris].[29]

But Possidius was also aware of a more public purpose for the book. In the same introduction he made reference to the authorial intention of the *Confessions*, its purpose of eliciting praise of God and (confirming Augustine's own stated expectations of his putative readers) prayer, from his fellow Christians: "He sought not his own praise for those things he had already received, but the glory of his Lord, because of the blessing of his own deliverance; and desired the prayers of his brethren for the things which he hoped to obtain" (*v. Aug.* Praef. 6). In saying this, he was reading the words of Augustine the author as if they were the intentions of Augustine the historical person. Not a very nuanced approach, but at least it was not hostile. Others were less sympathetic to the bishop of Hippo's theological approach. His adversary Pelagius lifted a single sentence from the *Confessions* to confect an attack, challenging its understanding of forgiveness, grace, and obedience to the divine will:

> Among my more modest works [*meorum opusculorum*] what is more often read, and known with greater pleasure [*delectabilius*] than the books of my confessions/*Confessions*? Although I published them before the Pelagian heresy even existed, in them I certainly said to our God, and said often, "Grant what you command, and command what you will [*da quod iubes, et iube quod uis*]." At Rome, when one of the brothers, a fellow-bishop, recounted these words of mine in his presence, Pelagius could not tolerate them: and denouncing them rather too vehemently almost came to cuffs with the man who had recounted them.[30]

In his old age, Augustine was writing to a court official, to recommend his reading the *Confessions*, in terms that reveal how well-known the book had become, and by that title. He was still exercised, so many years later, by people misdirecting their enthusiasm, and praising the writer, rather than the author or originator of the *Confessions* (God):

> My son, take up the books of my confessions/*Confessions* which you wanted [*libros, quos desiderasti, confessionum mearum*]. Regard what I am there, so that you do not praise me for being

---

[29] Possidius, *Vita Augustini*, Praef. 5 ("published" in 432 CE).
[30] Augustine, *persev.* 20.53; cf. *conf.* 10.29.40.

more than I am; do not believe what others say about me, but believe me instead. Observe me in that work, and see what I was in myself, for my own part – if anything about me there pleases you, join me in praising the one whose praises I longed for instead of my own. Do not praise me. For it is he who made us, and not we ourselves: we had lost ourselves, but he who made us remade us. So when you find me in that book, pray for me to be not defective but perfected. Pray, my son, pray [*ora pro me ne deficiam, sed perficiar; ora fili, ora*].[31]

The letter also clarifies what the title was intended to indicate about the contents: Augustine still meant it to be understood it as chiefly directed toward praise of God.

As well as in his preaching and letter-writing, he highlighted this point in his *Enarrationes in Psalmos*, in terms that suggest that his readers expected *confessio*-negative to predominate, and that they needed education in that specialized scriptural sense of declaring praise:

What does it mean, "I will confess to you for ever"? I will praise you for ever, because I have remarked that confession is concerned with praise, not just with admission of sins [*esse confessionem et in laudibus, non tantum in peccatis*]. So confess what you have done against God, and you will confess what God has done for you [*confitere ... quod tu fecisti in deum, et confiteberis quod tibi fecerit deus*]. What have you done? You have sinned. What has God done? When you confess your wrongdoing he forgives you your sins, so that afterwards you confess his praises for ever, and are no longer goaded by remorse for sin. (*en. Ps.* 29.2.22; cf. Ps 78:17; 94:4 [Vg])

RESONANCES: CONFESSING AND THE *CONFESSIONS*

The title *Confessions*, therefore, tells the reader to expect a conversation, which it depicts as a dialogue, in which the voice of the divine interlocutor is represented by evocations of Scripture. There is no trace of a belief that God's silence is an indicator of weakness or absence. The moments when Augustine draws attention to divine silence instead

---

[31] Augustine, *ep.* 231.6, written in 429 CE to Darius, an official at the court of Valentinian III.

throw into sharp relief his deviations from the path of proper converse, and so conversation:

> You see this, Lord, and remain silent. You are long-suffering, full of mercy and truth. But surely you will not always be silent [*numquid semper tacebis*]? (conf. 1.18.28)

> How enigmatic you are, God! You alone are great, and you dwell on high in the silence. (1.18.29 [Is 33:5])

> I was shaken about and poured away and spilled out and burned up by my sexual immorality; and you said nothing. How long you took, my Joy! You were silent then. (2.2.2)

> Were you really so silent toward me then? Whose words were they if not yours that you chanted into my ears through my mother, who was your faithful servant! (2.3.7)

This divine seeming-silence is most apparent in the early part of the *Confessions*, in which Augustine is expressing his inability to converse with God. When – in his role as author – he invokes the assistance of his divine interlocutor, he begins what will turn out to be a distinctively dialogic monologue: "Tell me, O Lord my God, by your mercies, what you are to me. Say to my soul, 'I am your salvation': speak in such a way that I may hear" (*conf.* 1.5.5).

The divine interlocutor is imagined, but it is Augustine who selects his words from the available scriptural sources. This becomes the standard way for him to realize that interlocutor for his readers, right from the point where the verb "to confess" is used for the first time in the text: "Or do you smile at me for asking these questions – and decree that I must praise you for what I do know about you, and confess my faith in you [*confiteri me tibi*]" (*conf.* 1.6.9)?[32]

God's imperative that Augustine must praise him (*confiteri*) finds an immediate response in the words of the protagonist – "I do make my confession to you [*confiteor tibi*], Lord of heaven and earth, and I sing your praises" (*conf.* 1.6.10). A thread of antithesis runs throughout the text as Augustine repeatedly contrasts the truest kind of speech, namely the positive speech-act he calls "confession," with negative speech-acts: "Do not let those whom I fear cry out against me any longer, O my God,

---

[32] Rhetorical questions are a device to create the impression of dialogue, reinforced by imagining God's responses: see C. T. Mathewes, "The Liberation of Questioning in Augustine's 'Confessions'," *Journal of the American Academy of Religion* 70 (2002), 539–560.

while I confess to you what my soul desires" (*conf.* 1.13.22). *Confiteor/confessus/confessio* language is present in all thirteen books of the *Confessions*: as the first example comes some way into the first book, so the final example is set shortly before the end of the last book: "Let my confession also be pleasing in your sight [*placeat ... coram oculis tuis*], by which I confess to you, Lord, that I believe you did not say this to no purpose" (*conf.* 13.24.36).

Augustine's confessions did not end with the completion of the *Confessions*. He felt that he was being compelled to express belief in this way, rather than doing so of his own volition, "You command me [*iubes me*] to make confession to you" (*conf.* 1.7.12). As he later commented on Ps 30:11 (Vg), confessing was woven into every interaction with the divine, "'For my life is spent with grief' [means] my life consists of confessing you, but it is spent with grief."[33] All that he went on to write after the *Confessions* was a working out of the case he had made so ably there, that life after his confessions/*Confessions* consisted, in every part, of divine praises.

Further Reading

Arts, M. R. "The Syntax of the Confessions of Saint Augustine." PhD dissertation, Catholic University of America, 1927.

Blaise, A. and H. Chirat, *Dictionnaire latin-français des auteurs chrétiens.* Turnhout: Brepols, 1954 (reprinted 1997).

Broeniman, C. S. "The Resurrection of a Latin Classic: The 'Confessions' of St. Augustine," *The Classical World* 86 (1993), 209–213.

Campbell, J. M. and M. R. P. McGuire, *The Confessions of Saint Augustine: Books I–IX (Selections).* Englewood Cliffs, NJ: Prentice-Hall, 1966 (reprint 2007).

Clark, G. *Augustine, Confessions: Books I–IV.* Cambridge: Cambridge University Press, 1995.

Condon, M. G. "The Unnamed and the Defaced: The Limits of Rhetoric in Augustine's 'Confessiones,'" *Journal of the American Academy of Religion* 69 (2001), 43–63.

Gibb, J. and W. Montgomery, *The Confessions of Augustine.* Cambridge Patristic Texts; Latin Texts and Commentaries. Cambridge: Cambridge University Press, 1908 (reprinted 1979).

Hagendahl, H. *Augustine and the Latin Classics,* two vols. Studia Graeca et Latina Gothoburgensia 20. Göteborg: Universitatis Gothoburgensis, 1967.

O'Meara, J. J. *The Young Augustine: An Introduction to the Confessions of S. Augustine.* London: Longman 1954 (second rev. ed. 2001).

---

[33] Augustine, *en. Ps.* 30.11 ("*quoniam defecit in dolore vita mea*": *quoniam vita mea est confiteri te, sed defecit in dolore*).

Rothfield, L. "Autobiography and Perspective in the Confessions of St. Augustine," *Comparative Literature* 33 (1981), 209–223.

Salway, B. "What's in a Name? A Survey of Roman Onomastic Practice from c. 700 B.C. to A.D. 700," *Journal of Roman Studies* 84 (1994), 124–145.

Thesaurus Linguae Latinae. *"Confessio,"* see www.degruyter.com/view/db/tll.

Verheijen, M. *Eloquentia Pedisequa: Observations sur le style des Confessions de Saint Augustin*. Nijmegen: Dekker & Van de Vegt, 1949.

2 Structure and Genre of the *Confessions*

ANNEMARÉ KOTZÉ

INTRODUCTION

Augustine's *Confessions* is arguably his most accessible, yet, at the same time, most confounding literary creation. Above all, modern scholars have not been able to reach consensus in pinpointing the genre of the work. This is hardly surprising in a highly complex and multi-layered work that is in many ways unlike anything preceding it, and that embodies a creative fusion of generic conventions from both pagan and Christian contexts.

The article aims to illuminate the central issues that provide challenges in terms of understanding the generic make-up of the *Confessions*. This is done through discussing first, in the next section, the issue of the "unity" of the *Confessions*, one that dominated scholarship on the work during the latter part of the previous century and is closely related to difficulties surrounding its structure (considered in the section titled "Describing the Structure of the *Confessions*") and its genre (examined in the section titled "Naming the Genres of the *Confessions*"). Although unity, structure, and genre are, in fact, inextricably intertwined aspects of the literary work, for the purposes of the current discussion, the section on unity focuses specifically on how aspects of structure and genre contribute to an explanation of the coherence of the work. The section on structure focuses mostly on various ways of categorizing the units of content within the work, including a concise overview of a variety of proposals that have been made in this regard. The section on genre highlights the generic labels that are most frequently attached to the work, suggests some others, and also points toward the innovative fusion of antecedent generic conventions that constitutes this rich and multidimensional work.

UNITY

Perplexity with the unity of the *Confessions* revolves primarily around a structural question: How do the autobiographical first ten books cohere with the exegetical last three? Thinking of the *Confessions* as a combination of two such disparate sections is what has made it difficult for modern readers to imagine the cohesion of the whole. In addition, because the first nine books follow the lines of Augustine's conversion story but Book 10 relates Augustine's state of mind at the time of writing (about ten years after the conversion and return to Africa, told in Books 8 and 9), scholars entertained the possibility that Book 10 was a later interpolation. Add to this the fact that Augustine seems to promise at a few points in the *Confessions* that he is moving toward a contemplation of Scripture as a whole, while the last three books only progress as far as the end of the conversion story in Gen 1–2:3, and it becomes understandable why some thought that the work may have been left incomplete (that there was no unity), or simply that *Augustin compose mal*[1] (that the structure and unity were flawed).

Scholarship has since come to a consensus that the *Confessions* does constitute a literary unity, even if not on what constitutes this unity. In the second half of the previous century, three German scholars, such as Grotz,[2] Holzhausen,[3] and Feldmann,[4] evaluated attempts in scholarship to come to grips with the unity of the *Confessions*. Grotz examines thirty-five proposals about unity (categorized into nineteen types of approach), using one criterion to test each: Does it provide a satisfactory explanation for Augustine's focus on specifically the creation story in Genesis in the last three books of *Confessions*? He focuses on the coherence between "autobiography" and "exegesis,"[5] a name-giving that I argue exacerbates bafflement about the unity the *Confessions*. Thirty years later, Holzhausen, tellingly still formulating the title of his article around the terms "biographer" and "exegete,"[6]

---

[1] H.-I. Marrou, *Saint Augustin et la fin de la culture antique* (Paris: Éditions E. de Boccard, 1958), 61 *et passim*.

[2] K. Grotz, "Warum bringt Augustin in den letzten Büchern seiner '*Confessiones*': Eine Auslegung der Genesis?" Doctoral Dissertation, the University of Tübingen, 1970.

[3] J. Holzhausen, "Augustin als Biograph und Exeget: Zur literarischen Einheit der *Confessiones*," *Gymnasium* 107 (2000), 519–536.

[4] E. Feldmann, "*Confessiones*," in *Augustinus-Lexikon*, eds. C. Mayer, I. Bouchert, R. Dodaro, et al. (Basel: Schwabe, 1994), vol. 1, 1134–1193.

[5] Grotz speaks about the unifying bond between life story and exegesis ("Lebensgeschichte und Genesisexegese") ("Warum bringt Augustin," 15).

[6] Holzhausen, "Augustin als Biograph und Exeget," 519.

points out that scholarship on the issue of the unity of the *Confessions* has either stagnated or resigned itself to the fact that no easy explanation will be found.

A concise and astute categorizing of scholarship's grappling with the unity of the *Confessions* into six approaches is provided by Feldmann, rendered by Kotzé (2004) as follows:

> 1) [studies] that see the unity provided by the notion of confession throughout; 2) studies that use information from Augustine's historical situation at the time of writing ... to provide a clue to its composition; 3) those that seek to find the unity in the exposition of specific theological problems that we know Augustine was concerned with at the time of writing; 4) those that go out from the presupposition that Books 11 to 13 are the actual goal of the *Confessions* and/or explain the rest of the work in the light of the Genesis exegesis; 5) those that show how the use of certain motifs contribute to the compositional unity; and 6) those few studies that have tried to examine the generic characteristics of the work.[7]

The unity of the *Confessions* no longer preoccupies scholarship, perhaps because the postmodern reader is more comfortable with the notion of complexity and with the absence of one solution accepted by all. Such a reader may well question whether scholarship was justified in seeking unity in an ancient work like the *Confessions*. Scholars' search for a structural explanation that would make sense to a modern mind may have contributed significantly to readers' inability to read the work on its own terms. The point is precisely that what constituted a comprehensible whole to an ancient writer or reader may not present itself as such to the modern reader. More pertinently, a more apt question would be what kind of "unity" an ancient author may have pursued.

Here, of course, Augustine's remarks in *retr.* 2.6 come into play. While he certainly did not regard the *Confessions* as an incomplete or unsatisfactory work – he was, in fact, quite pleased with it, both originally when he wrote and later when he read it again – his comment that he composed the first ten books about himself [*de me*] and the last three about holy Scripture [*de scripturis sanctis*] reinforced perceptions of two disjunct sections: autobiography and exegesis. But here the observations

---

[7] Free translation and summary from Feldmann, "*Confessiones*," 1144–1150.

by Marjorie Boyle are illuminating.[8] She contends that the *de* in these two phrases in *Retractations* must be understood as a technical term from the context of ancient rhetoric where it could refer to the *area* or *topic* around which a specific section of a work is composed (in contrast to literally meaning "about"). Further, Boyle points out that Augustine's combination of material arising from the story of a person (an instance of rhetorical invention "according to persons") and material arising from a text (rhetorical invention "from documents")[9] has an antecedent in Cicero's *De Legibus*. This means that an ancient reader may not have been perplexed by the combination of a *de personis* and a *de scripturis* section, assuming both to pertain to a central theme. Conventional naming of the parts of the *Confessions* may have complicated later understanding of the work. If *Confessions* is described, for example, as existing of a section composed around a person and a section around documents, both on the theme of God's presence in the life of, and his communication with, man, at least some of the perplexity may disappear and the readers' expectations may be preprogrammed to observe an organic whole when they start reading the *Confessions*.

Brian Stock provides a revealing lens through which to view the structure (and unity) of the *Confessions*.[10] He demonstrates how meaningful the theme of reading is throughout the first nine books of *Confessions*, arguing that Augustine's repeated emphasis on reading creates the image of a man slowly becoming a competent reader, this culminates in the life-changing reading of the letter to the Romans in the conversion scene of Book 8.[11] If the first nine books are seen as the story of the coming into being of a reader, that makes the reading of the creation story in Genesis in the following books, the section *de scripturis*, a most natural sequence to the preceding narrative.

Robert McMahon (whose work is also discussed later) addresses the unity between the first ten and the last three books by answering the objection in scholarship that Augustine seems to promise a reading of the whole of Scripture but then only offers an interpretation of Gen 1.[12] He suggests that, while the narrator and character Augustine thinks

---

[8] M. O. Boyle, "The Prudential Augustine: The Virtuous Structure and Sense of His *Confessions*," *Recherches Augustiniennes* 22 (1987), 129–150.

[9] Boyle, "The Prudential Augustine," 130.

[10] B. Stock, *Augustine the Reader: Meditation, Self-Knowledge and the Ethics of Interpretation* (Cambridge, MA: Harvard University Press, 1996).

[11] Stock, *Augustine the Reader*, 75.

[12] R. McMahon, *Augustine's Prayerful Ascent: An Essay on the Literary Form of the* Confessions (Athens: The University of Georgia Press, 1989).

that he is heading toward an interpretation of the whole, the implicit author knows from the beginning that what the character will find is the whole of Scripture represented in the text of Gen 1.

It may be wholesome to entertain the possibility that, if readers were to start reading the *Confessions* without expecting "autobiography" followed by "exegesis," or any of the other structural patterns that have come to circulate widely in the prolific scholarship on the work, they might experience it differently. Augustine writes a searching prayer, the report of a lengthy meditation ranging with unexpected twists and turns over unpredictable territory, as prayers tend to do, and not an orderly account of his life or a section of Scripture. The work surely does not start like an autobiography; it could also be described as presenting the reader with a growing number of interpolations of biographical information into the confessing contemplation only from *conf.* 1.6.7 onward.

Furthermore, Book 11 represents a transition to the last part of the work that minimizes the perception of it as an appendage, which the name "exegesis" causes the reader to expect. On the one hand, its tone perpetuates the searching and confessional mode of the preceding books, and, on the other, any first reading demonstrates the extent to which "exegesis" is a misnomer for describing what is offered here. What the reader will find, after the long prayer for divine assistance in reading holy Scripture (*conf.* 11.2.3–4), is that quotations from and explanations of the text of Genesis make up a miniscule portion of Book 11; the book is, after all, widely regarded as a discourse on the nature of time. Further support for an argument against calling the last part of the work exegesis is provided by the efforts of the narrator to engage the audience to meditate with him in the programmatic opening of Book 11 ("I do that to arouse my own loving devotion toward you, and that of my readers, so that together we may declare, *Great is the Lord, and exceedingly worthy of praise*").[13] His insistence is that what he will be doing in the last three books is *meditating* on Scripture [*meditari in lege tua*], as well as the preaching purpose he assigns to his discourse at the opening of *conf.* 11.2.2 ("you led me to this position where I must preach the word").

Another thought experiment that may have a salutary effect on readings of the *Confessions* might be to invert the normal assumption that Augustine's autobiographical narrative is frequently interrupted

[13] All translations quoted here are from M. Boulding, *Saint Augustine: The Confessions*, WSA I/1 (New York: New City Press, 1997).

with reflections on issues like human nature, the nature of sin, the nature of evil, or the nature of God, to name but a few. The work is, to an important extent, in the first place a reflection on the nature of God, a search for understanding God (the *scire et intellegere* prayed for in *conf.* 1.1.1), and a probing of how God acts in the life of a human being, even while the latter is moving away from him and unaware of his presence. It may be possible to see the events from his own life that Augustine chooses to narrate as the interpolations, called up when Augustine wants to illustrate how God works, mostly unobserved, but inexorably, toward the salvation of the sinful human being that was introduced in *conf.* 1.1.1. Readers may consider that the main purpose of the selected *exempla* from Augustine's life is to "lift [his own] mind and that of the reader" (*retr.* 2.6) up to God through demonstrating the mercy of God at work in the life of one human being. While specifics of Augustine's own story do emerge plainly from the narration, these are frequently made general, presented as constitutive of universal human experience, the story of everyman.

Another way to view the many varying proposals about the unity of the *Confessions* is to suppose that readers (including scholars) intuitively experience a coherence in the work that is so complex that they find it impossible to express concisely, or alternatively, a coherence that works on so many levels that no one study can express all its ramifications. Thus, while it is true that scholarship has not yet come up with one satisfactory explanation that adequately expresses the essence of the *Confessions* (and probably never will), the many different ways of explaining its unity all reinforce one another.

Further, just as O'Donnell's reading "against" the text of the *Confessions* was a wholesome and necessary exercise for opening up new perspectives on the historical events Augustine narrates in the *Confessions*,[14] so also an effort to read "with" Augustine, as free as possible from categories superimposed on the work by translators and scholars, may lead to an enhanced understanding of the *Confessions* as a unified work of art. While this is almost impossible to do today, conscious efforts in this direction may at least bear some fruit and may allow the reader to experience the organic unity of the *Confessions* as it meanders on through the prayer that it professes to be.

In this respect Lane Fox's suggestion that the *Confessions* may have been written in a relatively short period of time (over a number of

---

[14] O'Donnell speaks of reading *Confessions* "with resistance and imagination" (J. J. O'Donnell, *Augustine: A New Biography* [New York: Harper Collins, 2005], 6).

weeks),[15] instead of over four to five years as scholarship has generally supposed, supports the arguments for alternative ways of looking at it. Whether such a short period of composition is regarded as a realistic possibility or not, it aids thinking of the *Confessions* as a (very) long and wandering contemplative prayer rather than as consciously structured autobiography to which a formal piece of exegesis was added over a number of years. The art of Augustine may lie in the fact that, while there are many discernible patterns that form the backbone of a well-designed structure and whole,[16] the tone and atmosphere of prayer is sustained to such an extent that an impression of artlessness is achieved. The reader who is willing to follow Augustine on his meditative journey may not experience any sense of a lack of unity from the hesitant and searching beginning to the end. With the master rhetorician at work, the reader should certainly expect art so subtle that it seems artless rather than a botched composition.[17]

DESCRIBING THE STRUCTURE OF THE *CONFESSIONS*

First, it may prove salutary to regard the structural units, themes, or motives in the *Confessions* as representative of various *strands* that run through the work, constituting its intricate weave,[18] each interwoven with and complementing other strands. Each strand may be seen as forming part of the complex texture of the work that can be understood on an intuitive level by just reading *with* the text, but each may also be patiently unravelled when the text is reread repeatedly, as is owed to such an intricate work.

Here some of the strands of *Confessions* are discussed, with no attempt at being exhaustive. Apart from the Psalms that help create

---

[15] R. Lane Fox, *Augustine: Conversions to* Confessions (New York: Penguin, 2015), 522–539.

[16] McMahon speaks of a "deeply structured formal coherence" that exist over and above the thematic unifiers in the work (R. McMahon, *Understanding the Medieval Meditative Ascent. Augustine, Anselm, Boethius, and Dante* [Washington, DC: Catholic University of America Press, 2006], 65).

[17] While Stephany judges that "the first time reader of Augustine's *Confessions* is likely to feel that it is a botched-together affair," it may be, in fact, only the first-time reader of *interpretations* of the *Confessions* who may feel this (W. A. Stephany, "Thematic Structure in Augustine's *Confessions*," *Augustinian Studies* 20 [1989], 129–142, at 129).

[18] Many scholars resort to describing the *Confessions* through the imagery of weaving: for example, M. Djuth, "Collation and Conversion: Seeking Wisdom in Augustine's *Confessions*," *Augustinian Studies* 41 (2010), 435–451, at 436.

the timbre of the *Confessions*, certain other scriptural sections recur with high frequency, thereby constituting a binding factor throughout. Mt 7:7 is the source of the images of seeking and finding and those of knocking and opening as unifying images that become a vehicle for expressing Augustine's search to understand God. The allusions to Paul's letter to the Romans form another such strand,[19] as does the story of the prodigal son on which Augustine models his own journey away from and back to God.[20] Another strand running through *Confessions* and providing one of the mainstays for the design and purpose of the work are the echoes of Manichaean concepts and the associated goal to convert such readers to a Catholic point of view. While these may not be discernible on the surface to those without a background in Manichaean studies, any reader, even with a little knowledge of Manichaeism, may pick up the repeated allusions that, together with the explicit mentions of Manichaeans and Manichaeism, form another unifying strand throughout.

As implied earlier, describing the structure of the *Confessions* is a precarious activity because it is based on a procedure of relatively arbitrary name-giving. This depends on subjective interpretations of the contents, purpose, or coherence of smaller or bigger subsections of the work and is open to misunderstanding and conscious or subconscious manipulation. The flaws inherent in efforts to describe the structure of the *Confessions* notwithstanding, this approach may yield useful insights into the various facets of a multidimensional composition, as long as the limitations of this way of looking are kept in mind.

Anyone who reads any critical discussion or translation of *Confessions* must be aware that their understanding will be predisposed insidiously by the naming of its sections that commentators and translators typically use to delineate what is perceived as coherent subsections of the work.[21] Readers must remember that each heading conveys one possible interpretation of a section that may also have been represented differently and that different headings could give rise to a completely

---

[19] On this, see D. Jordaan, "The Intertextual Relationship between Augustine's *Confessions* and the Letter to the Romans," Doctoral Dissertation, Stellenbosch University, 2016.

[20] G. N. Knauer, "*Peregrinatio animae* (zur Frage der Einheit der augustinischen *Konfessionen*)," *Hermes* 85 (1957), 216–248.

[21] I have indulged in this type of procedure to allocate a neat structure to the last books of the *Confessions* (A. Kotzé, *Augustine's* Confessions: *Communicative Purpose and Audience*, Supplements to Vigiliae Christianae 71 [Leiden: Brill, 2004], 234–235), but such a modus operandi is open to criticism.

different representation of the patterns and the structure of the work. In general, one of the caveats in any reading of *Confessions* is to see the disjunct mosaic of parts that has been put into circulation by scholars over many years as just that. Each such presentation is open to criticism and the reader may benefit from trying to approach the *Confessions* with an open mind, allowing themselves to be guided or even "seduced" by Augustine's prose, rather than by the headings provided by others.

But let us consider some of the structuralist proposals (especially from the 1980s and 1990s).[22] Similar suggestions concerning the putative symmetrical patterns in the first nine books of *Confessions* have been forwarded by Levenson[23] and Stephany.[24] Although there are slight differences in their naming of the parts, both see Book 5 as the central point of Books 1–9, with the other books forming symmetrical pairs around it. Stephany's scheme presents Book 1 as corresponding with Book 9 (on physical and spiritual birth, respectively), Book 2 with Book 8 (with gardens as the common background to their narratives), Book 3 with Book 7 (on the life-changing readings of Cicero and the Platonists, respectively), and Book 4 with Book 6 (concerning friendship and the "use of the material world").[25] While the neatness of such proposals is compelling, it is clear that the naming of the various common denominators used to argue for the symmetry remains to a large extent arbitrary and requires a relatively reductionist naming of each book.

Two other interesting ways to look at the structure of *Confessions* are suggested by Crosson[26] and Starnes.[27] The former sees *Confessions* as composed around two central questions: first (in Books 1–7), "how God is to be understood as everywhere and yet as not in the world?" and, second (in Books 7–13), "how such a transcendent God who cannot appear in the world can act within the world, can speak audibly to us, can call us to Himself?"[28] Starnes, on the other hand, focuses on the

---

[22] This is by no means exhaustive and the scholars named are only a few of those that have contributed to this area.

[23] C. A. Levenson, "Distance and Presence in Augustine's *Confessions*," *The Journal of Religion* 65 (1985), 500–512.

[24] Stephany, "Thematic Structure in Augustine's *Confessions*" 129–142.

[25] Stephany, "Thematic Structure in Augustine's *Confessions*," especially 136–137.

[26] F. J. Crosson, "Structure and Meaning in St. Augustine's *Confessions*," *Proceedings of the American Catholic Philosophical Association* 63 (1989), 84–97.

[27] C. Starnes, *Augustine's Conversion: A Guide to the Argument of* Confessions *I–IX* (Waterloo: Wilfred Laurier University Press, 1990).

[28] Crosson, "Structure and Meaning in St. Augustine's *Confessions*," 94.

interlacing of Trinitarian patterns in *Confessions*: in his reading, Books 1–9 concern the first person of the Trinity, Book 10 the second person, and Books 11–13 the third person, while each of the bigger sections can be seen as consisting of three smaller sections, each in turn devoted to one of the three persons of the Trinity. He regards the three main sections as three separate confessions constituting one autobiographical whole. O'Donnell's analysis of "the perplexing structural problems"[29] of the last three books of *Confessions* reads Book 11 as constructed around the first person of the Trinity and then, like McMahon, Books 12 and 13 around the second and third persons of the Trinity, respectively.[30]

McMahon sees the *Confessions* as constructed around the notion of a Christian-Platonist ascent, with a return to the Origin as its goal. In this scheme the work moves upward in stages from the spiritual autobiography in Books 1–9 to what is ontologically prior and higher: to memory in Book 10, time in Book 11, the heaven of heavens and formless matter in Book 12, and finally to God's purpose with creation in Book 13.[31] He also regards Book 13 as providing the paradigm for the whole of the *Confessions*.

Further, thinking about the structure of an ancient work by an author who vies with predecessors like Vergil must include an evaluation of its opening and closing sections (which also pertains to how the unity of the work is understood). Taking seriously the prologue of the *Confessions* as the programmatic opening one may expect from a master rhetorician, may counteract the view of the work as an awkward combination of autobiography and exegesis and support efforts to read it on its own terms. The opening presents the reader with a confessing sinful man praying in a meditative searching way. Readers who allow themselves to be caught in the spell of this opening (as they are meant to) may be more ready to open themselves up to the central theme of man trying to understand who and what God is and – as puzzling a question – what man is to God than to expect autobiography in the modern sense of the word.

The other aspect of the opening that must be allowed its full value in determining the reading of the *Confessions* is the extent to which the

---

[29] J. J. O'Donnell, *Augustine:* Confessions (Oxford: Clarendon, 1992), vol. 3, 250.

[30] O'Donnell, *Augustine:* Confessions, vol. 3, 251.

[31] McMahon concisely recapitulates the arguments of *Augustine's Prayerful Ascent* in his later book, *Understanding the Medieval Meditative Ascent*, 69–71.

opening lines of the work sound like a reading from the Psalter, with all the implications of this. If the work starts by speaking in the words of the Psalms, this has important implications: such an opening would have determined the readers' first impressions and their expectations of what will follow.[32] Incidentally, it may do well to remember that both Augustine's fellow brethren (whom he names in *Retractions* as readers of the *Confessions*) and readers with a Manichaean background (whom many have argued were an important part of the intended audience of the *Confessions*)[33] were well versed in the Psalms of the Hebrew Old Testament or those from the Manichaean Psalm Book, respectively, both sets of which contained confessions of praise, of sin, and of faith, while also quoting words from other authoritative Scriptures. Of course, the number and character of the autobiographical sections that are inserted into the Psalm-like prayer in the rest of the *Confessions* far exceed in scope and unity the type of autobiographical moments that are offered in, for example, the Hebrew Psalms. Yet, Augustine manages to sustain the tone and feel of a prayer, and then of the Psalter, throughout (more about this later).

The saturation of his prose, not only in the opening lines, but throughout, with allusions to the Psalms makes the prayer a Psalm-like prayer throughout. A comparative study of the role of the Psalter in the early Church and the way in which the Psalms function in *Confessions* may perhaps contribute useful insights in the future. That the Psalm quotations also have implications for how the structural coherence of the *Confessions* is understood is demonstrated by Georg Knauer's seminal study.[34]

To get back to links between the opening and the closing sections of an ancient work, here it is mainly the recapitulation of the oblique allusion to Mt 7:7 in *conf.* 1.1.1 in the closing words of the work that may be pointed out as constituting a typical ring composition. Also the emphasis on an attitude of searching in the prologue of the work is prominent in its closing words. So is the idea of the searching heart finding rest that is recapitulated in *conf.* 1.1.1.

---

[32] Also, Lehman argues that the use of the language of the Psalms in the *Confessions* contributes in an important way to the "literary and theological integrity" as well as the generic distinctiveness of the work (J. S. Lehman, "'As I Read, I Was Set on Fire.' On the Psalms in Augustine's *Confessions*," *Logos* 16 [2013], 160–184, at 160).

[33] See Kotzé, *Augustine's* Confessions, 85–94.

[34] G. N. Knauer, *Psalmenzitate in Augustins Konfessionen* (Göttingen: Vandenhoeck & Ruprecht, 1955).

NAMING THE GENRES OF THE *CONFESSIONS*

The section on the generic characteristics of the *Confessions* aims to elucidate some of the generic labels that are commonly used in descriptions of the *Confessions*. It points out the disadvantages of some as well as ways in which others may be used fruitfully to describe the fusion of generic conventions of the *Confessions*. It is argued here that the reader's point of departure should be that the work did not originate in a generic vacuum – that is, it is generically less unique than is often implied. It deliberately makes use of conventions from a variety of antecedent genres in an artful fusion that has meaning, even if much of this may elude the modern reader. For, in spite of Pierre Courcelle's large-scale and groundbreaking work on the relationship between *Confessions* and the antecedent literary tradition,[35] scholarship has not yet exhausted the ways in which it incorporates preceding generic tropes.

While many of the generic labels commonly attached to the *Confessions* illuminate different aspects of this multidimensional work, it was argued earlier that the two most commonly applied labels, auto-biography and exegesis, have a detrimental effect on the understanding of the work and should be resisted. In the following, after some remarks on the concept of genre per se and some general labels that may be attached to the *Confessions*, the terms autobiography and exegesis are discussed first, followed by an examination of the usefulness of the labels apologetic and protreptic, also frequently used to refer to the *Confessions*. In addition to the use of the term "paraenetic," the conclusion concisely considers the use of the words Psalter, prayer, and song to describe the work.

While the term genre is highly problematic and used in a loose way by scholars, genre is a category that influences the reading of all texts fundamentally. Even though readers' expectations concerning the genre of whatever they read are mostly subconscious,[36] very little understanding of a text is possible without a whole set of such expectations and assumptions.[37] Thus, while the issue of the genre of *Confessions* has led

---

[35] Courcelle demonstrated authoritatively that a significant number of motifs and conventions from antecedent literature play an important role in the *Confessions* (P. Courcelle, *Les "Confessions" de s. Augustin dans la tradition littéraire: Antécédents et postérité* [Paris: Études Augustiniennes, 1963]).

[36] A. Fowler, *Kinds of Literature: An Introduction to the Theory of Genres and Modes* (Oxford: Clarendon, 1982), 25.

[37] See, for example, M. Chamberlain and P. Thompson, "Introduction," in *Narrative and Genre*, eds. M. Chamberlain and P. Thompson, Routledge Studies in Memory and Narrative 1 (London: Routledge, 1998), 1–22; A. J. Guerra, *Romans and the*

countless readers and scholars into *aporia* for centuries, it cannot be ignored.[38] If readers do not recognize that the names they attach to the work, including generic labels (e.g., autobiography or exegesis), fundamentally predispose their reading, and then consciously interrogate the connotations they attach to such labels, they may be led astray.

The issue of readers' expectations is a thorny one when it comes to ancient literary works. In John Swales' discussions of genre, he points to the "expert members" of a "parent discourse community" who are able to understand clues and codes in a work that may be lost on readers who do not belong to this community.[39] One of the – albeit flawed – ways in which modern readers may come closer to understanding how an ancient work may have functioned in its original context (and thus control their expectations) is through a study of antecedent and contemporary literature. While there is still much scope for work on this, some aspects of the issue are touched on in the later discussions.

Let us start with two nuanced descriptions of the *Confessions* that do not reduce it to autobiography and exegesis. Paula Fredriksen characterizes the work as "a brilliant and profoundly original work of creative theology [which] combines biblical interpretation, late Platonism, and anti-Manichaean polemic with haunting autobiographical narrative."[40] Also, Paul Rigby's perceptive formulation, because it simultaneously puts into play a great variety of terms with which to label the *Confessions*, avoids some of the most dangerous pitfalls of naming. It demonstrates both the richness of the *Confessions* and the wide spectrum of generic (and other) labels that can be attached to it:[41]

> Augustine's *confessio* draws on several genres: praise, hymn, lyric, lamentation, and repentance. It unites speculation with scriptural exegesis and exhortation with testimony, soliloquy with wisdom. *Confessio* culminates in the self-portrait of Augustine the bishop,

Apologetic Tradition: The Purpose, Genre and Audience of Paul's Letter, Monograph Series (Society for New Testament Studies) 81 (Cambridge: Cambridge University Press, 1995), 13.

[38] Here I differ fundamentally from C. Conybeare, "Reading the *Confessions*," in *A Companion to Augustine*, ed. M. Vessey (Oxford: Wiley-Blackwell, 2012), 99–110, at 99, who is of the opinion that "to read the *Confessions* through the lens of genre – any genre – is a mistake."

[39] J. Swales, *Genre Analysis: English in Academic and Research Settings*, Cambridge Applied Linguistics Series (Cambridge: Cambridge University Press, 1990), 58.

[40] P. Fredriksen, "The *Confessions* as Autobiography," in *A Companion to Augustine*, 87.

[41] It also demonstrates the looseness with which the term genre is often used.

seeker after wisdom, exegete, philosopher-theologian, seated in his study at Hippo Regius, immersed in these diverse genres as he writes his *Confessions* within the narrative of salvation history.[42]

To come to some objections to describing the *Confessions* as autobiography: while it can be said without controversy that the *Confessions* is predominantly a first-person narration, calling it "an autobiography" is more problematic. The overfamiliar word from a later era brings into play too many connotations that do not apply to *Confessions*: the contents, style, and aims of Augustine's narrative are hugely dissimilar to the majority of modern autobiographies, and the last part of the work, while continuing the first-person narration, cannot be described as autobiographical in the modern sense. Using the label autobiography today is, in fact, a hindrance to understanding the work.

On the other hand, an awareness of the nature and purposes of first-person and autobiographical narratives in antecedent literature may shed valuable light on the aims Augustine may have pursued in using a first-person narration and autobiographical details in the *Confessions*. Kotzé has argued that there is a significant intersection between autobiographical narration and apologetic, protreptic, and paraenetic aims in ancient literature (both pagan and Christian) from Plato's *Apology of Socrates* to Augustine's *Confessions* and beyond.[43] While a curiosity about the lives of famous people did seem to feature during Augustine's lifetime, the extant (preceding and contemporary) first-person and autobiographical narratives tend not to aim primarily at providing information about the life of the narrator, but rather to pursue communicative aims like defending life choices, trying to convert readers (outsiders) to a specific philosophy or religious group, or confirming the benefits of the choice for such a group and affirming the identity of insiders. Yet, the way in which the *Confessions* adopts and adapts generic conventions from preceding first-person narratives has not been fully explored.

Thinking about the historicity of the *Confessions* should also be seen in the light of these predominant aims of ancient autobiographical writing: historical accuracy is an issue that preoccupies modern readers and historians (especially when studying autobiography); ancient readers were probably in general more interested in the *way* in which

---

[42] P. Rigby, *The Theology of Augustine's* Confessions (Cambridge: Cambridge University Press, 2015), 6.

[43] A. Kotzé, "Perspectives on Three Instances of Greek Autobiographical Writing from the Fourth Century BCE," *Classical World* 109 (2015), 39–67.

the author presented well-known (or mythological) figures as *exempla* to follow or not. Readers may have expected a conversion story, like the one woven into the prayer of the first eight books of the *Confessions*, to have aims like defending, converting, or affirming rather than to provide a comprehensive life story. In the ancient world, the autobiography occurs in diverse genres and usually in service of other goals. Innovative as Augustine is, one cannot assume that expectations of this kind would have suddenly disappeared from the minds of the parent discourse community within which the *Confessions* first circulated, even if in hindsight we call his work "the first modern autobiography."

Describing the last part of the *Confessions* with the term "exegesis" is only possible if the observer looks at the work from a long distance, mostly because of the connotations of orderly, commentary-like discourse associated with the term, which is absent from Books 11–13. Readers who were to read *with* Augustine's text, without preconceived ideas, would, to my mind, not so easily infer at the opening of Book 11 that they have now embarked on reading exegesis, in the normal sense of the word. What distinguishes Augustine's discourse most from exegesis, is, of course, the fact that he is writing a prayer about reading Scripture, confessing "both what [he] know[s] and what [he] still find[s] baffling" (*conf.* 11.2.2), and he does this so convincingly through his lyrical emotive prose that readers have the impression of praying with him, much more than of reading exegesis. Whereas in the previous books of the *Confessions* Augustine describes himself as praising, confessing, and meditatively searching to understand God through looking at himself and the events of his life, from Book 11 onward he depicts himself as meditatively searching to understand God through knocking to fathom the hidden depths of Scripture. The approach and the tone is similar to that of the meditation on Ps 4 in Book 9 (*conf.* 9.4.7–11), clearly dissimilar to what most today would describe as exegesis.

Apologetics is another generic category sometimes associated with the *Confessions*,[44] with scholars regarding the work as part of an apology demonstrating how (and that) Augustine broke with Manichaeism.

---

[44] See, for example, J. D. BeDuhn, *Augustine's Manichaean Dilemma 1: Conversion and Apostasy, 373–388* C.E. Divinations: Rereading Late Ancient Religion (Philadelphia: University of Pennsylvania Press, 2010), 136, and *Augustine's Manichaean Dilemma 2: Making a "Catholic" Self, 388–401* C.E. Divinations: Rereading Late Ancient Religion (Philadelphia: University of Pennsylvania Press, 2013), 239–273.

First-person narration and autobiographical content are closely associated with apologetic aims from the earliest examples of autobiographical writing;[45] early readers may thus have expected the *Confessions* to potentially fulfill an apologetic purpose. Yet, the *Confessions* does not present itself as a defense, mostly because the narrative stance Augustine employs makes his all-knowing God the only addressee, a God before whom no explanation or defense is needed or even possible.[46] What apology there is present highly indirectly.

To move on to the next generic label: since Feldmann's *Augustinus Lexikon* article in 1994,[47] it has become something of a convention to call the *Confessions* a protreptic,[48] but I have argued that, because scholars use this term very loosely, it is not always clear what they mean when they call the *Confessions* a protreptic, partly because research on protreptic leaves a lot to be desired.[49] The point is that the most widely circulating definitions of protreptic assume that it is literature that aims to convert the not-yet-converted (outsiders), while the majority view on the *Confessions* is still that its intended audience is mainly insiders, Augustine's fellow *servi dei*. I have thus argued that, taking into account mainstream definitions of protreptic and the related term paraenetic, the *Confessions* would be more aptly called a protreptic-paraenetic writing.[50] The *Confessions* is aimed at a mixed

---

[45] Kotzé, "Perspectives on Three Instances of Greek Autobiographical Writing," 47, 51–54.

[46] In *conf.* 1.5.6, Augustine says explicitly that he cannot defend himself before God (his iniquity is indefensible): "I do not argue my case against you." Augustine's strategy is then the opposite of that of Socrates or Isocrates, who, in Plato's *Apology of Socrates* and the *Antidosis*, respectively, try to put the record straight about their past actions.

[47] Feldman, "*Confessiones*," 1134–1193.

[48] Scholars calling the *Confessions* a protreptic are, for example, C. P. Mayer, "Die *Confessiones* des Aurelius Augustinus: eine philosophisch-theologische Werbeschrift (Protreptikos) für christliche Spiritualität," *Theologie und Glaube* 88 (1998), 285–303; S. Lancel, *Saint Augustine*, trans. A. Neville (London: SCM, 2002), 210; W. Geerlings, "Christologie," in *Augustin Handbuch*, ed. V. H. Drecoll (Tübingen: Mohr Siebeck, 2007), 434–443, at 436; J. Lössl, "Augustine's *Confessions* as a Consolation of Philosophy," in *"In Search of Truth": Augustine, Manichaeism and other Gnosticism*, eds. J. A. van den Berg, A. Kotzé, T. Nicklas, and M. Scopello, Nag Hammadi Studies 74 (Leiden: Brill, 2011), 47–73, at 47–49.

[49] This is slowly being rectified by the recent publication by J. H. Collins, *Exhortations to Philosophy. The Protreptics of Plato, Isocrates and Aristotle* (Oxford: Oxford University Press, 2015) and the collected volume *When Wisdom Calls: Philosophical Protreptic in Antiquity*, ed. O. Alieva, A. Kotzé, and S. van der Meeren (Turnhout: Brepols, 2018).

[50] See, for example, A. Kotzé, "Protreptic, Paraenetic and Augustine's *Confessions*," in *"In Search of Truth,"* 3–23.

audience (including insiders but also potential Manichaean readers) and the exhortation to insiders is more aptly called paraenetic, while the urgent efforts in the work to convince Manichaean readers of their errors is what may be called protreptic.[51]

CONCLUSION

It will have become clear from the earlier arguments how elusive the genre of the *Confessions* is and that it is almost impossible to find one generic label or term to aptly categorize the work as a whole. It has also been argued here that understanding the generic innovativeness of the *Confessions* is of paramount importance but that there is still much work to be done in this field.

There are numerous ways in which the reader may conceive of the structural components of this highly complex literary work and its unity. Most importantly, the article argues that assumptions about structure and genre can fundamentally influence the reading of a text like the *Confessions* and that readers should interrogate the expectations with which they approach the work. For this reason, perhaps, the relatively imprecise labels, Psalterium, prayer, or song, used by Sieben, McMahon, and Conybeare, respectively,[52] do justice to the nature the *Confessions* as a whole, without predisposing readers in ways that may jeopardize their understanding. These terms take into account the role of language from the Psalms in creating a unity of tone or timbre throughout and encapsulate the pervasive presence of scriptural language (especially the language of the Psalms), the meditation on a section from the Old Testament, and the presence of autobiographical content, meditative prayer, and personal confession.

---

[51] This dichotomous distinction between protreptic and paraenetic did not exist in ancient literature, but the terms have developed in modern scholarship to denote two distinct types of audiences and communicative aims and may be used in this manner.

[52] H.-J. Sieben, "Der Psalter und die Bekehrung der VOCES und AFFECTUS: Zu Augustinus, *Conf.* IX, 4.6 und X, 33," *Theologie und Philosophie* 52 (1977), 481–497, at 484 suggests that *Confessions* may be called an amplified Psalterium; McMahon refers to the "meditative texture of its literary structure as a prayer" (*Understanding the Medieval Meditative Ascent,* 65); Conybeare emphasizes that "*Confessions* is, quite simply, a song" and "singing is its natural mode" ("Reading the *Confessions,*" 101).

Further Reading

BeDuhn, J. D. *Augustine's Manichaean Dilemma 2: Making a "Catholic" Self, 388–401 C.E,* Divinations: Rereading Late Ancient Religion. Philadelphia: University of Pennsylvania Press, 2013 (chapters 9 and 10, 314–402).

Brown, P. *Augustine of Hippo: A Biography.* Berkeley: University of California Press, 2000 (chapter 16, 151–177).

Kotzé, A. *Augustine's* Confessions*: Communicative Purpose and Audience.* Supplements to Vigiliae Christianae 71. Leiden: Brill, 2004.

Lane Fox, R. *Augustine: Conversions to* Confessions. New York: Penguin, 2015.

McMahon, R. *Understanding the Medieval Meditative Ascent: Augustine, Anselm, Boethius, and Dante.* Washington, DC: Catholic University of America Press, 2006 (chapters 2 and 3, 64–158).

O'Donnell, J. J. *Augustine: A New Biography.* New York: Harper Collins, 2005 (chapter 2, 35–62).

  Augustine: Confessions*: Commentary on Books 8–13,* three vols. Oxford: Clarendon, 1992 (especially the introduction and the introductory sections to books and sections of books).

Stock, B. *Augustine the Reader: Meditation, Self-Knowledge and the Ethics of Interpretation.* Cambridge, MA: Harvard University Press, 1996 (section 1, 21–122).

van Fleteren, F. *"Confessiones."* In *Augustine through the Ages: An Encyclopedia,* ed. A. D. Fitzgerald. Grand Rapids, MI: Eerdmans, 1999, 227–232.

Vessey, M. (ed.). *A Companion to Augustine.* Oxford: Wiley-Blackwell, 2012. (section 2 on the "Confessions," 55–110).

3 Anticipated Readers

JASON DAVID BEDUHN

Augustine anticipated certain readers for the *Confessions*, and composed it with them in mind. Yet, the complexity of its themes and concerns suggests more than one intended audience. James O'Donnell rightly has cautioned against "the assumption that there lies somewhere unnoticed about the *Confessions* a neglected key to unlock all mysteries. But for a text as multilayered and subtle as the *Confessions*, any attempt to find a single key is pointless."[1] Both the timing of its composition and the evidence of its content suggest that Augustine addressed the *Confessions* simultaneously both to his critics within the Catholic and Donatist churches of North Africa and to his former compatriots among the Manichaean community. By chronicling his passage from youthful Manichaean to mature Catholic, he could affirm the truthfulness of that transformation to those within the Church who doubted it, while at the same time making a compelling case for others to follow him into the Catholic fold.

As an apologia, the *Confessions* is addressed to critics inside the Catholic community, as well as to Donatists using him as an example of the questionable background of the new crop of Catholic bishops.[2] A significant number of Augustine's former Manichaean associates had found their way into positions of leadership in the Catholic Church in Africa and Numidia. This not only made an easy target for Donatist

---

[1] J. J. O'Donnell, *Augustine:* Confessions (Oxford: Clarendon, 1992), vol. 1, xxiii.

[2] Scholars stressing the apologetic context of the *Confessions* include: M. Wundt, "Augustins Konfessionen," *Zeitschrift für die neutestamentliche Wissenschaft* 22 (1923), 161–206, esp. 166–178; H. Chadwick, "On Re-reading the *Confessions*," in *Saint Augustine the Bishop: A Book of Essays*, eds. F. LeMoine and C. Kleinhenz, Garland Reference Library of the Humanities 1830 (New York: Garland, 1994), 139–160; P.-M. Hombert, *Nouvelles recherches de chronologie augustinienne* (Paris: Institut d'Études Augustinienne, 2000), 9–23.

critics, but also raised suspicions among the older Catholic leadership.[3] The Primate of Numidia, Megalius, had initially refused the request to ordain Augustine as (coadjutor) bishop of Hippo, committing his objections to a letter, which apparently highlighted lingering suspicions about his Manichaean connections (c. *Cresc.* 3.80.92; cf. 4.64.78–9; c. *lit. Pet.* 3.16.19; *Gesta coll. Carth.* 3.234–247; *Brev. conl.* 3.7.9). The "episcopal" or "holy" council (*in episcoporum concilio probare, c. Cresc.* 4.64.79; *sancto concilio, c. lit. Pet.* 3.16.19) Augustine mentions as the place where Megalius finally withdrew his charges would have been the episcopal commission empanelled to investigate them, which appears to have concluded its work in early 396.[4] It could not have done so without requiring a formal response from Augustine to the charges.[5] Given his predilections and talents, this defense would have taken a polished rhetorical form, and certain peculiarities in the structure and emphases of the *Confessions* suggest that it preserves large portions of this defense embedded in the larger, later work.

The formal opening of Book 5, with its stress on Augustine's twenty-ninth year (a year in which actually very little happened of significance to his spiritual development), and the expansive detail in this and the following books about a relatively short period of time (in contrast to the rapid pace of the previous four books), may reflect Augustine's earlier need to explain actions under scrutiny by the episcopal commission: his previous association with Manichaeism and the motives for his decision to leave Africa in 383 at a time of its intensified persecution, his Manichaean sponsors in Rome in 384 and the position they secured for him in Milan, his sudden resignation from his post in Milan and retirement into the countryside in 386, his baptism in 387, and his delay in returning to Africa until 388.[6] By telling a largely interior story, he could undercut the suspicious appearance of his conduct at the time, professing an agonized private struggle to find his way to God and truth. Apart from the question of how closely the account

---

[3] W. H. C. Frend, *The Donatist Church: A Movement of Protest in Roman North Africa* (Oxford: Clarendon, 1952), 236, 256–257; P. Brown, *Augustine of Hippo*, rev. ed. (Berkeley: University of California Press, 2000), 163.

[4] D. E. Trout, "The Dates of the Ordination of Paulinus of Bordeaux and of His Departure for Nola," *Recherches d'Études Augustiniennes* 37 (1991), 237–260.

[5] For comparison, the episcopal commission formed to look into charges against Instantius at Bordeaux a decade earlier is reported by Sulpicius Severus, *Chron.* 2.49: "Instantius was enjoined to plead his cause; and after he was found unable to clear himself, he was pronounced unworthy of the office of bishop."

[6] On the need to account for the entire period of his absence from Africa, see Wundt, "Augustins Konfessionen," 178.

may or may not have matched the actual course of his intellectual and moral development, its confessional self-criticism offered a brilliant rhetorical strategy for gaining a sympathetic hearing from his accusers.

As a protreptic, the *Confessions* offers in Augustine's own story a potential path for others to follow into the Catholic Christian faith. By structuring the entire work around confession of his human failings and the never-complete struggle for moral perfection, Augustine may have thought himself lighting the way for puritanical Donatist Christians. The work's Platonic themes might indicate that Augustine imagined "pagan" Platonists would find amenable the similar transcendent emphases of Christianity, and perhaps learn from his own account of how his spiritual ascent could only succeed when he surrendered his will to God (*conf.* 9.1.1), since he considered them to be those who "see where to go, but do not see how" (*conf.* 7.20.26). But the material Augustine wove into the *Confessions* to address both of these anticipated readers also would serve a third audience interested in the struggle for moral perfection and ascent to divinity: the Manichaeans. It is the potential Manichaean reader that the structure and much of the rhetoric of the work anticipates, as has been recognized by numerous scholars.[7]

[7] J. Gibb and W. Montgomery, *The Confessions of Augustine* (Cambridge: Cambridge University Press, 1927); A. Allgeier, "Der Einfluß des Manichäismus auf die exegetische Fragestellung bei Augustin," in *Aurelius Augustinus: Die Festschrift der Görres-Gesellschaft zum 1500 Todestage des heiligen Augustinus*, eds. M. Grabmann and J. Mausbach (Cologne: J. P. Bachem, 1930), 1–13; A. Pincherle, *Sant'Agostino d'Ippona. Vescovo e teologo* (Bari: G Laterza et Figli, 1930), 144–145; A. Adam, "Das Fortwirken des Manichäismus bei Augustin," *Zeitschrift für Kirchengeschichte* 69 (1958), 1–25; A. Vecchi, "L'antimanichaeismo nelle 'Confessioni' de Sant'Agostino," *Giornale di metafisica* 20 (1965), 91–121; R. J. O'Connell, *St. Augustine's Early Theory of Man, A. D. 386–391* (Cambridge, MA: Harvard University Press, 1968), 16 and 79; G. H. Tavard, "St. Augustine Between Mani and Christ," *Patristic and Byzantine Review* 5 (1988), 196–206; E. Feldmann, "Et inde rediens fecerat sibi deum (Conf. 7, 20). Beobachtungen zur Genese des augustinischen Gottesbegriffes und zu dessen Funktion in den *Confessiones*," in *Collectanea Augustiniana. Mélanges T. J. van Bavel*, ed. B. Bruning, M. Lamberigts, and J. Van Houtem (Leuven: Leuven University Press, 1990), 881–904; H. Chadwick, "The Attractions of Mani," in *Pléroma. Salus carnis. Homenaje a Antonio Orbe*, ed. E. Romero-Pose (Santiago de Compostela: Aldecoa, 1990), 203–222; C. Joubert, "Le Livre XIII et la structure des *Confessiones* de Saint Augustin," *Revue des sciences religieuses* 66 (1992), 77–117; J. van Oort, "Augustine's Critique of Manichaeism: The Case of *Confessions* III 6,10 and Its Implications," in *Aspects of Religious Contact and Conflict in the Ancient World*, ed. P. W. van der Horst, Utrechtse theologische reeks 31 (Utrecht: Faculteit der Godgeleerdheid, Universiteit Utrecht, 1995), 57–68 and *Augustinus' Confessiones: Gnostische en christelijke spiritualiteit in een*

Augustine had a unique opportunity to fuse polemic and protreptic in the *Confessions*, since, in criticizing himself and his own past errors, he placed himself back in the company of those he wished to reach. If the Manichaeans were prideful, delusional, carnal, chattering, or even insane, so once was he.[8] Erich Feldmann points to Augustine's apparently deliberate parallelism between the "sickness" he diagnoses in himself in Book 7 of the *Confessions* and that still afflicting the Manichaeans in his closing thoughts at the end of Book 13.[9] He took much of the argument he had developed in his previous anti-Manichaean writings, and found ways to insert them into the account of his own supposed ruminations as a dissatisfied Manichaean. In composing the *Confessions*, therefore, Augustine sympathetically reentered the Manichaean world view through his memory of it, and attempted to reason from its own premises to "Catholic" conclusions with the benefit of the hindsight of his own post-conversion intellectual development. This blending of familiar polemical critiques of Manichaeism with an account of his own self-discovery keyed to Manichaean themes made the *Confessions* "the most idiosyncratic, original and creative of Augustine's anti-Manichaean polemics,"[10] and perhaps for this reason it deserves the "supreme place" among his "anti-Manichaean" works.[11]

From the opening invocation of God at the beginning of the *Confessions* to its closing words, Augustine sent rhetorical signals he knew possessed special resonance for Manichaeans, even if they would pass with other readers for pious and worthy sentiments.[12] It was very much

---

diepzinnig dokument (Turnhout: Brepols, 2002); P. Fredriksen, "Excaecati Occulta Justitia Dei: Augustine on Jews and Judaism," *Journal of Early Christian Studies* 3 (1995), 299–324; V. Drecoll, *Die Entstehung der Gnadenlehre Augustins*, Beiträge zur historischen Theologie 109 (Tübingen: Mohr Siebeck, 1999), 255; A. Kotzé, *Augustine's Confessions: Communicative Purpose and Audience*, Supplements to Vigiliae Christianae 71 (Leiden: Brill, 2004); J. D. BeDuhn, *Augustine's Manichaean Dilemma 2: Making a 'Catholic' Self, 388–401 C.E.*, Divinations: Rereading Late Ancient Religion (Philadelphia, University of Pennsylvania Press, 2013), 314–402.

[8] See the analysis of this anti-Manichaean vocabulary of the *Confessions* in van Oort, "Augustine's Critique of Manichaeism," 60–62.

[9] Feldmann, "Et inde rediens fecerat sibi deum (Conf. 7, 20)," 889–890.

[10] Fredriksen, "Excaecati Occulta Justitia Dei," 309–310.

[11] Chadwick, "The Attractions of Mani," 204.

[12] Cf. Kotzé, *Augustine's Confessions*, 220: "The whole of the prologue of the *Confessions* is so strongly dominated by 'Manichaean concerns' that one cannot but see this as a significant indication of who a very important segment of the intended audience of the work may be." Similarly, van Oort, "Augustine's Critique of Manichaeism" adduces several examples of phrasing drawn from the Manichaean rhetorical repertoire both in the prologue and at key points throughout the work, of which, in some cases, "they alone would have heard the polemic wordplay" (67).

to his point that he could quote imagery and sentiments amenable to a Manichaean audience from the Old Testament Psalms, finding passages that echoed the famous hymnic repertoire of the Manichaeans. On the one hand, they demonstrated the remarkably similar devotional spirit underpinning both Manichaean and Nicene theologies; while in certain of their contents they provided valuable corrections of Manichaean errors. The same is true of Augustine's extensive references to Paul's rhetoric of the divided self in Book 8; with these he both evokes and corrects Manichaean readings of the Apostle. Augustine offered his analysis of his own interior vacillations in refutation of those "who on perceiving two wills engaged in deliberation assert that in us there are two natures, one good, the other evil, each with a mind of its own." "These same people," he continues, "will be good if they embrace true opinions and assent to true teaching, and so merit the apostle's commendation, 'You were darkness once, but now you are light in the Lord'" (*conf.* 8.10.22).

Augustine's knowing identification of God by the Manichaean title *deus veritas* (*conf.* 4.16.31), his heavy use of light imagery to represent the nature and action of God in dualistic contrast to darkness or gloom (*conf.* 13.2.3, 6.7, 8.9, 14.15), his characterization of personal transformation as an interior illumination dispelling darkness (*conf.* 8.12.29; 11.9.11), his references to the Manichaean motifs of God's redeeming right hand (*conf.* 3.11.19; 6.16.26; 8.1.2; 9.1.1; 10.41.66; 11.29.39),[13] the scattered and collected self (*conf.* 2.1.1; 4.8.13; 9.4.10; 10.29.40; 12.16.23),[14] and being "sealed" (e.g., *conf.* 9.4.11) – all serve to express Augustine's spiritual quest in terms familiar to a Manichaean audience. Similarly, his heavy use of Mt 7:7 throughout the *Confessions*[15] takes up a remarked upon Manichaean fondness for its image of knocking and opening, seeking and finding (*mor.* 1.17.31); he had employed it frequently before (e.g., *c. Acad.* 2.3.9; *sol.* 1.1.3; *lib. arb.* 2.2.6; *util. cred.* 1.1; *c. ep. Man.* 3.4) to chide them for prematurely ending their search for truth, confident they had found it. He summons them onward, to continue the quest they once shared, and not stop short amid the errors of the Manichaean faith.

Augustine recalls with sympathy and understanding the sentiments and motives that led him and his friends to embrace the Manichaean

---

[13] Cf. Augustine, *c. Faust* 15.5; *c. ep. Man.* 11.13; *c. Sec.* 1; *2Ps* 67.14–16; 69.5–7; 94.2; 108.17–19; 112.26–7; 153.4; *1Ke* 37.28–42.23; 148.18–20; 226.7–11.

[14] Cf. *1Ke* 178.13–23; Augustine, *c. Faust* 24.1.

[15] *Conf.* 1.1.1; 6.4.5; 11.18–20; 11.2.3, 22.28; 12.1.1, 12.15, 15.22, 24.33; 13.35.50, 38.53. See the discussion of Augustine's use of this verse in the *Confessions* in Kotzé, *Augustine's Confessions*, 134–147.

religion. They were, after all, truth-seekers. "Truth is loved in such a way that whoever loves something else wishes what he loves to be the truth," Augustine empathetically explained, "and because he does not wish to be deceived, neither does he wish to be proved wrong. And so men hate the truth for the sake of the thing they love as the truth" (*conf.* 10.23.34). Augustine suggests that the sweet bonds of friendship explained the solidarity of purpose, and all of the positive feelings, that came out of their Manichaean experience (*conf.* 4.8.13). Yet, nothing guaranteed that the solidarity friendship fosters necessarily leads to good; the Pear Incident reviewed in Book 2 serves in part to illustrate the potential joint misguidedness that friendship could bring (*conf.* 2.8.16–9.17), foreshadowing the much graver error of urging each other into Manichaeism. They had formed a mutually reinforcing clique of intellectual dilettantes, "seduced and seducers, deceived ourselves and deceivers of others ... in the company of friends who through me and with me were alike deceived" (*conf.* 4.1.1). Yet, the fulfillment of all that their friendship promised, with its pursuit of truth, could still be realized, once set on the correct path.

Augustine similarly showed empathy with the natural and under-standable desire the Manichaeans had for a world without punishment, and for a God who prevents rather than inflicts hurt, reflecting on his own fear of corporal discipline as a young schoolboy (*conf.* 1.9.14–15), until he learned the necessary role of punishment in driving him toward the good (*conf.* 1.12.19; cf. 2.2.4). Likewise, he empathetically recognized the emotional appeal of Manichaean myth, recounting his own youthful love and fascination for the drama of classical mythology and poetry (*conf.* 1.13.20–17.27), noting the way in which such tales play on emotions and passions, evoking sympathy for fictional characters and imaginary events (cf. *conf.* 3.2.2–4), and making the comparison explicit in *conf.* 3.6.11. Yet, he maintained, human tears and anxiety should be directed at ourselves in our sinful condition, motivating us to reform, rather than wasted on beings who for all we know may never have existed (*conf.* 1.13.21; 3.2.2–4, 4.5.10; cf. 9.6.14–7.15; 9.12.33–13.36).

On the basis of the good intentions evident in those who shared such sensibilities, Augustine even ventured to portray Manichaeism as a reasonable and valued stage in his own spiritual odyssey, even if it had to be left behind in the end. As Robert O'Connell has emphasized, Augustine acknowledged that the Manichaean appeal to reason, and criticism of those who mindlessly yielded to authority, helped him to "'stand up' on his own intellectual feet," and in several places we can see him "tacitly acknowledging a debt he owed to the Manichees, and to what was valid in the taunts they leveled against the 'blind faith' of African Catholics."[16] "On this issue," O'Connell continues, "Augustine clearly thought the Manichees were closer to the truth than the North African Catholicism he knew" as a child; "this was one of the reasons why Augustine could think of his 'conversion' to Manichaeism as a progressive step,"[17] away from the poorly conceived Christian faith of his youth, with its anthropomorphism, its ascription to God of the creation of a substantial evil, and its unsophisticated conception of Christ's incarnation (*conf.* 5.10.19–20). He acknowledged the role of "some kind of piety [*qualiscumque pietas*]" in leading him to reject the crude form of religion he had learned as a child for higher ideas. In short, he acknowledges in the Manichaeans an understandable, if ultimately misguided, attempt to know God, "more pious [*magis pius*]" than the common misunderstandings of ordinary Catholics. It was "better to believe [*melius credere*]" such things as the Manichaeans taught than to fail to advance out of the simple superstitions that the Manichaeans critiqued so effectively. Even Manichaean materialism is an understandable mistake within the limits of our embodied condition (*conf.* 7.1.2), until one discovers, perhaps only through divine revelation, a higher order of reality. Augustine even conceded that God could be perceived to some degree through material creation, according to the inductive method embraced by the Manichaeans (alluding to Rm 1:20) (*conf.* 7.10.16, 17.23, 20.26). But one must not stop at this preliminary stage of insight and intellectual progress: one must advance, must ascend, to higher ways of thinking.

This sympathetic treatment of Manichaeans, even in the midst of their errors, culminates in Augustine's portrait of the Manichaean leader in North Africa, Faustus. His surprisingly positive characterizations of him in Book 5 (in sharp contrast to his treatment of him in *De utilitate credendi* and *Contra Faustum Manicheum*, before and after the *Confessions*, respectively), is delivered with some self-consciousness that he risked offending less open-minded Catholic readers in being true to his positive impressions (*conf.* 5.6.11).[18] First of all, Faustus served as an example of a good person led astray by heresy; he possessed the foundations of genuine piety: modesty, awareness of his own ignorance,

---

[16] R. J. O'Connell, *Images of Conversion in St. Augustine's Confessions* (New York: Fordham University Press, 1996), 8.

[17] Ibid., 83, n. 12.

[18] See J. D. BeDuhn, *Augustine's Manichaean Dilemma 1: Conversion and Apostasy, 373–388 C.E.*, Divinations: Rereading Late Ancient Religion (Philadelphia: University of Pennsylvania Press, 2010), 106–134.

and a "disciplined, confessional mind" (*conf.* 5.7.12). In light of Augustine's subsequent narrative demonstration of the relative impotence of
knowing the right things, and the primacy of commitment to piety in
personal conduct and orientation to God, we can observe how he con-
forms Faustus to the type of the person of simple, uneducated piety,
whose success at commitment and self-discipline goaded an Augustine
still trapped in intellectual *curiositas* (*conf.* 8.8.19). It was this Manichaean bishop himself ("unwittingly and without intending it") who
"began to release me from the trap in which I was caught [*meum quo
captus eram relaxare iam coeperat*]" (*conf.* 5.7.12), providing the
turning point in Augustine's prodigal wanderings away from God, specifically by rebuffing his *curiositas*. Faustus, in fact, appears as one of
only two named ostensibly uneducated [*imperitus*] persons – the other
being none other than Monnica herself – who function in the *Confessions* to "thwart the proud" Augustine in all his prideful intellect.
Highlighting Faustus' indifference to fine points of Manichaean metaphysics, Augustine suggested that perhaps Manichaeans achieved whatever virtue they had in spite of, rather than because of, their doctrines.
Faustus's misplaced loyalty to the faith prevented him from seeing that
all of his spiritual goals could be reached within another faith unbur-
dened by such errors.

Augustine appears to have crafted much of the narrative of his own
conversion as a vivid demonstration of how the Catholic faith proved
itself in his own case by Faustus's own criterion of truth: its effective-
ness in transforming him into a self-disciplined, virtuous man.[19] It is
notable that the proof of that transformation comes in a commitment to
celibacy, at the time a moral ideal associated more with Manichaeism
than Catholicism. Quite tellingly, Augustine replaces the figure of a
beckoning *Philosophia* or *Sapientia*, found repeatedly throughout the
works composed around the time of his conversion, with *Continentia*
here in the *Confessions*, in this way reimagining his decision in the
garden as the attainment of the moral goal that Manichaeism set, but
could not itself effect in him.

Herein lies the Manichaean connection of the controlling theme of
the work: confession. Augustine encapsulated his inability to make
progress in the Manichaean faith in his arrogant resistance to a genuine

---

[19] See J. D. BeDuhn, "A Religion of Deeds: Scepticism in the Doctrinally Liberal
Manichaeism of Faustus and Augustine," in *New Light on Manichaeism: Papers
from the Sixth International Congress on Manichaeism*, ed. J. D. BeDuhn, Nag
Hammadi and Manichaean Studies 64 (Leiden: Brill, 2009), 1–28.

act of confession, which that religion regarded as essential to spiritual progress (*conf.* 5.10.18). He endeavored to show the Manichaeans through his own story that their spiritual goals could be reached only by abandoning Manichaeism for a system better suited to make the changes within them necessary for their salvation. He equated everything that needed correcting in Manichaean thinking with pride: the presumed divinity of the soul (*conf.* 3.8.16; 4.15.26), its heroic status as God's helper, its purity from sin (*conf.* 4.15.26; 7.3.4–5), and Manichaean claims to know the truth. Within this self-confidant system, they had shut themselves off from God. "Only to those whose hearts are crushed do you draw close. You will not let yourself be found by the proud" (*conf.* 5.3.3). Augustine had learned to hate something about himself (*conf.* 8.7.16), to be angry with himself (*conf.* 8.8.19), to have "disgust with myself" (*conf.* 10.2.2). It did no good to be angry at sin as some alien intrusion into one's divine perfection; one had to be angry at oneself as the agent of sin. Through the language of Ps 4:5 ("Be angry and do not sin"), Augustine sought to point out this essential reorientation of sentiment to his Manichaean readers, as Annemaré Kotzé has demonstrated in a close analysis.[20]

Augustine found himself "provoked with an intense and sharp grief [*vehementi et acri dolore indignabar*]" at the recalcitrance of his erstwhile Manichaean friends, and "pitied" them (*conf.* 9.4.8) – language far removed from the norms of polemic. In a disarming rhetorical move, he expresses the wish that they would overhear his ruminations on the Psalm, while he remained unaware of their presence, so that they could trust the sincerity of his sentiments, and so that that sincerity would not be tainted on his part by polemical self-consciousness (*conf.* 9.4.8). In this clever fashion, Kotzé observes, he "addresses the Manichaeans as directly as possible without completely breaking the prayer stance adopted throughout the rest of the *Confessions.*"[21] "Oh, if only they could have heard me" (*conf.* 9.4.9), "if only they would bring to me those hearts of theirs ... if only they would say, 'Who will show us good things?'" (*conf.* 9.4.10). Augustine was "frantic (*frendebum*) at my inability to show it to them" (*conf.* 9.4.10), yet, "I could find no way to help those deaf, dead folk among whom I had been numbered" (*conf.* 9.4.11), because of their rejection of the Old Testament containing the Psalm. That is why "to think of the enemies of that scripture caused me anguish [*tabescebam*]" (*conf.* 9.4.11). The Psalm commanded that one

---

[20] Kotzé, *Augustine's Confessions*, 97–115.
[21] Ibid., 97.

turn from falsehood, and so Augustine hoped that the Manichaeans, upon hearing its words, might turn from the falsehood of their doctrines, just as he had, to God. "They might perhaps be so shaken as to spew it out, and then you would hear them when they cried to you, because he who for us died a true death in the flesh now interceded with you on our behalf" (*conf.* 9.4.9). Implicitly, he suggested that Manichaeans did intend genuinely to cry to the real God, but had that cry muffled by the false beliefs that held them back from recognizing that the only real evil lay in themselves, in all humankind. "I had already learned to feel for my past sins an anger with myself that would hold me back from sinning again," Augustine says of his moral breakthrough. "With good reason had I learned this anger, since it was no alien nature from a tribe of darkness that had been sinning through me, as they maintain who are not angry with themselves" (*conf.* 9.4.10). As it says in Ps 4:1, "When I called, the God of my righteousness answered me" (*conf.* 9.4.8); and so, he professes to God, "you will answer them when they call out to you" (*conf.* 9.4.9). Augustine goes so far as to suggest that David had the Manichaeans providentially in mind in composing the Psalm: "It was addressed to the kind of people of whom I remembered that I had been one [*Talibus dicitur qualem me fuisse reminiscebar*]" (*conf.* 9.4.9).[22]

The very structure of the *Confessions* inverts the sequence of events in Augustine's development in order to accommodate Manichaean preferences. Immediately after his own conversion, Augustine had argued that faith and reliance on authority necessarily preceded understanding based in reason. He had noted at the time that the Manichaeans insisted upon the reverse order, with an intellectual persuasion necessary to justify trusting authority and obeying the moral precepts taught by that authority as the way to spiritual perfection. Augustine had already explicitly accommodated that preferred sequence in *The Morals of the Catholic Church* (*mor.* 1.2.3), and he brings up the same issue of priority at the opening of the *Confessions* (*conf.* 1.1.1). The reader finds, accordingly, that the *Confessions* gives an account of progressive steps of rationally obtained conclusions (culminating in Book 7) *before* faith is achieved and authority accepted (in Book 8), as the Manichaeans themselves preferred. Indeed, much of what Book 7 discusses demonstrably derives from Augustine's post-conversion work, and occasional anachronistic remarks expose the inversion of time in his narrative. For example, he says that he persisted steadfastly in his faith in Christ

---

[22] Ibid., 104.

"as I found it in the Catholic Church" (*conf.* 7.5.7), of a time before
he had joined that church; and similarly recounts holding fast to a series
of commitments to Catholic views of God, Christ, and scriptures,
"as I feverishly searched for the origin of evil" (*conf.* 7.7.11), again of a
period before he had embraced any of them. These anachronistic passages contradict *conf.* 7.18.24, where Augustine reports that he had not
yet embraced Christ.

The demonstrably fictitious reordering of some of his intellectual
development, therefore, served a protreptic purpose for Manichaean
readers. By displacing understandings developed after his conversion
to an earlier point in his narrative, he subordinated his personal story
to the protreptic purpose of the *Confessions,* accommodating the Manichaean predilection for prioritizing rational argument. Surreptitiously
reviewing the course of his own growing insight as a Catholic Christian
up to the present time, he laid out stepping stones by which the Manichaeans could catch up to him. Augustine took much of this material
from *Free Choice,* anachronistically projecting it back into a fictitious
pre-conversion deliberation (cf. *conf.* 7.3.4–5.7; 7.17.23 to *lib. arb.* Books
1 and 2).

An anticipated Manichaean audience also helps to resolve the
enigma of Augustine's inclusion of Books 11–13 in the *Confessions.*
Augustine himself indicates in *Gen. litt.* 8.2.5 that his previous allegorical readings of Genesis, including that in the *Confessions,* were
intended as responses to Manichaeans, and this is borne out by frequent
allusions to Manichaean objections to Genesis, or to alternative Manichaean conceptions of creation in this part of the work. James O'Donnell identifies both Augustine's long disquisition on time in Book 11,
and the conclusion of his Genesis exegesis in *conf.* 13.28.43–30.45, as
written against the Manichaeans.[23] Yet, refuting Manichaean views
does not necessarily entail anticipating them as readers. Identifying
more of a protreptic than polemical purpose, Annemaré Kotzé has
proposed that "Augustine's primary objective in books 11 to 13 is to
redeem the story of creation in the sight of his Manichaean reader."[24]
Catherine Joubert has taken a similar position: that Augustine seeks to
persuade Manichaean readers of the truth of the Genesis creation story

[23] O'Donnell, *Augustine:* Confessions, vol. 3, 252 and 343; C. P. Mayer, *Die Zeichen in
der geistigen Entwicklung und in der Theologie des jungen Augustinus* (Würzburg:
Augustinus Verlag, 1974), vol. 2, 151, concurs on the target of Book 11. Cf. Gibb and
Montgomery, *The Confessions of Augustine,* 332.
[24] Kotzé, *Augustine's Confessions,* 221.

by a combination of demonstrating its affirmation by authorities such as Paul the Manichaeans claim to recognize, and by finding in it worthy spiritual truths by means of allegory.[25] She and Robert O'Connell would include Neoplatonists as a second intended audience of Augustine's "ecumenical" allegorical reading of creation, and his choice of imagery often bridges the preferred tropes of both communities.[26] In doing so, Augustine returns to the Old Testament text that he himself had once found distasteful and unfathomable (*conf.* 3.5.9), yet whose depth of riches will open to the Manichaeans, too, if they will only heed their own slogan, to knock and to seek (*conf.* 11.2.3–3.4; 12.1.1).

Notably, however, Augustine does not actually put forward a definitive reading of Genesis, to which he might hope to persuade Manichaean readers. He repeatedly and emphatically denies that there is such a definitive reading (*conf.* 12.18.27, 20.29, 23.32–32.43). Rather, while repeating familiar answers to Manichaean critiques of the creation story, he demonstrates multiple possible interpretations of it that they should not find objectionable to their values and spiritual goals, even if they correct errors in their doctrines.

> Since, then, so rich a variety of highly plausible interpretations can be culled from those words, consider how foolish it is rashly to assert that Moses intended one particular meaning rather than any of the others. If we engage in hurtful strife as we attempt to expound his words, we offend against the very love for the sake of which he said all those things. (*conf.* 12.25.35)

Indeed, he would hope that God would have inspired in Moses words that would support diverse visions in his readers, as an *admonitio* or congruent call to different individuals, a "fountain for varied thirsts" (*conf.* 12.26.36).

Augustine concludes his effort in Book 13 by pointedly referring to the merely temporal and temporary value even of the scriptures, relative to ultimate spiritual aims (*conf.* 13.15.16–18, 18.23, 20.27–28, 21.31–23.34).[27] His purpose, therefore, would seem to be to disarm the creation story as an obstruction to Manichaean conversion, much as he used the biblical Psalms earlier in the *Confessions* to show how closely

---

[25] Joubert, "Le Livre XIII et la structure des Confessiones de Saint Augustin," 77–117.
[26] R. J. O'Connell, "The Riddle of Augustine's 'Confessions': A Plotinian Key," *International Philosophical Quarterly* 4 (1964), 327–372, at 369.
[27] See R. J. O'Connell, "The Plotinian Fall of the Soul in St. Augustine," *Traditio* 19 (1963), 1–35, at 17, and "The Riddle of Augustine's 'Confessions'," 362–369.

they approximate the devotional and confessional expression of Manichaean hymnody. To achieve this, he must fend off objections from within his own Catholic ranks (*conf.* 12.14.17–17.25). By constantly engaging Manichaean images and expressions in his allegorical exegesis, he demonstrates their interchangeability with perfectly acceptable Catholic discourse derived from the Bible, even while identifying unnegotiable differences of outlook that currently divide the two communities. Ultimately, he relativizes the very authority of the biblical text that he insists Manichaeans must acknowledge, reducing that acknowledgment to a mere formal gesture immediately mitigated by the rich latitude of possible interpretations.

Based on its discursive strategy, therefore, the *Confessions* appears designed to achieve, among other effects, an encapsulation of all that Augustine considered right and redeemable in the sentiments of the Manichaeans Augustine had known, while excising through critique (often cleverly as self-critique) the "fables and phantasms" of Manichaeism. Hence the confessional trope by which he contrasted the intention and outcome of Manichaean doctrine and practice; hence all of the Manichaean terminology and imagery, which he readily paralleled to the same sentiments in the Psalms of the Catholic Old Testament; hence the searching engagement with Paul's Manichaean-like self-dichotomies; hence the "ecumenical" demonstration of worthy views of God and cosmos hidden beneath the possibly objectionable phrasing of the Bible. These compositional elements served to point the way forward to the perfection of Manichaean aspirations through liberation from what Augustine regarded as the retarding elements of the Manichaean worldview. Just as Manichaeism had been an advance on the unsophisticated Christianity of Augustine's childhood, so the Nicene-Platonic sophistication of Milan offered an advance on Manichaeism, as a progressive purging of superstitious elements and ideas unworthy of God, on the way to a higher form of Christianity. Of course Manichaeism had been an advance on the crude, anthropomorphic view of God as inconstant and vengeful. Of course it was in the right in chiding blind, ignorant faith as an end in itself, in criticizing superstitious rites carried into Christianity from paganism. Of course it was wise in its ascetic self-discipline and desire to transcend the lure of the body. It represented an advance over all those aspects of popular Christianity that stemmed from the misunderstanding and bad habits of the mob, who did not know the supernal truths hidden within their own tradition. But the Manichaeans had stopped short. Confident in their reason and ability, they considered themselves already arrived at the truth. They did not realize there was further to go. Augustine beckons them forward with a masterful rhetorical performance in the *Confessions,* riddled with subtle signals only they would recognize.

Further Reading

BeDuhn, J. D. *Augustine's Manichaean Dilemma 2: Making a "Catholic" Self, 388–401 C.E.* Divinations: Rereading Late Ancient Religion. Philadelphia, University of Pennsylvania Press, 2013.

Chadwick, H. "On Re-reading the *Confessions.*" In *Saint Augustine the Bishop: A Book of Essays,* eds. F. LeMoine and C. Kleinhenz. Garland Reference Library of the Humanities 1830. New York: Garland, 1994, 139–160.

Feldmann, E. "Et inde rediens fecerat sibi deum (Conf. 7, 20). Beobachtungen zur Genese des augustinischen Gottesbegriffes und zu dessen Funktion in den *Confessiones.*" In *Collectanea Augustiniana. Mélanges T. J. van Bavel,* eds. B. Bruning, M. Lamberigts, and J. Van Houtem. Leuven: Leuven University Press, 1990, 881–904.

Joubert, C. "Le Livre XIII et la structure des *Confessiones* de Saint Augustin." *Revue des sciences religieuses* 66 (1992), 77–117.

Kotzé, A. *Augustine's Confessions: Communicative Purpose and Audience.* Supplements to Vigiliae Christianae 71. Leiden: Brill, 2004.

van Oort, J. "Augustine's Critique of Manichaeism: The Case of *Confessions* III 6,10 and Its Implications." In *Aspects of Religious Contact and Conflict in the Ancient World,* ed. P. W. van der Horst. Utrechtse theologische reeks 31. Utrecht: Faculteit der Godgeleerdheid, Universiteit Utrecht, 1995, 57–68.

Vecchi, A. "L'antimanichaeismo nelle 'Confessioni' de Sant'Agostino." *Giornale di metafisica* 20 (1965), 91–121.

Part II

Main Themes and Topics

4 Aversion and Conversion

MARIE-ANNE VANNIER

Augustine's *Confessions* is a continuous dialogue with God where the bishop of Hippo celebrates both the greatness of his Creator and God's wonderful actions in his life. By opening the book with the famous *inquietum cor* – in Augustine's own words: "Thou hast made us for thyself, and restless is our heart until it comes to rest in thee" (*conf.* 1.1.1) – and by ending the book with rest in God, with the "Sabbath of eternal life," Augustine emphasizes the importance of human active participation in God's doings. The cornerstone of human action is the *conversio*[1] that Augustine experienced over many years (between 372 and 387)[2] and what became the melting pot for his life and thought,[3] making him one of the great converts in the history of humankind.

[1] J.-M. Leblond, *Les conversions de Saint Augustin*, Théologie 17 (Paris: Aubier, 1950); F. Masai, "Les conversions de S. Augustin et les débuts du spiritualisme en Occident," *Revue du Moyen Âge latin* 67 (1961), 1–40; A. Mandouze, *Saint Augustin: L'aventure de la raison et de la grâce* (Paris, Études Augustiniennes, 1968); L. C. Ferrari, *The Conversions of Saint Augustine*, Saint Augustine Lecture Series (Villanova: Villanova University Press, 1984); M. Neusch, *Augustin: un chemin de conversion. Une introduction aux "Confessions"* (Paris: Desclée de Brouwer, 1986); G. Madec, "La conversion d'Augustin. Intériorité et communauté," *Lumen Vitae* 42 (1987), 184–194; G. Madec, "*Conversio*," in *Augustinus-Lexikon*, eds. C. Mayer, E. Feldmann, R. Dodaro, and C. Müller (Basel: Schwabe, 1994), vol. 1, 1282–1294; I. Bochet, "Le Livre VIII des *Confessions*: récit de conversion et réflexion théologique," *Nouvelle Revue Théologique* 118 (1996), 363–384; J. Oroz-Reta, "Conversion," in *Saint Augustin, la Méditerranée et l'Europe: IVe–XXIe siècle*, ed. A. Fitzgerald (Paris: Cerf, 2005), 377–382; and M.-A. Vannier, *Saint Augustin ou la conversion en acte*, Sagesses éternelles (Paris: Entrelacs, 2011).

[2] Cf. M.-A. Vannier, *'Les Confessions' de S. Augustin*, Collection Classiques du Christianisme (Paris: Cerf, 2007).

[3] A. Mandouze, "Du converti de Milan au convertisseur d'Hippone," in *Congresso Internazionale su S. Agostine nel XVI Centenario della Conversione : Roma, 15–20 settembre 1986 atti III Sezioni di studio V–VI*, Studia ephemeridis "Augustinianum" 26 (Rome: Institutum Patristicum Augustinianum, 1987), vol. 1, 89–98; M.-A. Vannier, "La conversion d'Augustin, comme principe herméneutique de son œuvre," in *De la conversion*, ed. J.-C. Attias, Centre d'études des religions du Livre (Paris: Cerf, coll. "Patrimoines," 1997), 281–294.

A VERBAL PLAY ON WHAT CONSTITUTES ONE'S BEING

As a rhetorician, Augustine played on words he used and set up, in an original way, the dialectic between the *aversio a Deo* ["aversion from to God"] and the *conversio ad Deum* ["conversion to God"]. He did so in his first commentary on Genesis, *De Genesi contra Manichaeos* (388–389), and after that developed it in the last three books of the *Confessions*, as well as in his *De Genesi ad litteram*. Augustine began with the verb *vertere*,[4] which comes from the Greek word *strephein*. By adding to it a particular prefix gives us *epistrophē*, which means "change, reversal, turning around." In Latin, adding of *alpha*-privative [*a/versio*] marks certain remoteness and, adding the prefix *con-* [*con/versio*] evokes, in turn, the sense of togetherness and completion. In the *Confessions*, the term *aversio* is never alone. It is always dialectically linked to *conversio*. While for human beings living in time there is a perpetual process or movement from *aversio* to *conversio*, the angels make their choice and are fixed in their being for eternity (*conf.* 12.9.9).

Indeed, for Augustine, this verbal play on *aversio/conversio* was neither a mere empty rhetorical trick nor an echo of neoplatonic emanation and return, but the result of his personal experience of first painfully facing his separation from God and, after that, finding joy in his conversion. So, as Augustine talked about the constitution of the human subject, unlike Manichaeans, Augustine affirmed both human freedom of will and createdness in God's image. This made him, Augustine, a creature who was an *esse ad* – a being oriented toward God. Such being was not constituted merely by one's own efforts, but by the synergy of freedom and grace in one's conversion. In other words, having moved away from Manichaeism (*conf.* 7.3.4), Augustine endeavored to highlight the fundamental role of human freedom, as well as the reality of being created. For him, both of these were important realizations that enabled him either to fulfill his being fully human by his *conversio ad Deum* or to destroy himself and his being human by his *aversio a Deo*, if he refused God. It also highlighted his personal responsibility, the relevance of which he had eventually become aware of and understood. An echo of all this is found in *conf.* 4.10.15, where he wrote in the wake of his friend's death:

> For wherever a person's soul turns, everywhere it is pierced with enduring pains except in you – even if it is stuck in things which are

---

[4] H. Jacobsohn, "*Conversio et converto*," in *Thesaurus Linguae Latinae* (Leipzig: Teubner, 1906-9), vol. 4, 853–856 and 858–869.

beautiful but are separate from you ... They arise and pass away; and in arising they begin to exist, so to speak; and they grow so that they may reach perfection; and once they are perfected they grow old and perish. So when things arise and strive for existence, the faster they grow into being, the more they hasten toward annihilation: this is their nature.[5]

The *aversio a Deo* is here synonymous with dispersion, suffering, and precariousness. Only the *conversio ad Deum* leads to eternal stability. Accordingly, Augustine invited his readers to *conversio*:

Stand with Him, and you will stand fast indeed. Take your rest in him, and you will find peace ... [Christ] calling us to return from here to him, into that secret place which he came forth to us ... First come down, so that you may then ascend [*descendite, ut ascendatis*], and that your ascent may indeed be to God. (*conf.* 4.12.18–19)

He also invited his readers to find God, like he had done, in *intimo meo* ["more inward than my most inward part"] and in *superior summo meo* ["greater than the best of me"] (*conf.* 3.6.11).

Even if Augustine was inspired by Hilary of Poitiers' account of his conversion (*Trin.* 1.1–14), unlike his predecessor, he highlighted the role of one's will in *aversio a Deo* and clarified that conversion was a continuous process, a reoccurring decision. Later he also came to understand the importance of humility, which led him to reconsider the Platonic theme of homeland and the way to it, as well as the contrast between two cities.

HUMILITY VERSUS PRIDE

As something of a fundamental significance for Augustine's conversion, the dialectic between the *aversio a Deo* and the *conversio ad Deum* was linked with the topics of humility and pride, with homeland and the way to it, as well as with the topic of two cities.

The Homeland and the Way to It

Augustine described his parting of the way with Platonists with the following words: "Those people ... who can see the homeland from a

[5] *Augustine: Confessions*, trans. C. J.-B. Hammond, LCL 26 (Cambridge, MA: Harvard University Press, 2014), vol. 1, 157.

long way off, and from the mountain of pride on the opposite side of the valley, scorn humility; that's why they don't stick to the way" (*s. Dolbeau* 26.61)[6] – the "way" being Christ. Next, he explained what the *aversio a Deo* was by using an image from the practice of "paganism":

> Any who deviate from this way will stumble upon a mountain of tangled and impenetrable thickets, placing himself in the way, destructively and deceitfully intruding himself as a mediator through countless sacrilegious rites, through soothsayers, augurs, fortune-tellers, astrologers, magicians. People who are sold on these don't come down to the way, but wander around on a kind of wooded mountain, from which some of them lift up their eyes and see the homeland, but they can't reach it, because they don't keep to the way. Those on the other hand who do not keep to the way; that is, to the true and trustworthy Mediator, the Mediator who leads along the way and doesn't block it, the Mediator who purges away guilt and doesn't involve us in it, these persevere in walking along in the faith they hold. Because some of them too can see the homeland, some of them can't. But let those who can't yet see the homeland not depart from the way, and they will reach exactly the same place as those who can. You see, some people have such sharp eyes that they can see things from a long way off. It does these no good to see where they are going and not know how to get there. But if they know the way, being able to see from afar the place they have to reach is not so much use to them as knowing how to get there. Those of the other hand who are not so sharp-sighted, if they walk along together with others, are going to arrive together with them ... In [Christ] we have the bodily creation, which he also took to himself in the flesh; in him we also have the spiritual creation. (*s. Dolbeau* 26.61)

While reading the *Libri platonicorum*, Augustine discovered the spiritual nature of the transcendent God – the "homeland" – and this was a major step forward in his intellectual conversion [*epistrophē*]. However, he only found the access to such God by encountering Christ the Savior – the "way." Encountering Christ the Way enabled him to move from pride to humility, from the *aversio a Deo* to the *conversio ad Deum*, which constituted his moral conversion [*metanoia*]. This is to

[6] *Augustine: Sermons*, trans. E. Hill, WSA III/11 (New York: New City Press, 1997), 226 (English modified).

say that Christ had a decisive role in both his turning toward God and finding the way to God. Augustine wrote:

> I was pontificating like an expert, and unless I was seeking your way in Christ our Savior I was not so much expert as destined to expire. I had already begun to want to appear wise: I was filled with a torment of my own making, and instead of shedding tears I grew bloated with learning. Where was that love that which builds up from a foundation of humility, namely Christ Jesus? After all when were all those books of mine going to teach me that? Because of this, I believe it was your will that I should come across those books before I gave my attention to your Scriptures, so that it would be imprinted on my memory how I was affected by them. Then afterward, when I grew to be gentile by means of your books, and my wounds felt the touch of your healing fingers, I discerned and remarked what a difference there was between presumption and confession [*inter praesumptionem et confessionem*], between those who see what direction they should go but do not see how [to go there], and the Way who leads to the land of bliss [*ad beatificam patriam*]. (*conf.* 7.20.26)

This passage contains more than just various pious expressions, such as, the tears of confession, Christ's loving sacrifice, Augustine's troubled spirit, broken and contrite heart, and God's healing. The following passage, *conf.* 7.21.27, adds the heavenly city (Rev 21:2), the pledge of the Holy Spirit (2 Cor 5:5), and the cup of our ransom (Mt 20:28). The core of the matter was that it was Christ who converted him and enabled him to take the passage from pride to humility.

Two Cities

In the end of his life, Augustine tackled the same issue in another way; namely, by operating with the image of two cities. So, more than two decades after composing his *Confessions*, Augustine wrote:

> Two cities, then, have been created by two loves: that is, the earthly by love of self extending even to contempt of God, and the heavenly by love of God extending to contempt self. The one, therefore, glories in itself, the other in the Lord; the one seeks glory from men, the other finds its highest glory in God, the Witness of our conscience. The one lifts up its head in its own glory; the other says to its God, "Thou art my glory, and the lifter up of mine head." In the Earthly City, princes are as much mastered by the lust for mastery as the nations which they subdue are by them; in the

Heavenly, all serve one another in charity, rulers by their counsel and subjects by their obedience. The one city loves its own strength as displayed in its mighty men; the other says to its God, "I will love Thee, O Lord, my strength" Thus, in the Earthly City, its wise men, who live according to man, have pursued the goods of the body or of their own mind, or both. Some of them who were able to know God "glorified Him not as God, neither were thankful; but became vain in their imagination, and their foolish heart was darkened. "Professing themselves to be wise" (that is, exalting themselves in their wisdom, under the dominion of pride), "they became fools, and changed the glory of the incorruptible God into an image made like to corruptible man, and to birds, and fourfooted beasts, and creeping things" ... "and they worshipped and served the creature more than the Creator, Who is blessed forever." In the Heavenly City, however, man has no wisdom beyond the piety which rightly worships the true God, and which looks for its reward in the fellowship not only of holy men, but of angels also, "that God may be all in all." (*civ. Dei* 14.28)[7]

Without explicitly saying so, Augustine emphasized that the city that was closed on itself lived the *aversio a Deo*; while the other city, the city of God, always knew the *conversio ad Deum* and thus found its eternal fulfillment. The first was locked in in its pride; the second was humble and received its life from God.

THE DIALECTIC OF THE *FORMATIO*

While pondering and reflecting, Augustine did not consider the matter only from an ethical point of view (according to the free choice of the will, the twists-and-turns of his conversion), but also and in various ways from an ontological point of view.[8] Here one encounters another verbal play on words – no longer on the verb *vertere* and not the dialectic of *magis* and *minus esse* ["more" and "less being"], but on the word *forma*.[9] The *forma*, given to each one at his/her creation can be

---

[7] *Augustine: The City of God against the Pagans*, trans. R. W. Dyson, Cambridge Texts in the History of Political Thought (Cambridge: Cambridge University Press, 1998), 632–163.

[8] E. Zum Brunn, *Le dilemme de l'être et du néant chez Saint Augustin* (Paris: Études Augustiniennes, 1969).

[9] Cf. M.-A. Vannier, *Creatio, conversio, formatio chez S. Augustin*, second ed. (Fribourg: Éditions Universitaires, 1997), 14–19, 148–172.

obtained fully by one's *conversio ad Deum*. If so, it becomes *forma formosa*, the form of the beautiful. On the other hand, if the *forma* is obliterated by *aversio a Deo*, it can degrade and become *deformis forma*, the form of the ugly. Given the importance of this whole topic, Augustine dealt with it both in the last three books of the *Confessions* and in *Trin.* 15.3.14, where he gave his full attention to *formatio* while reading again the Apostle Paul. Augustine wrote: "'We are being transformed,' he said, we are being changed from form to form, and are passing from a blurred form to a clear one. But even the blurred one is the image of God, and if image then of course glory, in which men were created surpassing the other animals" (*Trin.* 15.3.14).[10]

When the most excellent of the created "things" – the human being – is converted by its Creator from its godlessness and justified, it is transformed from an ugly form [*deformis forma*] into a beautiful form [*forma formosa*]. The more damnable something is in its godlessness, the more admirable is its change into God-likeness. Apostle Paul said: "from glory to glory" (2 Cor 3:18), meaning a movement from the glory of creation to the glory of justification. However, the phrase "from glory to glory" can also be understood in another way: a movement from the glory of faith to the glory of sight; from the glory by which we are sons of God to the glory by which "we shall be like him," because "we shall see him as he is" (1 Jn 3:2).

Arriving at the climax of his thought, Augustine highlighted both the goodness of the creation and its transformation into the new creation as a fulfillment. Such result was not only the consequence of the conversion of the human being and his/her achievement, but it presupposed, just like creation, a first gift, an initiative of the Creator, and the mediation of the *Forma omnium* (i.e., Christ, the Word and the Principle). Christ had a determinative role in any kind of conversion. So, Augustine wrote in *conf.* 11.8.10:

> everything that begins to exist and begins to end actually begins to exist, and begins to end, at the particular time when eternal Reason (where there is no beginning nor ending) knows that it should begin and come to an end. That eternal reason is your Word, who is the Beginning, because he also speaks to us. That is what he says in the gospel, speaking in the incarnate self, and it resounded in people's outward hearing so that they would also believe, and seek it within,

[10] *Saint Augustine: The Trinity*, trans. E. Hill, WSA I/5 (New York: New City Press, 1991), 406.

and find it in eternal Truth, where the one good teacher instructs all
his disciples ... After all, what is actually teaching us if not the
steadfast Word? Even when instruction comes to us from some
mutable creature, we are let to your steadfast truth, where we
really learn, when we stand and listen to him and rejoice greatly
to hear the Bridegroom's voice, and then we restore ourselves to the
source of our being. This is why he is the Beginning: because if he
did not stand fast when we went astray, there would be nowhere for
us to return to. So, when we turn back from our mistakes, it is
through recognizing them that we can turn back; but he teaches us
to recognize those mistakes, for he is the Beginning and he speaks
to us.

As the Word and Principle, the *Forma omnium* of Christ is the Creator
of the creation and the Re-creator of the new creation.

THE DIALECTIC OF FREEDOM AND GRACE

Conversion is never just one's own choice. Already before the maturing
of his doctrine of grace during the Pelagian controversy, Augustine
emphasized that it was God who brought about one's conversion (e.g.,
Sol. 1.3 and other Cassiciacum dialogues). This conviction shows itself
frequently in the *Confessions* (e.g., 8.12.30), as well as in many other
texts, such as *en. Ps.* 79.4, where Augustine wrote, "We are turned away
from you, and unless you turn us around, we shall not be converted."[11]
This means that one's conversion is the result of a synergy between the
Creator and the created being, so that the initiative is always on the side
of God who seeks out the lost humankind.

   In any case, for Augustine, the uneven synergy between human
freedom and God's grace – his conversion – lasted for some fourteen
years. It required his intellectual and volitional transformation and his
acceptance of God's plan for his life – a "full" renovation, which was
both *epistrophē* [intellectual conversion] and *metanoia* [moral
conversion].

   As Augustine talked about his intellectual conversion, the bishop of
Hippo noticed his Creator's deliberate action in his change of mind.
This is evident from the passage in *conf.* 7.10.16 where Augustine
evoked his spiritual experience:

---

[11] *Saint Augustine: Exposition of Psalms*, trans. M. Boulding, WSA III/18 (New York:
   New City Press, 2002), vol. 4, 143.

All this warned me to come back to myself. I entered deep within myself under your guidance, for you became my helper. I entered and saw, as it were with the eye of my soul, above that same eye of my soul, above my mind, the unchangeable light. It was not this ordinary light, which all flesh can behold, nor was it a grander version, as it were, of the same kind, as if it had the power to light everything up much, much more brightly, and to fill the whole with its abundance. That light was not like this; it was something else, something utterly different from all these things. It was not above my mind in the way that oil floats above water or sky above land; it was greater than that, because it made me, and I was lesser because I was its creation. One who knows the Truth knows this light, and one who knows it knows eternity too. Love knows it . . . When I first recognized you, you lifted me up, to let me see that there was something I must see, but I was not yet capable of seeing it.

Augustine finally realized who God, the giver of this Light, was. Nevertheless, Augustine was still morally "unformed [*informitas*]" and thus in the "a place of unlikeness [*regio dissimilitudinis*]."

Augustine's *formatio*, as a constantly renewed gift of the Creator, took place gradually. In *conf.* 13.2.2–3.3, Augustine pointed out that creation, conversion, and *formatio* were the expression of the overabundance of God's love. He confessed that a created being "owed the fact that it was alive at all, and the fact that it was living a life of bliss, to your grace alone, after being converted by a change for the better" (*conf.* 13.3.4). Everything was grace. The fact that Augustine was established in his new life was grace as well. In *conf.* 11.30.40, he wrote, "I shall stand fast and be established in you, in the pattern for my life, which is your truth [*Stabo and solidabor in te, in forma mea, veritate tua*]" (cf. *s.* 26.5, 12, 14–15). As one can see, it was not enough for Augustine to be converted. He also had to be firmly grounded in God. And this too was the work of the Holy Spirit (*conf.* 13.8.9).

A RERUN OF THE DIALECTIC OF THE MORNING AND EVENING METAPHOR

To give his conversion a universal significance, Augustine used parables and metaphors to describe his experience(s). Among those were the parable of the lost sheep and the lost drachma, and especially the parable of the prodigal son (Lk 15) (*conf.* 4.16.30), where both the *aversio* and the *conversio* had such a striking significance.

Augustine also employed other metaphors, including those of "morning knowledge" and "evening knowledge." Morning was the time when human beings were supposed to experience the *conversio ad Deum*, while the evening before was the time when they experienced the *aversio a Deo*. But these images also had a deeper, ontological meaning. Augustine deliberated in *Gn. litt.* 4.22.39:

> Just as ... it turned from its own formlessness towards the creator and thus was formed, so too, after evening, morning was made, meaning that after acknowledgement of its proper nature, of its not being what God is, it goes back to praising the light which is God himself, and by which it is formed as it gazes upon it.[12]

Evidently, "morning knowledge" is synonymous with *conversio ad Creatorem*. A few lines later, Augustine reiterated:

> While the morning after that evening ... means its turning to refer what it was created as to the praise of the creator, and to receive from the Word of God knowledge of the creature which is made after itself; that is, of the firmament ... This morning again marks the conversion of this light in the same way; that is, the turning of this day to the praise of God for his work of making the firmament, and to its reception from his Word of knowledge of the creature to be fashioned after the firmament. (*Gn. litt.* 4.22.39, modified)

One can almost detect here, in the "morning knowledge," a trinitarian pattern: the Holy Spirit makes the conversion to the Father possible, which in turn leads to gaining of knowledge in the Word. In any case, when the creatures turn to their Creator, they receive an understanding of the hidden things that are given to them by the Word. Augustine picked up again the idea of the Inner Teacher, to which he gave an important place already in his *De magistro*.

Augustine only uses the metaphor of "morning" and "evening knowledge" for better communication. From this generally accessible figure of speech he developed a more complicated dialectic of the *formatio*. The latter concerned the constitution of the subject and contributes to the *magis esse* ["more being"], which was received by one's turning to the Creator and receiving life from Him. It was a kind of dialectic of grace and freedom that concerned everyone.

---

[12] *Saint Augustine: On Genesis*, trans. E. Hill, WSA I/13 (New York: New City Press, 2002), 263–264.

THE DIALECTIC OF *DISTENTIO* AND *INTENTIO*

One finds an echo of the dialectic between "extension [*distentio*]" and "intention [*intentio*]" in Augustine's analysis of time (*conf.* 11.23.30). The *distentio*, which marks the very nature of time as a "particular type of extension" (*conf.* 11.23.30), is synonymous with degradation, scattering, or, as we would say today, entropy. It corresponds to the *aversio a Deo* – not so much as a rejection of God, but as being indifferent to, or having moved away from God. The *conversio ad Deum*, on the other hand, corresponds to *intentio*, to the role of one's consciousness, which recapitulates time, transforming its negative existence to positive existence in "the present of the things present" (*conf.* 11.20.26).

Here we see the originality of the Augustinian reflection, which impacted the discussions for centuries after him. He contended that, although time as such escaped us, it was nevertheless recapitulated in the present moment; for example, in the *momento aeternitatis* of the vision that was granted to Augustine in Ostia. Even here conversion had an essential role. It transformed the *distentio* into *intentio* (*conf.* 11.29.39). Augustine "wants, through *exercitatio animi*, to allow his reader to realize that time is inside the soul,"[13] and that the only true time is the present time. In his own way, Augustine seems to anticipate Bergson's analyses of duration, introducing, as it were, eternity within time.[14]

Conversion, which is apprehended by mind, is constitutive of a subject. It enables one's movement from nonexistence to existence, just like one's scatteredness in time yields to the unity of the "timeless" present.

CONCLUSION

Augustine was definitely a thinker who gave conversion such a crucial significance. Dialectically pairing *aversio a Deo/conversio ad Deum*, he also indicated that, in this life, conversion was never a completed "thing." By God's grace, the ongoing conversion marked both his life and thought. This, in short, is the meaning of this unique work, the *Confessions*, in the history of humankind. The constant rethinking (or "conversion") is also evident in Augustine's *Retractationes*, where he reviews his writings one by one. Thus, postulating the dialectic of

---

[13] P. Hadot, "Patristique latine," *Annuaire de l'EPHE* 78 (1967–1968), 176–185, at 181.
[14] H. Bergson, *Les données immédiates de la conscience* (Paris: Felix Alcan, 1889).

aversio a Deo and *conversio ad Deum*, and revising his works in *Retractaiones*, Augustine basically had the same goal – to highlight the foundational importance of conversion, which comprised both the gift of God's grace and the responsibility of a human being. The pair *aversio a Deo/conversio ad Deum* constitutes a continuous dialectical process until the *conversio ad Deum* of human beings will find its fulfillment.

Further Reading

Ferrari, L. C. *The Conversions of Saint Augustine*, Saint Augustine Lecture Series. Villanova: Villanova University Press, 1984.

Leblond, J.-M. *Les conversions de Saint Augustin*, Théologie 17. Paris: Aubier, 1950.

Madec, G. *"Conversio."* In *Augustinus-Lexikon*, eds. C. Mayer, E. Feldmann, R. Dodaro, and C. Müller. Basel: Schwabe, 1994, vol. 1, 1282–1294

 La patrie et la voie: le Christ dans la vie et la pensée de saint Augustin. Paris, Desclée, 1989.

Mandouze, A. *Saint Augustin: L'aventure de la raison et de la grâce*. Paris, Études Augustiniennes, 1968.

Masai, F. *"Les conversions de S. Augustin et les débuts du spiritualisme en Occident,"* *Revue du Moyen Âge latin* 67 (1961), 1–40.

Oroz-Reta, J. *"Conversion."* In *Saint Augustin, la Méditerranée et l'Europe: IVe–XXIe siècle*, ed. A. Fitzgerald. Paris: Cerf, 2005, 377–382.

Vannier, M.-A. *Creatio, conversio, formatio chez S. Augustin*. Paradosis 31. Fribourg: Éditions universitaires, 1991 (rev. ed. 1997).

 Les Confessions de Saint Augustin. Collection Classiques du Christianisme. Paris: Cerf, 2007.

 Saint Augustin ou la conversion en acte. Sagesses éternelles. Paris: Entrelacs, 2011.

Zum Brunn, E. *Le dilemme de l'être et du néant chez Saint Augustin*. Paris: Études Augustiniennes, 1969.

5 Creation and Recreation

MATTHEW DREVER

INTRODUCTION

The theme of creation and recreation is at the heart of the *Confessions*, tracing its way through Augustine's account of his spiritual formation in both his autobiographical narrative in Books 1–9 and his expansive accounts of temporality and creation in Books 11–13. Augustine characterizes creation and recreation as two moments in God's relation to the world that are distinct and yet inseparable. The way these moments come together offers Augustine fundamental insights into both God and humanity. On one hand, creation and recreation beckon toward their unity within the trinitarian God: the Father forms creation through the eternal Word (Son) and within the Spirit's love, and recreates through the eternal Word incarnate in Christ. On the other hand, creation and recreation disclose the fundamental ontological and moral character of human existence. It is for this reason that a creation–recreation dynamic spans the *Confessions*, providing Augustine with a theological framework to plumb the existential depths of his spiritual and self-identity formation.

CREATION FROM NOTHING

One way to see how Augustine's accounts of creation and recreation unfold in the *Confessions* is by beginning with the final books where he traces the broader foundations of his accounts of creation and recreation, and then move through the earlier books to examine how these accounts shape his autobiographical narrative. We can begin in Book 12 where Augustine develops his doctrine of *creatio ex nihilo*. This allows us a glimpse behind the veil to the foundation of his tale of the malleable and fluid nature of his soul, an oft-lamented theme in the *Confessions*. In Book 12, Augustine associates this condition with the soul's created origin. Here he often opts for a preposition *de* rather

than *ex* to describe the movement of creation "from" nothing.[1] There is
little warrant for any technical distinction between *ex* and *de* within
either the biblical or wider Christian Latin traditions.[2] Yet Augustine
adopts *de nihilo* explicitly at key moments to signal connections with
both his accounts of creation and recreation. Foremost, it provides him a
trinitarian solution to differentiate the temporal and mutable origin of
creation that comes out of nothingness [*de nihilo*] from the eternal and
immutable origin of the Son who comes out of God's own substance [*de
Deo*].[3] Augustine is searching for a way to articulate the distinct origins
of creation and the Son, while also maintaining God's relation to both.
In *On the Nature of the Good*, a text written in 399, around the same
time as the *Confessions*, Augustine fills in the picture he is developing
in the *Confessions*. There he distinguishes *ex* and *de* to differentiate a
causal and a substantial relation between God and creation: creation
comes from [*ex*] God's power but not from [*de*] God's substance.[4] This
allows Augustine to maintain a qualitative distinction between God
and creation, which he needs to avoid Manichean dualism.[5] But it also
renders Augustine's position logically treacherous. If the cosmos is *de
nihilo* in contrast to the Son who is *de Deo* and this is interpreted
substantially, it means the cosmos is created from the substance of
nihil. This would land Augustine in a dualism reminiscent of Manichaeism and require him to hold that nothingness is actually something. Augustine is aware of this problem and warns against interpreting
nihil as a substance, but he struggles with how to describe it (*nat. b.* 25).

---

[1] Augustine, *conf.* 12.6.6, 7.7–8.8, 22.31, 28.38–29.40; 13.33.48. See also: *Gn. litt. imp.*
1.1.2; *nat. b.* 1; *Gn. litt.* 7.28.40, 43; 10.4.7; *Gn. adv. Man.* 1.2.4, 6.10, 7.11; 2.7.8,
29.43; and *civ. Dei* 12.5.

[2] Latin writers often adopt *ex nihilo* and *de nihilo* interchangeable, and both phrases
mean generally: a movement away or out of something; or the underlying cause of a
movement. For a good overview of this issue, see: N. J. Torchia, *Creatio ex nihilo and
the Theology of St. Augustine: The Anti-Manichaean Polemic and Beyond* (New
York: Peter Lang, 1999), 111–115.

[3] Augustine, *conf.* 12.5.6, 7.7, 11.11. See also *nat. b.* 1; *Gn. litt.* 7.28.43.

[4] *Nat. b.* 19, 25, and 27. Augustine's choice of terminology is closely associated with his
interpretation of the divine name [*ego sum qui sum*] in Ex 3:14, which he takes to
indicate divine immutability. Creation, however, is mutable because it is brought
into existence from [*ab/ex*] God's power not from [*de*] God's substance. See
Augustine, *vera rel.* 49.97; *conf.* 7.10.16; 13.31.46; *Gn. litt.* 5.16.34; and *Trin.* 5.2.3;
7.5.10.

[5] Created things derive their goodness from (*ex*) God, but do not share essentially in,
and so cannot alter, God's goodness. In this way, the ontological mutability of the soul
de nihilo opens the space, as it were, for Augustine to formulate how the soul rebels
against God without undermining divine goodness or immutability (Augustine, *nat.
b.* 1 and 10).

In the *Confessions*, this difficulty surfaces in his account of the mutability of creation, which he connects with its *de nihilo* origin. Here Augustine describes mutability as: a "nothing something [*nihil aliquid*]" and what "is and is not [*est non est*]" (*conf.* 12.6.6).[6]

As Augustine goes on to describe the nature of mutability, his choice of *de nihilo* offers a vivid, and I think intentional, illustration of its existential ramifications. *De nihilo*, with its substantial intimations, underscores the continued "presence" of *nihil* (mutability) in human existence.[7] *Nihil* is not a condition from which we are created and leave behind, but rather is more like the abiding foundation, or lack thereof, that affects our identity formation throughout our lives. This means that humans rely continually on God's power for their existence, having no resources – no foundation – in themselves that can substitute for God, even as their origin *de nihilo* deconstructs anything other than God as the source of stability and identity for human existence. This also unites the dual quests for understanding human identity and overcoming the precarious condition of mutability in an ever-necessary search to transcend human origins and find unity in God.

The potential instability Augustine associates with our origin *de nihilo* also signals a close relation between creation and recreation. Angels avoid danger by adhering to God and sublating, as it were, their *de nihilo* origin (*conf.* 12.11.12). This is in contrast to humans who turn from the immutable God to their mutable origin and become lost in and torn by the vicissitudes of time and creation.[8] We will see that Augustine's account of time, friendship, and his attempted ascents to God illustrate how sin corrupts and threatens us with the nothingness of our origins. We will also see that the soteriological answer to this plight returns us to where we started, namely, to the distinction between our origin *de nihilo* and the Son *de Deo*. The Son is of the same immutable substance as the Father, but becomes incarnate in mutable creation to

---

[6] Despite the substantial undertones to his use of *de nihilo*, here and elsewhere Augustine prefers *esse* to *substantia* to describe the mutability inherent in creatures and the existence of unformed matter. Here, in *conf.* 12.6.6, Augustine postulates a formless something on the first day of creation, breaking with the essentialism of classical metaphysics that derived all being from *essentia* (*species/forma*) (J. Brachtendorf, "Orthodoxy without Augustine: A Response to Michael Hanby's *Augustine and Modernity*," *Ars Disputandi* 6/1 [2006], 297–304, see paragraph 9).

[7] In *nat. b.* 27, Augustine offers the example of the child who is born from (*de*) her parents to illustrate the substantial and enduring nature of the relation he associates with the preposition *de*.

[8] *Conf.* 4.10.15; 12.11.13; 13.2.3; see also *Gn. litt.* 1.1.2.

provide a bridge that moves us from the troubles that assail our mutable condition to peace in unity with the immutable God.

TEMPORALITY

Augustine's account of temporality in Book 11 offers further evidence of how creation and recreation are interwoven in his thought. It also illustrates how creaturely mutability, which itself is a product of God's good creation, morphs in sinful human existence to threaten the fabric of human identity. Although commentators often focus on Augustine's well-known account of the "extension or stretching of the mind [*distentio animi*]," which provides his solution to time's measurement, Augustine begins his account of time elsewhere with the question of its created origin. He argues that time has a qualitatively distinct origin from the eternal and immutable nature of God. This is important to recognize because it connects to his claims in Book 12, drawing implicitly on the contrast he formalizes between the *de nihilo* origin of mutable creation and the immutable nature of God (*conf.* 11.4.6–5.7). Divine eternity is more than simply a long succession of time; it transcends all temporal succession.[9] Locating God outside of time, then, positions time itself within the *de nihilo* origin of creation and means that time shares the mutable characteristics of creation.[10]

The origin of time within creation frames Augustine's examination into the nature of human temporality, which he takes up when he shifts from the question of time's origin to its measurement. This leads Augustine to a spatial account of time. What type of space gives time its duration and allows us to distinguish past, present, and future? Augustine answers with his famous *distentio animi* and a psychological reduction of time: the soul itself is stretched through its threefold capacity to expect (future), attend (present), and remember (past) (*conf.* 11.26.33, 28.37). This solution to time's measurement initially does not carry negative connotations, but by the conclusion of his account the *distentio animi* has become more a metaphor for the effects of time on the sinful soul (*conf.* 11.29.39).[11] The shift here is indicative of time's

---

[9] *Conf.* 11.7.9; 10.12–11.13. In contemporary parlance, the distinction between "everlasting" and "eternity" is often used to parse this difference.

[10] *Conf.* 11.5.7: "There was nowhere for it to be made before it was brought into existence [*quia non erat, ubi fieret, antequam fieret, ut esset*]." Augustine again prefers the verb *esse* to describe time's origin, giving it echoes of his account of mutability and the origins of human existence in Book 12.

[11] G. O'Daly, "Time as *Distentio* and St. Augustine's Exegesis of *Philippians* 3, 12–14," *Revue des Études Augustiniennes* 23 (1977), 265–271.

origin *de nihilo* and where it finds the space for its existence (duration); namely, within the mutable nature of the soul. Augustine foreshadows the dangers lurking in this shift when he positions his assessment of the *distenio animi* between a biblical allusion to Josh 10:12 – where the day (time) is stopped by God, allowing victory for the Israelites – and a plea to God for help against the ravenous effects of time.[12] As such, even his initial, supposedly neutral analysis of time is framed within a biblical and soteriological account of God's redemption of humanity from the sinful effects of time.

Augustine concludes his account of time by focusing it through a Pauline framework. Here he draws on the term *extentio*, which appears in his Latin version of Phil 3:12–14 and elicits for him connotations of an extension toward the immutable God that gathers and unifies the soul, to contrast with the way *distentio* scatters and stretches the soul within the mutable world.[13] This sets up Augustine's final prayer-in Book 11 where he contrasts the sinful distention of the soul with the hope of finding extension and unity in Christ's love (*conf.* 11.29.39–30.40). It also returns Augustine to the question of time's origin and his hope of salvation in Christ who bridges temporal, mutable humanity and the eternal, immutable God. Creation and recreation, working between the poles of creation's origin *de nihilo* and the Son's origin *de Deo*, are again brought together: time's created origin bears the marks of *creatio de nihilo* and finds its place (duration) within human mutable and sinful temporality, leading to the cry for recreation within the incarnation of the Son in Christ.

THE BOOK OF GENESIS AND THE CHURCH

The *Confessions* concludes in Book 13 with an exegesis of Gen 1. For Augustine, the opening chapters of Genesis disclose humanity's created and sinful origins, and so anchor his autobiography within the wider dynamics of creation and recreation (*conf.* 13.12.13). In particular, Augustine argues that God's grace of salvation and its vehicle the Church is already found symbolically and mystically within God's grace of creation. For example, he argues that in Gen 1 the separation of light from dark is also the delineation of the elect (*conf.* 13.14.15, 18.22, 19.25), while the creation of the waters and earth signals the work of

---

[12] J. J. O'Donnell, *Augustine:* Confessions (Oxford: Clarendon, 1992), vol. 3, 289.
[13] O'Daly, "Time as *Distentio*," 269–271.

the Church in the sacraments (waters/baptism) and preaching (earth/scripture) (*conf.* 13.17.20–18.22, 20.26–21.30). Despite skepticism contemporary biblical exegetes may have toward such moves, they advance and bring to a culmination key theological claims in the *Confessions*.

First, they signal that divine providence in both its soteriological and creative role is eternal. In Augustine's account of time we have seen that he distinguishes divine eternity from created temporality in an absolute, qualitative sense, holding divine immutable eternity as the soteriological goal that reunites the sinful fragmentation of mutable temporality. In Book 13, Augustine builds on this claim, arguing that God's soteriological plan is present from the beginning of creation, deriving from divine eternity.

Second, Augustine's exegetical claims on Gen 1 underscore that his search for his origins is not simply a question about his past, or even a question about the enduring influence of his past on his present identity. It is also a question about the future – his own and all other Christians. The origins of creation contain God's eternal providential plan for the cosmos' recreation and in this frame the *telos* of Augustine's personal and religious self-formation. This also invites the reader into Augustine's self-narration insofar as we too are caught up in God's eternal creative and redemptive providence. Here, the performative dimension of the *Confessions* comes to the fore: as Augustine performs his own confessions to God, so also he invites the reader to do so within a shared "self-narrative" guided by God's eternal providence.

In Book 13, Augustine anchors his account of God's eternal providence to his pneumatology through his explication of Gen 1:2. Here Augustine returns to the mutable, fluid state of creation *de nihilo*, arguing that the Spirit's love is what brings form and life from the inchoate and chaotic abyss (*conf.* 13.4.5, 7.8). As in Books 11 and 12, Augustine juxtaposes the incorruptible and immutable God with the mutable and fluid condition of unformed matter, which is symbolized by the Spirit hovering over the waters (*conf.* 13.4.5). The Spirit orders and forms creation, giving everything a place to find rest and peace (*conf.* 13.9.10). The human place is constituted through its love, and its proper place is found in the Spirit's love. In this, Augustine now qualifies the causal relation between God and creation he developed in Book 12: God creates all things *de nihilo* through the Spirit's love. This also brings together the conclusion of Book 11, where Augustine prays for unification in Christ's love of fragmented human temporality, with the Spirit's initial creative act, borne in love, that draws form and existence from the nothingness of the depths (Gen 1:2). Divine love is the unifying force underlying the Spirit's creation and Christ's recreation.

Divine love also signals, then, another important juncture where Augustine's accounts of creation and recreation come together. He develops this theme as he moves onto Gen 1:3 – the formation of light – which he takes to be the formation of intellectual creatures (i.e., angels and human souls) (*conf.* 13.2.3–4.5). Augustine describes creation here as the conversion of the creature to God that brings both form (existence) and happiness (goodness).[14] He argues these are distinct moments in the creature's life – to live and to live well – but they come together in the Spirit's loving act of creating a good creation. Creatures that turn toward the Spirit's love receive their proper form, which is also their blessedness. Creatures that reject the Spirit's love retain their life but fall out of blessedness (*conf.* 13.7.8–8.9). In this, Augustine juxtaposes the movement of creation with that of human sin, arguing that human sinful love moves us from the forming love of the Spirit and back toward the [*de nihilo*] abyss from which we were created (*conf.* 13.9.10). This risk is the reality of temporal fragmentation Augustine faces in Book 11, and his prayer for unity in Christ's love is now given its pneumatological and ecclesiological foundation. That is, Augustine's search for the Church in the Genesis creation narrative is also his account of the abiding presence of the Spirit's love in both creation and recreation: the Spirit's love forms us in the Father's creative act and reforms us in Christ's soteriological act as it is mediated through the Church. Thus, the love of Christ that unifies us from our temporal fragmentation (Book 11), a condition borne from our sinful appropriation of our mutable origins *de nihilo* (Book 12), finds its eschatological resolution within our participation in the Church that brings with it the Spirit's forming and reforming love (Book 13).

ORIGINS

When Augustine grounds the human place – its rest and peace – within the Spirit's forming and reforming love, he also returns to the opening lines of Book 1 where he claims all humans search for rest in God (*conf.*

---

[14] Cf. Augustine, *Gn. litt.* 1.1.2; *Enn.* 1.6.8; 5.1.12, 8.11; 6.5.7, 9.7. For an overview of Augustine's philosophical sources, see A. Solignac, "Analyse et sources de la Question De Ideis," in *Augustinus Magister* (Paris: Études Augustiniennes, 1954), vol. I, 307–315. Solignac speculates that Augustine's concept is dependent on Plotinus, Celsus, and Albinus.

1.1.1). This return signals the wider creation–recreation framework within which Augustine's narration of his self-formation in the first nine books of the *Confessions* unfolds. In the opening two books, Augustine focuses much of his narration around the question of language acquisition and formation, a discussion contemporary critics sometimes allege is at best simplistic and naïve and at worst a gross mischaracterization.[15] The problem with such critiques, couched as they often are within secular scientific and philosophical parameters, is that they ignore the creation–recreation framework within which Augustine develops his analysis of language. This framework is signaled already in the opening lines of Book 1 in Augustine's chosen method of analysis – namely, confession and his presentation of the basic truth and dilemma of human existence: humans desire to find rest in God but there is a gap between human understanding and divine wisdom that results in our restless dislocation from God (*conf.* 1.1.1). Augustine's analysis of language seeks to discern how we acquire the words to traverse this gap and reunite with God. Here already the dynamics of creation and recreation are at play. A gap exists between creation and the uncreated wisdom of God, one that is made foreign and dangerous by sin, and so calls for our recreation. The *Confessions* seeks to bridge what discursive reason cannot; namely, the difference between the eternal, immutable, good God and temporal, mutable, sinful humanity. Thus, his account of language is from the beginning an attempt to confess: the difference between God and creation *de nihilo*; the effects of sin on creation; and the route for mutable humanity back to the immutable God.

Augustine's ensuing discussion of language plays out the consequences of this gap and our desire to overcome it. He moves between the eternal, immutable divine Word (Wisdom), who is creator and redeemer, and temporal, mutable human words (restlessness). This is evident in the way Augustine opens his account of language with a confession of faith in the incarnation, arguing that the words needed to praise God come when the Son bridges the gap between God and humanity in the incarnation (*conf.* 1.1.1). This allows us to voice praise for the immutable, mysterious, and incomprehensible God (*conf.* 1.4.4), a voice only possible because God called first to us in the incarnation (Word) to give us words to call to God (*conf.* 1.5.5).

---

[15] Such criticism is found, for example, in Wittgenstein and those following his lead (L. Wittgenstein, *Philosophical Investigations*, trans. G. E. M. Anscombe [Oxford: Blackwell, 1997], 1–4).

From here, Augustine turns to his infancy, intertwining epistemic, psychological, and moral arguments about how he acquires language and his motives behind it. Augustine's claims on inner infant psychology, especially his contention of his own sin, often strike modern readers as artificial and misguided. But note again where Augustine begins; namely, with a petition for God's mercy to allow Augustine to speak about his mortal life [*vitam mortalem*] that has become a living death [*mortem vitalem*] (*conf.* 1.6.7).

That is, the starting point for Augustine's speech is not the inner developmental psychology of his own infancy, but rather God's mercy, which is also to say the divine Word incarnate. Augustine seeks the origin of language within himself but never within his own capacity as a self – in the development of his infancy. Rather, he seeks the origin of language in the way he as a self exists in relation to God, and the clue to this relation comes in Augustine's play on how mortal (*mortalem*) life becomes a living death [*mortem*]. This is the problem of language's origin tied into the problem of sin's origin; that is, language's origin read through Gen 3 where Adam's original sin leads to him receiving a coat of skins that Augustine interprets as symbolically representing the reception of a mortal body, which, in Book 7, he connects to the incarnation where the divine Word takes on a dying body in order to redeem humanity (*conf.* 7.18.24).[16]

The consequences of Gen 3 and of a mutable creation sinfully unmoored from the safe harbor of divine immutability reverberate throughout Augustine's discussion of language. We see it, for example, in the way he describes human customs as a river [*flumen moris humani*] that carries "the sons of Eve into the great and fearful ocean which can be crossed with difficulty only by those who have embarked on the wood of the cross" (*conf.* 1.16.25). Here Augustine opts for metaphors of instability, fluidity, and change to evoke creaturely mutability under the condition of sin. Human language in written and spoken form contributes to this river that carries us away from God. In particular, Augustine brings charge against the way schools teach rhetoric and Greco-Roman mythology (*conf.* 1.16.25–17.27). He argues

---

[16] Augustine draws on the language of Gen 3:21 to describe the eternal Word's participation in human mortality and to connect this to humanity's original fall into sin and mortality, which he argues occurs between Gen 3:7 and 21. In *Gn. litt.* 11.31.40–32.42, Augustine argues that Adam and Eve's realization of their nakedness signals that death and disease have entered the human body, which leads God to fashion coats of skin – mortal bodies – for Adam and Eve to replace the fig leaves in Gen 3:7.

that the stories of Greek mythology he was taught stirred up illicit emotions and sinful loves that focused on the fictitious suffering and death of Dido and masked his own sinful, mortal death (*conf.* 1.13.20). He describes his dalliances with Greek mythology as a type of fornication, an initially strange assessment but one that finds its deeper meaning in Augustine's famed pear tree story where he characterizes also his theft of fruit as an act of fornication (*conf.* 2.6.14). With allusions to the original theft of fruit in the Garden of Eden, Augustine anchors his account of fornication to the Genesis story of original sin and the illicit loves that drive Adam and Eve to imitate falsely the creative acts of God. Augustine's connection between fornication and false imitations of God suggests the power and danger of improper creative acts that result from temporal and mutable human words (books) and actions that distort the proper imitation of God we find as the divine image (Gen 1:28) within the Spirit's creative and redemptive love.

In this way, the Genesis creation narrative offers an archetypal framework for Augustine's critique of classical learning. But it is also only a partial framework that Augustine fills out as he moves on to unravel the problem of original sin and its solution in Christ. The connection to Augustine's account of language comes in the previous quote in his contrast between the river of human custom that sweeps us away from God and the wood of the cross that floats us back to God. This reminds us that language (and culture) is not evil as such; after all, our salvation flows through the incarnation of the divine Word within human language and culture, and the driving force of the *Confessions* is to find proper human words of praise and confession to help unite us with the divine Word.[17] In turn, this unity – this recreation – reconnects us to our created origins, which God forms through speaking the eternal, divine Word (Augustine, *Gn. litt.* 1.2.4–6). In these ways, language in both divine and human form plays an intrinsic role in the drama of human creation and recreation. Augustine's critique of classical learning and language, then, is really a critique of human mutability unmoored from the goodness of divine immutability, and his ambivalence toward language is a product of the way it contributes to sin and salvation. This ambivalence is on display in the closing lines of Book

---

[17] One of the important ways Augustine comes to confess God properly is through the teaching and preaching (rhetoric) of Ambrose. In this, Ambrose stands as an important example and contrast to Greek mythology on the morally efficacious role of language (*conf.* 5.14.24).

1 where Augustine repeatedly returns to God in words of praise only to then bring charge against words for leading humans astray into sin (*conf.* 1.20.31).

All of this points to the fact that Augustine's inquiry into language acquisition is really religious confession in search of how to voice both his own mutable humanity rendered mortal through sin and the immutable, immortal God rendered alien as a result of sin (*conf.* 1.6.10–7.11). As such, Augustine's claims on the sins of his infancy are less a psychological or phenomenological statement about infant development or experience and more an archetypal, theological claim about human existence in and through Adam. The problem is the sin that haunts our origins, that precedes our conscious recollection of ourselves, and that inhibits our confession of praise to God.

THE JOURNEY HOME

Augustine's discussion of language is crucial to the analysis of his origins and highlights how the dynamics of creation and recreation come together. As he moves beyond the opening books of the *Confessions* and into the account of his journey home to God, we see this dynamic continue to unfold. In this context, Augustine's relations with other people constitute an intimate part of his journey and capture well the creation–recreation dynamic. His relations serve as a cautionary tale of the dangers friendship can pose, as well as play a vital role in his return to God. The well-known contributions of Ambrose and Monica in helping Augustine reunite with God are counterbalanced by his account of the death of his unnamed friend. Both sets of accounts, in turn, connect into the creation-recreation themes we have traced in the final books of the *Confessions*.

We can begin in Book 4 and Augustine's account of the death of his friend. He argues that his grief transcended mere sorrow for his loss and threatened to tear apart his soul because he chose to love his friend apart from rather than through the Spirit's love (*conf.* 4.4.7). Here Augustine traces the disastrous consequences of human love thus directed, foreshadowing his discussion of the creation–recreation dynamic in Books 11–13. In Book 4, Augustine notes already how his grief led him to confront the dissipating and fragmenting experience of sinful temporality (Book 11) that arose from his attempt to ground his love within the mutable nothingness (*nulla*) of creation (Book 12) (*conf.* 4.8.13, 10.15). In this condition, the soul remains restless and agitated because its love has exchanged immutable divine eternity for creaturely mutability, which when unmoored from God leads to the soul's dissipation within the nothingness of creation's origin (Book 13) (*conf.* 4.13.20–14.22). The soul has no resources within itself to rectify this problem and so must be repositioned and raised up through the Spirit's love that descends to us in Christ (*conf.* 4.12.19).

Both the problems and solution Augustine discovers through his grief lead him on a quest to discern the road back to God and the role others play in this journey. We see this unfold, for example, in his attempts to reunite mystically with God, which culminate in his conversion to Christianity. We can begin here with Book 7 where Augustine frames the first two mystical ascents within a Platonist hierarchical model of inward rational movement from mutable creation to the immutable God (*conf.* 7.10.16).[18] He complicates this model, however, by overlaying it with a Christian creation-recreation framework in his attempt to recast and understand it within a Christian trinitarian structure. Augustine cues this overlay in the first ascent narrative when he argues that beneath and before his reading of the Platonist books, God's soteriological action in Christ is the real guide, an action Platonism fails to grasp (*conf.* 7.9.13–15).[19] In particular, and citing Rm 1:18–23, Augustine contends that rational speculation alone cannot transcend the created order and achieve lasting unity with God because our immoral loves generate idolatrous relations with creation that drag us away from God (*conf.* 7.9.14–15).[20] Augustine's answer to this problem interweaves themes of creation and recreation: God's incarnation in creation recreates us, restoring us to a proper relation with the created world that allows us to transcend this order and

[18] Contemporary scholarship often focuses on this Platonist framework. For example, Courcelle argues the ascents are a failed attempt at Plotinian ecstasy (P. Courcelle, *Recherches sur les Confessions de saint Augustin* [Paris: Boccard, 1950], 157–167). O'Donnell accepts the basic Plotinian structure of the ascents and agrees that Augustine fails in his first mystical ascent (*conf.* 7.10.16), but thinks he is successful in his second one (*conf.* 7.17.23), at least on Plotinian grounds (O'Donnell, *Augustine: Confessions*, vol. 2, 435). Louth argues for the Plotinian character of the ascents but contends that Augustine's search for a more permanent reunion with God leads him from a Plotinian model of ecstasy to a Christian model of the beatific vision (A. Louth, *The Origins of the Christian Mystical Tradition*, second ed. [Oxford: Oxford University Press, 2009], 133).

[19] Although Courcelle finds Plotinian echoes in the passage, O'Donnell notes that the language of *duce te* ("you as my guide") that opens the ascent narrative, anchored as it is in divine initiative, moves in the opposite direction of Plotinus (*Augustine: Confessions*, vol. 2, 437–438).

[20] TeSelle speculates that Augustine's critique here may be anti-Porphyrian (E. TeSelle, *Augustine the Theologian* [New York: Herder and Herder, 1970], 242–258).

become united with the creator God. Against this backdrop, Augustine's first mystical ascent echoes ambiguously the brief success of a Platonist ascent against the warnings of Rm 1:21–23 that such an ascent fails to achieve permanent reunion with God because of distortions in human love (*conf.* 7.9.14–10.16). This tension between God's love and human sinful loves also frames the second mystical ascent narrative (*conf.* 7.17.23). Here again, Augustine overlays a basic Platonist ascent with a warning from Rm 1:20–23 that visible creation should elevate humans toward God but on account of sin fails to do so. This leads to his claim that love must be reformed through Christ before humans can permanently unite with God (*conf.* 7.9.13–15, 18.24).

Augustine concludes the second ascent with a return to the Genesis creation narrative that he now juxtaposes with our recreation through the incarnation. Here he draws on the language of Gen 3:21 to argue that in the incarnation the Son participates in our "coat of skin" – our mortality. This reference serves as an important bridge to his conversion narrative in Book 8. In particular, Augustine's reference to Gen 3:21 connects with his story of the fig tree and its allusions to Gen 3:7 where Adam and Eve cover themselves with fig leaves, symbolizing their sin and loss of innocence. Augustine's use of the fig tree positions his own conversion story within the Genesis creation narrative as he seeks after lost innocence and to uncover the origins of where human mutability becomes sinful mortality (*conf.* 8.12.28). Toward this end, in Book 8, Augustine finds himself under a fig tree at a crucial moment after a long conflict within his will in which his deviant loves ripped at his "clothing of flesh [*vestem carneam*]," threatening to tear him from God's love (*conf.* 8.11.26). This "clothing of flesh" returns Augustine to the conflict of loves that undermined his mystical ascents, even as it alludes to the solution in Christ who takes on our coat of skin (Gen 3:21). This solution begins to present itself in Augustine's encounter with Lady Continence, who helps him confront his sinful loves, especially his deviant sexual loves, that have prevented him from permanent reunion with God (*conf.* 8.11.27). This healing encounter leads Augustine to the fig tree and the place, or moment, where created mutability became sinful mortality (*conf.* 8.12.28). It also leads Augustine back to the opening books of the *Confessions* as he finds the words (confession) that lead to his conversion in reading the eternal Word of Scripture that now comes to him within a love reformed through the incarnation (*conf.* 8.12.29).

Augustine's conversion leads into his final mystical ascent at Ostia. Here we find both an interesting contrast to the ascents in Book 7 and an important claim on the soteriological efficacy of human relations when they are ordered properly through divine love. Admittedly, the contrast between the Ostia vision and Augustine's prior visions is not apparent initially given that the Ostia vision still fails to achieve permanent union with God. But beneath this, important differences unfold. Foremost, unlike the prior visions that Augustine experiences alone, the Ostia vision occurs with his mother, a person who in the *Confessions* stands as a paragon of Christian virtue (*conf.* 9.10.23–25). This signals the Christian communal context in which the Ostia vision occurs, a context that now repositions the ascent within a new framework of the pilgrim Church and its eschatological hope for reunion with God. This allows Augustine to understand the Ostia vision, which is fleeting like those in Book 7, as fertile rather than futile because it offers him the "first-fruits of the Spirit" (Rm 8:23) that symbolize the promise and hope of a future permanent union with God (*conf.* 9.10.24).[21] As importantly, Augustine states that their exit from the vision entailed a return to the noise of finite human speech, which suggests that their experience of the Spirit occurred outside finite human speech and so within the eternal divine Word. Here again, we are brought back to Augustine's search for the appropriate speech, divine and human, that leads people to God, which Augustine now finds in the Ostia vision. That is, he encounters the Spirit's love at its point of soteriological efficacy, namely in Christ (the divine Word) as he is mediated through others (the Church).

This implicit trinitarian and ecclesiological framework is important not only in how it shapes Augustine's evaluation of the Ostia vision, but also in the way it presages his ensuing account of his Mother's death. In particular, the soteriological dynamic that accompanies this framework, which couches permanent reunion with God as eschatological promise, underscores that the way humans continue to suffer their mutability as mortality is a slow-dying threat overcome only through a lifetime of reformation in Christ (*conf.* 10.30.42). Augustine's juxtaposition of the Ostia vision with Monica's death is a dramatic reminder of this and of love's possibilities in helping to reform human beings. This reforming process is evinced in Augustine's grief over Monica's death, which offers an important counterpoint to his earlier grief over the unnamed friend's death. This latter grief threatened the dissolution of his soul (*conf.* 4.8.13–10.15), which brought to light the universal, if

---

[21] See also Augustine, *en. Ps.* 31.2.20, 37.5, 50.19, and *Trin.* 2.17.29 where Augustine connects Rm 8:23 with the soteriological hope of permanent reunion with God.

often unrecognized, condition of sinful temporal finitude (*conf.* 11.29.39). Augustine's grief over his Mother's death brings him again to experience and confront this condition, a condition he traces to his mortal finitude and the way he attaches to and forms habits around finite relations that pass away (*conf.* 9.12.30–13.34). But Augustine can draw now on a soteriological framework that allows for a new confession of his grief and his mortal condition. One can see this unfold as Augustine searches to remember both Monica's sin and her pious devotion to God (*conf.* 9.13.34–35). His prayer eulogizing his mother traces the tension between immoral and moral love, but now within a context in which divine grace offers the hope of love's reform and with this the promise eternal reunion with God.

This is the same tension that sculpts the contours of Augustine's own inner-religious conversion. As in the case of the unnamed friend, Monica's death returns Augustine to his mortal condition but now under the hope of finding unity in God. In this, both deaths bring to the fore the importance of human relations in Augustine's spiritual journey. They not only expose the inner condition of his soul, which often lies hidden to him, but also help him understand both the threat of eternal judgment and the hope of eternal peace. Beyond this, Monica also gives us insight into Augustine's wider vision of the Church's place in human spiritual reformation. We have already glimpsed this in his account of the Ostia vision, and he returns to it in describing his grief over his mother's death. In particular, one needs to take note of the way Augustine positions his direct confession of grief to God between a hymn he ascribes to Ambrose, who represents Orthodox Catholicism and the Church hierarchy, and an appeal to the wider Church body to remember Monica in the right way. Here Augustine begins with a hymn of Ambrose that he acknowledges as an important turning point in his grieving process that allows him to remember God's love and grace (*conf.* 9.12.32–33). The hymn highlights the God of creation ("Creator of all things") and recreation ("So rest restores exhausted limbs"), positioning his grief within the Christian dynamic of creation and recreation as it is expressed through the Church's liturgy. This hymn also returns us to Augustine's grief over his unnamed friend's death where he cites it as a counterpoint and critique of his wayward love (*conf.* 4.10.15).

The hymn in Book 9 precipitates Augustine's direct confession of grief to God that he offers privately to God in order to bypass how people might judge his expression of sorrow (*conf.* 9.12.33). Augustine's avoidance of other people's judgment is also an attempt to place himself

under divine judgment, but one directed through grace. In this, Augustine seeks to push beyond finite words toward the eternal Word, and
beyond finite loves toward the immutable Spirit's love. This does not
mean, however, that Augustine abandons human relations, only that he
repositions them. Here Augustine again returns to an ecclesiological
context as he transitions from his private memory and confession of his
mother to a collective memory and public confession of her in an appeal
to his readers and the Church to remember Monica in the right way;
that is, through love – "pious affection [*affectu pio*]" – properly formed
through confession to God – "at your alter [*ad altare tuum*]" (*conf.*
9.13.35–37). In this, Augustine moves from an individual to a collective
memory of Monica within a context where human words are formed
within the Church, and so elevated through the Spirit's love toward the
eternal divine Word.

This, then, returns us to Augustine's answer to the problems that
assail human mortal mutability. As the sinful love of his friend in Book
4 portends the temporal dissolution of the soul in Book 11, so the proper
love of others leads toward the unifying of the soul, a unity Augustine
seeks in the concluding prayer to Christ in Book 11 and glimpses with
Monica in the first-fruits of the Spirit in the Ostia vision. Finally, it is
this difference in how Augustine's love for others is positioned within
God's love for us that distinguishes his grief over the death of his mother
from his grief over the unnamed friend. Augustine still grieves deeply
for the loss and separation that accompanies the mortal condition, but it
is a grief not lost in the nonexistence that threatens any creature turned
from the forming power of God. Rather, Augustine is now sustained
within God's power of creation and recreation, and so can face the
lingering consequences of sinful love where the fragility and fleeting
nature of life *de nihilo* finds real hope of reunion, where the fleeting
vision of God is not the voice of condemnation – a sign that we exist in
the region of dissimilarity – but where it is now the voice of hope – the
first fruits of the Spirit – and a sign of our future permanent likeness and
union to God.

Further Reading

Brachtendorf, J. "... damit sie weinen lernen im Tal der Tränen. Augustin und
    die christliche Rehabilitation der Affekte." In *Unruhig ist unser Herz.
    Interpretationen zu Augustins Confessiones*, ed. M. Fiedrowicz. Trier: Pau-
    linus, 2004, 123–139.
Harrison, C. "The Role of *Creatio ex Nihilo* in Augustine's *Confessions.*" *Studia
    Ephemeridis Augustinianum* 85 (2003), 415–419.

O'Daly, G. "Time as *Distentio* and St. Augustine's Exegesis of *Philippians* 3, 12–14." *Revue des Études Augustiniennes* 23 (1977), 265–271.

Ortiz, J. *"You Made Us for Yourself": Creation in St Augustine's Confessions.* Minneapolis: Fortress, 2016.

Torchia, N. J. *Creatio ex nihilo and the Theology of St. Augustine: The Anti-Manichaean Polemic and Beyond.* American University Studies VII, Theology and Religion 205. New York: Peter Lang, 1999.

Torrance Kirby W. J. "Praise as the Soul's Overcoming of Time in the *Confessions* of St. Augustine," *Pro Ecclesia* 6/2 (1997), 333–350.

Werpehowski, W. "Weeping at the Death of Dido: Sorrow, Virtue, and Augustine's *Confessions*," *Journal of Religious Ethics* 19/1 (1991), 175–191.

Williams, R. "Good for Nothing? Augustine on Creation," *Augustinian Studies* 25 (1994), 9–23.

6 Sin and Concupiscence

JOHANNES VAN OORT

INTRODUCTION

What is the subject of Augustine's *Confessions*?[1] Many people think it is the famous story of a saint who confesses his sins to God. The reader perceives how the godly man once committed many offenses in which sexual concupiscence played a pivotal role. After all, does not the book tell the life story of the man who once prayed, "Grant me chastity and continence, but not yet" (*conf.* 8.7.17)?

In the past decades, innumerable studies have shown that Augustine's *Confessions* deals with many more subjects and is aimed at a variety of different readers. But all of the deeper insights into the ingeniousness of this literary masterpiece do not obliterate the fact that, indeed, much of it concerns sex and sin.

The present chapter seeks to uncover this aspect anew. It will discuss how Augustine conceived the sins of his youth and even earliest days; it will show how sex and sin were determinative in his illustrious conversion story; it will also focus on the reflections on his sinful state at the time when he wrote the book. After these and other main aspects have been discussed – for the sake of convenience I follow the sequence of the *Confessions* – I will seek to fathom what, exactly, concupiscence and sin meant to Augustine.

SIN AND CONCUPISCENCE IN AUGUSTINE'S EARLY YEARS

Modern readers are often struck by the following passages in the first book of the *Confessions*:

[1] The *Confessions* are quoted according to the critical text in *Sancti Augustini Confessionum libri XIII, quos post Martinum Skutella iterum*, ed. L. Verheijen, CCL 27 (Turnhout: Brepols, 1981). All translations are mine and footnotes are kept to a minimum. An elaborated version of this chapter will appear in the specialist journal *Augustiniana*.

Who reminds me of the sin of my infancy? For "none is pure from sin before You, not even an infant of one day upon the earth" (Job 14:4–5 LXX). Who reminds me? Some little mite who is a tiny child now, in whom I see what I do not remember in myself?
(*conf.* 1.7.11)

If "I was conceived in iniquity and in sins my mother nourished me in her womb" (Ps 50:7), I ask You, my God, I ask, Lord, where and when Your servant was innocent? (*conf.* 1.7.12)

These are the first statements about what Augustine later termed original sin. With reference to a text from the biblical book of Job, it is first confessed that even an infant of one day is not free from sin. This sin, so we may infer from Augustine's thinking during the time he authored the *Confessions*, is inherited through the child's generative descent from Adam. The same is expressed in the second statement with reference to Ps 50:7.

The two quotations are indicative of the negative tone that pervades the beginning of the *Confessions*. If already an infant (a child unable to speak, *in-fans*) is not without sin, how much more will this apply to an older child! No wonder that Augustine, after his *infantia*, describes his *pueritia* with even darker colors. He goes so far as to summarize his boyhood period as, "So little a boy and so great a sinner [*tantillus puer et tantus peccator*]" (*conf.* 1.12.19). Looking for the sins he has in view, one finds them particularly described at the end of Book 1. They consist of

countless lies with which I deceived the slave who took me to school and my teachers and my parents, and all because of my love for play [*amor ludendi*], my passion for frivolous spectacles [*studium spectandi nugatoria*], and my restles urge to imitate comic scenes [*imitandi ludrica inquietudo*]. (*conf.* 1.19.30)

Moreover, so Augustine recalls,

I also used to steal from the cellar of my parents and from their table either out of gluttony [*gula imperitante*] or to have something to give to other boys who, certainly, enjoyed our play as much as I did, and who would sell me their playthings in return. Even in this game I often lay in wait to dominate by fraudulent victories, because I was myself dominated by a vain desire [*cupiditas*] to win. (*conf.* 1.19.30)

Commentators have often seen this last passage as an anticipation of the famous pear theft.[2] It has also been detected that Augustine's tripartite arrangement of sins in accordance with 1 Jn 2:16 (the concupiscence of the flesh; the concupiscence of the eyes; the pride of life, which division of sins becomes most clear in his reflection in *conf.* 10.30.41) already forms the background of the description of his boyhood errors. The concupiscence of the flesh presents itself in his youthful demands of gluttony, the concupiscence of the eyes in his passion for frivolous spectacles, and the pride of life in his vain desire to win. In actual fact, we may see the same tripartite pattern in the brief indications of his early sins in *conf.* 1.10.16: his love of games (*amor ludendi*) reflects the concupiscence of the flesh; his curiosity (*curiositas*) with regard to the public shows is caused by the concupiscence of the eyes; his pride of winning (*superbae uictoriae*) is constituted by the pride of this world.

Another element in Book 1 is also indicative of the whole work. Already in *conf.* 1.18.28, one finds Augustine's identification with the younger son of Lk 15. The prodigal son went to live in a far country, and "to live there in lustful passion is to live in darkness and to be far from Your face." "The lustful passion [*affectus libidinosus*]" is here also mentioned as "the dark passion [*affectus tenebrosus*]." This *affectus* is nothing but the sexual libido, which arose in humankind as a punishment for Adam's sin.[3]

SIN AND CONCUPISCENCE IN AUGUSTINE'S EARLY ADOLESCENCE

If Augustine considers his baby- and boy-hood to be so filled with sin, how much more does this apply to his adolescence! The reader of Book 2 is introduced to this harsh truth by the very first sentence, "Now I want to call to mind the foolish deeds I committed and the carnal corruptions [*carnales corruptiones*] of my soul" (*conf.* 2.1.1). What did these deeds of sin consist of? Augustine first indicates them briefly as "various and shadowy love affairs" (*conf.* 2.1.1). They

---

[2] E.g., L. C. Ferrari, "The Pear-Theft in Augustine's 'Confessions'," *Revue des Études Augustiniennes* 16 (1970), 233–242; cf. J. J. O'Donnell, *Augustine:* Confessions (Oxford: Oxford University Press, 1992), vol. 2, 100.

[3] See, e.g., *civ. Dei* 14.21, "It was only after their sin that such lust arose [*post peccatum quippe orta est libido*]." That this *libido* is *sexual* lust is clearly evident from *conf.* 1.16.26 (Terentius' words stimulating sexual lust) and from another remark in *conf.* 1.18.28, referring the lusts [*libidines*] described in the works of the grammarians.

comprise the passions of the sixteenth year of his life when, having completed school in Madauros, he spent a year in idleness at home. By then "the clouds from the mud of carnal concupiscence [*concupiscentia carnis*]" obscured his heart (*conf.* 2.2.2), "the frenzy of lust [*uesania libidinis*]" (*conf.* 2.2.4) and "the thornbushes of lust [*uepres libidinum*]" arose above his head (*conf.* 2.3.6). All this becomes evident through Monnica's strict warning that he should not fall into fornication and, above all, should not commit adultery with any man's wife (*conf.* 2.3.7). The adolescent Augustine, however, throws her admonitions to the winds and, seeking to impress his comrades, even pretends [*fingebam*] to have done things he had not done (*conf.* 2.3.7). In all of this, he now considers himself to have wandered through the streets of Babylon,[4] while everywhere there was a dark fog [*caligo*] that cut him off from the brightness of God's truth (*conf.* 2.3.8). From the beginning of the book, the reader may know what this "dark fog" was: nothing other than "the darkness of [sexual] lust [*caligo libidinis*]" (*conf.* 2.2.2).

The next part of Book 2 (paragraphs 9–18) deals with the famous pear theft. Much ink has been spent on this story and its interpretation. One of the insights gained from these many studies is that Augustine's lengthy reflection on his deed seems to be especially aimed at his (former or actual) Manichaean readers.[5] It remains curious, however, that his adolescent life of sin finds its fullest expression in this episode, although in his reflection Augustine repeatedly stresses that *alone* he would never have committed the crime (*conf.* 2.8.16–9.17). Sensual pleasure [*uoluptas*] and desire [*cupiditas*] stand in the background as causes for his evil doing (*conf.* 2.8.16). One may read the story as a metaphor for sexual sin.

SIN AND CONCUPISCENCE IN AUGUSTINE'S LATER ADOLESCENCE

The following books until Book 7 deal with the later years of Augustine's adolescence. When he came to study at Carthage, a "cauldron of scandalous loves [*sartago flagitiosorum amorum*]" hissed all around him (*conf.* 3.1.1). What does Augustine mean with "scandalous loves"? He described it as being "sweet to love and to be loved, the more so if

---

[4] On the metaphor in its context, see J. van Oort, *Jerusalem and Babylon: A Study of Augustine's* City of God *and the Sources of his Doctrine of the Two Cities* (Leiden: Brill, 1991 [repr. 2013]), 119.

[5] E.g., Ferrari, "The Pear-Theft in Augustine's 'Confessions,'" 233–242.

I could also enjoy the body of the beloved," and he adds, "I therefore polluted the vein of friendship [*uena amicitae*] with the dirts of concupiscence [*sordes concupiscentiae*], and I clouded its purity by the hell of lust [*tartarus libidinis*]" (*conf.* 3.1.1).

Augustine is dealing here with concupiscence and lust in the context of his friendship relations; that is, friendships with male adolescents. The aforementioned quotations may best be read as indications of homoerotic relationships, and the same probably goes for his remark that God "besprinkled that sweetness with much vinegar" and that he was "flogged with the glowing iron rods of jealousy, suspicion, fear, anger, and quarrels" (*conf.* 3.1.1). Latent or actual homoerotic feelings may also be suspected behind Augustine's remark that he even dared to pursue his desires [*concupiscere*][6] in the church during the service and that he was "struck with severe punishments" (*conf.* 3.3.5). But Augustine leaves no misunderstandings about his current judgment:

> Therefore shameful acts [*flagitia*] which are contrary to nature, such as the acts of the Sodomites, are everywhere and always to be detested and punished ... The fellowship [*societas*] which should exist between God and us is violated when the nature of which He is the author is polluted by the perversity of lust [*libido*].
> (*conf.* 3.8.15)

The fact that Augustine in all these instances in Book 3 has homoeroticism in view, seems to be corroborated by his account in Book 4 of how he once loved a "very dear" Thagastian friend in a friendship "sweet to me beyond all the [other] sweetnesses of life that I had experienced" (*conf.* 4.4.7). He compares it to the friendship between Orestes and Pylades (*conf.* 4.6.11), which is often taken as the archetype of the homoerotic pair.

But all these likely homoerotic affairs were only transient. Although Augustine recalls, at the beginning of Book 4, that – because of the liberal arts – he was concerned with "the follies of the stages and the intemperance of lusts [*intemperantia libidinum*]," he also tells that in those years he lived with one woman (*una*), whom he had tracked down by his restles passion [*uagus ardor*]. This unnamed Una "was the only one [*una*] and I was faithful to her" (*conf.* 4.2.2).

---

[6] Curiously, Chadwick translates *concupiscere* in *conf.* 3.3.5 with "lust after a girl," but the latter is simply made up (H. Chadwick, *Saint Augustine, Confessions* [Oxford: Oxford University Press, 1991], 37).

In Book 5, we again come across a short remark about original sin [*peccatum originale*] "by which we all die in Adam" (*conf.* 5.9.16, quoting 1 Cor 15:22). Book 6 tells that Augustine, by then the official state rhetorician in Milan, feels himself "dragging along, under the goads of the desires [*sub stimulis cupiditatum*]" (*conf.* 6.6.9). The same book also contains a brief sketch of the life of Alypius – his integrity is stressed, but so also his former lust [*uoluptas*] for the circus (*conf.* 6.7.12) and the pleasures (*uoluptates*) of the gladiatorial games (*conf.* 6.8.13). As regards Augustine himself, he sees his former years as well as his present life in Milan full of "vain desires [*uanae cupiditates*]" (*conf.* 6.11.18). Later in Book 6, he describes himself as "bound by the disease of the flesh [*morbus carnis*] and its death bringing sweetness [*mortifera suauitas*]" (*conf.* 6.12.21). From the context we may be sure that this fleshly disease, also described as "the glue of that pleasure [*uiscum illius uoluptatis*]" (*conf.* 6.12.22), is nothing else than his addiction to sex. Unlike Alypius, he is tortured by the habit of satisfying his insatiable concupiscence [*insatiabilis concupiscentia*] (*conf.* 6.12.22). After he has dismissed his Una, and because his new fiancée is not marriageable, he takes an interim concubine because he is "a slave of lust [*libidinis seruus*]" (*conf.* 6.15.25). In retrospect he sees the time of his transition from adolescence to early manhood as the time when he was absorbed in an abyss of carnal lusts [*uoluptatum carnalium gurges*] while living in perpetual bodily prurience [*in perpetua corporis uoluptate*] and an over-flow of carnal lusts [*affluentia carnalium uoluptatum*] (*conf.* 6.16.26).

SIN AND CONCUPISCENCE IN AUGUSTINE'S EARLY MANHOOD AND THE TIME OF HIS CONVERSION IN MILAN

In Book 7, Augustine begins the narration of his early manhood [*iuuen-tus*]. His first words on this period are by no means flattering, "By now, my evil and wicked adolescence was deceased and I was entering the period of early manhood. But as I advanced in years, the more shameful I became in vanity" (*conf.* 7.1.1). His most important intellectual prob-lem is the question of how to think about God and, related to this difficulty, the immense issue of the origin of evil. According to August-ine, the cause of sin is human's free choice of the will (*conf.* 7.3.5). At this time, in the thirty-first year of his life, he experiences that he is drawn toward God because of God's beauty, but dragged away from God by his own weight. "And this weight was my carnal habit [*et pondus hoc consuetudo carnalis*]" (*conf.* 7.17.23). In other words, it was his sexual habit that kept him away from God. From his reading of the apostle Paul, he learns about "the law of sins, which is in his members" and also that only Christ "will free him from this body of death (Rm 7:23–5)" (*conf.* 7.21.27).

Book 8 deals with the most memorable period of Augustine's life, the time of his conversion in Milan. By then, he is in his thirty-second year. "Still in tight bondage to a woman," he feels himself constrained to the conjugal life (*conf.* 8.1.2). He is very negative about sexual lust. In his opinion, the perverted will causes the *libido*; when this *libido* is served, it becomes a habit; and when this habit is not resisted, it becomes a necessity (*conf.* 8.5.10). From his own experience he now understands Paul's words that the flesh desires against the spirit and the spirit against the flesh (Gal 5:17; *conf.* 8.5.11), and that there is a law of sin in his members (Rm 7:23; *conf.* 8.5.12). The effect of the famous story told by his African compatriot Ponticianus is introduced as follows: "I will now tell how You delivered me from the chain of my desire for copulation [*uinculum ... desiderii concubitus*], by which I was tightly bound, and from the slavery of worldly affairs" (*conf.* 8.6.13). Once – in all likelihood, when he was a Manichaean *auditor*, impressed by the Manichaean Elect's sexual abstinence – he had prayed: "Grant me chastity and continence [*castitas et continentia*], but not yet," for he was afraid that God would hear his prayer quickly and that too rapidly he might be healed from his disease of sexual lust (*morbus concupiscentiae*) (*conf.* 8.7.17). Now he is almost torn apart by the inner struggle between his two wills. The bad will is not caused by an evil spirit (as the Manichaeans opine), but is the punishment caused by Adam's sin (*conf.* 8.10.22). To Augustine, sexual abstinence [*continentia*] is the great ideal to be pursued (e.g., *conf.* 8.11.27). The essential result of his conversion is described at the end of Book 8 as follows: "For You so converted me to You that I sought neither a wife, nor any hope of this world" (*conf.* 8.12.30).

After his conversion, Augustine and a number of his fellows prepared themselves for baptism. First he had to withdraw from his worldly duties, the former pursuit of which he describes in general terms as scratching the itch of lust [*scabies libidinum*] (*conf.* 9.1.1). He no longer has the desire [*cupiditas*] to teach (*conf.* 9.2.4). One of those preparing himself for baptism along with Augustine is Adeodatus, his son according to the flesh, begotten of his sin [*peccatum*], "for I contributed nothing to that boy other than sin [*delictum*]" (*conf.* 9.6.14). Another hint at original sin may be found at the end of Book 9 in the statement that every soul dies in Adam (cf. 1 Cor 15:22; *conf.* 9.13.34). Earlier, in the famous Ostia conversation with his mother, both had reached the conclusion that the delight of the bodily senses [*carnalium sensuum delectatio*] could in no way be compared to eternal life (*conf.* 9.10.24).

SIN AND CONCUPISCENCE IN AUGUSTINE
AS A BISHOP

A new phase in Augustine's speaking of concupiscence and sin is reached in Book 10. Here Bishop Augustine discusses his present state when composing the *Confessions*. The discourse appears to be unique, for where else in earlier Christian times and even throughout antiquity does one find a person who searches his inner self in such depth and detail? First comes Augustine's famed passages on memory (*conf.* 10.6.8–27.38). After his penetrating analyses of this part of the inner self, he elaborates on other aspects of the human interior that – like memory – are connected with the human senses (*conf.* 10.30.41–34.53).

In his first and lengthy exposition on sinful concupiscence, Augustine proceeds from 1 Jn 2:16 (*conf.* 10.30.41). According to this biblical text, there is "the concupiscence of the flesh [*concupiscentia carnis*]," "the concupiscence of the eyes [*concupiscentia oculorum*]," and "the worldly ambition [*ambitio saeculi*]." Although the second and third lusts (the latter mainly meaning "worldly arrogance") will receive extensive treatment, Augustine's first and most detailed attention goes to the problem of carnal lust. Immediately after his opening quote of 1 Jn 2:16, he remarks:

> You commanded me to abstain from copulation[7] and, in regard to marriage itself, You instructed a better way of life than You have allowed (cf. 1 Cor 7:38). And because You gave it, it was done, even before I became a dispenser of Your sacrament. But in my memory of which I have spoken at length, there still live images of such things which were fixed there by my habit [*consuetudo*]. They rush into my thoughts, though strengthless, when I am awake; but in sleep they do not only arouse pleasure [*delectatio*], but even obtain consent, to something closely akin to the act they represent. The illusion of the image within my soul has such a force upon my flesh that these unreal visions influence me, when sleeping, unto that which the real visions are not able when waking. Am I not myself at that time, Lord my God? (*conf.* 10.30.41)

---

[7] *Concubitus*, in this context, means "extra-marital intercourse."

In fairly explicit terms, Bishop Augustine speaks here about his sexual dreams. In the next chapter he even more openly tells that these dreams may lead to nocturnal emissions ("up to the flow of the flesh [*usque ad carnis fluxum*]"). In modern parlance, these "flows" may be labeled with the informal term "wet dreams." According to Augustine, they are caused by the lascivious motions of his sleep [*lasciuos motus ... mei soporis*], which in turn he sees provoked by the glue of lust (*concupiscentiae uiscum*) (*conf.* 10.30.42).

There are also other forms of sinful concupiscence. Augustine is dealing with the temptations of the flesh in accordance with the classical five senses and, thus, after his discussion of the sense of touch (i.e., sexual pleasure), he continues with expositions of the other senses. First he reviews the lust [*uoluptas*] of eating and drinking (*conf.* 10.31.43). Although food and drink are necessary as "medicines," the snare of concupiscence [*laqueus concupiscentiae*] lies in wait (*conf.* 10.31.44). The transition from hunger to satiety is itself a pleasure (*uoluptas*). While the upkeeping of one's health is the reason for eating and drinking, a dangerous pleasantness [*periculosa iucunditas*] joins itself to the process and tries to take first place. In this context, Augustine warns against the deceitful pleasure-seeking desire [*uoluptaria cupiditatis fallacia*] (*conf.* 10.31.44). Texts on *concupiscentia* and *uoluptas* from Jesus Sirach (18:30; 23:6) are quoted to support his opinion (*conf.* 10.31.45). Most likely in polemics with his former Manichaean fellow believers, he remarks that it is not the uncleanness of food he fears, but that of uncontroled desire [*inmunditia cupiditatis*] (*conf.* 10.31.46). Although he has been able to completely cut away sexual intercourse [*concubitus*], his daily struggle against uncontroled desire [*concupiscentia*] in eating and drinking has remained (*conf.* 10.31.47).

Augustine discusses the allurement of odors only briefly (*conf.* 10.32.48, "With the allurement of odours I am not much concerned. When absent, I do not look for them; when present, I do not reject them. I am prepared to do without them all the time") before he comes to the delights of the ears [*uoluptates aurium, conf.* 10.33.49]. May we conclude, on the basis of his scant self analysis regarding the sense of smell – that is, only one full Latin sentence in the leading editions – that Augustine's olfactory organ was less developed?[8] In contrast to this,

---

[8] After his famous outburst *Sero te amaui* ["Late have I loved You"] (*conf.* 10.27.38), Augustine also makes mention of God's fragrance, but the passage seems to be strongly influenced by Manichaean descriptions of God (cf. J. van Oort, *Augustinus' Confessiones: Gnostische en christelijke spiritualiteit in een diepzinnig document*

he seems to have had an exceptional feeling for sounds and music. The remark that opens his two fairly long paragraphs on the sense of hearing may refer to his adolescent years as a Manichaean – "the pleasures of the ears had a more tenacious hold on me and held me under their spell" (*conf.* 10.33.49). Once he sang Manichaean songs and had difficulty with their metrical art (cf. *conf.* 3.7.14, "And I sang songs [*et cantabam carmina*]"); this past period of his life in which the alluring Psalms and hymns of the Manichaeans were so important, still seems to affect his appreciation of music. A great danger to Augustine remains to be carried away by the sweetness of the tones without fully observing the holy words; this is "a delight of the flesh [*delectatio carnis*]" (*conf.* 10.33.49). After some consideration he is prepared to allow melodic singing in the church; "yet when it happens to me that the singing moves me more than the subject of the song, I confess myself to commit a sin deserving punishment [*poenaliter me peccare confiteor*]" (*conf.* 10.33.50).

Concupiscential sin is also considered to be present in "the delight [*uoluptas*] of the eyes of my flesh" (*conf.* 10.34.51). The sensual pleasure of the sense of sight is discussed by Augustine as the last temptation of the lust of the flesh [*concupiscentia carnis*]. He prays that "beautiful and varied forms, glowing and pleasant colors" may not hold upon his soul – God is his good, not these (*conf.* 10.34.51). Corporeal light (venerated by the Manichaeans) is seen in contrast with noncorporeal light; typically, the blind Tobit and a number of Old Testament patriarchs are mentioned as those who saw it (*conf.* 10.34.52). It is difficult not to discern anti-Manichaean polemic in the choice of only Old Testament examples (and the striking absence of any New Testament text as accepted by his former coreligionists). On account of beauty of form, it is God the creator who must be praised; He is the highest Beauty from whom the artists and admirers of beauty draw their power to appreciate it. This (Neo)Platonic way of understanding God and Beauty is accompanied by the typically Augustinian warning: be mindful of "the (Christian) mode of use [*utendi modus*]" (*conf.* 10.34.53).[9]

In addition to the concupiscence of the flesh [*concupiscentia carnis*], "which inheres in the delight [*delectatio*] given by the pleasures

[Turnhout: Brepols, 2002], 21–24 and 58–60). Other passages in which Augustine speaks of fragrance and smell are mostly inspired by biblical texts, although in *conf.* 10.8.13 he notes that he can distinguish between the smell of lilies and the smell of violets (cf. *conf.* 10.9.16).

[9] For earlier passages based upon the underlying distinction between *uti* and *frui*, see *conf.* 1.20.31; 4.16.30; and 8.10.24.

[*uoluptates*] of all the senses," there exists in the soul – through the medium of the same bodily senses – a concupiscence that does not take delight in carnal pleasure, but in perceptions acquired through the flesh. This is, according to 1 Jn 2:16, the concupiscence of the eyes [*concupiscentia oculorum*]. Augustine devotes a long discussion to this form of concupiscence that he sees exemplified in the *curiositas* (*conf.* 10.35.54–57). Essential to human curiosity is "a lust [*uoluptas*] for experimenting and knowing," which however often becomes "a morbid craving [*morbus cupiditatis*; litt. "a malady of desire"]" (*conf.* 10.35.55). As such it is a grave sin. But falling into sin also threatens "through many most minute and contemptible things" that arouse our curiosity – "how often we slip, who can count?" (*conf.* 10.35.57).

Finally there is, as the third kind of temptation, the worldly ambition [*ambitio saeculi*]. Part of it is the lust [*libido*] for self-justification, the first sinful concupiscence from which Augustine confesses he has been cured (*conf.* 10.36.58).

In the remaining three books, Augustine does not further thematize his concepts of concupiscential sin. An echo of his expositions based on 1 Jn 2:16 can be found near the end of the *Confessions*. In *conf.* 13.21.30, it sounds one last time, "but haughtiness of pride [*fastus elationis*], the pleasure of lust [*delectatio libidinis*], and the poison of curiosity [*uenenum curiositatis*] are the passions [*motus*] of a dead soul."

CONCLUSIONS AND FURTHER REMARKS

Based on our analytical reading of the *Confessions*, I'd like to make the following observations:

First, in the descriptions of both his past and present state (*conf.* 1–9; *conf.* 10), Augustine continuously stresses his sinfulness. Although in regard to his early years as an adolescent he sometimes exaggerates his sins – in *conf.* 2.3.7, he tells that he invented stories of sexual prowess to impress his playmates; another case is the broad drawn-out story of the pear theft in *conf.* 2.4.9–10.18 – Augustine without a doubt displays a profound conviction of sin throughout the whole work of his *Confessiones*. This conviction is based, on the one hand, on his (by the time only slightly systematized) concept of original sin, and on his view of concupiscence on the other. Original sin – meaning in all evident instances in the *Confessions* (1.7.11–12;

5.9.16; 9.13.34; cf. *delictum* in 9.6.14), the sin in which Adam's progeny is involved – may be viewed as the starting point and lasting basis of Augustine's sinful state; "concupiscence" is thus the actual state in which Augustine lived his past life and in which he still existed.

Second, in the vocabulary of the *Confessions*, "concupiscence" is indicated by a whole plethora of words. Among these the noun *concupiscentia* occurs sixteen times, supplemented by the verb *concupiscere* in three cases. The *concupiscentiae* of which is spoken of in 1 Jn 2:16 form an important reference point for Augustine to define *concupiscentia* (e.g., *conf.* 10.30.41). Also, *concupiscentia carnis* is rather generally described as "the lust of the flesh which inheres in the delight given by the pleasures of *all* the senses [*concupiscentiam carnis, quae inest in delectatione omnium sensuum et uoluptatum*]" (*conf.* 10.35.54). However, in most references *concupiscentia* has an outspoken sexual meaning or, at least, a strong sexual connotation. This begins with Augustine's depiction of his early adolescence in which "the clouds from the mud of carnal concupiscence [*concupiscentia carnis*]" obscured his heart (*conf.* 2.2.3). He also "befouled the spring of friendship with the filth of concupiscence [*sordes concupiscentiae*]" (*conf.* 3.1.1) and he even pursued his sexual desires (*concupiscit*) within the walls of the Church (*conf.* 3.3.5). Books 6 and 8 are on his later adolescence, but *concupiscentia* has an outspoken sexual meaning also in the narrative of those years – Augustine describes himself as fully addicted to sexual intercourse ("my habit of satisfying an insatiable sexual desire [*consuetudo satiandae insatiabilis concupiscentiae*]" [*conf.* 6.12.22]). His famous prayer, "Grant me chastity and continence, but not yet [*da mihi castitatem et continentiam sed noli modo*]" is spoken within the context of his fear that God would "too rapidly heal me from the disease of concupiscence [*morbus concupiscentiae*]" (*conf.* 8.7.17). From the contexts of their quotations, one also gets the impression that, for Augustine, well-known Pauline texts such as Gal 5:17 ("the flesh lusts against the spirit [*caro concupiscit aduersus spiritum*]") (*conf.* 10.13.33; cf. 8.5.11) and Rm 13:14 ("But put on the Lord Jesus Christ and make no provision for the flesh in its lusts [*sed induite Iesum Christum et carnis prouidentiam ne feceritis in concupiscentiis*]") (*conf.* 8.12.29) have an outspoken sexual ring. Up to and including the narrative of *conf.* 10.30.42, *concupiscentia* with the meaning of "burning desire" always denotes sexual desire.[10]

Third, the observations made in regard of the new Christian word *concupiscentia* (mainly translating the Greek noun *epithymia*) turn out to be even more distinctly sexual in the case of the classical word *libido*. This noun appears some twenty-five times in Augustine's *Confessions* and nearly always denotes a strong sexual concupiscence or lust.[11] I already indicated the evident instances in the subsequent books of the *Confessions*; here I'd like to emphasize the fact that, according to Augustine, he was for many years a slave of his libido [*libidinis seruus*] (*conf.* 6.15.25). He considered this sinful libido (caused by his perverted will) leading to a habit [*consuetudo*[12]], and this habit becoming a necessity [*necessitas*] (*conf.* 8.5.10, "The perverted will causes the *libido*; when this *libido* is served, it becomes a habit; and when this habit is not resisted, it becomes a necessity [*Quippe ex uoluntate perversa facta est libido, et dum seruitur libidini, facta est consuetudo, et dum consuetudini non resistitur, facta est necessitas*]"). He even describes his addiction to sex as a sinful disease [*morbus animae meae*] (*conf.* 6.15.25).[13]

Fourth, contrary to what might be expected from modern word usage, *uoluptas* (the word occurs over forty times in the *Confessions*) seldom denotes sexual concupiscence. The first evident case in point is in *conf.* 4.7.12, where Augustine speaks of his – also homoerotic? – "pleasure(s) of bed and couch [*uoluptas cubilis et lecti*]." The second one is in the so-called *uita Alypii* in Book 6: Alypius wondered why Augustine was "stuck so fast in the glue of

---

[10] The only exception is in *conf.* 3.4.7, where Augustine relates his emotion after having read Cicero's *Hortensius*, "With an incredible desire of the heart I began to long for immortal wisdom [*et immortalitatem sapientiae concupiscebam aestu cordis incredibili*]."

[11] Most notable exceptions are: "harmful desire [*libido nocendi*]" (*conf.* 3.9.17) and "desire of (self)-justification [*libido uindicandi*]" (*conf.* 10.36.58). One is reminded of the well-known concept of *libido dominandi* or "lust of power" in *De civitate Dei* (e.g., 1 *praef.*; 1.30; 3.14).

[12] Cf. *conf.* 6.12.22, "To a large extent what held me captive and tortured me was the habit of satisfying with vehement intensity an isatiable sexual desire [*magna autem ex parte atque vehementer consuetudo satiandae insatiabilis concupiscentiae me captum excruciabat*]" (Chadwick, *Saint Augustine, Confessions*).

[13] Cf. *conf.* 6.12.21, "By the fastening of the flesh's disease [*et deligatus morbo carnis*]"; *conf.* 8.7.17, "by a disease of desiring [*a morbo* concupiscentiae]"; cf. also "the weaknesses of my soul [*omnes languores* (Ps 102:3) *animae meae*]" in the context of *conf.* 10.30.42.

that pleasure [*ita haerere uisco illius uoluptatis*]" (*conf.* 6.16.22) –
uoluptas here being his morbid tendency to sex mentioned in the
preceding paragraph. This disease is also meant by the subsequent
phrase "overpowered by the lust of that pleasure [*uictus libidinis
talis uoluptatis*]" (*conf.* 6.16.22). Apart from these evident cases,
one may wonder whether and to what extent the sinful *uoluptates carnales*, or *carnis*, or *corporis* spoken of at several occasions
(*conf.* 4.15.25; 6.16.26 [2x]; 8.7.17; and 11.2.4) should be understood in a sexual sense.

Fifth, concupiscential sin in the *Confessions* is also indicated by a
few other words. *Cupiditas* occurs over thirty times, nearly
exclusively in a negative sense, and at least in two cases it has
an evidently sexual meaning (*conf.* 2.2.2, "through the abysses of
lust [*per abrupta cupiditatum*]"; *conf.* 4.16.30, referring to the
Prodigal Son of Lk 15, "in order to waste it [my strength, *for-
titudo*, cf. Ps 58:10] in the quest for meretricious lusts [*ut eam
dissiparem in meretrices cupiditates*]"). *Fornicatio* is always
used in a very negative sense, and carries an explicitly sexual
meaning in *conf.* 2.2.2 ("I boiled up by my fornications [*ebullie-
bam per fornicationes meas*]") and *conf.* 2.3.7 ("that I should not
fall into fornication, and above all that I should not commit
adultery with someone else's wife [*ne fornicarer, maximeque
ne adulterarem cuiusquam uxorem*]"). In other places (*conf.*
1.13.21; 2.6.14; 4.2.3; and 5.12.22) it is used – as so often in
Augustine's œuvre[14] – in the biblically inspired sense of "adultery." Some other words denoting concupiscential sin include
ignis (very likely with a sexual meaning in *conf.* 3.2.2 ["of my
fire" (i.e., "of my passion") [*ignis mei*]] and *ardor* – clearly sexual
in *conf.* 4.2.2 ["whom my wandering concupiscence, void of
prudence, had tracked down (*sed quam* [i.e., Una] *indagauerat
uagus ardor inops prudentiae*)"]).

Although many modern studies of the multilayered concept of
"concupiscence" in Augustine's oeuvre acknowledge its sexual com-
ponent,[15] a close reading of the *Confessions* points to the central place it

---

[14] J. van Oort, "*Fornicatio*," in *Augustinus-Lexikon*, ed. C. Mayer (Basel: Schwabe,
1986–), vol. 3, 52–55, at 52–53.
[15] E.g., G. Bonner, "Concupiscentia," in *Augustinus-Lexikon*, vol. 1, 1113–1122
(although he sees its sexual meaning as special for Augustine's later anti-Pelagian
writings); G. Bonner, "Cupiditas," in *Augustinus-Lexikon*, vol. 2, 166–172;
N. Cipriani, "Libido," in *Augustinus-Lexikon*, vol. 3, 981–985.

assumed already in this work. Much in the story of its protagonist concerns sex and sin. This feature entitles us again to be fully aware of one of the essential meanings of *confessio* to which the title *Confessiones* refers; that is, the confession of *sexual* sins. Apparently, the cantus firmus of Augustine's *confessio laudis* is best heard against this background.

Further Reading

Beatrice, P. F. *The Transmission of Sin: Augustine and the Pre-Augustinian Sources*, trans. A. Kamesar. New York: Oxford University Press, 2013.

Bonner, G. "*Concupiscentia*." In *Augustinus-Lexikon*, ed. C. Mayer (Basel: Schwabe, 1986–), vol. 1, 1113–1122.

Cipriani, N. "*Libido*." In *Augustinus-Lexikon*, ed. C. Mayer (Basel: Schwabe, 1986–), vol. 3, 981–985.

Couenhoven, J. "St. Augustine's Doctrine of Original Sin," *Augustinian Studies* 36 (2005) 359–396.

Nisula, T. *Augustine and the Functions of Concupiscence*. Supplement to Vigiliae Christianae 116. Leiden: Brill, 2012.

O'Donnell, J. J. *Augustine:* Confessions. Oxford: Clarendon, 1992 (reprint 2012), three vols.

Van Oort, J. "Augustine and Mani on *Concupiscentia Sexualis*." In *Augustiniana Traiectina. Communications présentées au Colloque International d'Utrecht, 13–14 novembre 1986*, eds. J. den Boeft and J. van Oort. Paris: Études Augustiniennes 1987, 137–152.

"Augustine on Sexual Concupiscence and Original Sin." *Studia Patristica* 22 (1989), 382–386.

"Was Julian Right? A Re-Evaluation of Augustine's and Mani's Doctrines of Sexual Concupiscence and the Transmission of Sin." *Journal of Early Christian History* 6 (2016), 111–125.

"Sin and Concupiscence in Augustine's Confessions: An Analytical Overview of the Relevant Texts and Some Conclusions." *Augustiniana* 68 (2018), 193–207.

7 Grace

VOLKER HENNING DRECOLL

A THEOLOGY OF PRAYER

At the end of his life, Augustine, once again, felt obliged to defend his theology of grace. Some of his followers and readers in Gaul had pointed out that he himself would have supported their view about the origin of faith in former times. Augustine agreed and conceded that he had corrected an error in his writing *Ad Simplicianum*.[1] At the same time, however, he pointed out that already in *De libero arbitrio* he had emphasized original sin and its weakening effect on all humans.[2] Furthermore, he pointed to all the writings of his episcopacy. It may be that one aim of writing the *Retractationes* was to show how intensively he had dealt with grace even before the Pelagian controversy (therefore *Ad Simplicianum* was set as the starting point of all his writings as a bishop).[3] In *De dono perseuerantiae* (which should rather be named Book 2 of *De praedestinatione sanctorum* according to the manuscript tradition[4]), Augustine referred to his *Confessions*. He was well aware that this was his most famous work. In fact, it was published before the Pelagian controversy. In this context, he mentions that the book was previously (presumably around 405) read in Rome, apparently in a group of people. Pelagius, who participated in the reading group, was immediately concerned with the prayer in Book 10: "*Da quod iubes et iube quod uis* [Give what you are commanding, and command what you

---

[1] Cf. Augustine, *praed. sanct.* 1.3.7–4.8.
[2] Cf. Augustine, *praed. sanct.* 2.11.27 (olim *De dono perseuerantiae* 11.27).
[3] Cf. Augustine, *praed. sanct.* 2.21.55 (olim *De dono perseverantiae* 21.55).
[4] The new critical edition of *De dono perseuerantiae* in *CSEL* that I prepared in the last decade is already in press and will be published in 2019. The title of *De praedestinatione sanctorum* and *De dono perseuerantiae* will be changed to *De praedestinatione sanctorum liber I et liber II*.

want]" (*conf.* 10.29.40).⁵ Pelagius could not support this prayer.⁶ Indeed, the prayer sums up in a very concise manner the core of Augustine's theology of grace. The prayer is especially relevant for the question where faith comes from. Augustine's answer is: faith is an action of the human will, but this will can direct himself toward God only if God himself grants this to it. That is why humans can only pray for faith; they cannot achieve it by themselves. Praying as such, however, is a gift of God, thus the first impulse to pray is already an effect of God's operative grace. Augustine's theology of grace is a theology of prayer. Humans have to seek, to pray, and to wait for God's grace.

This is why the *Confessions* is written as a long prayer. *Confessio* means to address God – to speak about one's own sins, to express one's own thankfulness, and to praise God for all his operations. The *confessio peccati* ["confession of sins"] is intertwined with the *confessio laudis* ["confession as praise"]. To confess means to pray. Therefore, Augustine addresses God himself from the beginning of the work onward. This is not just a literary trick, but the core of the whole thing. He presents himself to the reader as the object of God's grace. His life is not interesting as such, but as the place where God's grace operates.⁷

In the context of Book 10, the famous prayer "*da quod iubes et iube quod uis*" is a prayer for chastity. Augustine quotes Wisd 8:21 as biblical witness: no one can become chaste unless God grants it, and it is already a sign of wisdom to know where this gift comes from. Augustine uses the literal meaning of the Latin word *continentia* ["being held/bound together"]: "Through continence we are gathered and lead back to the One [*Per continentiam quiippe colligimur et redigimur in unum*]" (*conf.* 10.29.40). The contrast between God as the One and the world as a multitude makes clear that one's love of God is less intense if anything else is loved apart from God. Therefore, the author prays for more love: God is asked to shed light upon the love. Continence as a form of highly concentrated love to God is an example for the effect of grace.⁸

---

⁵ For the question what may have been the source for Augustine's knowledge of the scene, see J. J. O'Donnell, *Augustine:* Confessions (Oxford: Clarendon, 1992), vol. 3, 201.
⁶ Cf. Augustine, *praed. sanct.* 2.20.53 (olim *De dono perseverantiae* 20.53).
⁷ Cf. E. Feldmann, "*Confessiones*," in *Augustinus-Lexikon*, ed. C. Mayer (Basel: Schwabe, 1994), vol. 1, 1134–1193, at 1158.
⁸ This explains why Pelagius reacted immediately to this prayer. His reluctance could not be understood if the prayer would only ask for the realization of what was recognized before (as Brachtendorf assumes [J. Brachtendorf, *Augustins* "Confessiones" (Darmstadt: Wissenschaftliche Buchgesellschaft, 2005), 187]).

Of course, this example is chosen deliberately. Augustine stresses that he pursued an ascetic lifestyle even before becoming a priest (*conf.* 10.30.41). This fits the apologetic character of the *Confessions* very well. By describing the effects of God's grace in his own life, Augustine defends himself against attacks that were derived from Donatists, but presumably also from Manichaeans.[9] At the same time, he provides a positive description how Christians should think of God and his grace. At the beginning of Book 10, Augustine claims that nobody except God can see what is going on in one's mind and soul (*conf.* 10.3.3). It is clear from this text that Augustine had to struggle with people who mistrusted him and who argued that, due to his past, he would not be an adequate candidate for a bishop. The *Confessions* is an admirable defense against these attacks. Augustine did not justify his behaviour, but confessed his past as sin and highlighted how God led him step by step to the priesthood and bishopric in Hippo. Thus, continence is an important part of Augustine's authority that is confirmed by the *Confessions*.

Augustine insists on the fact that continence is not just the external behavior that avoids any impure behavior. What is going on in the interior of the mind is more important, especially in the memory. Here, Augustine adds that the images and impressions of sexual intercourse and lust are always vivid (*conf.* 10.30.41). When one is awake, these memories are weak, but they have power in the dreams during sleeping and evoke joy and consent. Such a dream can have corporeal effects, even if one would consent while being awake (*conf.* 10.30.41). Thus, the dreams in which the memories are active show that humans do not have their minds under control. Therefore, it is the effect of God's grace when these memories disappear little by little. It is God himself who heals the weakness of the soul and extinguishes any lasciviousness that may be present in the soul. God increases his own gifts so that the soul can overcome all the internal struggles, sexual emotions, and any assent to them. Grace works on emotions. These emotions cannot be changed simply by a conscious decision, nor by rational arguments or insights, but only by grace. The prayer *"da quod iubes et iube quod uis"* shows exactly this: it expresses thankfulness for all the gifts that God already granted, it confesses all the sins that are always present in one's life and

Rather he understood the prayer as general sentence about how grace evokes someone's will.

[9] Cf. J. J. O'Donnell, *Augustine, Sinner and Saint: A New Biography* (London: Profile Books, 2005), 53.

mind, and it hopes for more grace and the final perfection that consists in perfect peace and that can be reached only by God's mercy.

A THEOLOGY OF CONVERSION

Augustine's own conversion in the garden of Milan became one of the most famous scenes of Latin literature. With tears in his eyes and the codex of Paul on his knees, Augustine sits under a fig tree, inspired by the voice: *Tolle, lege* ["Pick up and read!"] (*conf.* 8.12.29). This scene stands at the end of Book 8 in which Augustine describes how he was led by God to his conversion. He states: "*Convertisti enim me ad te* [You converted me to yourself]" (*conf.* 8.12.30). He begins this book praying to God: "My God, let me thankfully remember and confess what you have done in your mercy to me [*Deus meus, recorder in gratiarum actione tibi et confitear misericordias tuas super me*]" (*conf.* 8.1.1). A description of his own past and a prayer are intertwined in Book 8. The beginning of this book picks up the situation in which Augustine found himself after the events of Book 7. Books 7 and 8 belong together and describe the decisive moments of Augustine's conversion in Milan in 386. It is exactly the mode of Augustine's conversion that illustrates his understanding of grace.[10] Grace brings humans to God, by shaping their mind, by eliminating any reluctance, by giving new emotions and convictions. All this is prepared by information, knowledge, examples, and encounters.

In Book 7, Augustine describes how he reached the proper understanding of God, but this was not sufficient for him to be converted. Conversion is not just the correct understanding or a new intellectual insight. At the end of Book 7, Augustine is simply desperate. It takes various further encounters, thoughts, experiences, and finally the direct influence of God himself to lead to his conversion. For the overall intention of the *Confessions*, this is crucial. The right concept of God is important and necessary, but grace is not limited to information and help, rather it is a deep and direct influence of God on the most internal part of one's soul.

For his path to the true understanding of God, Augustine mentions two sources: 1) Ambrose and 2) the books of the Platonists.[11] Of course,

---

[10] V. H. Drecoll, "Gratia," *Augustinus-Lexikon*, vol. 3, 182–242, at 200.

[11] In *b. vita* 1.4, Augustine mentions *Plotini paucissimi libri* ("very few books of Plotinus"). The idea that an eclecticism of Christianity and Neoplatonism represented a kind of intellectual milieu (of a "circle of Milan") (P. Courcelle,

speaking about Ambrose is part of the apologetic strategy of the *Confessions*. Ambrose as the bishop who baptized Augustine appears as a kind of spiritual father and was one of the most famous Latin Christian authors in 400 – the time when the *Confessions* was published. Augustine was introduced to the Christian faith not by anybody, but by this prominent figure of Christian theology and spirituality.[12] Even according to Augustine's description, however, Ambrose's skepticism toward the high official of the (Homoean) court and the former Manichaean (and one might imagine the doubt whether he was really only a former Manichaean) is obvious. His advice to read Isaiah (given after his registration as candidate for baptism) (*conf.* 9.5.13) – in fact, hard stuff for a rhetorician such as Augustine – may be understood as Ambrose's attempt to check how seriously this son of the pious mother would deal with the Christian, pro-Nicene faith. In fact, for Augustine, reading Isaiah was of no help. What was a substantial help was Ambrose's concept of God. It became clear to Augustine that God was spirit. This meant: God cannot be found in the world, or by any efforts that are linked to material or external things. Only a way into one's interior could be helpful. The reading of the books of the Platonists promised exactly such a way into one's own mind.[13]

Augustine provides more than one description of how he tried such a way to find God in himself. He says that he noticed through the eye of his soul an immutable light over his mind, a light that was different from any visible light. It was not simply above, but superior because, when looking at it, it became immediately clear that the light was a creative power, and he, Augustine, was created by it.[14] Thus, looking at this light makes clear: this light has permanent and real existence; it *is* in the fullest sense of the word, while the observer is weak and nearly

---

Recherches sur les Confessions de saint Augustin [Paris: Boccard, 1968], 252–254) was criticized by G. Madec, "'Platonisme' et 'Christianisme': Analyse du livre VII des 'Confessions'," in *Lectures Augustiniennes*, Collection des Études Augustiniennes, Série Antiquité 168 (Paris: Paris Institut d'Études Augustiniennes, 2001), 121–184, at 151; and C. Markschies, *Ambrosius von Mailand und die Trinitätstheologie: Kirchen- und theologiegeschichtliche Studien zu Antiarianismus und Neunizänismus bei Ambrosius und im lateinischen Westen (364–381 n.Chr.)*, Beiträge zur historischen Theologie 90 (Tübingen: Mohr Siebeck, 1995), 79–80.

[12] O'Donnell, *Augustine, Sinner and Saint*, 54–55.

[13] Cary contends that *conf.* 7 is rather a description of Augustine's understanding of Plotinus in ca. 400 than in 386 (P. Cary, *Augustine's Invention of the Inner Self: The Legacy of a Christian Platonist* [New York: Oxford University Press, 2000], 35–37).

[14] Cary, *Augustine's Invention of the Inner Self*, 38–39.

nonexistent. The light is so strong that it repels by its beam the weak observer who trembles and feels love and dismay at the same time. Augustine felt himself *"in regione dissimilitudinis* [a place of unlikeness]," far away from God (*conf.* 7.10.16).[15] Everything in the world exists only in a limited way, not in the fullest sense of being. It is different from God and thus exists less and is affected by corruption (*conf.* 7.11.17–12.18).

When he returns to this experience[16] of not being able to grasp the light (namely, God), he says that his own weight [*pondus*], his fleshly conduct and habit [*consuetudo carnalis*], prevented him from remaining in permanent contact with God – "The corruptible body burdens the soul" (Wisd 9:15). At the same time, Augustine was sure that the invisible side of God could be recognized through the created things (cf. Rm 1:20). Therefore, he sought the source of beauty and assumed that this should be an immutable and eternal truth above his own mind. Thus, he tried to ascend from all bodies to the soul that has all the sensations of the beautiful things, from these sensations to the rational part of the soul that makes judgments about beauty, and from anything that is confusing and provides illusions to what is absolutely immutable.[17] The highest goal is what can be seen only in the blink of an eye.[18] The result is the same as before: Augustine was not able to maintain this moment and felt repulsed to his normal, material life. Only the memory of God remained in him (*conf.* 7.17.23). Thus, these experiences of thought did not lead directly to God, but at least confirmed his new conviction that God is absolutely different from any corporeal or material being, the truth above all, the real being.[19]

The reading of the books of the Platonists revealed how to think about God. They showed that only God as the real being is the ultimate

[15] For the biblical background of this expression, see O'Donnell, *Augustine: Confessions*, vol. 3, 443.
[16] This is retrospective because, in *conf.* 7.17.23, Augustine uses the pluperfect *inueneram* (V. H. Drecoll, *Die Entstehung der Gnadenlehre Augustins*, Beiträge zur historischen Theologie 109 [Tübingen: Mohr Siebeck, 1999], 287).
[17] For the Plotinian themes in this description, see Drecoll, *Entstehung*, 288–293.
[18] O'Donnell, *Augustine:* Confessions, vol. 2, 457 highlights 1 Cor 15:52 as the biblical background for *in ictu trepidantis aspectus* ("with the stroke of one trembling glance") in *conf.* 7.17.23.
[19] K.-H. Ruhstorfer, "Die Platoniker und Paulus. Augustins neue Sicht auf das Denken, Wollen und Tun der Wahrheit," in *Die Confessiones des Augustinus von Hippo. Einführung und Interpretation zu den dreizehn Büchern*, eds. N. Fischer and C. Mayer, Forschungen zur europäischen Geistesgeschichte 1 (Freiburg: Herder, 1998), 283–341, at 291–292.

goal of any human effort. This goal, however, was not reached by knowledge. Augustine uses the contrast between knowledge and love for this. He was proud of his knowledge, but love was lacking (*conf.* 7.20.26). He could see God from far away but not reach a stable communion with him. Only later, by reading the Bible, especially Paul, did he understand what was lacking. What was lacking was the humble, Incarnate Christ (*conf.* 7.20.26). It may be true that the books of the Platonists confirm the Christian idea of the eternal *logos*, but the meaning of the incarnation was hidden to them. This meaning consists in the deep insight that nobody can become strong enough so that God can be reached, but rather it is God who proves humbleness and rescues human beings in spite of their weakness in order to bestow peace (*conf.* 7.9.14, 18.24). Thus, at the end of Book 7, Augustine both reduces the importance of any rational ascent as it can be found in the writings of the Platonists, and describes the operation of grace in terms taken from Paul (*conf.* 7.21.27).

Whatever is said in Scripture is said as a recommendation of grace: even one who gets an idea of God, does so only because God bestowed it. This is confirmed by 1 Cor 4:7 ("What do you have that you did not receive?" [*conf.* 7.21.27]).[20] In his writing *Ad Simplicianum*, exactly the later verse is used in order to express the main intention of Paul (*Simpl.* 1.2.2, 2.21). Later on, Augustine could refer especially to the former verse as witness for his own doctrine of grace (*praed. sanct.* 1.3.7). Here, he uses both verses in order to elucidate the difference between an abstract concept of God, who may be touched by a rational process for a split second, and the permanent communion with God. Grace allows not only seeing, but also holding tight to what was seen and finding the way to the homeland. With the words of Rm 7, he compares the abstract knowledge about God with the law that is already accepted by the inner man and the other, different law in the flesh that is reluctant.[21] This human condition is due to the sins of human beings, to the just judgment of God, and to the punishment; that is, submission to the devil and death. With words of Rm 7:25, he asks: "Who will deliver me from this body of death, if not your grace through Jesus Christ?" Jesus Christ is not only the coeternal Word that was present at the creation (about

---

[20] Cf. P.-M., Hombert, *Gloria Gratiae: Se glorifier en Dieu, principe et fin de la théologie augustinienne de la grâce*, Collection des Études Augustiniennes, Série Antiquité 148 (Paris: Institut d'Études Augustiniennes, 1996), 36–37.

[21] Drecoll, *Entstehung*, 298; I. Bochet, "*Le firmament de l'écriture*": *L'herméneutique Augustinienne*, Collection des Études Augustiniennes, Série Antiquité 172 (Paris: Institut d'Études Augustiniennes, 2004), 228.

this eternal mind of God the books of the Platonists may be right), but also the Incarnate one that was killed by the devil without being guilty, the handwriting of ordinances being killed (cf. Col 2:14). These aspects cannot be found in the books of the Platonists[22] – neither the incarnation, nor the sacrifice of Jesus Christ; neither the sorrow of the human spirit, nor the contrite heart; neither the gift of the Holy Spirit, nor the Eucharist are contained in them. This redemption by grace is granted to the Christians, not to the Platonists. The Platonists see the homeland, they know where to go, but they do not know the way to get there. The way is only accessible by grace. When this became clear to Augustine through reading Paul, he was well prepared for his conversion (*conf.* 7.21.27).

The conversion described in Book 8 is a highly emotional process. Throughout the first nine books of the *Confessions*, Augustine mixes passages that reflect on the soul and God's actions with narrative passages about his past. In Book 8, this is more complicated: some of the reflective passages do not concern Augustine at all, but are quite general; some of them, however, describe what was going on in his soul in 386. Furthermore, within the narrative passages about the past various stories are embedded. These stories within the stories provide models of conversion and prepare the garden scene. Thus, there are four levels: (1) general reflections, (2) reflections of Augustine's own situation in the past, (3) the narrative of what happened in summer 386, and (4) the stories embedded in the narrative.[23]

Let us first consider the general reflections: Augustine deals at some length with the idea of two wills in one soul. He rejects the Manichaean assumption that two wills in one individual are caused by the presence of two different natures in two minds with opposite wills in the soul. They assume that the better part of their soul is directly a part of God's substance, whereas the bad one belongs to the bad nature. Both sides stem from the two principles (*conf.* 8.10.22, 24). Augustine refutes this by arguing that also two good wills or two bad wills could conflict with each other and that there could even be more than two competing wills (*conf.* 8.10.23–24). Therefore, the observation of two different wills in one individual does not confirm the Manichaean system. Different wills can belong to one will. This anti-Manichaean passage fits with the overall apologetic structure of the *Confessions*. Augustine has the Manichaeans as possible readers in mind and develops arguments

---

[22] Cf. O'Donnell, *Augustine: Confessions*, vol. 2, 479.

[23] Drecoll, *Entstehung*, 301.

against their theology.[24] Furthermore, it shows an important aspect of how grace operates. The difference between knowledge and love causes a struggle within the soul because it causes two directions of will. Thus, it is not the struggle between mind and flesh, or soul and body, but a struggle within the will of one soul that is crucial.

Augustine pursues the question where this struggle comes from. If there are not two distinct authorities in the soul that can be responsible, then it is just the soul itself that causes this struggle. Augustine wonders why the will can directly rule the limbs of the body but is not capable of asserting itself against itself, if there were to be another competing will. This question, however, already includes the answer: because it is not the whole will that wills, but rather two parts of it. The will is not entirely willing and, therefore, it is weak and cannot simply accomplish what it wants (*conf.* 8.9.21). Thus, the struggle of the will can only be brought to an end by a new unity of the will. The will to realize an ascetic life devoted to God must take possession of the whole of the will. Only then will the reluctant will disappear step by step. The last step, then, makes it possible that the now unified will puts its will to practice. This process is not a series of conscious decisions, nor is it sufficient simply to will something. The process of conversion is a series of experiences in which the will gets its new unity and the reluctant will finally disappears.

It is exactly this process which Augustine describes. He tells of two visits, their influence on his soul, and the final garden scene as the last step. Both visits provide conversion scenes that become models for Augustine's own conversion.[25] The conversion of Marius Victorinus, which was told by the priest Simplician, shows how an important rhetor, a significant member of the "pagan" society (as Augustine was himself in 386), decided not only to share ideas with Christianity, but also to receive baptism and confess his faith in public (*conf.* 8.2.5). The conversion of two high officials [*agentes in rebus*] in Trier to an ascetic life highlights the connection between conversion and chastity that

---

[24] Ibid., 303–305. According to Kotzé, Augustine has Manichaeans in mind not only as enemies, but also as a considerable part of his audience (A. Kotzé, *Augustine's* Confessions: *Communicative Purpose and Audience*, Supplements to Vigiliae Christianae 71 [Leiden: Brill, 2004], 88–94). Since the idea of two souls is clearly a polemical invention Manichaeans would not agree with (cf. V. H. Drecoll and M. Kudella, *Augustin und der Manichäismus* [Tübingen: Mohr Siebeck, 2011], 148–149), such proposal is at least not very plausible for *conf.* 8.10.22–24.

[25] For the comparison of the motives of all three conversion stories of Book 8, see Drecoll, *Entstehung*, 312–313; Bochet, *Firmament*, 282–286.

became crucial for Augustine. It also introduces the conversion of Anthony and the reading of Athanasius' *Vita Antonii*, even though Anthony's own conversion is not yet explained. Furthermore, this story, which is told by the high official Ponticianus, who congratulates Augustine for reading Paul and outs himself as having been a Christian for years, shows that monastic life in the West at this time is quite new. Augustine mentions that he was not aware of the monastery outside of the city that Ambrose was responsible for (*conf.* 8.6.14–15). The conversion of these two former fellows of Ponticianus is caused by their insight that they contend and fight all their lives, but all that they can hope for is a high reputation with the emperor, a fragile and dangerous thing. Thus, they are struck by reading the *Vita Antonii* and touched in their soul. The one of the two was "changed internally where God sees [*mutabatur intus, ubi tu uidebas*]" (*conf.* 8.6.15), thus turning away from any secular and external goal. They chose an ascetic, eremitic lifestyle, and gave up their wedding plans. When the brides heard about the decisions of their partners, they too decided to become nuns (*conf.* 8.6.15). By these two examples, two sides of Augustine's own conversion are covered: his job and profession as rhetor, and his wedding plans.[26] Thus, in the case of Augustine, conversion is not simply a new insight or a new will, but the decision to begin a new life that cuts off important things that were previously important: career and partnership.[27]

Above all, the two stories provided models of conversion that made clear to Augustine what his goal was. Partially, he wanted exactly such an ascetic life: to give up his rhetoric position at the emperor's court and call off his engagement with the woman that he should marry, to find a new life, to practice philosophy, and think about God. But this was only a partial will in itself. His prayers run: "Give me chastity, but not yet!" (*conf.* 8.7.17). Thus, knowing and willing what he should do also humiliated him at the same time. He felt weaker than the ascetics that he knew about now, he felt ashamed because he was not strong enough to bring about his will, he was confronted with his own emotions that were reluctant (*conf.* 8.11.27). He felt them urging: can you really dismiss us; that is, live without sex (*conf.* 8.11.26)? He expressed this feeling through a direct short speech of his conscience. Augustine looked back to all the years since he had begun to read Cicero's

---

[26] Cf. Augustine, *b. vita* 1.4: "*uxoris honorisque inlecebra detinebar* [I was bound by the lure of having a spouse and a honorable position]."
[27] Feldmann, "*Confessiones*," 1160–1162.

Hortensius and had decided to look for truth and to avoid any delusion. His conscience confronted him with his internal struggle: the right way is already given, others came to a decision without decades of searching and hesitating. What about you (*conf.* 8.7.18)? The emotions of humiliation, desperation, and shame are combined with hope, expressed in prayers, and a kind of certainty that the chosen goal is right. Directly before the garden scene he introduces an internal dialogue with the continence that admonished him by questions and imperatives to hand himself over to God and promises that God will rescue him.[28]

In the garden scene, Augustine describes a sight where this conflict of emotions is resolved. He describes how he shared his feelings with his friend Alypius (*conf.* 8.11.27), a witness who is still alive at the time of publication of the *Confessions*. While both were in the garden, Augustine, in tears, hides himself from his friend, going away a few yards (*conf.* 8.12.28). This is the situation where he listens to the voice of a child: "*Tolle lege* [Pick up and read!]"[29] He started to wonder if this could be a song that children sing while playing, but he could not remember anything similar. Thus, he could not interpret it in any other way than as divine command: pick up the codex and read what occurs first! This idea came to him because he had heard about the conversion of Antony earlier. Antony was struck by a biblical verse that was read exactly in the moment when he entered the Church and had felt that he was directly addressed. Augustine went back to Alypius who had the codex of Paul on his knees. He opened the codex and read the first verse that came to his eyes: "Not in rioting and drunkenness, not in affairs and impudence, not in struggle and pretense, but put on the Lord Jesus Christ, and do not take care of the flesh with its desires" (Rm 13:13–14). He stated that he did not want to read further, nor was it

---

[28] The passage is crucial for the analysis of Byers (S. C. Byers, *Perception, Sensibility, and Moral Motivation in Augustine: A Stoic-Platonic Synthesis* [Cambridge: Cambridge University Press, 2013], 37–39). She focuses upon the imperatives and interprets them as the reception of the Stoic idea of the perception of impulsive (*hormetic*) impressions linked to sayings [*lekta*]. For the internal character of the speaking continence (against the theory of Courcelle [*Recherches*, 192], who was in favor of the appearance of a personalized allegory), see Byers, *Perception, Sensibility, and Moral Motivation*, 4. For the Stoic concept of *akrasia/incontinentia*, see J. Müller, *Willensschwäche in Antike und Mittelalter: Eine Problemgeschichte von Sokrates bis Johannes Duns Scotus*, Ancient and Medieval Philosophy, Series I, 40 (Leuven: Leuven University Press, 2009), 164–193.

[29] L. F. Pizzolato, "Libro ottavo," in *Sant' Agostino. Confessioni (Libri VII–IX)*, Fondazione Lorenzo Valla, Scrittori greci e latini (Milan: Arnoldo Mondadori, 1994), vol. 3, 282–297.

necessary. By reading this verse, Augustine felt immediately sure. It was as if light of certainty was infused into him. Any doubts of when to start with his new life were gone (*conf.* 8.12.29). Something similar happened to Alypius, as he read Rm 14:1: "Receive the weak in faith!" He joined Augustine in his decision. They told about their decisions to Monica who was happy. God has done more than she had asked for in her prayers. "*Conuertisti enim me ad te* [You have converted me to you]", is Augustine's conclusion (*conf.* 8.12.30).

The garden scene shows how Augustine sketches the internal way to his new motivation. It is not caused by himself, but he is very active in it. It is he who is in tears, hears the voice, thinks about it, gives an interpretation, remembers the conversion of Antony, and reads the verse. At the same time, however, it is not a way of decisions, but a way in which God operates with him: externally and internally. In addition to external signs (the voice, the *Vita Antonii*, and the verses of Paul) God's grace operates directly in the mind of Augustine.[30] The wondering about the voice, the idea that this should be a divine command, the interpretation that could not be given in another way, the sudden idea that this is similar to what happened to Antony, the feeling that Rm 13:13–14 cut off any doubts are all in the mind of Augustine, but this was not due to a conscious decision of his own will, the ideas rather came to his mind, they appeared suddenly.[31] In his *Ad Simplicianum*, Augustine says that grace is not only operating externally (by a

---

[30] Drecoll, *Entstehung*, 321–324; C. Köckert, "Therapie der Affekte: Augustins Confessiones als Dokument christlich-philosophischer Seelsorge," *Zeitschrift für Kirchengeschichte* 127 (2016), 293–314, at 306–307.

[31] Byers emphasizes that, in *conf.* 8.11.27, God's agency is explained (*Perception, Sensibility, and Moral Motivation*, 184). This is even more true for the garden scene. Brachtendorf understands God's activity in *conf.* 8.11.25–12.30 as (1) "*gratia subsequens et cooperans* [the subsequent and cooperative grace]" and (2) doubts that the "*gratia praeueniens* [the prevenient grace]" can be experienced in life or can be told in a narrative (*Confessiones*, 184–185). Thus, the conversion in the *Confessions* does not illustrate Augustine's understanding of grace. Although it is true that Augustine does not use the terminology of the exegesis of Paul nor the anti-Pelagian arguments in describing the garden scene, God's agency in it seems to be minimized by reducing it to a *gratia subsequens et cooperans* (Augustine never used the phrase *gratia subsequens*; for the *cooperari*, see Augustine, *gr. et lib. arb.* 17.33). The idea that it was simply Augustine's own decision (not caused by God's activity) to end the internal struggle in his soul by asking for God's help in the beginning of *conf.* 8.12.29 does not fit with the description of the motivational and emotional process as described by Byers and with Augustine's literary strategy in *conf.* 7–8 (cf. *conf.* 8.1.1: *dirupisti uincula mea ... quomodo dirupisti ea, narrabo*). See Köckert, who highlights the transformative dimension of this strategy for the author as for the reader ("Therapie," 308–309).

congruous vocation or an appropriate arrangement of signs), but also in the mind where nobody controls what suddenly appears there.[32] This is exactly what he describes in the garden scene.[33] The *Confessions* is an illustration of how grace operates, because Augustine explains this in detail in the case of his own conversion.

A THEOLOGY OF ETERNAL REST

From the very first lines of the *Confessions* up to the last paragraphs of his work Augustine deals with eternal rest. It is the goal that every soul longs for. The famous phrase at the beginning *"inquietum est cor nostrum donec requiescat in te* [our heart is restless until it finds peace in you]" (*conf.* 1.1.1) is part of a praise to God and refers to God as the creator. God made not only the soul of humans (*"quia fecisti nos ad te* [because you made us toward yourself]"), but also heaven and earth; that is, everything (*conf.* 1.1.1–2.2). God fills heaven and earth, everything by himself, or *vice versa*: whatever is, is in God. This is true also for humans: they cannot find God in any other way than in themselves; that is, in their memory, but God is not simply an object that is there in one or another place of the memory.[34] The soul is in God and he is the only one who can grant peace and salvation (cf. *conf.* 10.25.36–28.39). Therefore, already at the beginning of the *Confessions*, Augustine prays: *"Dic animae meae: salus tua ego sum* [Tell my soul: I am your salvation!]" (*conf.* 1.5.5). "God is active and resting [*semper agens, semper quietus*]" (*conf.* 1.4.4). God remains who God is, and leads the whole creation to the goal that he determined. This aspect shows an important

---

[32] Augustine, *Simpl.* 1.2.21; cf. Augustine, *spir. et litt.* 34.60. Byers assumes that, after *Ad Simplicianum*, Augustine fell back to his former doctrine of grace and only during the Pelagian controversy discovered it again step by step (*Perception, Sensibility, and Moral Motivation*, 210–211), but the coherence of *spir. et litt.* 34.60 with *Ad Simplicianum* is very striking, See D. Marafioti, *L'uomo tra legge e grazia: Analisi teologica del De spiritu et littera di S. Agostino*, Aloisiana 18 (Brescia: Morcelliana, 1983), 216–225; V. H. Drecoll, "De spiritu et littera (Über den Geist und den Buchstaben)," in *Augustin Handbuch*, ed. V. H. Drecoll (Tübingen: Mohr Siebeck, 2007), 328–334, at 332; D. Ogliari, *Gratia et Certamen: The Relationship between Grace and Free Will in the Discussion of Augustine with the So-Called Semipelagians*, Bibliotheca Ephemeridum Theologicarum Lovaniensium 169 (Leuven: Leuven University Press, 2003), 255–257.

[33] P. Fredriksen, "The Confessions as Autobiography," in *A Companion to Augustine*, ed. M. Vessey, Blackwell Companions to the Ancient World (Chichester: Wiley-Blackwell, 2012), 87–98, at 97.

[34] T. Fuhrer, *Augustinus*, Klassische Philologie kompakt (Darmstadt: Wissenschaftliche Buchgesellschaft, 2004), 128–131.

aspect of grace: grace is the way God continues his creation and leads it to the final goal. Grace is the execution of the eternal predestination and it has an overall goal: eternal rest.

Thus, it is not by chance that the subject of Augustine's talk with Monica in Ostia a couple of days before her death is not only about what God is, but also about what the eternal life of the saints is (*conf.* 9.10.23). Augustine describes a kind of ascent that happens only in thoughts. In this talk they reached the region of abundance without any defect [*regio ubertatis indeficientis*], where life is wisdom and where there is no time; that is, there is neither past nor future (*conf.* 9.10.24). It was not possible for Augustine and Monnica to stay there, but they left, as Augustine says, their first fruits as a deposit [*primitiae*] there (cf. Rm 8:23).[35] This allusion to Paul is not the only one. Augustine characterizes the discussion as reaching forth unto those things that are before and forgetting those things that are behind (cf. Phil 3:13).[36] Thus, it is not a mystical ascent that establishes a new communion (or union) with God, but rather Augustine and Monica got a preliminary idea of how the eternal life will be; it is a brief glance at the promised future (*conf.* 9.10.25: "*ut talis sit sempiterna uita, quale fuit hoc momentum intellegentiae* [so that eternal life would be just what that moment of understanding had been]"). Monica concludes that there is no reason for her to stay on earth any longer since she has seen her beloved son become a Christian who has given up all secular aims (*conf.* 9.10.26).

Reading the *Confessions* as an illustration of Augustine's concept of grace elucidates the overall structure of the work.[37] It can explain why Augustine combines the reflection of his own life with an exegesis of Gen 1. What happens in one's life is only part of what God does in general. Grace is deeply linked to creation.[38] Both are actions in time, but time is not simply what humans imagine. The concept of time, therefore, shows that, from the perspective of humans, there is neither time as an abstract or physical principle, nor a present that does not also become a past and a subject of memory (*conf.* 11.27.36–29.39). Only God can immediately understand the temporal extension of what happens in the order of the creation (but God does not know the order as a human mind that pursues the series of facts as the notes in a song)

---

[35] The term *primitiae spiritus* ["first-fruits of the spirit"] does not refer to the Holy Spirit here, but to the human mind. See O'Donnell, *Augustine:* Confessions, vol. 3, 132–133.
[36] Cf. conf. 9.10.23, cf. O'Donnell, *Augustine:* Confessions, vol. 3, 125.
[37] Fredriksen, "The Confessions as Autobiography," 91.
[38] Bochet, *Firmament*, 244–245.

(*conf.* 11.31.41). Augustine expresses this at the end of the *Confessions* as the execution of the predestination: you have begun to realize in time what was predestined. The "pre"destination was made "before" any time. The effect of this is not only the realization of the creation, but also the justification of the impious, the distinction between believers and unbelievers, and the gathering of the Church in which merciful actions [*opera misericordiae*] or alms are performed (*conf.* 13.34.49). Gen 1 can be read not only as report of creation, but also as announcement of God's grace. The saints are the lights or stars in the firmament that enlighten the impious people. God established visible sacraments and miracles, as well as the Bible. The life of the saints is shaped when their affections are ruled by the power of chastity; thus, the mind of the believers is subordinated exclusively to God, not to human authorities. Therefore, the soul is renewed in God's image and likeness (cf. Gen 1:26) (*conf.* 13.34.49).[39] Augustine compares this new order within humans to the subordination of women to men (while emphasizing that men and women have the same nature in regard to the rational capacities of their mind) (*conf.* 13.32.47: "*feminam, quae haberet quidem in mente rationalis intellegentiae parem naturam* [Woman ... having an equal nature in terms of her mental capacity for rational intelligence]"). The insight of the believers into the temporal order of what happens in the world or in anybody's life is based on scripture and leads back to prayer: God is asked to give peace and rest (*conf.* 13.35.50).

Augustine ends his *Confessions* with an allegorical interpretation of the seventh day of Gen 1. This seventh day has no evening, which means that it lasts forever. It signifies the eternal permanence that is announced by the Bible; that is, the eternal life in which "we" – that is, Augustine and his faithful readers – will find rest (*conf.* 13.36.51). Thus, God's grace is activity and rest at the same time [*semper operaris et semper requiescis*] (*conf.* 13.37.52). God's grace is active in the world in its temporal extension, in everybody's life, and it provides the final rest of eternal life as the goal of the whole process. Therefore, in the *Confessions*, the theology of grace is not only a theology of prayer and a theology of conversion, but also a theology of time and eternity, creation, and predestination, as well as of the longing of humans and their final peace in God. Grace is what leads Augustine to his faith (and bishopric) – and every believer to his final rest – that is, eternal life. Thus, the search for this rest will reach its goal. The last words in the

---

[39] See the comparison of Augustine's allegorical exegesis with the full text of Gen 1 in O'Donnell, *Augustine:* Confessions, vol. 3, 416–417.

Confessions (13.37.53) are: to him who knocks, it will be opened (Mt 7:7).[40]

Further Reading

Bochet, Isabelle, *"Le firmament de l'écriture": L'herméneutique Augustinienne. Collection des Études Augustiniennes. Série Antiquité 172.* Paris: Institut d'Études Augustiniennes, 2004.

Brachtendorf, J. *Augustins "Confessiones."* Darmstadt: Wissenschaftliche Buchgesellschaft, 2005.

Byers, S. C. *Perception, Sensibility, and Moral Motivation in Augustine: A Stoic-Platonic Synthesis.* Cambridge: Cambridge University Press, 2013.

Drecoll, V. H., *Die Entstehung der Gnadenlehre Augustins.* Beiträge zur historischen Theologie 109. Tübingen: Mohr Siebeck, 1999.

Feldmann, E. "Confessiones," in *Augustinus-Lexikon,* ed. C. Mayer. Basel: Schwabe, 1994, vol. 1, 1134–1193.

Fredriksen, P. "The Confessions as Autobiography." In *A Companion to Augustine,* ed. M. Vessey. Blackwell Companions to the Ancient World. Chichester: Wiley-Blackwell, 2012, 87–98.

Köckert, C. "Therapie der Affekte: Augustins Confessiones als Dokument christlich-philosophischer Seelsorge." *Zeitschrift für Kirchengeschichte* 127 (2016), 293–314.

Kotzé, A. *Augustine's* Confessions: *Communicative Purpose and Audience.* Supplements to Vigiliae Christianae 71. Leiden: Brill, 2004.

Madec, G. "'Platonisme' et 'Christianisme': Analyse du livre VII des 'Confessions'." In *Lectures Augustiniennes.* Collection des Études Augustiniennes. Série Antiquité 168. Paris: Institut d'Études Augustiniennes, 2001, 121–184.

O'Donnell, J. J., *Augustine. Confessions,* three vols. Oxford: Clarendon, 1992.

Augustine, Sinner and Saint: A New Biography. London: Profile Books, 2005.

Pizzolato, L. F. "Libro ottavo." In *Sant' Agostino. Confessioni (Libri VII–IX).* Fondazione Lorenzo Valla. Scrittori greci e latini. Milan: Arnoldo Mondadori, 1994, vol. 3, 229–292.

---

[40] For Mt 7:7 in the *Confessions,* see Kotzé, *Augustine's* Confessions, 134–147.

8 God

PAUL VAN GEEST

INTRODUCTION

Anyone who wishes to discover God in the *Confessions* will first have to acknowledge that the genre of this work is anything but clear. For a start, Augustine's "intellectual autobiography" is cast in the form of a *confessio*. In a *confessio fidei*, Augustine praises God as the Most High. In a *confessio peccatorum*, he confesses his sins. And, as if in a single movement with the other forms of *confessio*, in a *confessio laudis* he gives thanks and praise to God for his creation and his blessings.[1] This means that Augustine does not speak *about* God very often; as he seeks God and desires God, he prays to God, but without attempting to comprehend God in some theory.

But precisely by asking God questions in prayer, Augustine does in fact speak about God; for instance, in apologetic passages against the Manichaeans, who think that the good God is made of matter and that he created the world using existing matter. Augustine confidently rejects this – paradoxically, by asking questions – and describes God as the Creator "out of nothing," so as to avoid any misunderstanding about the origins of matter. As he discusses "theory" or "theology" in these apologetic passages, he is more self-assured about God's being and his works than when he invokes [*inuocat*] God in his *confessio* (*conf.* 1.1.1).

Finally, there are also passages in which Augustine strives to [re] create the experience of his readers by presenting his own experience: a

---

[1] J. J. O'Donnell, *Confessions: Introduction, Text and Commentary* (Oxford: Oxford University Press, 1992), vol. 1, xxxiii. Cf. P. Courcelle, *Recherches sur les Confessions de Saint Augustin* (Paris: Boccard, 1968), 29–40, esp. 37–40. See also E. Feldmann, "Das literarische Genus und das Gesamtkonzept der Confessiones," in *Die Confessiones des Augustinus von Hippo. Einführung und Interpretationen zu den dreizehn Büchern*, ed. N. Fischer and C. Mayer, Forschungen zur europäischen Geistesgeschichte 1 (Freiburg: Herder 1998), 11–59.

goal that characterizes protreptic texts as a distinctive form of oratory.[2] Like in his *confessio* and his invocations of God, which are formulated as pithily as they are made casually, his aim in these passages is to heighten a particular awareness of God rather than to augment orthodox knowledge about God. Whenever his purpose is to increase knowledge, he underlines God's omnipotence and the fact that he transcends time and space. But in his attempts to arouse awareness of God, he underlines God's tenderness and mercy. Of course it is not always possible to draw a sharp distinction between the genres and the different emphases.

In the questions that he never ceases to formulate, he often tries to persuade his readers that the human intellect is unable to truly comprehend God. By using various genres, Augustine not only endeavors to preserve the tension between knowing about God and seeking God. Above all, he tries to intensify the awareness that God is most likely best "comprehended" in paradoxes: in all his exaltedness and hiddenness, God is near and very present (cf. *conf.* 6.3.4: "For you, most highest and most near, most hidden and most present [*Tu enim, altissime et proxime, secretissime et praesentissime*]").

SPEAKING ABOUT GOD TO GOD: THE MORE APOLOGETIC PARTS

When he does speak about God in the more apologetic parts of the *Confessions*, Augustine stresses that God is not material and is therefore not bound to time and space.[3] Moreover, he contends that God is simple or uncompounded [*simplex*]. Finally, he regards God as the origin of all being and of all that lives. This kind of language about God reveals not only Augustine's debt to Scripture, with which he had become ever more familiar from 387 onward. The neo-Platonist Plotinus' fundamental philosophical conception is another source for his image of God. And yet it is primarily his familiarity with the prologue of John's Gospel that

---

[2] Cf. A. Kotzé, *Augustine's* Confessions: *Communicative Purpose and Audience*, Supplements to Vigiliae Christianae 71 (Leiden: Brill, 2004), 117–196. See also O. Alieva, "Protreptic: A Protean Genre," in *When Wisdom Calls: Philosophical Protreptic in Antiquity*, ed. O. Alieva, A. Kotzé, and S. Van der Meeren, Monothéismes et Philosophie 24 (Turnhout: Brepols, 2017), 29–45; P. van Geest, "Protreptic and Mystagogy: Augustine's Early Works," in *When Wisdom Calls*, 349–364. See E. Feldmann, "Confessiones," in *Augustinus-Lexikon*, ed. C. Mayer (Basel: Schwabe, 1994), vol. 1, 1134–1193, at 1167; 1134–1139 (historiography) and 1185–1193 (bibliography).

[3] See, in general, G. Madec, "Deus," in Augustinus-Lexikon, vol. 2, fasc. 1/2 (1996), 314–322; fasc. 3/4 (1999), 322–366, esp. 334–337.

taught him to accept the Word as God incarnate; a belief that could not be encountered in the books of the Platonists.

In the *Confessions*, Augustine regularly recalls that, when he was still a follower of the Manichaeans, he was expected to imagine God as a mass of unlimited extension who permeates and delimits all parts, great and small, in the entire mass of the world, but is not himself delimited by them. God was boundless but material, so that, logically, a large part of the earth contained more of God than a small part (*conf.* 3.7.12; 5.2.2, 10.19; 6.4.5; 7.1.1–2, 4.20). Augustine's lifelong aversion to anthropomorphic representations of God was due to the Manichaeans. They accused the Catholics of taking Scripture literally and of seeing God as a human being writ large on the basis of certain pericopes. Around 383, Augustine still vaguely believed that there had to be something human about God, because God had created human beings in his own image (*conf.* 6.3.4–4.6; Gen 1:26–28). But, in the *Confessions*, he primarily expresses his horror at the fact that the Manichaeans' material image of God could give rise to a notion of God in which God is limited, as a human being has physical limits (*conf.* 6.11.18; cf. 5.3.5).

It must be noted here that material images of God were quite common in the second and third centuries, including among Christians. The Stoics taught that all being, not excepting the spirit, presupposed matter. Tertullian (c. 160–c. 230) asked rhetorically who could deny that God was body (*Adv. Prax.* 7.8). By contrast, Origen considered any image of God as material to be "manifestly impious [*manifeste impium*]," all the more so because this assumption could lead to anthropomorphically inflected belief in God.

It was not Origen but Plotinus who convinced Augustine that God was "not diffused through space," but purely immaterial: outside time and space, eternal and imperishable, untouchable and unchanging (*conf.* 7.10.16; e.g., Plotinus, *Enn.* 3.9.4; 5.5.8–9).[4] In fact, he already acknowledged then that "being" was not an adequate term for God's being, because "being" usually refers to "being" in time and space. Like Plotinus, Augustine thought that God always "was," fully and everywhere (*ubique totus*), but not materially or physically (cf. *conf.* 6.3.4; 7.1.1; Plotinus, *Enn.* 6.3.4, 5.1–2, 5.4). The allegorical-spiritual interpretation to which Ambrose introduced him around 388 helped him to see that those words in Scripture that described God's essence or activity must not be taken literally, because that would imply doing an injustice to

---

[4] Cf. R. Ferwerda, "Plotinus' Presence in Augustine," in *Augustiniana Trajectina*, eds. J. den Boeft and J. van Oort (Paris: Études Augustiniennes 1987), 107–118.

God. They invited associations with things in the spatiotemporal reality (*conf.* 6.3.4). Thanks also to his new hermeneutics, Augustine was able to contest the Manichaean view that a large part of the earth contained more of God than a small part (cf. *conf.* 7.1.2–4). He also challenged their idea of God as a mass of matter, and of the Son as a mass of supremely lucid matter (*conf.* 5.10.20: *de massa lucidissimae molis*). Incidentally, it is very clear from the image of God that Augustine outlines in the apologetic parts of Books 5–7 that the questions he asks God in *conf.* 1.3.3 about the way in which God fulfills (parts of) heaven and earth are the prelude to a final reckoning with the Manichaean, material image of God; the image, in other words, that he himself had once espoused.

Augustine's indebtedness to Plotinus is evident also in his thinking about God as "the one [*simplex*]." For Plotinus, the One, the Good, is the truly simple, beyond any ordinary simplicity (*Enn.* 2.9.1; 5.3.16): even beyond being (*Enn.* 5.6.6) and, therefore, perfectly unknowable; the supreme being is not the One, but the Nous (Intellect). But there are echoes of the Plotinian notion that the entire hierarchy of being emanates from this Simplicity (*Enn.* 5.5.9; cf. 6.3.4) when Augustine says that all physical entities derive their being from the One (*conf.* 13.2.2). For Plotinus, multiplicity entails egress from the One (*Enn.* 6.6.1). Returning to the One therefore is the purpose of life (*Enn.* 3.6.6). When Augustine writes that the return to God is supported by Christ as the Mediator (see later) between the One and us, the many, then this is to characterize the Father in Plotinian terms, probably with the noble aim of convincing neo-Platonists of his image of God (*conf.* 11.29.39). But at the same time he postulates that this *simplicitas*, which implies immutability and eternity, cannot be imagined on earth (*conf.* 7.1.1; cf. Plotinus, *Enn.* 5.3.15).

In the more apologetic passages of the last books of the *Confessions*, Augustine mainly speaks of God as the Creator. There is a reason for this: he is eager to disprove the Manichaeans' creation myth on the basis of his exegesis of Gen 1:1–2:3.[5] The Manichaeans believed that God was not, like Genesis says, the creator of the cosmos, but that the Prince of Darkness, the antithesis of Light, had brought forth the cosmos through an act of copulation.[6] In their eyes, God was not the creator of matter, which was the root of all evil (cf. *conf.* 7.14.20).

---

[5] Kotzé, *Augustine's* Confessions, 30. Cf. Feldmann, "Confessiones," 1134–1193, at 1167.

[6] Cf. G. M. Van Gaans, "The Manichaean Bishop Faustus: The State of Research after a Century of Scholarship," in *Augustine and Manichaean Christianity: Selected Papers*

Augustine countered this by contending that God was the Creator who was eternally prior to matter, and who created everything, including matter, out of nothing [*creatio ex nihilo*] (*conf.* 7.9.13, 11.17; 11.5.7; 12.7.7, 17.25, 29.40).[7] Whereas Plotinus thought that the universe had always existed and had no real beginning (*Enn.* 2.1.1), Augustine instead followed his mentor Ambrose's position, who argued that the Word of Christ was able to create out of nothing what had not existed before (*myst.* 9.52). Both thus followed Origen, who had already ruled out preexistent matter because this would imply a denial of God's omnipotence. Augustine therefore did not trace evil to matter, which had been created by God, but to the wickedness of the human will, which, in choosing evil, deformed its own nature (*conf.* 3.8.16; 7.5.7, 16.22).

There was another difference between Augustine and Plotinus: on the former's view of God as the Creator of time. Augustine shared Plotinus' idea that changes imply the genesis of time (*Enn.* 3.7.11).[8] But whereas for Plotinus time was inherent to the One, the Intellect [*Nous*] and the World Soul that created and ordered, for Augustine God "was" outside time, creating time together with matter, so that time for him had a very specific origin (*conf.* 11.13.15–16, 30.40). God is outside time, even transcends time because time, together with matter, implied change, and there was no change in God (*conf.* 12.49.40; 13.1.1). Ambrose had already contended that there was no time before the creation of the world, and that time was inherent to the world rather than to God (*hexaem.* 1.5.18; 1.6.20). Neither Ambrose nor Augustine therefore thought that there had been time before the creation.

As far as creation was concerned, Plotinus assumed that the One simply emanated without itself having a will (*Enn.* 3.2.1; 5.1.6; cf. 6.8.13). For Augustine, God's attribute of being *simplex* did not exclude the possibility that God wanted the creation, although God's will cannot be compared to the human will, because God's will paradoxically does not negate his *simplicitas*. For Augustine, God's act of

from the First South African Conference on Augustine of Hippo, *University of Pretoria, 24–26 April 2012*, ed. J. van Oort, Nag Hammadi and Manichaean Studies 83 (Leiden: Brill, 2013), 197–227, esp. 210.

[7] A.-I. Bouton-Touboulic, *L'ordre caché. La notion de l'ordre chez saint Augustin*, Collection des Études Augustiniennes & Série Antiquité 174 (Paris: Études Augustiniènnes, 2004), 49–55.

[8] See J. Brachtendorf, *Augustins "Confessiones"* (Darmstadt: Wissenschaffliche Buchgesellschaft, 2005), 254; E. P. Meijering, *Augustin über Schöpfung, Ewigkeit und Zeit: das elfte Buch der Bekentnisse*, Supplements to Vigiliae Christianae (Leiden: Brill, 1979), 4–37; 113–114.

creation was based on a plan, in which the creature was created on behalf of the creature (*conf.* 13.1.1, 2.2, 4.5); creation is not a matter of near-automatic emanation from the generosity of the One alone (cf. Plotinus, *Enn.* 4.8.6; 5.4.1). But whereas Plotinus believes that generosity was the foundation of creation, Augustine thinks it was God's goodness (*conf.* 13.2.2). Only in Book 13 of the *Confessions* does he reveal that God's ultimate motive in creating the world was love: Christ himself (*conf.* 13.7.8; Rm 5:5).

Augustine thus deviates from Plotinus in believing that creation happened according to a prior plan. But Plotinus traces the order *in* creation to the One and to the formative principle (*logos*; *Enn.* 5.5.9), and Augustine traces it to the Word (*conf.* 7.13.19). For both, God's creation therefore is a thing of harmony (*conf.* 7.13.19; *Enn.* 3.2.1).[9] Augustine's comparison of creation to musical harmony can even be traced literally to Plotinus (cf. *conf.* 12.29.40).[10]

The sequence of Books 11–13 in the *Confessions* betrays that for Augustine God the Creator is a Triune God. Book 11 describes God as the Eternal One, Book 12 as the Word, and Book 13 as God who acts through the Church.[11] From *conf.* 11.1.1 onward, the reader is invited to experience him- or her-self as created in the image of the triune God, as Augustine has already done in the previous books: living in time, addressed by the Word, and redeemed by the Holy Spirit in the Church.[12] But Augustine emphasizes that any understanding of the almighty Trinity escapes the human intellect (*conf.* 13.11.12).

In the more apologetic passages, too, Augustine points out that the creation is the work of the Trinity. God the Father created heaven and earth in his Wisdom – that is, in the Son, who is equal to and co-eternal with the Father (*conf.* 13.5.6; cf. 11.5.7; 12.3.3, 7.7, 11.11, 19.28; cf. Phil 2:6–11). Augustine's familiarity with Plotinus' One is at the basis of his reflections on the Father, just like his acquaintance with the Plotinian *Nous*, the Intellect, is evident from his vision on the Son.[13] But Augustine differs from Plotinus because he accepts the emptying of the Word in

[9] P. van Geest, "Ordo," in Augustinus-Lexikon, vol. 4, fasc. 3–4 (2014), 374–379.
[10] A. Alexandrakis, "The Notion of Beauty in the Structure of the Universe: Pythagorean Influences," in *Neoplatonism and Nature: Studies in Plotinus' Enneads*, ed. M. F. Wagner, Studies in Neoplatonism: Ancient and Modern 8 (New York: State University of New York Press, 2002), 149–156, esp. 153.
[11] O'Donnell, *Confessions*, vol. 2, 250–252.
[12] Ibid., 251–252.
[13] O. Du Roy, *L'intelligence de la foi en la Trinité selon saint Augustin. Genèse de sa théologie trinitaire jusqu'en 391* (Paris: Études Augustiniennes, 1966), 419.

the incarnation (see later). He does emphasize, however, that the creation in the Son is incomprehensible to human beings on earth, both in word and in thought (*conf.* 11.9.11: *Quis comprehendet? Quis enarrabit?*; cf. 11.31.41).

In order to be able to approach the mystery of the Trinity at least to some extent, Augustine uses triads. The triad Eternity/Truth/Love expresses the essence of the Father, the Son, and the Holy Spirit respectively.[14] He uses the Plotinian triad of Measure/Number/Weight to describe the Father as the ultimate Measure, the Son as the Number that structures the cosmos, and the Spirit as the Weight of love, as he does in previous works (*conf.* 1.7.12; 13.9.10).[15] He also draws a comparison with being, knowing, willing (*conf.* 13.11.12: *esse, nosse, velle*) to indicate that the image of the triune God is reflected in the creation of human beings. It is impossible to separate being, knowing, and willing from each other, and yet they are distinct. But because God's being is an immutable knowing and willing; and God's knowing is an immutable being and willing; and God's willing is an immutable being and knowing, therefore the triune God is also incomparable to human being, knowing, and willing: no one can understand this with the intellect (*conf.* 13.11.12: *Trinitatem omnipotentem quis intelleget?*).

In comparison to his treatises on God the Creator, Augustine has little to say about the Holy Spirit. He equates the Spirit who floats above the waters in Gen 1:2 with the Holy Spirit, who he defines as *caritas,* following Paul (Rm 5:5), and who rests upon people so that they find rest in God (*conf.* 13.4.5; cf. 13.9.10). But he adds that the creator is the Father, the Son, and the Spirit, who are indivisible (*conf.* 13.4.5: *Ecce trinitas meus, pater et filius et spiritus sanctus, creator uniuersae creaturae*). Moreover, like with the Father and the Son, he also stresses in respect of the Holy Spirit that his floating above the waters cannot be compared to the floating that a human being might do, on account of God's unimaginable and immutable exaltedness (*conf.* 13.9.10 "But if [we understand] the changeless supereminence of the divine Being above every changeable thing, then Father, Son, and Holy Spirit 'moved' over the waters [*si autem incommutabilis diuinitatis eminentia super omne mutabile, et pater et filius et spiritus sanctus superferebatur super aquas]"*). As it turns out, this denial of every comparison between the human and the divine reality contains a form of knowledge of God for Augustine – even more so than in the more apologetic passages.

---

[14] Ibid., 72–81.
[15] Van Geest, "Ordo," 376–377.

In relation to God the Son, Augustine acknowledges that the Manichaeans recognize Christ, but he argues that they have not understood him as truly human (*conf.* 3.4.8; 5.9.16). He said the Platonists taught him that everything came into being through the Word, which he immediately equates with the Word of whom John writes that it was with God and that it was God (*conf.* 7.9.13, 10.16, 11.17, 13.19; cf. 11.29.39, where he even calls God "the One" in this context). However, for Augustine the crucial difference between the Plotinian *Logos* and Christ is that he believes, in conformity with the Nicene Creed, that the Word, God, became flesh and took on the form of a slave (*conf.* 7.9.13–14; cf. Jn 1:13; Phil 2:6).[16] In the incarnation, God demonstrates his humility. Augustine even appears to hold it against the Platonists that they had no notion of this dimension of God (cf. *conf.* 7.9.13).

But even in relation to the eternal Word that is God, and that all created things obey (*conf.* 4.10.15), Augustine emphasizes the difference with a human word, specifically because of the eternal nature of the first Word (*conf.* 4.11.16–17), which, paradoxically, calls the soul back home and teaches human beings the unshakeable truth (*conf.* 4.11.17; cf. 7.7.11; 11.7.9). The word that is God was never spoken, and cannot therefore be compared to perishable fleeting words that are spoken and that consist of passing syllables. Speaking these words implies time, and time passes. Unlike the divine Word, they are not permanent (*conf.* 11.6.8). For Augustine, the unimaginable nature of the Word that is God is situated in the fact that it is co-eternal, imperishable, immortal, and was "spoken" eternally (*conf.* 11.7.9). Human words cannot therefore be compared with the Word that God spoke eternally and silently and that remains for ever: "It was different, totally different [*Alius est longe, longe aliud est*]" (*conf.* 11.6.8; cf. 11.11.11; 13.11.12). Augustine also follows the *via negativa* in respect of the Word: the way that leads to insight into God as mystery precisely through the denial that any word or thought about God might be capable of expressing God's essence.

Augustine's familiarity with John's gospel and Paul's epistles often inspires him throughout the *Confessions* to confess Christ as Truth, Wisdom, and Love (*conf.* 1.9.11, 18.28; 4.5.10; 6.5.7; 8.10.24 *deus uerax*; 10.43.68; 11.3.5, 9.11; 13.29.44 *tu uerax et ueritas*; 13.43.68 *uerax*

---

[16] B. Studer, "Credo in Deum Patrem omnipotentem. Zum Gottesbegriff des Heiligen Augustinus," in *Congresso Internazionale su S. Agostino nel XVI centenario della conversione, Roma, 15–20 settembre 1986*, Studia ephemeridis Augustinianum 25 (Rome: Institutum patristicum "Augustinianum," 1987), vol. 1, 163–188.

mediator; 13.29.44; cf. Jn 3:21, 33; 8:32, 40; 14:6; 1 Cor 1:24).[17] It is entirely possible that when he describes Christ as the truth, he is trying to speak to Manicheans, Christians, and neo-Platonists each at their own level.[18] He expresses the "neo-Platonic" notion of elevation – an intellectual reflection focused on the good and the beautiful – through the neo-Platonic-philosophical *abstracta* ("truth," "eternity"). By equating Christ with the truth and with eternity, he effectively adds a new layer of meaning to the Plotinian concept of "truth," in the hope that they might also accept this Christian denotation in which, as we have seen, God's humility is a crucial element.

Once the Word, Christ, had become man, Augustine regards it as the Mediator between God and humankind, between the One and the many (in Plotinian terms). But as the Word, he is equal to God (*conf.* 10.43.68; 11.29.39); or to put it in the classic doxological formulation: "sits at the right hand of God" (*conf.* 11.2.4). That this incarnation is the expression par excellence of God's humility and love is made clear in the descriptions – and exclamations – of Christ as *medicus*, physician.[19] Origen (c. 185–254) had already described the exomologesis in thera-peutic terms, and as the instrument of the *medicus animae*.[20] For Augustine, the incarnation and, subsequently, the suffering of Christ is the antidote to each individual human being's pride, including his own. But, according to him, the immense power of the crucified God also creates the antidote to the pandemic form and extent of the pride that has determined human history from the first man onward. August-ine believes that human beings can become receptive to the person of

---

[17] P. van Geest, *The Incomprehensibility of God: Augustine as a Negative Theologian,* Late Antique History and Religion 4 (Leuven: Peeters, 2010), 99–108. See also: L. Ladaria, "Presentación," in *La incomprehensibilidad de Dios. Agustín como teólogo negativo,* ed. P. van Geest (Bogota: Universitaria Agustiniana, 2014), 13–14.

[18] For *deus-veritas* in Manichean circles, see E. Feldmann, "Christus-Frömmigkeit der Mani-Jünger. Der suchende Student Augustinus in ihrem 'Netz'?'," in *Pietas: Festschrift für Bernhard Kötting,* eds. E. Dassmann and K. Suso Frank, Jahrbuch für Antike und Christentum, Ergänzungsband 8 (Münster: Aschendorff, 1980), 198–216.

[19] Cf. P. C. J. Eijkenboom, *Het Christus-medicusmotief in de preken van Sint Augustinus* (Assen: Van Gorcum & Co, 1960), viii–xiv; T. Martin, "Paul the Patient: *Christus Medicus* and the '*Stimulus Carnis*' (2 Cor 12:7): A Consideration of Augustine's Medicinal Christology," *Augustinian Studies* 32 (2001), 219–256, at 222; M. Dörnemann, *Krankheit und Heilung in der Theologie der frühen Kirchenväter,* Studien und Texte zu Antike und Christentum 20 (Tübingen: Mohr Siebeck, 2003), 219–256, at 222.

[20] Cf. H. J. Vogt, "Gott als Arzt und Erzieher. Das Gottesbild der Kirchenväter Origenes und Augustinus," in *Origenes als Exeget,* ed. W. Geerlings (Paderborn: F. Schöningh, 1999), 289–299.

Christ by imitating him in his humility, which has become evident in his descent to humanity, and in his vanquishing of death for the sake of humankind (cf. *conf.* 7.20.26). This means that it is in the opposite of pride – which Christ discredited in his incarnation and suffering – that human beings can "comprehend" God. Augustine accuses himself of not having been humble enough to hold on precisely to the humble Jesus and to admit the physician of his interior into his heart (cf. *conf.* 7.8.12; cf. 5.9.16; 6.9.14, 11.20; 7.8.12; 9.8.18, 13.35; 10.43.69; as well as 10.3.4 *medice intimus meus*; cf. 10.28.39). He acknowledges that the pain that goes with the gradual appropriation of this attitude to life can be alleviated by the medicine of meditation on Christ's suffering, which is also the medicine against pride. The motif of Christ the Physician would become a fundamental theme in his work.[21]

To sum up: in the apologetic passages of his *Confessions*, Augustine is very much indebted to Plotinus. But once he has come to a pivotal point in this work, the middle of the seventh book, he concisely formulates an image of God that he had clung to, more subconsciously than consciously, in his quest for God before his baptism. He says he wants to believe in God's existence, God's immutable essence, God's care for people, and God's judgment. In Christ, Scripture, and the Church he recognizes the way to salvation that God has prepared for humanity – a way that leads to life beyond this death (*conf.* 7.7.11). He invites everyone to travel along this way, just as he invites his readers in his exclamations to experience God in a certain way together with him. This brings us to the following point.

CHARACTERIZING GOD IN INVOCATIONS

In the invocations, or the summary characterizations of God that he gives in these, Augustine's aim is not so much to increase knowledge about God, as to heighten a particular consciousness of God. These especially demonstrate that Augustine experiences God as an unfathomable but ever-present person, for whom it is more fitting to long than to have fear. Although the description of God's attributes in the longer explanatory passages is not essentially different from the summary descriptions of God in these short prayers, the invocations, much more than the explanations, serve to intensify the awareness that God is merciful above all.

---

[21] Vogt, "Gott als Arzt und Erzieher," 289–299.

Even the invocations that Augustine expresses at the beginning of the first book to address God as the creator and *ordinator* of everything in nature, already heighten a sense of trust in God because he links God's creating with God's mercy. Augustine impresses the consciousness upon his readers that humankind, which is part of creation, should trace mortality to the sinfulness with which it is riven. But even this does not make the tone morose. Augustine confronts his readers with the truth that God has created people in such a way as to make them capable of finding joy in praising God despite their sins (*conf.* 1.1.1: "carrying the evidence of his sin ... you have prompted him, that he should delight to praise you [*circumferens peccati sui; tu excitas, ut laudare te delectet*]"). Precisely because Augustine follows up the *confessio peccatorum* with the *confessio laudis* of God the Creator – and not *vice versa* – it is clear that his intention is to inspire confidence in God's mercy rather than despair at human imperfections (*conf.* 1.6.10, 10.16: "And yet I sinned, O Lord my God, ruler and creator of all natural things ... Look down on these things with mercy, O Lord, and deliver us [*Et tamen peccabam, domine deus, ordinator et creator rerum omnium naturalium ... vide ista, domine, misericorditer et libera nos*]"; cf. 3.8.16).

The purpose of invoking God as the Creator therefore is to heighten the awareness that God is merciful (*conf.* 1.7.12, 20.31; 4.15.24; 9.12.32). Certainly, Augustine succinctly describes God as a God of retribution who must be feared. But at the same time he also characterizes God as the source of mercy, the cause of joy. It is precisely the order of words that places the final emphasis on the latter aspect. Augustine is consistent in his choice of this word order (*conf.* 4.4.7: "At once a God of vengeance and a source of mercies [*deus ultionum et fons misericordiarum simul*]"; cf. 9.4.9: "I trembled with fear and warmed with hope and rejoiced in thy mercy, Father [*inhorrui timendo ibidemque inferui sperando et exultando in tua misericordia, pater*]"; cf. *conf.* 8.12.28). Even his warning that vices such as pride, ambition, lust for power, or envy obscure a person's view of God is embedded in an exposition about God as an exalted, praiseworthy, awesome, and loving being (*conf.* 2.6.13). It is no wonder therefore that he regularly briefly but explicitly refers to God for instance as "source of mercies [*fons misericordiarum*]," whom human beings may praise rather than fear – at least we assume that this is Augustine's intention (*conf.* 6.16.26; cf. 5.1.1, 8.14, 9.17; 6.5.7; 7.8.12; 8.1.1, 3.6, 9.21; 9.1.1, 4.9; 11.29.39). In his short prayers, Augustine frequently also mentions God's loving-kindness (*conf.* 1.20.30: *dulcedo mea*; 2.1.1, 6.13; 3.6.10; 4.3.4; 9.1.1 *suavitas*;

10.17.26). Even his brief reference to God's omniscience is not oppres-
sive; instead, he stresses that this omniscience leads more to forgiveness
than to retribution (cf. *conf.* 12.26.36; cf. 2.2.2–4; 3.3.5, 4.7; 5.7.13–14;
10.43.60; 11.1.1).

In sum: Augustine tries in his invocations and summary characterizations to convince his readers of human guilt and imperfection, but in
such a way as to make their newly kindled sense of guilt inspire them to
realize all the more urgently that God is merciful and therefore worthy
of praise. The same principle applies whenever Augustine specifically
addresses Christ. Referring often to the Manichaean *deus-veritas*, but
even more often to Jn 6:14, he invokes Christ so that his readers may
praise him, all the more so because he is victor precisely through his
victimhood on the cross (e.g., *conf.* 5.3.5). The Spirit is also mentioned
as the consoler, although this does not happen quite as often (*conf.* 5.5.8;
9.4.9; 12.7.7; cf. Jn 14:16–17). Similarly, Augustine rarely addresses the
Trinity (*conf.* 13.5.6).[22] But his short prayer to truth, love, and eternity is
evidently intended to call to mind the Son, the Spirit, and the Father
(*conf.* 7.10.16).

When Augustine articulates the essence and activity of God in short
formulas, he does so in language indebted mainly to Scripture. Quotations from the Psalms or from Ambrose's hymn *deus creator omnium*
appear frequently. Thus, at the very start of the first book, Augustine
quotes the Psalms verbatim to express God's greatness (*conf.* 1.1.1; Ps
95:41, 144:3). And when he immediately after this confesses before God
that God's Wisdom is immeasurable (*conf.* 1.1.1), he does this in a literal
quotation from Psalm 146:5 ("your wisdom [is] without number [*sapientiae tuae non est numerus]*"), with *virtus* and *sapientia* being references
to Christ ("*Christum Dei virtutem et Dei Sapientiam* [1 Cor 1:24]"), as
they are in Paul's letter; when Augustine goes on to address *Domine*
(*conf.* 1.1.1) in the remainder of the *Confessions*, this refers not only to
the Creator of heaven and earth, but also to the Lord who descended to
our pride (cf. *conf.* 1.1.1; cf. 1.11.17).

And yet it must also be emphasized that Augustine in his short
prayers and in a number of brief questions is eager to convince his
readers that the human intellect is unable to truly comprehend God.
God is a merciful and loving God, but precisely in his nearness he is also
inaccessible: hidden, dwelling in silence, most mysterious and simultaneously near, ineffable (*conf.* 1.18.29: "How mysterious you are, who

---

[22] For the frequency of this invocation in other works and for the way in which this
occurs, see O'Donnell, *Confessions*, vol. 2, 309.

dwellest on high in silence [*Quam tu secretus es, habitans in excelsis in silentio*]"; cf. 4.4.8, 12.19; 5.6.11: "Guiding me by the secret impulse of your providence [*abdito secreto providentiae tuae*]"; 5.7.13; 6.3.4; 7.10; 8.1.1; 9.1.1, 7.16; 10.42.67, 43.68; 11.6.8, 31.41; 12.16.23 *ineffabilia*). By evoking these apparent contradictions, Augustine tries to heighten the awareness that his thinking about God is ineffable because God is unknowable (*conf.* 1.4.4: "most hidden and most present [*secretissime et praesentissime*]").

In addition to the *via negativa*, Augustine in his invocations also uses the *via eminentiae* to impress God's incomprehensibility upon his readers: the *via* in which God's essence and activities are described in superlatives. He uses assonance and alliteration to express this insight in a way that plays to the emotions:

> What are you then, my God? ... You are most high, excellent, most powerful, omnipotent, supremely merciful and supremely just, most hidden and yet intimately present, infinitely beautiful and infinitely strong, steadfast yet elusive, unchanging yourself though you control the change in all things, never new, never old ... ever active, ever at rest ... You love without frenzy, you are jealous yet secure, you regret without sadness, you grow angry yet remain tranquil ... After saying all that, what have we said, my God, my life ... What does anyone who speaks of you really say? Yet woe betide those who fail to speak, while the chatterboxes go on saying nothing![23]

The impasse is often expressed poignantly in the invocations: whenever people speak of God, neither form nor content are adequate to the task. They almost call condemnation down upon themselves: their speech is inarticulate. The same apophatic note is present in all books of the *Confessions* whenever Augustine speaks about God or addresses God.

---

[23] Augustine, *conf.* 1.4.4 (*The Confessions*, trans. M. Boulding, WSA 1/1 [Hyde Park, NY: New City, 1997], 41) (assonance and alliteration): *Quid es ergo Deus meus? ... Summe, optime, potentissime, omnipotentissime, misericordissime et iustissime, secretissime et praesentissime, pulcherrime et fortissime, stabilis et incomprehensibilis, immutabilis, mutans omnia, numquam novus, numquam uetus, innovans omnia ... semper agens, semper quietus ... Amas nec aestuas, zelas et securus es, paenitet te et non doles, irasceris et tranquillus es ... Et quid diximus, Deus meus, uita mea, dulcedo mea sancta, aut quid dicit aliquis, cum de te dicit? Et vae tacentibus de te, quoniam loquaces muti sunt.*

BY WAY OF CONCLUSION

Whether Augustine is eager to increase knowledge of God, to refute heterodox ideas – even ideas that he himself once espoused – about God the creator of matter, space, and time, or whether his aim is to heighten a particular awareness of God: he tries to convince his readers that God is present in creation and in themselves (cf. Books 1–10), and is close to humankind (cf. Books 11–13) in healing. But as a Person who is incomprehensible to human beings, God is always as much hidden as he is near. In this tension between certainty at the "existence of God" and the awareness that human beings may trust particularly in God's mercy on the one hand, and God's hidden nature on the other, Augustine intensifies human longing for this most hidden and simultaneously most near God, who precisely in this longing appears as even more hidden and even nearer than the human mind could ever have imagined.

In the *Confessions*, Augustine explores many avenues to make it possible – almost – to experience God. Thus he asks in the tenth book of the *Confessions* who it is that he loves when he loves God.[24] He acknowledges that when he loves God, there is no physical beauty to love, no majesty of time, no shining light, no delightful melodies, scent, or embrace (*conf.* 10.6.8). Once again, he is a faithful follower of Plotinus who believes that it is dangerous for the soul to come under the spell of that beauty that is perceptible to the senses, given that the soul, according to him remains pure, when determined by intellectual pursuits and virtues (*Enn.* 1.6.1–2, 4–5). According to the Platonic and patristic *via eminentiae*, it appears that Augustine first calls to mind the beauty of bodies in order to then radically distinguish this beauty from the Beauty that is God, as the latter form of beauty is not comparable with the former, because God is absolutely transcendent and therefore unfathomable. But he immediately adds that what he loves when he loves God is something like the light, something like the sound of a voice, something like a scent, something like food, something like an embrace, because God is light and voice and scent and food and embrace of his inner being (*conf.* 10.6.8). This shows us a side of Augustine that is much more sophisticated than his indebtedness to Plotinus might lead us to expect. He does not equate the experience of God and the perception of the senses. But he does assume that a human being must have

---

[24] Cf. van Geest, *The Incomprehensibility of God*, 88–99; P. van Geest, "Sensory Perceptions as a Mandatory Requirement for the *via negativa* towards God. The Skilful Paradox of Augustine as Mystagogue," *Studia Patristica* 49 (2010), 200–208.

tasted, seen, felt, smelled, to be able to form some image of God. He regards sense perception and affective experiences as indispensable for the increase of both knowledge about God and receptiveness to God, even though he acknowledges that sense perception and emotions, as changeable experiences, are thoroughly unlike any "experience" of the immutable God. Augustine is eager not to leave any human experience unused to give his readers as accurate an image of God as possible: an image of God as hidden as he is near.

Further Reading

Bouton-Touboulic, A.-I. *L'ordre caché. La notion de l'ordre chez saint Augustin.* Collection des Études Augustiniennes. Série Antiquité *174*. Paris: Études Augustiniènnes, 2004.

Brachtendorf J., *Augustins "Confessiones."* Darmstadt: Wissenschaffliche Buch-gesellschaft, 2005.

Courcelle, P. *Recherches sur les Confessions de Saint Augustin.* Paris: Boccard, 1968.

Feldmann, E. "Confessiones." In *Augustinus-Lexikon,* ed. C. Mayer. Basel: Schwabe, 1994, vol. 1, 1134–1193.

Fischer, N. and C. Mayer (eds.), *Die Confessiones des Augustinus von Hippo: Einführung und Interpretationen zu den dreizehn Büchern.* Forschungen zur europäischen Geistesgeschichte 1. Freiburg: Herder, 1998.

Kotzé, A. *Augustine's* Confessions: *Communicative Purpose and Audience.* Supplements to Vigiliae Christianae 71. Leiden: Brill, 2004.

Madec, G. "Deus," in *Augustinus-Lexikon,* ed. C. Mayer. Basel: Schwabe, vol. 2, fasc. 1/2 (1996), 314–322; fasc. 3/4 (1999), 322–366.

O'Donnell, J. J. *Confessions: Introduction, Text and Commentary.* Oxford: Oxford University Press, 1992, two vols.

Van Geest, P. *The Incomprehensibility of God: Augustine as a Negative Theologian.* Late Antique History and Religion 4. Leuven: Peeters, 2010.

9 Happiness and Friendship*

ANNE-ISABELLE BOUTON-TOUBOULIC

Aristotle notes that friendship is generally taken to be essential to happiness (*NE* 8.1; 1155a5–15). The *Confessions* suggest that Augustine too is unable to conceive of happiness without friends. However, it took Augustine some time to settle on a notion of happiness that he regarded as authentic, and also to have a resolve to conform his life to this notion. Friendship[1] proved to be an experience that was essential to this process, although it was also one that was somewhat paradoxical:

> This is the happy life and this alone: to rejoice in you, about you and because of you. This is the life of happiness, and it is not be found anywhere else. Whoever thinks there can be some other is chasing a joy that is not the true one. (*conf.* 10.22.32)[2]

Augustine subscribes to classical eudaemonism. He holds that the ultimate goal of human beings is happiness and that this demands the acquisition of wisdom.[3] As a Christian, Augustine identifies wisdom with God and maintains that our relations with others should be ordered in accordance with our love for God. Nevertheless, he does

---

* Translated by Lucy Sheaf.

[1] *Amicitia* "most often designates friendship in the strict sense; i.e., the bonds uniting two persons in mutual sympathy" "rather that the sentiment itself," which is expressed by *amor, caritas, beneuolentia* (M. A. MacNamara, *Friendship in Saint Augustine*, Studia Friburgensia 20 [Fribourg: The University Press, 1958], 193–195). According to Konstan, unlike other Christian authors, "Augustine exploits the traditional terminology" and does so especially in the *Confessions* (D. Konstan, "Problems in the History of Christian Friendship," *Journal of Early Christian Studies* 4/1 [1996], 87–113, at 102–103).

[2] *Et ipsa est uita beata, gaudere, ad te, de te propter te: ipsa est et non est altera. Qui autem aliam putant esse, aliud sectantur gaudium neque ipsum uerum* (*Saint Augustine: The Confessions*, trans. M. Boulding, WSA I/1 [New York: New City Press, 1997], 218).

[3] See Chapter 14 by Phillip Cary in this volume.

not hold that friendship is reducible to charity.[4] This search for an "ordered love [*ordinata dilectio*]"[5] runs through the *Confessions*, and takes the form of a conversion [*conuersio*]. What role does friendship play in the account of this conversion? In what ways does Augustine align himself with classical notions of friendship? For example, does he accept the hierarchical distinctions Aristotle makes between friendship that is based on pleasure, friendship that is based on self-interest, and friendship that is based on virtue (*EN* 8.2; 1155b)? And does he appeal to the contrast that Plato draws between "friendship" and "genuine friendship" (*Lysis* 214d)? We can note at the outset that Augustine's loyalty to the Roman tradition is evident in his youthful[6] appropriation[7] of the definition of friendship given in Cicero's *De Amicitia*: "For friendship is nothing else than an accord in all things, human and divine, conjoined with mutual goodwill and affection."[8] This definition is not found in

<hr />

[4] Luigi Pizzolato studies the interaction between friendship and charity, as well as the movement from one to the other. Charity directs us to be selfless: it places an obligation on us to love all human beings. Friendship is a love that is not obligatory: it is spontaneous, and freer than charity. As long as it is subordinated to *caritas*, it is safeguarded from egoism (L. F. Pizzolato, *L'idea di amicizia nel mundo classico e cristiano* [Torino: G. Einaudi, 1993], 312). See also H. Pétré, *Caritas: Étude sur le vocabulaire latin de la charité chrétienne*, Études et documents 22 (Louvain: Spicilegium Sacrum Lovaniense, 1948).

[5] Augustine, *doc. Chr.* 1.27.28; see A.-I. Bouton-Touboulic, *L'ordre caché. La notion d'ordre chez saint Augustin*, Collection des études augustiniennes, Série Antiquité 174 (Paris: Institut d'Études Augustiniennes, 2004), 574–579.

[6] Augustine, *c. acad.* 3.6.13: "This agreement is the clearest indication of a true friend, if friendship has been correctly and properly defined as agreement on human and divine matters combined with charity and good will" (*Against the Academicians and the Teacher*, trans. P. King [Indianapolis: Hackett, 1995], 64). Augustine comments solely on the notion of agreement and not on the "ethical" and "affective" tensions that can be found in *beneuolentia* and *caritas*, respectively, as L. F. Pizzolato puts it in his "L'amicizia in S. Agostino e il 'Laelius' di Cicerone," *Vigiliae Christianae* 28 (1974), 203–215, at 207. Augustine takes this "agreement on divine matters" to be related to the agreement on *religio*. For Cicero, the agreement in question is intellectual, ideological, and political (Pizzolato, "L'amicizia in S. Agostino," 206–207).

[7] This results from the inversion of the order of objects (*rerum humanarum/rerum diuinarum*), which corresponds to a dialectical progression. See M. Testard, *Saint Augustin et Cicéron* (Paris: Études Augustiniennes, 1958), vol. 1, 270; T. J. Van Bavel, "The Influence of Cicero's Ideal of Friendship on Augustine," in *Augustiniana Traiectina: communications présentées au colloque international d'Utrecht, 13–14 novembre 1986*, eds. J. den Boeft and J. van Oort (Paris: Études Augustiniennes, 1986), 59–72, at 60. Ambrose formulates his own definition in which the notion of the *alter ego* plays a central role (*Off.* 3.134) (cf. Pizzolato, *L'idea di amicizia*, 270).

[8] Cicero, *Amic. (Laelius)* 6.20 (*De senectute; De amicitia; De divinatione*, trans. W. A. Falconer, LCL 154 [London: Heinemann, 1964], 131). Jean-Claude Fraisse speaks of "a rational agreement which is humanised by affective benevolence" (*Philia: La notion*

the *Confessions*,[9] but Augustine cites it in a letter that was probably written shortly afterward. This letter is addressed to a friend, Marcianus, who has finally converted. Augustine tells him that until this point they had not been united by a genuine friendship, because agreement on human matters is in fact conditioned by agreement on divine mattes. Thus, their friendship was "lame" "for one who holds things divine in contempt necessarily evaluates things human otherwise than he should."[10]

In the *Confessions*, a similar understanding of the relation between friendship and happiness is embedded in the narrative – not only in the sense that our progress on the path of happiness involves a transformation of friendship, but also in the sense that friendship itself allows us to make progress on the path of authentic happiness. In fact, although the affective experience of friendship resonates throughout the *Confessions*, the role ascribed to friendship in this account must be seen in the context of Augustine's desire to affirm the primacy of divine grace in salvation. This raises the question of the conditions under which friendship can contribute to genuine happiness (i.e., happiness that is anchored in eternal life).

THE VALUE OF FRIENDSHIP AND ITS SWEETNESS

Unity and Sweetness

In order to explain the attraction of friendship, Augustine often appeals to the concept of "sweetness [*dulcedo*]," relating this to bond that unites many souls: "Friendship which draws human beings together in a tender bond is sweet to us because of out of many minds it forges a unity" (*conf.* 2.5.10). In fact, as the *De ordine* indicates,[11] the ontological principle of unity is identified with God. Friendship is one of

---

d'amitié dans la philosophie antique. Essai sur un problème perdu et retrouvé, Bibliothèque d'histoire de la philosophie [Paris: J. Vrin, 1984], 392). Cicero's source is Panetius (who, in turn, draws on Aristotle). A discussion of *eunoia* can be found in Aristotle's *NE* 9.5; 1166b 20. Willing the good of the other, and reciprocity are the distinguishing features of *philia*.

[9] There are also echoes of *De amicitia* in the section of the *Confessions* in which Augustine recalls his discussions of aesthetics in *De pulchro et apto* (see Testard, *Saint Augustin et Cicéron*, vol. 1, 63–65).

[10] Augustine, *ep.* 258.2 (*Augustine: Letters 211–270, 1*–29**, trans. R. J. Teske, WSA II/4 [New York: New City Press, 2005], 195).

[11] Cf. Augustine, *ord.* 2.18.48, "And what else do friends strive for but to be one?" (*Divine Providence and the Problem of Evil*, trans. R. P. Russell, FC 5 [Washington, DC: Catholic University of America, 1948], 325).

the manifestations of this aspiration to unity that marks all created beings, from stones to human beings whose rationality allows them to practise dialectic. It is a natural aspiration that also illustrates Augustine's view that human beings are social creatures. As such, it is among the goods given to us by our creator, although it should not be preferred to greater or higher goods (such as truth and the divine law), as such a preference could lead to sin (*conf.* 2.5.10). This also implies that friendship is to be valued more highly than carnal love, as Augustine opposes the "bright boundary of friendship"[12] and the "mud of fleshly desires" (*conf.* 2.2.2). The latter involves seeking satisfaction in the other person's body, but, in the former, satisfaction is sought in their soul. The fact that Augustine takes friendship to be a philosophical "good" is also consistent with the sensibility he manifests in relation to this judgment, as the different stages of the *Confessions* show.

Cicero, whose understanding of friendship influenced Augustine profoundly, had emphasized the "sweetness [*suauitas*]"[13] of discourse and character, "which gives flavour to friendship." In contrast to "seriousness and gravity," friendship should be "more unrestrained, genial and agreeable [*remissior, liberior, dulcior*]."[14] What are the elements of this *dulcedo*? Perhaps the best description is the quasi-phenomenological one that Augustine gives in connection to his relationship with his Manichean friends in Carthage. Augustine claims that being with them enabled him to find consolation after the recent death of a friend from Thagaste (which is related in Book 4 of the *Confessions*, and will be discussed later). What strikes him is that, despite the vanity of the common "fiction [*fabula*]" they share thanks to their allegiance to Manichaeism[15] – a fiction that blinds them to God ("in whose company I loved what I was loving as a substitute for you" [*conf.* 4.8.13]) – their friendship is essentially based on the joys deriving from mutual benevolence [*amare et redamare*] and a shared life. He is particularly preoccupied/charmed with this latter fact:

[12] On this "moral metaphor" see G. P. O'Daly, "Friendship and Transgression: *Luminosus limes amicitiae* (Augustine, *Confessions* 2.2.2) and the Theme of *Confessions* 2," in *Reading Ancient Texts, Aristotle and Neoplatonism*, eds. S. Stern-Gillet and K. Corrigan, Brill's Studies in Intellectual History 162 (Leiden: Brill, 2007), vol. II, 211–223, at 212.

[13] Cicero, *Amic.* 6.22: "What is sweeter than to have someone with whom you may dare discuss anything as if you were communing yourself?"

[14] Ibid., 18.66: "To this should be added a certain affinity of speech and manner, which gives no mean flavour to friendship."

[15] The Ciceronian definition is thus respected, at least when that definition is taken at face value.

There were other joys to be found in their company which still more
powerfully captivated my mind – the charm of talking and laughing
together [*colloqui et corridere*] and kindly giving way to each
other's wishes, reading elegantly written books together, sharing
jokes and delighting to honor one another, disagreeing occasionally
but without rancor, as a person might disagree with himself
[*tamquam ipse homo secum*] and lending piquancy by that rare
disagreement to our much more frequent accord. We would teach
and learn from each other, sadly missing any who were absent and
blithely welcoming them when they return. Such signs of
friendship sprang from the hearts of friends who loved and knew
their love returned, signs to be read in smiles, words, glances and a
thousand gracious gestures. So were sparks kindled and our minds
were fused inseparably, out of many becoming one [*quasi fomitibus
conflare animos et ex pluribus unum facere*]. (*conf.* 4.8.13)

The ideal of unity underlies this passage: all these activities are
opportunities to manifest reciprocal love, and to allow the fusing of
souls in the same fire. One seeks the physical presence of the friend in
order to multiply the (extralinguistic) signs of a fusion of souls that is,
strictly speaking, impossible, and to alleviate the difficulty of seeing
into another person's mind (a difficulty that Augustine had always
lamented).[16]

The Manichean error notwithstanding, in Book 4, Augustine explicitly argues that it is precisely this ardor of love that should be safeguarded. His argument is presented in the context of the discussions of
Cicero's *De finibus malorum et bonorum* that Augustine had with
Alypius and Nebridius in Milan. Augustine writes that he "would have
given the palm" to Epicurus, were it not for Epicurus' denial of immortality. At that time, Augustine's ultimate ideal was immortality and
uninterrupted bodily pleasure:[17]

Nor did I in my wretchedness consider what stream it was whence
flowed to me the power to discuss even these distasteful things with
my friends and still find sweetness in our talk, or whence came my
inability to be happy … without my friends. (*conf.* 6.16.26)

---

[16] Cf. J. Pépin, "Le problème de la communication des consciences chez Plotin et saint
Augustin," *Revue de Métaphysique et de Morale* 55/2 (1950), 128–148.

[17] Cf. T. Fuhrer, "Contro I Platonici con Epicuro. Agostino sulla fisiologia del corpo
umano," *Eikasmos* 26 (2015), 303–318, at 303.

Augustine's pitiful moral and spiritual condition did not stop him enjoying the benefits of friendship, which he explicitly took to be an indispensable element of happiness. Thus friendship does not "imply virtue" (Aristotle, *NE* 8.1; 1155a). We should note that in Book 3 the same term "stream [*uena*]" is applied to friendship itself, which had degenerated into pseudo-compassion (which was, in fact, pleasure taken at the representation of another person's suffering). Such pseudo-compassion stoked his desire to watch tragic scenes (*conf.* 3.2.2–3). In spite of this new error – opting for the ideal of life favored by the Epicureans – friendship leads Augustine to the path of a love that is reciprocal and disinterested (*gratis*) (*conf.* 6.16.26). The distant model for this is God's love for his creatures, which is characterized by the couplet "love/love back [*amare/redamare*]."[18]

The Death of a Friend
The aporetic character of this contradiction reveals itself precisely at the time of the death of a childhood friend, which is recounted in Book 4 of the *Confessions*. This anonymous friend had initially followed Augustine on the path of Manichaeism, but was baptized and converted to Catholicism on the day before he died. It was a loss that affected Augustine on two levels. His appropriation of the classical tradition relating to grief over the loss of an *alter ego* can be seen as the first level. He feels as if he is only "half alive [*dimidius uiuere*]," and writes, "Still more amazed that I could go on living myself when he was dead" (*conf.* 4.6.11). He describes a lack of stability that is felt in the very depths of his being, and that is described in strikingly physical terms. His soul is said to be "torn and wounded [*concisa* and *cruenta*]" – a characterization that foreshadows the "torn heart [*cor concisum*]," which results from the forced separation from his concubine (*conf.* 6.15.25). However, he rejects the heroic tradition of Orestes and Pylades (*conf.* 4.6.11),[19] as he is overwhelmed by the fear of death. Yet it is this very fear that allows him to properly understand the value of this friendship. Indeed, in Book 4, his commitment to Manichaeism and his excessive attachment to this friend are errors that are linked not only by the narrative, but also conceptually. The intensity of his grief can be explained by the fact that, thanks to the *dilectio* that characterized this love, he had failed to understand that the object of his love

---

[18] Augustine, *cat. rud.* 4.7. Cicero uses the neologism *redamare* in *Amic.* 14.49.
[19] This example of friendship is praised by Cicero, *Amic.* 7.24.

could be lost. For this reason, it was a loss that brought him misery (*conf.* 4.6.11).

Through comparing this love to the love that is due to God, who of course cannot be lost (*conf.* 4.9.14), Augustine is able to see the folly of the love he had for his friend, and to contrast the divine solidity with the "sand" of this friendship (*conf.* 4.8.13). As he declares, "Blessed is he who loves You, and loves his friend in you and his enemies for you sake" (*conf.* 4.9.14), he points toward a more authentic friendship, made possible by charity. In the absence of charity we cannot talk of "genuine friendship [*uera amicitia*]," but only of friendship: "Friendship is genuine only when you bind fast together people who cleave to you through *the charity poured abroad in our hearts by the Holy Spirit who is given to us* (Rm 5:5)" (*conf.* 4.4.7).

God is not a distinct object of friendship: God is the very source of it. Augustine picks up Aristotle's suggestion that virtue is the principle source of a fully realized friendship, and the cause of its stability.[20] The principle of such stability is in God, who enters every relationship of authentic friendship through charity. It is in this framework that we should understand the rejection of Augustine by his friend, who felt he had been made a mockery of by the baptism he had received the day before his death – a baptism that occurred while he had lost consciousness, but that was nonetheless valid (*conf.* 4.4.8). Augustine's later interpretation of Cicero's *De amicitia* can shed light on his friend's attitude: the lack of "agreement on divine matters" brings an end to their "mutual dependence [*nimis pendamus ex inuicem*]." To some extent, Augustine finds himself in a situation parallel to the one Marcianus seems to be in: although Marcianus was always full of "benevolence [*beneuolentia*]"[21] toward Augustine, he nonetheless desired only a "mortal well-being [*salus mortalis*]" for him (*ep.* 258.2).

Augustine's grief, described in poignant and quasi-elegiac terms, finds no relief in "hope" placed in God, as long as he represents God as a *phantasma*. The account of this period foreshadows Book 9 of the *Confessions*. It points toward Augustine's baptism in Milan in 387, and toward the change in his outlook that was brought about by the death of Monnica.[22] Nonetheless, in Book 4, the "sweetness" of this old

---

[20] Friendship unites those who are "similar according to virtue" (Aristotle *NE* 8.4; 1156b), and for the virtuous person "his friend is another self" (Ibid., 9.9; 1170b).

[21] Without benevolence there is no friendship in the proper sense of the term (Cicero, *Amic.* 8.26).

[22] A.-I. Touboulic, "De la mort de l'ami à la présence divine (*Conf.* IV, 4, 7–12, 19)," *Vita Latina* 153 (1999), 58–69, at 57–58.

friendship is underlined, even though it cannot be seen as *uera amicitia*. Augustine's account includes certain elements that feature in the *De amicitia* – for example, a commonality of tastes and of interests ("similarity of outlook lent warmth to our relationship [*(amicitia) cocta feruore parilium studiorum*]" [*conf.* 4.4.7]) – and that Cicero takes to constitute the foundation of friendship.[23] Still, as we have seen, Augustine led this friend along the path of Manichaeism, which can lead only to misery ("Already this man was intellectually astray along with me"), just as Caius Blossius would have been willing to burn down the Capitol if Tiberius Gracchus had asked him. Cicero condemns this attitude on the basis that friendship should be founded on virtue.[24]

An "Unfriendly Form of Friendship [inimica amicitia]" (conf. 2.9.17)

Aristotle distinguishes three kinds of friendship, according to the object on which the friendship is founded – that is, pleasure, utility, and virtue. The first and lowest kind is described in Book 2 of the *Confessions*, which famously recounts how his theft of some pears prompted Augustine to reflect on the depths of evil.[25] Regardless of the appeal the pears had, Augustine is aware of a "company [*consortium*]" between those who commit the theft with him and of the "stimulation of conspiracy" (*conf.* 2.8.16),[26] a companionship in sin, which is the determining factor in this theft.

> On my own I would not have perpetrate that theft in which I felt no desire for what I stole, but only for the act of stealing; to do it alone would have aroused no desire whatever in me, nor would I have done it. What an exceedingly unfriendly form of friendship [*O nimis inimica amicitia*] that was! It was a seduction of the mind hard to understand, which instilled into me craving do harm for sport and fun. (*conf.* 2.9.17)

---

[23] Cicero, *Amic.* 4.15: *uoluntatum, studiorum sententiarum summa consensio* ("The most complete agreement in policy, in pursuits and opinions"), trans. W. A. Falconer, LCL 154 (London: Heinemann, 1964), 125.

[24] Cicero, *Amic.* 8.27.

[25] For example, Augustine's friendship with Manichaeans in Rome was partially based on utility (see *conf.* 5.10.18–19).

[26] *Confricatione consciorum animorum accenderem pruritum cupiditatis meae*. The term "itching [*pruritum*]" is also found in *Gn. adv. Man.* 2.15.23, in relation to the "itch" that gave rise to Adam's and Eve's desire for pleasure, and led them to lie after they had committed the first sin [*Folia uero fici pruritum quemdam significant*].

His friends (who are never named individually) were the "adjuvants [*adminicula*]" to his wicked deed, and this friendship that reenacts the temptation that led to the first sin can be described as a friendship that is orientated toward evil.[27] To this extent, it is similar to the case of the "friends" who dragged Alypius to the games at the amphitheater at Carthage, where the fall of a gladiator was the occasion of Alypius's own fall (*conf.* 6.8.13). There is no doubt that the kind of life that Augustine envisaged at this point was opposed to authentic happiness.

FRIENDSHIP AND PROGRESS

On one hand, these friendships illustrate Augustine's progress on the path of a life that is in harmony with God, and throw this progress into relief. On the other hand, they are at the same time elements that enable this progress.

Friendship and Progress toward Wisdom

After Books 2 and 4, which were concerned with the negative or aporetic character of friendship, and with the period in his life when Augustine became ever more distant from God, Book 6 describes a more focused search for a happy life and wisdom. This book also describes the first stage of the process of the return of the "prodigal son" (*conf.* 1.18.28). "Though I was so enamoured of a happy life [*amans beatam uitam*] I feared to find it in its true home, and fled from it even as I sought it" (*conf.* 6.11.20). Augustine had to "abandon worldly ambition and apply ourselves singleminded to the search for God and a life of happiness" (*conf.* 6.11.19), but this aspiration seemed doomed to failure once his mother insisted that he enter an "arranged marriage" (*conf.* 6.13.23).

This problem notwithstanding, in Book 6, Augustine presents us with a friendship that will allow both parties to progress toward wisdom. In so doing, he returns to certain themes in ancient philosophy. For example, Cicero suggests that friendship has been given to us by nature for the perfection of virtue,[28] as we cannot attain to this perfection on our own. As such, friendship can produce a "comradeship

---

[27] R. Lane Fox analyzes it as a "misapplied friendship," and emphasizes that "Augustine is the first Christian writer to explore friendship, rather than love, for a neighbour or for God." (*Augustine: Conversions to Confessions* [London: Penguin Books, 2016], 68–69). On this topic, see T. Nawar, "Augustine's on the Dangers of Friendship," *The Classical Quarterly* 65/2 (2015), 836–851.

[28] Cicero, *Amic.* 22.83.

[*comitatus*]" oriented toward the supreme good. In this respect, Books 6 and 9 complement each other, since the latter resolves the difficulties raised in the former (namely, the question of what kind of life to follow, and the place in that life that should be given to women). First, we should note that the discussions with Nebridius and Alypius that are recounted in Book 6 bear on the question of the supreme good and testify to their common search for happiness. Their search may be misguided, but they rightly take it for granted that there can be no happiness without friendship. Augustine's "awarding the palm" to Epicurus (*conf.* 6.16.26) is perhaps an acknowledgment of the central role ascribed to happiness in the Epicureans' account of the goods that are necessary to happiness.

It is well known that, in the course of his discussions with a dozen or so friends in Milan, Augustine conceived the project of a communal life "far removed from the crowd" and devoted to "live a life of leisure [*otiose uiuere*]" (*conf.* 6.14.24). Such a project has parallels both in Pythagoreanism[29] and in the communities set up by the first Christians: in both cases we find an emphasis on communal ownership, with each member renouncing their private property in the name of "the sincerity of our friendship [*amicitiae sinceritas*]" (*conf.* 6.14.24),[30] and a certain rudimentary political structure (in which administrative responsibility lies with two "magistrates," following Roman custom). It is clear that this project was made viable by the financial assistance of Romanianus (who was a patron of Thagaste, and Augustine's benefactor). However, there was no consensus on whether "womenfolk" could be admitted to this community (some of Augustine's friends were married, and others had been married before), and so the project ended in failure (*conf.* 6.14.24).

Augustine's framework for understanding progress toward wisdom is consistent with his position in the *Soliloquies* (387 CE): love for one's friends is to be proportioned to their inclination toward wisdom (*sol.* 1.12.20).[31] The first person to find wisdom can easily lead the others onto the same path (*sol.* 1.12.20). This project comes to completion during the time Augustine spent at Cassiciacum after his conversion.

---

[29] See I. Hadot, "*Amicitia*," in *Augustinus-Lexikon*, ed. C. Mayer (Basel: Schwabe, 1986–), vol. 1, 287–293, at 290.

[30] See Konstan, "Problems in the History of Christian Friendship," 112.

[31] This ascetic model, drawn from neoplatonism, is discussed by Hadot, "*Amicitia*," 292 and Pizzolato, *L'idea di amicizia*, 309. Here, the problem of friendship is seen in terms of its relation to wisdom, rather than to charity. Friendship is an instrument that puts ultimate truths within our grasp.

There, he enjoyed "leisured freedom [*libertas otiosa*]" (*conf.* 9.3.6) and was able to "rest in God" alongside friends and family (Monnica was the only woman in the group), far from the tumult of the age [*aestus saeculi*] (*conf.* 9.3.5).

We should also recall that Augustine was interested in the cenobitism of St. Anthony, which had inspired ascetic vocations. Book 8 of the *Confessions* recounts how he heard about this from Ponticianus before the fateful day in the garden in Milan. Indeed, Augustine presents the new stage of his life that begins at Cassiciacum as the end of his attachment to the "world" and as an aspiration toward asceticism.[32]

The villa close to Milan was the property of Verecundus, who worked as a grammarian there. To his great disappointment, Verecundus was cut off from this *consortium*, as he was married,[33] and believed that a Christian way of life must involve the kind of continence to which Augustine was now committed (*conf.* 9.3.5).[34] Nonetheless he "generously [*benigne*]" gave his friends the use of this villa as a sign of his *beneuolentia* and his friendship. Verecundus died shortly afterward, but not before finally being baptized. Augustine asserts that, thanks to this baptism, Verecundus would now be able to enjoy the "delights of paradise" (*conf.* 9.3.5).[35] God becomes the horizon of communal friendship after the turning point of Book 8, and offers the promise not just of a happy life, but of eternal life – that is, true happiness. Friendship is thus no longer understood in terms of a classical "dyad," but rather in terms of a relation to something "inward," which is shared by each participating person and that feeds their charity.[36]

The image of the *iter* from which Verecundus is excluded shows that Augustine's friends accompany him in their communal progress

---

[32] Folliet argues that this aspiration toward "being deified in leisure [*deificari in otio*]" (Augustine, *ep.* 10.2), synonymous with asceticism and purification through the virtues, is characteristic of Porphyrianism (G. Folliet, "'Deificari in otio', Augustin, *Epistula* 10, 2," *Recherches Augustiniennes* 2 [1962], 225–236).

[33] Hindered by this, he was unable to set out on the path (*iter*) chosen by the others (*conf.* 9.3.5).

[34] This group was enriched by new arrivals such as Evodius, who had converted before Augustine and shared his "holy agreement [*placitum sanctum*]."

[35] In a play on words, Augustine expands on the "mountain of rich pasture [*mons incaseatus*]" of Ps 67:16.

[36] Pizzolato, *L'idea di amicizia*, 311–312. Cf. Augustine, *conf.* 10.3.3: "Charity believes all things" (1 Cor 13:7), "at least among those who are bonded together by charity" (cf. Col 3.14). In contrast, van Bavel suggests that there is a "triadic" structure to Cicero's account of friendship: on the one hand, the two friends, on the other hand, nature (or virtue) as a divine, impersonal power ("The Influence of Cicero's Ideal of Friendship on Augustine," 64–65).

toward the good, and together they form a society that can be seen as a foretaste of the city of God. In Book 9, before recalling his time at Cassiciacum, Augustine reflects on the moral progress made by the friends who were with him in Milan. By means of a narrative prolepsis,[37] which looks beyond the events currently being related, he allows us to see the spiritual destiny of Nebridius, who moved from docetism to the Catholic faith, and died before Augustine's return to Africa in 391. In a quasi-elegy, Augustine takes pleasure in imagining him in "the bosom of Abraham" (Lk 16:22): "There my Nebridius is living, to me a friend most tenderly loved, to you, Lord, a freedman adopted as you son" (*conf.* 9.3.6).

There are two aspects to the bond that Augustine describes, friendship and spiritual affiliation, and these give rise to two distinct points of view. On the one hand, the friendship continues regardless of Nebridius' spiritual state, but, on the other hand, it becomes an enlightened friendship after his conversion. From that point onward, Nebridius' thirst for knowledge is filled by wisdom as he enjoys happiness without end (*sine fine felix*) (*conf.* 9.3.6). Yet, beyond the *eschaton*, friendship returns for Augustine and does not stop being reciprocal. It continues even as it is transformed by its relation to God: "Yet I cannot believe that he is so inebriated as to forget me, since you, Lord, from whom he drinks, are mindful to us" (*conf.* 9.3.6).

An episode at Cassiciacum that is described in Book 9 points toward the framework in which friendship will now be understood. When Augustine is afflicted by toothache, he asks the friends who are with him to "pray [to God] for [him]" (*conf.* 9.4.13).[38] As he can no longer speak, he writes his request on a wax tablet. As soon as they fall on their knees in supplication, an almost miraculous healing takes place (*conf.* 9.4.13).

The Case of Alypius: A Communal and Progressive Appropriation of the Good

Thanks to his long-established and ongoing friendship with Augustine, and his role in the genesis of the *Confessions*,[39] Alypius seems well placed to play the role of a friend who is an *alter idem* for Augustine.

---

[37] This literary device is also used in the account of Augustine's friendship with Verecundus, which is cited earlier.

[38] See MacNamara, *Friendship in Saint Augustine*, 211.

[39] Cf. Augustine, *ep.* 27.33 (to Paulinus of Nola); cf. P. Courcelle, *Recherches sur les Confessions de Saint Augustin* (Paris: Boccard, 1968), 45.

He could also throw into relief Augustine's apprehension of an authentic conception of friendship – one that not only offers consolation in the face of the trials of their age, but that can also contribute to happiness in the next life. But does Augustine escape the temptation to project onto his friend an ideal self?[40]

Their friendship is initially marked by a certain inequality: Alypius is younger than Augustine, and is his pupil in Carthage, but at the same time he belongs to a higher social class. Here Augustine breaks with the Aristotelian tradition that regards inequality as an obstacle to friendship (*conf.* 6.7.11).[41] The strength of their friendship is all the greater because it triumphs over obstacles – notably a disagreement between Alypius's father and Augustine. Its complementarity and reciprocity reveal the foundations of this friendship: "I seemed to him good and learned, while I for my part was fond of him on account of his great nobility of character" (*conf.* 6.7.11). The model that is relevant here is one in which friendship is founded on complementarity rather than resemblance.[42] We have an example of friendship in which one party is oriented toward knowledge, and the other oriented toward virtue.[43] In the *Confessions*, however, there are echoes of Cicero's suggestion that friendship develops when *beneuolentia* is kindled through contact with a virtue that is embodied by another person.[44] Endowed with an honorable character, Alypius already possesses the humility that will lead to his baptism (*conf.* 9.6.14)[45] and, being motivated by *continentia*, he is no longer attracted to women. Does this friendship allow its protagonists to make mutual progress on the path of authentic happiness?

The events that led to Alypius being freed of his passion for circus games are well known.[46] At first, Augustine cannot offer a "warning [*monitio*]" because the "goodwill of friendship [*amicitiae*

---

[40] For an assessment of this relationship, see A.-I. Bouton-Touboulic, "Alypius, l'ami sceptique d'Augustin?," in *Augustin philosophe et prédicateur. Hommage à Goulven Madec: Actes du colloque international organisé à Paris les 8 et 9 septembre 2011*, ed. I. Bochet, Collection des Études Augustiniennes, Série Antiquité 195 (Paris: Institut d'Études Augustiniennes, 2012), 295–314.

[41] Aristotle, *NE* 8.8; 1158b.

[42] When Plato defines friendship in *Lysis* 222a5, he substitutes the idea of "belonging [*to oikeion*]" for the notion of "being like [*homoiotēs*]."

[43] See Bouton-Touboulic, "Alypius, l'ami sceptique d'Augustin?" 309.

[44] Cicero, *Amic.* 8.28.

[45] Alypius goes as far as walking on icy ground with bare feet.

[46] Conversely, we must note that Nebridius challenges some of Augustine's Manichaean ideas, as well as his attraction to astrology and divination (see *conf.* 4.3.6; 7.2.3, 6.8).

beneuolentia]" has not yet been firmly established (*conf.* 6.7.11); the correction [*correctio*] that comes later is clearly attributed to divine Providence, which already sees a future "minister" of God in Alypius. Augustine, the *magister*, is simply God's instrument as he expounds a scriptural text (Prov 9:8). Alypius takes this text to be addressed to him and is "healed" of this passion (*conf.* 6.7.12).[47]

On the other hand, Alypius is unable to dissuade Augustine from seeking marriage on the basis that this would stop them being able "to live together in the carefree leisure and devote ourselves to philosophy, as we had long desired" (*conf.* 6.12.21). Augustine insists that marriage is not incompatible with such a life; marriage does not preclude the possibility of cultivating wisdom and obtaining some merit before God, "having faithfully kept their friends and loved them dearly" (*conf.* 6.12.21). As we have seen, the problem of the incompatibility of these two ways of life will ultimately prove decisive. To a great extent this is due to the fact that, far from desiring "the good of marriage,"[48] Augustine is in fact a hostage to the "carnal fever" of concupiscence. Because his assumption that life without a woman is a "punishment" rather than a "life,"[49] Augustine even plays the role of "serpent" in his relationship with Alypius. Namely, he provokes Alypius's desire to seek marriage through eliciting his "curiosity," or rather his "mimetical desire."

In the remarkable sequence of their conversion, Augustine hears the refrain "Take and read [*Tolle, lege*]!" in the garden in Milan while he is away from Alypius (an episode recounted in Book 8).[50] Alypius is not led on to the same path by anything Augustine says to him after his conversion, but rather by his own reading of Rm 14:1, even if this passage comes immediately after the one Augustine had just read (i.e.,

---

[47] Cf. the *exemplum* of Polemon coming to Xenocratus' school (Diogenes Laertius, *V. phil.* IV.3.16); Courcelle, *Recherches sur les Confessions*, 59.

[48] This is recounted in *conf.* 6.12.22: "the glory of wedlock in terms of guiding the course of a marriage and bringing up children [*coniugale decus in officio regendi matrimonii et suscipiendorum liberorum*]." In *b. conjug.* 9.9, Augustine describes *amicitia* as a *bonum*, and suggests that marriage is a good that is necessary for friendship, as it supports the propagation of the human race. He conceives "a certain relationship and kinship [*amicalis quaedam et germana coniunctio*]" (*b. conjug.* 1.1) between Adam and Eve before the carnal relationship that was initiated after their sin (*Augustine: Marriage and Virginity*, trans. R. Kearney, WSA I/9 [New York: New City Press, 1997], 33).

[49] Here Augustine does not mean the "happy life."

[50] See A.-I. Bouton-Touboulic, "Body Language in Augustine's *Confessiones* and *De doctrina christiana*," *Augustinian Studies* 49/1 (2018), 1–23, at 21.

Rm 13:13–14): "He in return told me what had been happening to him without my knowledge" (*conf.* 8.12.30). It is indeed the divine Word in Scripture that plays the role of *admonitio* in relation to Alypius, who was "weak in faith" (Rm 14:1) (*conf.* 8.12.30), as he had wrongly attributed the heresy of Apollinarianism to the Catholic Church (*conf.* 7.19.25)[51] (whereas Augustine himself had evidently yielded to Photinianism).

Alypius's and Augustine's conversion mirrors the conversion of the two officials in Trier. It should also be seen as the culmination of a series of parallels that have been drawn between these two friends, with Augustine leading the way in regard to knowledge, and Alypius leading the way in regard to morals [*mores*].[52] This common quest for wisdom will finally lead them to ministry in the Church; indeed, these friendships validate the foundations of their communal life in Thagaste, before they are fully realized in the heart of the Church.

CONCLUSION

In the *Confessions*, Augustine suggests that the quest for happiness is inseparable from the quest for wisdom. Friendship plays a major role here, not least in showing the social and affective dimensions of these quests. Augustine lays particular emphasis on the point that the sweetness of the bond of friendship is directly related to divine charity. The intersubjectivity manifested in the guidance and warnings that friends give each other is the fruit of a divine *dispensatio*. Augustine's understanding of friendship is certainly informed by classical ideas, but ultimately he is concerned to present friendship as the cornerstone of a Christian community that is yet to be founded.

Further Reading

Bouton-Touboulic, A.-I. "Body Language in Augustine's *Confessions* and *De doctrina christiana*." *Augustinian Studies* 49/1 (2018), 1–23.

[51] See E. Feldmann, "Alypius," *Augustinus-Lexikon*, vol. 1, 246–267, at 248; G. Van Reyn, "*Ad christianam fidem pigrius mouebatur* (*Conf.* VII.20.(25)): Alypius' More Reluctant Move to the Christian Faith (Compared to Augustine). Part. 2: Between Conversion and Baptism," *Augustiniana* 60/3–4 (2011), 193–234. Alypius enjoins Augustine not to mention the name of Christ in the Dialogues of Cassiciacum (*conf.* 9.4.7).

[52] Cf. teacher of words/teacher of morals (*magister uerborum/magister morum*) in Augustine, *ord.* 2.10.28.

"Alypius, l'ami sceptique d'Augustin?" In *Augustin philosophe et prédicateur. Hommage à Goulven Madec: actes du colloque international organisé à Paris les 8 et 9 septembre 2011*, ed. I. Bochet. Colletion des Études Augustiniennes, Série Antiquité 195. Paris: Institut d'études Augustiniennes, 2012, 295–314.

L'ordre caché. La notion d'ordre chez saint Augustin, Collection des études augustiniennes, Série Antiquité 174. Paris: Institut d'Études Augustiniennes, 2004.

Courcelle, P. *Recherches sur les* Confessions *de saint Augustin*. Paris: Boccard, 1968.

Folliet, G. "'Deificari in otio', Augustin, Epistula 10, 2." *RechAug* 2 (1962), 225–236.

Fuhrer, T. "Contro I Platonici con Epicuro. Agostino sulla fisiologia del corpo umano." *Eikasmos* 26 (2015), 303–318.

Hadot, I. "*Amicitia.*" In *Augustinus-Lexikon*, ed. C. Mayer. Basel: Schwabe, 1986–, vol. 1, 287–293.

Konstan, D. "Problems in the History of Christian Friendship." *Journal of Early Christian Studies* 4/1 (1996), 87–113.

Lane Fox, R. *Augustine: Conversions to Confessions*. London: Penguin Books, 2016.

MacNamara, M. A. *Friendship in Saint Augustine*. Studia Friburgensia 20. Fribourg: The University Press, 1958.

Nawar, T. "Augustine and the Dangers of Friendship." *The Classical Quarterly* 65/2 (2015), 836–851.

O'Daly, G. P. "Friendship and Transgression: *Luminosus limes amicitiae (Augustine, Confessions 2.2.2) and the Theme of Confessions 2.*" In *Reading Ancient Texts, Aristotle and Neoplatonism*, eds. S. Stern-Gillet and K. Corrigan. Brill's Studies in Intellectual History 162. Leiden: Brill, 2007, vol. II, 211–223.

Pépin, J. "Le problème de la communication des consciences chez Plotin et saint Augustin." *Revue de Métaphysique et de Morale* 55/2 (1950), 128–148.

Pétré, H. Caritas: *Étude sur le vocabulaire latin de la charité chrétienne*. Études et documents 22. Louvain: Spicilegium Sacrum Lovaniense, 1948.

Pizzolato, L. F. "L'amicizia in S. Agostino e il "Laelius" di Cicerone." *Vigiliae Christianae* 28 (1974), 203–215.

L'idea di amicizia nel mundo classico e cristiano. Turin: G. Einaudi, 1993.

Testard, M. *Saint Augustin et Cicéron*. Paris: Études Augustiniennes, 1958, vol. 1.

Touboulic, A.-I. "De la mort de l'ami à la présence divine (*Conf.* IV, 4, 7–12, 19)." *Vita Latina*, 153 (1999), 58–69.

Van Bavel, T. J. "The Influence of Cicero's Ideal of Friendship on Augustine." In *Augustiniana Traiectina: communications présentées au colloque international d'Utrecht, 13–14 novembre 1986*, eds. J. den Boeft and J. van Oort. Paris: Études Augustiniennes, 1986, 59–72.

10 Love, Will, and the Intellectual Ascents

SARAH CATHERINE BYERS

> Beloved eternity: you are my God.
> (*conf.* 7.10.16)

Augustine's accounts of his so-called mystical experiences in *conf.* 7.10.16, 17.23, and 9.10.24 are puzzling. The primary problem is that, although in all three accounts he claims to have seen "that which is," we have no satisfactory account of what "that which is" is supposed to be. I shall be arguing that, contrary to a common interpretation, Augustine's intellectual "seeing" of "being" in Books 7 and 9 was not a vision of the Christian God as a whole, nor of one of the divine persons, each of whom is equally God, according to Augustine. This becomes clear when we attend to the fact that Augustine is appropriating a specific meaning of "that which is" or "being" used by Plotinus in his account of the lover of Beauty. This resolution, however, leads to a second question. Is there *anything* distinctively Christian about any, or all, of Augustine's ascents? On the one hand, it would be odd if there were not, given that the *Confessions* are addressed to the Christian God. On the other hand, upon close inspection we find that the allegedly specific "Christian" characteristics that modern commentators have identified in the ascents of *conf.* 7 and 9 also occur in the Neoplatonists. I will argue that there is in fact one important difference between Augustine and the Neoplatonists here that has not been pointed out in these prior interpretations.

PROBLEMATIC INTERPRETATIONS OF THE ASCENTS IN *CONF.* 7 AND 9

Augustine claims that as a young man he repeatedly attained intellectual vision of "being [*id quod est, esse*]." These reports are located in three famous passages of the *Confessions*. In *conf.* 7.10.16, he recounts: "When I first came to know you, you raised me up to make me see that what I saw was, and that I who saw was not yet [*Et cum te primum cognovi, tu adsumpsisti me ut viderem esse quod viderem, et nondum me esse qui viderem*]."[1] In *conf.* 9.10.24, Augustine similarly reports:

We ascended even further by internal reflection and dialogue and wonder at your works, and we entered into our own minds. We moved up beyond them ... There life is the Wisdom[2] through which all creatures come to be, both things which were and things which will be. But Wisdom itself is not brought into being but is as it was and always will be. Furthermore, in this Wisdom there is no past and future, but only being (*esse*), since it is eternal ... we touched it [Wisdom] in some small degree by a moment of total concentration of the heart [*et adhuc ascendebamus interius cogitando et loquendo et mirando opera tua. et venimus in mentes nostras et transcendimus eas ... ibi vita sapientia est, per quam fiunt omnia*

---

[1] Latin texts are taken from J. J. O'Donnell, *Augustine:* Confessions (Oxford: Clarendon, 1992), vol. 1. All English translations are from H. Chadwick, *Saint Augustine:* Confessions (Oxford: Oxford University Press, 1991), but sometimes, as here, these have been amended. There is an implausible alternate translation of this phrase; namely, "that I might see that there was something/being/an existing thing to see" (see P. Constantine, *Confessions*: A New Translation [New York: Liveright, 2018], 128; M. Boulding, *Saint Augustine:* The Confessions, WSA I/1 [New York: New City Press, 1997], 173; E. Tréhorel and G. Bouissou, *Les Confessions. Livres I–VII*, BA [Paris: Études Augustiniennes, 1992], 617; F. Sheed, *The Confessions of St. Augustine*, Books I–X, Ancient and Modern Library of Theological Literature 1 [New York: Sheed and Ward, 1942], 129), which was followed in E. Zum Brunn, *St. Augustine: Being and Nothingness*, trans. R. Namad [New York: Paragon House, 1988 (original 1978)], 69). The following authors rightly reject the alternate reading in favor of the one cited in the main text: Chadwick, *Saint Augustine:* Confessions, 123; J. P. Kenney, *Contemplation and Classical Christianity: A Study in Augustine.* Oxford Early Christian Studies (Oxford: Oxford University Press, 2013), 87; S. MacDonald, "The Divine Nature," in *The Cambridge Companion to Augustine*, eds. E. Stump and N. Kretzmann (Cambridge: Cambridge University Press, 2001), 71–90, at 88, n. 30; J. Burnaby, *Amor Dei: A Study of the Religion of St. Augustine* (London: Hodder and Stoughton, 1938), 36; O. du Roy, *L'Intelligence de la foi en la Trinité selon St. Augustin* (Paris: Études Augustiniennes, 1966), 76, n. 1. The reasons why the latter authors are correct are as follows (cf. the section titled "The Plotinian "Love" Context of All Three Ascent Passages"). It would not make sense for Augustine to present the mere realization that there was something to see as a dramatic ascent; for that information was available in simply reading the Neoplatonic books; but he presents his ascent as *subsequent* to reading the books, and as a deliberate act of trying to attain contemplation according to the method laid out in the Neoplatonic books. The alternate reading would make Augustine say that he had not actually attained intellectual contact with the objects proposed for contemplation in the Neoplatonic books; this contradicts his claims to have known, seen, or touched something transcendent.

[2] It will become clear momentarily why I have capitalized "wisdom."

*ista, et quae fuerunt et quae futura sunt, et ipsa non fit, sed sic est
ut fuit, et sic erit semper. quin potius fuisse et futurum esse non est
in ea, sed esse solum, quoniam aeterna est ... attingimus eam
modice toto ictu cordis*].[3]

In *conf.* 7.17.23, Augustine says:

> Step by step I ascended from bodies to the soul which perceives
> through the body, and from there to its internal power to which
> bodily senses report external sensations,[4] this being as high as the
> beasts go. From there again I ascended to the power of reasoning to
> which is to be attributed the power of judging the deliverances of
> the bodily senses. This power ... had no hesitation in declaring that
> the unchangeable is preferable to the changeable ... And in the flash
> of a trembling glance it attained to that which is [*gradatim a
> corporibus ad sentientem per corpus animam atque inde ad eius
> interiorem vim, cui sensus corporis exteriora nuntiaret, et
> quousque possunt bestiae, atque inde rursus ad ratiocinantem
> potentiam ad quam refertur iudicandum quod sumitur a sensibus
> corporis. Quae ... cum sine ulla dubitatione clamaret
> incommutabile praeferendum esse mutabili ... et pervenit ad id
> quod est in ictu trepidantis aspectus*].

These three passages are obviously parallel in their claims that Augustine saw "what is [*id quod est*]." Although some scholars have wanted to
partly contrast the surrounding presentation in *conf.* 9.10.24 with that
of the two passages in Book 7, claiming that it is in some ways uniquely

---

[3] De La Peza long ago showed that the term "heart [*cor*]" in Augustine often, as here,
refers to the same set of capacities as "mind [*mens*]" (E. De La Peza, *El Significado de
"cor" en San Agustín* [Paris: Études Augustiniennes, 1962], 66–67, 73–76, 81–82).
Hence Augustine's statements that he "heard within the heart" and "touched being
with the heart" (*conf.* 7.10.16 and *conf.* 9.10.24, respectively) indicate that these
experiences were acts of *intellectual* contemplation. Grammatically, Augustine's *in*
plus ablative (*in sapientia*) need not be a locative; it could be asserting simply that, in
the case of Wisdom, only the present tense – not the past or future – obtains. This is
something that Augustine asserts about the Son (a.k.a. Wisdom, for Augustine) in *f. et
symb.* 6 *ad fin*. Hence some of the translators render the *in sapientia* of *conf.* 9.10.24
this way (Sheed: "it [= Wisdom] simply is"). Most, however, have retained the literal
construction "in" with the locative sense (*BA*, WSA). The literal construction is more
accurate, given that the context of Augustine's claims to have seen "being" is, as he
tells us, the "Platonic books"; see footnotes 23 and 24.

[4] This internal power is the internal sense [*sensus interior*] of *conf.* 1.20.31, as well as
lib. arb. 2.3.8 and 2.4.10, on which, see S. Byers, "Augustine's Debt to Stoicism in the
Confessions," in *The Routledge Handbook of the Stoic Tradition*, ed. J. Sellars
(London: Routledge, 2016), 56–69 at 58–59.

Christian,[5] their claims do not pertain to the "being" itself of *conf.* 9.10.24. It is not controversial to treat all three passages as commonly describing an apprehension of "that which is." The question is: *What is* "that which is"?

No doubt because Augustine's reports that he saw "that which is" are obscure, many writers have chosen not to address the question of *what* the intentional object of his intellectual visions *was*, and instead concentrated on the visions' role in his philosophical maturation (his rejection of materialism and Manichaeism). Those who do allude to the object seen typically say that it was God, without arguing for the claim that Augustine's "being" is equivalent to "God" or analyzing fully the implications of asserting that it is.[6]

Textually, the interpretation that Augustine is claiming to have seen God is based upon his statements in *conf.* 7.10.16 and 9.10.24. In the former text he says that he saw a light, the light had made him, one who knows the light knows the truth, and truth is God. He says these things immediately before reporting that what he saw "was." Then, after his asseveration that he saw "what was," Augustine associates the divine name of Ex 3:14 with his contemplation: "You cried to me from afar, 'I am who am.'" This framework certainly *seems* at first glance to say that he had seen God. Commentators then infer that the "being" of *conf.* 7.10.16 is God, and apply this meaning to 7.17.23 as well. In *conf.* 9.10.24, Augustine says that he touched being in Wisdom, and Wisdom for Augustine is the second Person of the Trinity, who is equally God with the Father and Holy Spirit.

---

[5] See the section titled "Second Problem: Christian or Neoplatonic Mysticism?"

[6] R. Lane Fox, *Augustine: Conversions to Confessions* (New York: Basic Books, 2015), 252; J. P. Kenney, *The Mysticism of Saint Augustine: Rereading the* Confessions (London: Routledge, 2005), 59; C. Vaught, *Encounters with God in Augustine's* Confessions: *Books VII–IX* (Albany: State University of New York Press, 2004), 53; R. J. O'Connell, *St. Augustine's* Confessions: *The Odyssey of the Soul*, third ed. (New York: Fordham University Press, 2000), 76, 79; Boulding, *Saint Augustine:* The Confessions, 217, n. 56, and 228, n. 103; MacDonald, "The Divine Nature," 82; J.-L. Marion, *God without Being*, trans. T. Carlson, Religion and Postmodernism (Chicago: University of Chicago Press, 1991 [original 1982]), 73 and 215, n. 50, following E. Zum Brunn, "L'exégèse augustinienne de 'Ego sum qui sum' et la 'métaphysique de l'Exode'," in *Dieu et l'être* (Paris: Études Augustiniennes, 1978), 141–164; M. Pellegrino, *Les Confessions de Saint Augustin* (Paris: Études Augustiniennes, 1960), 167. Exceptions are Masnovo and du Roy, but both are vague as to what Augustine did see. Masnovo, cited in Pellegrino, *Les Confessions*, 169, says only that immutable "being" must be a "reflection" of God rather than God. Du Roy says that Augustine saw Truth, which is God himself, but not the ultimate in God, which is eternity; eternity is known by truth, which is access to true Being (*L'Intelligence de la foi*, 74–75).

However, earlier than and contemporaneously with the *Confessions*, Augustine indicates that the contemplation of the divine nature is reserved to the afterlife and requires complete moral purification.[7] Given that in the *Confessions* Augustine presents himself as a living and morally corrupt contemplator (*conf.* 7.20.26–21.27; 10.30.42–42.67), how could he be claiming to have seen God? Although scholars continue to be interested in Augustinian "mysticism,"[8] this problem has not been pointed out previously, and so it has not been resolved.

THE PLOTINIAN "LOVE" CONTEXT OF ALL THREE ASCENT PASSAGES

In each of these passages, Augustine describes his experience in terms that give us no reason to doubt that he is indebted to Plotinus' descriptions of intellectual love [*erōs*]; namely, the desire to embrace some beauty, directed to intelligible reality (see *Enn.* 3.5.1). Plotinus' account is adapted from Diotima's "ladder" of love objects in Plato's *Symposium*, of course.[9] In *conf.* 7.10.16, Augustine contrasts bodily light seen

---

[7] The *Confessions* is dated to 397–400/1. Augustine says or implies that it is impossible to contemplate God's invisible nature without dying, as early as *Gn. adv. Man.* 5.6 (dated 388/389) and *f. et symb.* 9.20 (dated 393), where he cites 1 Cor 13:12, "We see now through a mirror obscurely; but then face to face. Now I know in part." See also his distinction between the soul's ability to know God fully, which comes only in the afterlife, and partially, which is in this life for those who are morally purified, *sol.* 1.7.14 (dated 386/387); *vera rel.* 7.13 (dated 391); *c. Faust.* 5.4 (dated 397/398), and *Gn. litt.* 8.19.38, 8.27.50 (quoting 1 Tim 6:16) (begun in 401). In the *retr.* 1.19.1–2, he regrets that he said in *s. Dom. mon.* 1.4.12 (dated 394) that it was possible for people like the Apostles to achieve in this life the complete purity of heart necessary for the vision of God. But note that even this correction addresses what he had said about the attainment of a necessary condition (*non nisi;* cf. also *c. Adim.* 9), not a sufficient one.

[8] Kenney, Contemplation and Classical Christianity; J.-L. Marion, "*Idipsum*: The Name of God according to Augustine," in *Orthodox Readings of Augustine*, eds. G. E. Demacopoulos and A. Papanikolaou (Crestwood, NY: St. Vladimir's Seminary Press, 2008), 167–189; R. Sorabji, "Time, Mysticism, and Creation," in *Augustine's Confessions: Critical Essays*, ed. W. Mann (Oxford: Rowman and Littlefield, 2006), 209–235, esp. 215–218; P. King, "Augustine's Encounter with Neoplatonism," *The Modern Schoolman* 82/3 (March 2005), 213–226; M. Gorman, "Augustine's Use of Neoplatonism in *Confessions* VII: A Response to Peter King," *The Modern Schoolman* 82/3 (March 2005), 227–233; Kenney, The Mysticism of Saint Augustine. On these works, see footnotes 1, 15, 16, 19, 28, and 40.

[9] According to Plotinus, all human beings are sensitive to beauty, though to greater and lesser extents. The lover matures by progressing from love of beautiful corporeal things to love of morally pure souls and sound ethical codes, to love of the various branches of scientific knowledge, to intellectual contemplation and love of immutable Beauty and Goodness themselves (cf. Plato, *Symp.* 210a–211c).

by sensory eyes with the immutable light that he saw with the interior eye of his soul, that is to say, his mind. He also says that this kind of light is seen by someone who loves: love knows it [*caritas novit*]. He reports that during the vison he was "shocked [*reverberatus*]" and "trembled with love and awe [*contremui amore*[10] *et horrore*]." In *conf.* 7.17.23, Augustine similarly says that he saw the "beauty [*decus, pulchritudo*]" of the "invisible things" "in the flash of a trembling glance." All of these characterizations are rather close to Plotinus' treatise *On Beauty* (*Enn.* 1.6.4):

> But about the beauties beyond, which it is no more the part of sense to see, but the soul sees them and speaks of them without instruments – we must go up to them and contemplate them and leave sense to stay down below . . . There must be those who see this beauty by that with which the soul sees things of this sort, and when they see it they must be delighted and overwhelmed and excited much more than by those [bodily] beauties we spoke of before, since now it is true beauty they are grasping. These experiences must occur whenever there is contact with any sort of beautiful thing, wonder [*thambos*] and a shock [*ekplēsis*] of delight and longing and love [*erōs*] and a happy excitement. One can have these experiences by contact with invisible beauties, and souls do have them, practically all, but particularly those who are more passionately in love with the invisible, just as with bodies all see them, but all are not stung as sharply, but some, who are called lovers, are most of all.[11]

Also present in Augustine's descriptions are features evocative of Plotinus' treatise *On Love*, which asserts that "the eternal nature is that which is primarily beautiful" (*Enn.* 3.5.1, line 45). In *conf.* 7.10.16, Augustine speaks of "beloved eternity [*cara aeternitas*]" and in 9.10.24, he writes with erotic overtones of a rapid insight by which he

---

[10] The various terms for "love" in Augustine are not mutually exclusive technical terms denoting different kinds of loves differentiated by different kinds of objects. Hence, in the *Confessions*, he speaks of philosophical love of transcendent reality by the terms *amor* and *caritas*, and he also calls the desire for money *pecuniae caritas* (*conf.* 5.12.22). See further discussion and texts in S. Byers, *Perception, Sensibility, and Moral Motivation in Augustine* (Cambridge: Cambridge University Press, 2013), 95–99.

[11] *Plotinus:* Enneads, trans. H. Armstrong, LCL 440 (Cambridge, MA: Harvard University Press, 1966–1988), in English, amended. All translations of Plotinus are taken from this work, sometimes with amendments.

made contact with that which he "loved"; that is, an "eternal" object for which he was sighing. Clearly, what Augustine "saw" – namely, "that which is" – was also intelligibly beautiful, and hence an object of philosophical love.

These similarities between Augustine and Plotinus are not surprising. Augustine says that he undertook his contemplative exercises in 384–386 in Milan under the tutelage of "Platonic books" (*conf.* 7.9.13–14, 10.16),[12] and we know for a fact that he read "books of Plotinus" in particular (in Latin translation) by 386.[13]

Now these parallels between Augustine's texts and those of Plotinus allow us to figure out what "that which is" should be. Plotinus is talking in these two texts about seeing the intelligible ideas inside the Divine Intellect, the second divine entity (*hypostasis*[14]) of his tritheistic[15] hierarchy. He says in *Enn.* 1.6.9, lines 34–37:

> First the soul will come in its ascent to Intellect and there will know the Forms, all beautiful, and affirm that these, the Ideas, are Beauty; for all things are beautiful by these, by the products of Intellect and Being.

---

[12] Augustine, *conf.* 6.11.18 gives his age for the move to Milan as thirty (i.e., the year 384), and the contemplative experiences are said to occur before his decision to be baptized (in July 386: *conf.* 8.11.26–27).

[13] In *b. vita* 1.4 (dated 386), Augustine says that he read books of Plotinus (*libri Plotini*); he also mentions Plotinus in *sol.* 1.4 (dated 386/387), *c. Acad.* 3.18 (dated 386). Presumably these were the (nonextant) translations of Marius Victorinus (see *conf.* 8.2.3). So, *pace* M. Nussbaum, *Upheavals of Thought: The Intelligence of Emotions* (Cambridge: Cambridge University Press, 2001), 531, n. 3, there is no doubt that Augustine read works by Plotinus (in a Latin translation). See O'Donnell, *Augustine: Confessions*, vol. 2, 421, and J. Rist, "Plotinus and Christian Philosophy," in *The Cambridge Companion to Plotinus*, ed. L. Gerson (Cambridge: Cambridge University Press, 1996), 386–413.

[14] Porphyry calls Plotinus' three Gods "hypostases" in his headings in the fifth *Ennead*.

[15] *Pace* P. Athanassiadi and M. Frede, "Introduction," in *Pagan Monotheism in Late Antiquity*, ed. P. Athanassiadi and M. Frede (Oxford: Clarendon Press, 1999), 1–20, at 3 (cf. Kenney, *Contemplation and Classical Christianity*, 14), the monarchist polytheism of Plotinus is not accurately redescribed as monotheism. The point at issue in whether a theistic system is monotheistic or polytheistic is whether there is more than one god who is "divine" *in the same sense*. Neoplatonists like Plotinus think that immutability is the necessary and sufficient condition for being a God, and that there is more than one immutable entity, hence more than one God. To give just one of many examples, Plotinus begins *Enn.* 1.2.1 by asking "to which God" (mentioning the World Soul and Divine Intellect as two options) we are made similar by virtue. In contrast, Christian Neoplatonists such as Augustine assert that there is only one immutable entity, hence only one God; all creatures are mutable and therefore cannot be divine in the same sense as God, even if they can become "godly" by participation in the holiness of God (cf. *f. et symb.* 9.16).

Similarly, in *Enn.* 3.5.1, lines 32–36, Plotinus asserts that the eternal nature, which is primarily beautiful, is an "archetype" known by recollection. So *prima facie*, given Augustine's use of Plotinus, we should expect the object seen in the contemplative ascents in the *Confessions* to be a Form in the Divine Intellect.

This is in principle a plausible reading of Augustine's mystical ascents in the *Confessions*. Augustine had said just before writing the *Confessions*, in his *83 Questions* (compiled in 388–395), that the Platonic Forms are the proper objects of contemplation (*div. qu.* 46.2 *ad fin*), and that these are contained in the Divine Intellect [*divina intelligentia continentur*], also called the Wisdom of God or Son of God (*div. qu.* 46.2 with questions 16, 23, 78 [a gloss on Jn 1:3, "all things were made through him"], and 80). Then, in *conf.* 7, Augustine alludes to this Christianized Neoplatonic model when he says that the Platonists helped him to accept the Nicene account of the Son.[16] Thus it is possible that in our passages of *conf.* 7 and 9 he is telling us that he accessed Form within the second hypostasis or person of the Christian Trinity,[17] who is

---

[16] What he literally says is that the Platonists had an account of the Son as having the same nature as the Father (*conf.* 7.9.14), a reference to the Council of Nicaea's (325 CE) doctrine of "consubstantiality." The literal statement is inaccurate; Plotinus says clearly that the One/Good/Father (cf. Augustine's Father) is essentially superior to the Divine Intellect (cf. Augustine's Son/Wisdom) (e.g., *Enn.* 5.1.6, line 39). Either Augustine does not mean this literally, but means that Neoplatonism was an aid to his accepting the Nicene account of consubstantial Father-Son (I incline to this interpretation), or he is genuinely confused (presumably because he had not read all of the *Enneads*) and thinks Plotinus actually believed that the One and Divine Intellect were "consubstantial," as in Nicaea. A third possibility, that Augustine's "Platonists" is meant to include Marius Victorinus' pro-Nicene treatises on consubstantiality, seems to be ruled out by the fact that Augustine says the Platonists did not believe in the Incarnation, something to which Victorinus refers in these treatises. (For more on Victorinus' treatises and Augustine's eventual knowledge of them hinted at later in the *Confessions*, see the section titled "Which Form(s) Did Augustine See?") King takes Augustine literally, and supposes that he understood Plotinus' three divine principles to be triune, the same as the Father, Son, and Holy Spirit ("Augustine's Encounter with Neoplatonism," 216–218). Gorman takes issue with King, arguing that the passage is not really about all three persons of the Trinity, but about the divinity of the Son, and that in any case King has not shown how Augustine would have interpreted the three Plotinian hypostases as anything other than three distinct entities (i.e., tritheism rather than triunity/Trinitarianism), given what King himself says about the meaning of *hypostasis* at the time of Augustine, and what Augustine says about its Latin translation in *De Trinitate* ("Augustine's Use of Neoplatonism in *Confessions* VII," 230–232). King's article could have benefited from the work of Ayres cited in footnote 45.

[17] For these terms *hypostasis* and *persona*, see Augustine, *Trin.* 7.4 and 15.3; Marius Victorinus, *Adv. Ar.* 3.4.

called Wisdom in the Bible,[18] and who Augustine considers analogous to the second Plotinian hypostasis, which Plotinus also called "Wisdom [*sophia*]" (e.g., *Enn.* 5.8.4, line 36–5.8.5, line 25).

But why should Augustine use the term "that which is" or "being" to refer to transcendent Form? The answer to this is not difficult to discover; it lies in Plotinus' *Enn.* 5.8–9. It has been missed, however, by commentators who have assumed that Augustine was talking about seeing the nature of God and thus tried to make comparisons with texts wherein Plotinus describes contemplation of the One or the Good.[19] In fact, Plotinus states emphatically that the One or the Good is "*beyond being/s.*"[20] So texts about vision of the One or Good are not actually relevant to Augustine's claims to have seen "being."[21]

Plotinus' *Enn.* 5.8.1, *On the Intelligible Beauty*, asks how it is possible to ascend to contemplation of Forms in Divine Intellect, as distinct from seeing the Good that is superior to Divine Intellect. At various points in *Enn.* 5, Plotinus refers to a single Form as a "being [*to on*]," and to the multiple Forms as "beings [*ta onta*]."[22] The Forms are contained in the second divine hypostasis, Divine Intellect or Wisdom (e.g., *Enn.* 5.9.5, lines 24–25). Thus, in this idiom, the participle "being" is not typically a *generic* term meaning "immutability" or "immutable existence," but rather is used with the definite article, and in the plural, to designate the specific immutable Forms such as Prudence, Justice, *et cetera*. Hence Plotinus says of ascent to the vision of a Form in Divine Intellect:

> All those who are able to see look at him [Divine Intellect] and what belongs to him when they see; but each does not always gain

---

[18]   1 Cor 1:24 ("Christ the power of God and the wisdom of God").

[19]   So Sorabji, "Time, Mysticism, and Creation," 217; R. J. O'Connell, *St. Augustine's Early Theory of Man* (Cambridge: Belknap, 1968), 207; P. Henry, *Plotin et l'Occident* (Louvain: Spicilegium Sacrum Lovaniense Études et Documents, 1934), 112–115; Burnaby, *Amor Dei*, 34, n. 1, citing *Enn.* 6.7.36. See the *loci classici* (but these themselves cite earlier studies): P. Courcelle, *Recherches sur les Confessions de Saint Augustin* (Paris: De Boccard, 1968), 157–167; Solignac's notes and commentary in the *Bibliotheque Augustinienne* translation: *Les Confessions*, second ed. (Paris: Études Augustiniennes, 1992), vol. 1, esp. 679–689.

[20]   E.g., Plotinus, *Enn.* 1.6.9, lines 37–39; *Enn.* 5.1.8, lines 6–8 (referencing Plato).

[21]   O'Connell came the closest to seeing the centrality of Plotinus' *Enn.* 5.8, but like the other commentators he made no use of *Enn.* 5.9, and by including references to other *Enneads* that are not relevant, he showed that he did not quite see what is at issue (*St. Augustine's Early Theory of Man*, 207–217).

[22]   E.g., Plotinus, *Enn.* 5.1.7, lines 21–23; 5.8.9, lines 40–42; 5.9.5, line 12; 5.9.6, line 3; 5.9.10, line 14. *Ōn, ousa, on* is the (masculine, feminine, and neuter nominative singular) present participle of the infinitive "to be [*einai*]." The neuter plural is *onta*.

the same vision, but one, gazing intensely, sees the source and nature of Justice, another is filled with the vision of Prudence.

(*Enn.* 5.8.10, lines 11–14)

The historical-philosophical context for Plotinus' language of "beings" "in" Wisdom is twofold. First, as Plotinus himself notes, this use of the present participle "being" as a term of art for Form goes back to Plato, who called Form "being [*on*]" (e.g., *Enn.* 6.2.1; cf. Plato, *Rep.* 484c, 507b, 509b). Second, Plotinus is taking a position on the epistemological and metaphysical debate between Plato and Aristotle about whether Forms separated from matter exist extramentally or only in the mind.[23] Plotinus famously synthesized the two by holding that there are transcendent Forms that are in a Divine Intellect. Hence he, along with Porphyry after him, makes clear that the multiple "beings" or Forms are "in" Divine Intellect, Wisdom, or Beauty in the sense of within [*endon*] as opposed to outside of [*ouk exō*] it.[24]

Augustine's phrase "that which is [*id quod est*]" in *conf.* 7.17.23 is equivalent, in Latin, to the Greek participle *to on* ("the thing which is"). His verbal noun "being [*esse*]," which he says is "in Wisdom" in *conf.* 9.10.24, could in principle be a rendering of this Plotinian "being" as well, given that classical Latin has no proper present participle for the verb "to be."[25] So, it is plausible that Augustine is saying he saw a Form, called a "that which is," or a "being," by Plotinus. But in what sense is a Form a "being"?

---

[23] Aristotle used the language of the "place of the forms [*topos eidōn*]" in *Anim.* 3.4 429a27–28.

[24] E.g., Plotinus, *Enn.* 5.5.1, lines 50–56; 5.9.8, lines 11–15; cf. Porphyry, *Vita Plotini*, 18.

[25] As is pointed out in a work sometimes attributed to Augustine, *gramm.* 4.31. Cf. the discussion in E. Bermon, "Grammar and Metaphysics: About the Forms *essendi*, *essendo*, *essendum*, and *essens* in Augustine's *Ars grammatica breviata* (IV, 31 Weber)," *Studia Patristica* 54 (2012), 1–10. On one occasion, Augustine hesitantly gives *essens* when searching for a translation for the Greek participle "being" (*loc. in Hept.* 3.32 [Lev 13:46]). But the fact that Augustine does not elsewhere make use of *essens* shows that he does not really countenance it. Bermon suggests that Victorinus, through an oral tradition via Simplicianus, is the/a source for this term *essens* in Augustine (Bermon, "Grammar and Metaphysics," 5 and 9); but this is hard to reconcile with the facts that (a) Victorinus himself gives *ens* rather than *essens* as a translation in *Expl. Cic. Rhet.* 1.28, and (b) if Victorinus were the purveyor of *essens*, we would expect to see him using it in his anti-Arian works, where in fact he instead leaves the participle in Greek (*Adversus Arrium* and *Ad Candidum Arrianum* [= *De generatione divini verbi*]), although he sometimes does translate the plural *ta onta* into Latin, as *ea quae sunt*.

"Being" has, in principle, veridical, existential, and predicative senses. The veridical (something is the case, a proposition is true) is rather clearly the incorrect sense for our present *Confessions* passages. Augustine's presentation in these particular passages differs substantially from others wherein he describes his seeing *that* some *propositions* he had read in the "Platonic books" were true.[26] Among other dissimilarities, here in *conf.* 7.10.16, 9.10.24, and 7.17.23, he says that what he saw had made him; that he touched Wisdom in which is being, and that he saw in a flash the invisible realities of God. He can hardly be saying that he was made by true propositions, or that there are propositions in God (since propositions are not simple). Furthermore, the explicit context of the "Platonic books" indicates that this would be a misunderstanding. As we have already noted, to see "that which is" in a Neoplatonic context would not be to recognize *that* God is immutable and immaterial; it would be to see an eternal Form, each of which is a divine idea.

As for the existential sense, we will be especially tempted to assume that "being" is equivalent to "God" in these passages if we classify Augustine as a figure to be grouped with medieval "onto-theologians" for whom "being" means "existence." Aquinas, the most famous defender of this thesis, carefully distinguished existence [*esse*] from nature or essence [*essentia*], and then asserted that these two are united in the case of God, who is defined as pure existence [*esse tantum*], a subsistent thing whose essence is its existence.[27] However, we should not assume that Augustine's "being" in Books 7 and 9 means "existence," given that he has told us he attempted these ascents on the basis of what he read in the Platonic books.[28]

---

[26] So Augustine, *conf.* 7.11.17–12.18, 15.21; cf. footnote 1.

[27] Aquinas, *De ente et essentia* 1.1, 4.6, 5.1 (chapter divisions cited here are according to the numbering in A. Maurer, *Thomas Aquinas: On Being and Essence*, second ed. [Toronto: Pontifical Institute of Mediaeval Studies, 1968]).

[28] Marion is correct that, for Augustine, God is not "being" in the way that he is for Aquinas ("*Idipsum*," 184–185); but Marion does not parse out the possible senses of the term nor avert to the fact that Augustine's glossing of *esse* and *idipsum* as connoting immutability is derived from Platonic ontology. Moreover, Augustine's presentation cannot be characterized as Biblical *rather than* ontological or metaphysical (so Marion, "*Idipsum*," 179–180, and 184). For Augustine this would be a false dichotomy, since he thought that the primary author of Scripture is God, who knows (Platonic) metaphysics and intends to tell us about it in verses such as Ex 3:14 and Ps 121:3 (LXX).

In fact, the Platonic technical term "being" for the Forms uses the predicative sense of "is."[29] It is a term of art for things that stably remain *what* they are. Clearly, the only thing that *fully* has the characteristic of "being," when "being" is thus defined, is an immutable object that eternally remains the same kind of thing that it is. In other words, only an immutable subsistent form is fully "being" in this sense. Accordingly, it is because Justice is just absolutely and eternally that it is called the "being [just]" in which all just particulars participate. What the individual Forms have in common, then, is that they are all being absolutely and eternally whatever it is that each one is being; hence they are called "beings."[30] Although it is counterintuitive for English speakers, when Platonists say that something "is" without qualification, they assume the listener will ask "Is what?", allowing them to mention the predicative adjective.[31]

So existence is not at issue in Plotinus' use of the present participle "being." The objects of the transcendent realm exist, and the objects of the mutable spatiotemporal realm exist; only the former are called "beings," while the latter are said to be "becoming." This latter term of art "becoming [*genesis*]" again goes back to Plato (*Tim.* 27d–28a) and designates objects that are subject to any sort of change – not just coming into existence, but the gain or loss of a quality, a quantity, a relation, and so on (e.g., Plotinus, *Enn.* 5.9.5, lines 32–48).

Notice in this regard that all our focus passages from the *Confessions* have the Plotinian motif of being *versus* becoming. Augustine says

---

[29] See, for example, the use of "is" and "to be" in Plato's *Rep.* 479b–c within a discussion of the predication of properties (beautiful, just).

[30] Kahn's discussion, citing Lesley Brown's study of Plato's *Sophist* and *Laws*, is apropos here: "She [Brown] shows that the relation between *einai* in sentences of the form *X is* and *X is Y* is like that between the verb *teaches* in *Jane teaches* and *Jane teaches French*. This seems true not only for Plato but also for Aristotle and for the language generally. Adding a predicate to *einai* does not change the meaning of the verb any more than adding a direct object to *teaches* changes the meaning of the verb *to teach*. From the point of view of transformational grammar, the longer form is more basic: *X teaches* is derived from *X teaches something* by zeroing the direct object. Similarly, I suggest, *X is* can be derived from *X is Y* by zeroing the predicate ... Logically speaking, every absolute or existential sense of *einai* can be seen as an abridged form of some predication" (C. H. Kahn, *The Verb "Be" in Ancient Greek: With a New Introductory Essay*, second ed. [Indianapolis: Hackett, 2003], ix–x).

[31] This is the source of the problem of self-predicating Forms, raised by Plato in *Parm.* 132a. It is because the sense in which the Form of largeness is a "being" is assumed to be its "being large" that the so-called third man problem arises. Plotinus, for his part, has no qualms about asserting that a human being here in this world below *is* human, and the Form/"being" Human Being contained in Divine Intellect *is* human, although one as image and the other as paradigm (*Enn.* 6.2.22, lines 42–46).

in the excerpt from *conf.* 7.10.16 quoted in the section titled "Problematic Interpretations of the Ascents in conf. 7 and 9" that what he saw was [*esse*], and that he who saw was not yet [*nondum esse*]. If we took "to be" in the existential sense rather than as the first of a pair of Platonic terms of art, then by this self-description Augustine would be saying that he *did not exist yet*. This of course is absurd. The correct reading is that "not yet" is a reference to the term of art "becoming." Augustine is saying that he, the seer, belonged to the realm of coming-to-be-and-passing-away, whereas what he saw did not. Compare *conf.* 9.10.24, where he says that, unlike the items in temporality, Wisdom does not come to be [*fieri*]: "those things come into being, both those things which were and which will be. But Wisdom itself is not brought into being but is as it was and always will be." The passage in *conf.* 7.17.23 similarly contrasts "that which is" immutably, with the objects of this changeable realm.

AUGUSTINE WAS KNOWING ONE DIVINE IDEA

Turning now to the details of these *Confessions* passages, let us consider four types of evidence for our theory that, when Augustine says that he saw "that which is," he does not mean that he contemplated God, but that he contemplated a Form within God. We have already mentioned the high antecedent probability that the contemplative achievements recounted in the *Confessions* are intended to be the intellectual "seeing" of Form, given what he said in his *div. qu.* 46.2,[32] and given that "that which is" is a technical term for Form in Neoplatonism. In the same text, as well as in works he wrote after the *Confessions*, Augustine makes clear that he held that there are multiple Forms in the Divine Intelligence (*div. qu.* 46.2). (He does not address the question of *how* God is still simple while having multiple divine ideas, although it is clear that he does hold this [see *conf.* 4.16.29].) Augustine must hold, then, that, if someone were to see one of the Forms, she would not be seeing the Godhead itself.

First, there are a number of distinctive items in Plotinus' accounts of Divine Intellect, or Beauty, and of ascent to this intelligible realm,

---

[32] Note the absence here of "being" as a name for Form. The reason is that in *De diversis quaestionibus* Augustine is not working directly off of Plotinus or Porphyry, but instead references a doxography offering a history of philosophy (perhaps it was Varro's *De philosophia*). Augustine signals his Neoplatonism here, however, by saying the Forms are contained in the Divine Intellect (*divina intelligentia*).

which appear also in Augustine's ascent passages in the *Confessions*. These distinctive elements occur in *Enn.* 5.8–9, where Plotinus also calls Form "that which is." Augustine repeatedly says that what he accessed was "there [*ibi*]" (*conf.* 9.10.24, twice). This is reminiscent of the way that Plotinus uses the word "there [*ekei*]" as a technical term to refer to the place of the Forms, Divine Intellect (e.g., *Enn.* 5.8.4, 9.6, 9.10). Again, Plotinus says that Divine Intellect is a light that "shines bright and fills those who come to be there"; it is as if it is "dawning upon them from on high" and "illuminates everything and fills it with his rays," "shocking" their intellectual power of sight (*Enn.* 5.8.10, lines 5–7 and 25–26).[33] This language of a superior light is also used by Augustine, who says that, when he saw a "being," he saw "an immutable light higher than his mind," which shone with radiant rays and "gave a shock to his mental sight" (*conf.* 7.10.16, 17.23). Plotinus compares the contemplative vision of a Form to eating nourishing food: truth is the food of those who contemplate the beings rather than things that are coming to be (*Enn.* 5.8.4, lines 1–4). Augustine similarly says that the being, truth, or light that he saw was "the food of the fully grown" on which he was "feeding" (*conf.* 7.10.16).[34] And when Augustine says that the transcendent light, or Wisdom, made all things (*conf.* 9.10.24), this too is already in Plotinus, who says that Divine Intellect or Wisdom has made all things that come into being and pass away (*Enn.* 5.8.5).

Notice, second, that in all three passages Augustine says things that seem to imply that he was *not* seeing the nature of God itself. He does not in fact claim to have seen "your invisible nature," *pace* Chadwick's and Constantine's translations of *conf.* 7.17.23. Augustine says that he saw "your invisible things [*invisibilia tua*]," a phrase more suggestive of the Plotinian invisible "beings" known by the lover of intelligible

[33] The suggestion of Theiler that Augustine's "shock of sight [*ictus aspectus*]" (*conf.* 7.17.23) is from Plotinus' *Enn.* 5.5.7, line 10 [*athroōs*] would be convincing were it not for the fact that 5.8.10 has the same idea [*exeplēxe*, line 7] in addition to the other similarities to *conf.* 7.10.16 and 7.17.23 that are already noted (W. Theiler, *Forschungen zum Neuplatonismus* [Berlin: De Gruyter, 1966], 237).

[34] Cf. Augustine, *conf.* 7.17.23 *ad fin.*; 9.10.24. The parallel between eating in the two texts was noticed by O'Connell, *St. Augustine's Early Theory of Man*, 212. Kenney suggests that there is a Eucharistic allusion here (*The Mysticism of Saint Augustine*, 58). The phrase most suggestive of Eucharistic imagery is Augustine's claim that he would be transformed into what he was eating; but in fact this seems to mean that he would become wise by seeing an Idea in Wisdom, beautiful by seeing a Beauty (cf. Plotinus, *Enn.* 5.8.11). For Augustine next says that the food *became* incarnate. So the "food" is the eternal truth, metaphysically prior to the Incarnation and therefore to the Eucharist.

beauty, than it is of the singular nature of the Trinitarian Godhead. In *conf.* 7.10.16, Augustine asserts distance between himself, the seer, and God – when he says that in the very moment of the vision, the speaker of "I am who am" called to him from afar. This would be odd if he meant that he attained union with God himself. Furthermore, he says that he was struck by "rays of" God and that God "showed him that what he saw was." Both of these suggest that the "being" he saw was not strictly identical to God. Finally, in *conf.* 9.10.24, Augustine claims that he touched Wisdom in some small degree [*modice*], and says that he "sighed [*suspirare*]" after it. Taking into account the philosophical context, "some small way" most plausibly means that he had seen partial content of the Divine Mind, rather than the whole of it. The term "sighed [*suspirare*]" was shown by Courcelle to indicate an incompletely satisfied desire (*conf.* 9.10.24–25).[35] Now clearly, to see partial content of the Divine Mind, that is, to see a Form, would not be entirely satisfying, given Augustine's repeated assertion in the *Confessions* that our hearts were made to rest in the contemplation of the "face" of God. A Form would be analogous to one of God's features rather than his face, to continue the metaphor. Notice, too, that to describe the knowledge of a single Form as incompletely satisfying would be in agreement with Plotinus, who actually says that contemplation of a single Form is not a satiating experience, because there are other Forms to know: "There is a lack of satisfaction in the sense that fullness does not cause contempt for that [i.e., being/Form] which has produced it: for that which sees goes on seeing still more" (*Enn.* 5.8.4, lines 31–33).[36] Clearly, if Augustine describes his experience as unsatiating, then he cannot be saying that he saw the Son,[37] even momentarily. He thinks the Son is

---

[35] Courcelle, *Recherches sur les Confessions*, 224–245, cited in O'Donnell, *Augustine: Confessions*, vol. 3, 130.

[36] Plotinus here describes Divine Intellect's knowledge of its own discrete Forms; but the description would certainly apply, and apply preeminently, to human minds, which must know each Form successively if they know more than one.

[37] A view put forth, notably, by S. Menn, *Descartes and Augustine* (Cambridge: Cambridge University Press, 1998), 140–141, 154–155. This interpretation also seems to be implied by: H. Chadwick, *Augustine, Past Masters* (Oxford: Oxford University Press, 1986), 23; Burnaby, *Amor Dei*, 37–38, 41; Zum Brunn, *St. Augustine: Being and Nothingness*, 71. Note that in *conf.* 9.10.24, Augustine says that he and Monnica ascended *in idipsum*, literally into *idipsum*, into God (specifically, into the Son/God's Mind), and does not say that he saw *idipsum*. In *en. Ps.* 121.5–6 (cited by Marion, "Idipsum," 180–183), which is not about "seeing" being, Augustine actually calls the Son "being" [*esse, id quod est, idipsum*], in the same way that Plotinus sometimes uses synecdoche of part for whole ("being" for Divine Intellect as a whole, *Enn.* 5.3.5, lines 26–28). Augustine's usage in *en. Ps.*

God,[38] and that contemplative union with God is sufficient for happiness (e.g., *conf.* 1.5.5).

Third, Augustine's citation of Ex 3:14 ("I am who am [*Ego sum qui sum*, in Augustine's Latin]") in *conf.* 7.10.16 very likely signals that he is partly indebted to Marius Victorinus's anti-Arian treatises here. Victorinus, writing in the late 350s after having become a Christian, had "Niceanized" the Neoplatonic hypostases by making the Son or Divine Logos the site of the Platonic "beings" or Forms, explicitly citing Ex 3:14.[39] Victorinus' justification for the attribution was that the (Plotinian, Porphyrian) immutable "beings [*onta*]" are proper to the second hypostasis, and that the Septuagint of Ex 3:14 used this participle "being" when it said "I am he who is [*egō eimi ho ōn*]."[40] Augustine tells us plainly that he wanted to imitate Victorinus as soon as he heard about the famous man's conversion to Christianity from Simplicianus, Victorinus's much younger friend (presumably pupil), and that this occurred after he had already read Victorinus's translations of "the Platonists" (*conf.* 8.2.3). What would have been more natural than for Simplicianus to recommend that Augustine read the works that Victorinus had written as a Christian, the anti-Arian treatises, and for Augustine to follow up the suggestion eagerly? Augustine even seems to hint that he did so: Victorinus's anti-Arian treatises explain and rebut Photinus' position (*Adv. Ar.* 1A.28, 2.2), and Augustine tells us that he learned how Photinus' account of the Incarnation differed from the standard Christian view somewhat after [*aliquanto posterius*] he read the Platonists (*conf.* 7.19.25);[41] he tells us this shortly before he

---

121.5–6 is probably not directly from Plotinus, however, but from Victorinus, *Ad Cand.* 14, lines 25–27, where again "seeing" being is not at issue.

[38] We know that he held this from very early in his writing career, prior to the *Confessions*; it is evident throughout the *On True Religion*, for example.

[39] For Victorinus explicitly equating "being [*on*]" in the Son with Form (*forma*), see *Adv. Ar.* 2.4, lines 19–22. By "Niceanized," I mean the creed of the Council of Nicea in 325, which called the Son "consubstantial" with the Father.

[40] Victorinus, *Ad Cand.* 14, lines 22–27: "This is Jesus Christ. For he himself said, 'If it will be asked: who sent you? Say, 'He who is [*ho ōn*].' For only that being [*on*] which is always being [*on*] is he who is [*ho ōn*]'" (M. T. Clark, *Theological Treatises on the Trinity*, FC 69 [Washington, DC: The Catholic University of America Press, 2001]), in English. *Pace* Theiler there is no reason to think that Philo of Alexandria's mention of Ex 3:14 in *Life of Moses* 1.75 is relevant to Augustine in *conf.* 7 (*Forschungen zum Neuplatonismus*, 237).

[41] Note that B. Dobell's thesis in his *Augustine's Intellectual Conversion* (Cambridge: Cambridge University Press, 2009), 75–107 that Augustine was a Photinian until 395 is problematic, for more than one reason; see Byers, *Perception, Sensibility, and Moral Motivation in Augustine*, 185, n. 61.

introduces Victorinus himself in *conf.* 8.2.2. We also have a textual reason to think that Augustine had read Victorinus's anti-Arian treatises before the *Confessions*, perhaps much earlier. Augustine had already asserted that the Son of God was the subject of Ex 3:14 in his *f. et symb.* 4.6, written a few years before he started the *Confessions*; and he had done so in the same context as Victorinus.[42] So it looks like Augustine is using Victorinus's exegesis of Ex 3:14 in the *Confessions* as well as *On Faith and the Creed*. This in turn makes it likely that the "being" Augustine claims to have seen in *Confessions* refers to Form contained in the Divine Intellect or *Logos*, rather than to the *nature* common to all three persons or hypostases of the Godhead.

WHICH FORM(S) DID AUGUSTINE SEE?

We have seen a few reasons to conclude that when Augustine tells us in Books 7 and 9 of the *Confessions* that he saw "that which is," he is not claiming to have seen God as a whole or one of the divine persons, each of whom is equally God, but that he understood an eternal standard that God is also eternally understanding, thereby achieving a *union with God in the knowing of one divine idea*. This is a union that provides momentary intellectual possession or "embrace" of an intelligible beauty, because the Forms are intelligible beauties. The quest for this possession is therefore moved by love in the sense of desire to possess beauty [*erōs; caritas, amor*].[43]

Well then, which Form(s) did Augustine allegedly see? In *div. qu.* 46, where he says that only very few people can attain to contemplation of the Forms, the examples he gives are the Form of a human being and the Form of a horse.[44] It will not be surprising if the answer is along these lines.

---

[42] Victorinus' gloss (*Ad Cand.* 14) occurs in the midst of an account of how the Son is generated from the Father, and this is also the context in Augustine's *f. et symb.* 4.6. Victorinus' presentation is notably like Plotinus' discussion of the One's "generation" of Divine Intellect in *Enn.* 6.7.15–17, except that Victorinus is arguing for consubstantiality. This similarity between Augustine's *f. et symb.* 4.6 and Victorinus' *Ad Cand.* 14 inclines me to the thesis of L. Ayres in his *Augustine and the Trinity* (Cambridge: Cambridge University Press, 2010), 26–41 (partly citing Cipriani), that Augustine knew Victorinus' anti-Arian works from early on.

[43] See footnote 10.

[44] Cf. Plotinus, *Enn.* 5.1.4 lines 20–21. This parallel between Augustine in *De diversis quaestionibus* and Plotinus (which was not noted by P. Henry, *La vision d'Ostie: Sa place dans la Vie et l'Œuvre de saint Augustin* [Paris: Vrin, 1938]) suggests that Henry was right (on other grounds) to think that this (i.e., *Enn.* 5.1.4) played a role in

It seems clear that, in Book 7, it is the transcendent Form or pattern of a human being that Augustine is claiming to have seen. In *conf.* 7.10.16, he says that he saw that there was a contrast between the being that he contemplated and his own status as something in the realm of coming to be and passing away; and in *conf.* 7.17.23, he says that he turned his mind from sense-based representations and reflected on the power of reasoning, noting that reason is the specific difference of human beings. The latter statement evokes Plotinus's and Porphyry's method of attaining vision of the Form of oneself by abstracting from all images of one's accidental characteristics such as one's physical size (*Enn.* 5.8.9, 8.11; Porphyry, *Sent.* 40). Furthermore, if what Augustine saw was the archetypal pattern of human being, then it would have been germane for him to mention his having been made by God according to this pattern; and in fact he does say that what he saw "made him."

As for the object of contemplation in the other ascent (*conf.* 9.10.24), all we know is that it was the grasping of an eternal pattern of some created thing, as he indicates when he says that he ascended by wonder at the sun, moon, stars, and all mutable things and observed that all the things of creation say, "we did not make ourselves, but he made us who abides forever in eternity" (*conf.* 9.10.25). Augustine is again consistent with Neoplatonic methodology: in *Enn.* 5.8.9, Plotinus recommends starting from the sun, the moon, and the stars, and Porphyry cites the authority of Plato for starting the mystical ascent from the perceptible world, and continuing on to the intelligible.[45]

Given all this, the best way to understand Augustine's statements in *conf.* 7.10.16 that he saw a light, the light had made him, one who knows this light knows the truth, and truth is God is that he means God is incidentally "seen" by anyone who "sees" a Form and who also knows that the Forms are in God's Mind. Anyone who has seen London has in fact seen England, since London is in England, despite the fact

---

Augustine's presentation in *conf.* 9.10.24; see Henry in J. Pépin, "*Ex Platonicorum Persona*": *Études sur les lectures philosophiques de Saint Augustin* (Amsterdam: Adolf M. Hakkert, 1977), 137, n. 4.

[45] Porphyry, *Marc.* 10. If Porphyry's *Ad Marcellam* and *Sententiae* are being used by Augustine here, they are being used in conjunction with and secondarily to Plotinus. For, while Porphyry's texts do carry over Plotinus's terminology of "beings" for the Forms and his account of the contemplation of one's Form, they do not contain anything that we find in Augustine's accounts that is not already in Plotinus (see the sections titled "The Plotinian "Love" Context of All Three Ascent Passages", "Augustine Was Knowing One Divine Idea," and "Which Form(s) Did Augustine See?"). Furthermore, some of the points of similarity between Augustine and Plotinus are not found in these Porphyrian works.

that she has not seen the entirety of England. Similarly, if "the beings" are within God, then it will be true to say that whoever has seen a being has in fact seen God. Hence, because Augustine thinks that the beings or Forms are inside of God, he can address God as the locus of what he saw when he recounts his experiences. And because there are multiple Forms inside of God's Mind, no one of which exhausts the nature of God, he can say that he saw *a* Form without contradicting his position that one must be completely purified and must die to see God's nature itself.

CHRISTIAN OR NEOPLATONIC MYSTICISM?

Some commentators have wanted to say that all of these so-called mystical experiences are in some way Christian *as opposed* to Neoplatonic. Augustine's statement that he was "lifted up" by God [*tu adsumpsisti me*] to one of the visions in Book 7, for example, might seem to be a particularly Christian ingredient. Is this not a case of his general insistence on the human being's need for grace and the insufficiency of the human will damaged by original sin to accomplish any worthwhile action?[46] It turns out that the notion that seeing a Form requires divine aid is not particularly Augustinian or Christian, however; Plotinus himself describes ascent to Divine Intellect as a gift necessarily preceded by petitionary prayer (*Enn.* 5.1.6, lines 8–12; 5.8.9, lines 13–14). Notice, too, that Augustine presents his and Monnica's mystical experience in Book 9 without any suggestion of passivity on their part. He says that he and Monnica *stretched themselves* and thereby succeeded in touching "being" in eternal Wisdom (*conf.* 9.10.25, *extendimus nos*). This means that they willed to attain this vision; their ascent was moved by impulse to action.[47] Plotinus similarly says that in order to see the content of Divine Intellect we must "stretch ourselves out with our soul" (*Enn.* 5.1.6, line 10).[48]

---

[46] Du Roy, *L'Intelligence de la foi*, 72, 76; O'Donnell, *Augustine:* Confessions, vol. 2, 437; cf. Boersma's comments on Augustine's *De vera religione* (G. Boersma, *Augustine's Early Theology of Image: A Study in the Development of Pro-Nicene Theology*, Oxford Studies in Historical Theology [Oxford: Oxford University Press, 2016], 225).

[47] On will (*voluntas*) as impulse to action (the Stoic sense of *hormē* in Augustine, Seneca, and Cicero, see Byers, *Perception, Sensibility, and Moral Motivation*, 88–99, 217–231.

[48] The parallel "stretching out" was noted in Pépin, "*Ex Platonicorum Persona*," 139, n. 1.

We might think instead that the "mystical experience" in Book 9, by which point both Augustine and Monnica are baptized Christians, is Christian in a way unlike those recounted in Book 7, which are Neoplatonic. Book 9, it has been suggested, describes a "hearing" rather than a "seeing," and there are biblical verses that mention "hearing."[49] But this contrast will not work, on two accounts. First, Augustine calls his first ascent in Book 7 a "hearing" in addition to a "seeing;" and he identifies himself and Monnica as being in the role of a "seer [*spectator*]" in Book 9. Second, Plotinus himself describes mystical ascent as "hearing voices from on high" (*Enn.* 5.1.12, lines 15–21). Perhaps, then, Augustine's ascent in Book 9, because it was with Monnica, is being presented as an experience of Christian community, rather than a Plotinian communing of the "alone with the Alone."[50] But this contrast is complicated by the fact that in Porphyry we already have a model of a man and a woman united in contemplation of an intelligible Form/being (Porphyry, *Marc.* 10). If Augustine did not know this text, then it may be right that in Book 9 he *intends* to differentiate himself from what he knew of the Neoplatonists. Nevertheless it remains true that conceptually there is nothing particularly Christian about the idea of intimate friends jointly aiming for vision of the intelligible Forms.

In fact, the only substantive difference between Augustine and Neoplatonism here is one to which these commentators have not drawn attention. Augustine stipulates that the light in which he saw "being" "was superior because it made me, and I was inferior because I was made by it" (*conf.* 7.10.16). This sets him apart from Plotinus. The latter recommends, as part of the process of ascent, consideration of the fact that one's own soul *itself made all the things in nature* when it was with Plotinus' third God, Soul, prior to its fall into matter (*Enn.* 5.1.2–3). Thus, even when presenting the ascents prior to his baptism, in Book 7, Augustine insists upon a radical differentiation of creature from Creator. This is how he disagrees substantially from the Neoplatonic accounts that inspired him to attempt intellectual ascent to Divine Beauty.

---

[49] O'Donnell, *Augustine: Confessions*, vol. 3, 128, 133.

[50] J. Rist, *Augustine: Ancient Thought Baptized* (Cambridge: Cambridge University Press, 1994), 85, referencing Plotinus, *Enn.* 5.1.6. Cf. J. P. Kenney, *Contemplation and Classical Christianity*, 151.

Further Reading

Ayres, L. *Augustine and the Trinity*. Cambridge: Cambridge University Press, 2010.

Boone, M. "The Role of Platonism in Augustine's 386 Conversion to Christianity." *Religion Compass* 9/5 (May 2015), 151–161.

Brittian, C. "Attention Deficit in Plotinus and Augustine: Psychological Problems in Christian and Platonist Theories of the Grades of Virtue." *Proceedings of the Boston Area Colloquium in Ancient Philosophy* 18 (2003), 223–263.

Byers, S. "Augustine and the Philosophers." In *A Companion to Augustine*, ed. M. Vessey. Oxford: Blackwell, 2012, 175–187.

Cooper, S. "The Platonist Christianity of Marius Victorinus." *Religions* 7/122 (October 1, 2016), 1–24.

Kenney, J. P. *Contemplation and Classical Christianity: A Study in Augustine*. Oxford Early Christian Studies. Oxford: Oxford University Press, 2013.

Menn, S. *Descartes and Augustine*. Cambridge: Cambridge University Press, 1998.

Rist, J. M. *Augustine: Ancient Thought Baptized*. Cambridge: Cambridge University Press, 1994.

  "Plotinus and Christian Philosophy." In *The Cambridge Companion to Plotinus*, ed. L. Gerson. Cambridge: Cambridge University Press, 1996.

Sorabji, R. "Time, Mysticism, and Creation." In *Augustine's Confessions: Critical Essays*, ed. W. Mann. Oxford: Rowman and Littlefield, 2006, 209–235.

11 Memory, Eternity, and Time

LENKA KARFÍKOVÁ

MEMORY

Augustine's *Confessions* can be regarded as a "work of memory" in the broadest sense: it captures a new kind of personal identity created by narration that relies extensively on memory.[1]

The unity of Augustine's narration is created not only by the memory of his own experiences [*memoria sui*], or by his effort to acquire self-knowledge and integrity, but also, and perhaps foremost, by his testimony to the ways in which God treated him and his desire to know God [*memoria Dei*].[2] This is the reason why the exploration of memory – which Augustine undertakes in *conf.* 10.8.12–26.37, as soon as the account of his previous life is finished (Books 1–9) and a report of his current Christian existence begins (*conf.* 10.27.38–43.70) – does not take the shape of searching for oneself (even though he does find himself during this investigation), but searching for God.

During this process, Augustine arrives "in the fields and vast mansions of memory [*in campos et lata praetoria memoriae*]," from where, with his will, he elicits what he is currently looking for. In this way, he can gradually retrieve whole sequences of past events and give an account of them. Some of them are retrieved easily, while others require more effort (*conf.* 10.8.12).[3] But not even his own memories can be fully controlled by Augustine, because "from what point, by what path" they go, what they retain, and what they leave behind is determined, as he

---

[1] See J.-M. Le Blond, *Les conversions de saint Augustin* (Paris: Aubier, 1950), 6 and 16. On narrative identity, see P. Ricoeur, *Soi-même comme un autre*, Éditions Points (Paris: Éditions du Seuil, 1990), 167–180.

[2] J. A. Mourant, *Saint Augustine on Memory*, Saint Augustine Lecture Series (Villanova: Villanova University Press, 1980), 62–70.

[3] For the Latin text of Augustine's *Confessions*, I use the critical edition by L. Verheijen, CCL 27 (Turnhout: Brepols, 1981); *Saint Augustine: The Confessions*, trans. M. Boulding, WSA I/1 (New York: New City Press, 1997), in English, at times slightly modified.

himself says, by God (*conf.* 9.7.16). They do not succumb to the will in the sense that they sometimes "come tumbling out in disorderly profusion" when we are looking for something else, and with our "mental hand" we have to "push them out of the way" of our "effort to remember" (*conf.* 10.8.12). This motif of an unprompted memory is prominent in Augustine's account (see also *ep.* 7.3.6; *ord.* 2.2.7) and represents the reverse side of the proverbial coin: namely, his preoccupation with the will, which is noticeable in all of his work.

All this takes place in "the immense court of my memory [*in aula ingenti memoriae meae*]," where, Augustine goes on to say, "I also meet myself [*mihi et ipse occurro*]"; that is, my actions, their circumstances, and my feelings (*conf.* 10.8.14). Thus, Augustine's narration is conditioned by memory, but does he also find his God in his memory? In order to answer this question, Augustine must explore the basic types of contents of memory, especially images of things perceived by the senses, intelligible things, and notions of one's own emotions.

Images of Things Perceived by the Senses

Images [*imagines*] of things perceived by the senses that are stored in the "courts" of memory are arranged according to the senses they belong to: visual perceptions of light, colors, and forms; auditory perceptions of various sounds; olfactory perceptions of odors, and gustatory and tactile perceptions. All images enter through their gateways and are preserved in memory in order to be available to the thought that recalls them (*illic praesto sunt cogitationi reminiscenti eas*) (*conf.* 10.8.13). The images can be recalled from the "huge repository" of memory even if the things that left them behind are no longer present. It is possible to recall an image of white and black, of a song, of the scent of lilies and violets, and of the taste of honey and grape juice without confusing one image with another and without losing the ability to choose one over another (*conf.* 10.8.13).

Intelligible Things Themselves

In addition to this vast treasury of images representing things that are no longer present, memory also contains the things themselves, specifically the contents of liberal arts based on meanings (*trivium*) and numbers (*quadrivium*).

Although these items (related, for example, to the questions of "whether something exists," "what it is," and "what qualities belong to it") are also mediated by the senses, they are not present as images, but as things themselves [*res ipsae, quae illis significantur sonis*] (*conf.*

10.10.17). They did not enter memory from the outside through sensory perception, but they have always been in one's own heart (*ibi erant et antequam ea didicissem*), because otherwise one would not be able to affirm them as true (*conf.* 10.10.17).

The intelligible *res* have always been in our memory, albeit "so remote ... that unless they had been dug out by someone who reminded me, I would perhaps never have been able to think about them" (*conf.* 10.10.17).[4] "Lying hidden, dispersed, and neglected [*sparsa et neglecta latitabant*]," they must be "collected together" by thinking and "placed ready-to-hand by our attention [*animadvertendo*]." This is called learning. In this context, Augustine posits an etymological connection between *cogito* ("I cogitate") and *cogo* ("I compel"); thinking is then some kind of iterative compelling (*conf.* 10.11.18).

In addition to the logical contents, there are mathematical definitions and laws. Augustine also counts other things that have always been in our memory and wait to be discovered, such as, geometrical entities that we recognize within ourselves with our inner sight and the "numbers by which we count [*quibus numeramus*]," different from the "numbers counted in things [*quos numeramus*]"; that is, perceived by the senses (*conf.* 10.12.19).[5] Although these mathematical objects are also expressed in sensory signs, they cannot be perceived by the senses: they are objects of thought. Unlike their names, they are not part of any language (*conf.* 10.12.19).

Augustine also contends that we remember true and false arguments that we have heard about the intelligible objects, and we can discern the true from the false in our memory (*conf.* 10.13.20).

Notions of Emotions

As for the emotions of our soul [*affectiones animi*], memory does not store them in the way in which our soul experiences them. I may recall my joy, grief, fear, and desire, but such a memory does not necessarily evoke the same emotion. When Augustine, after many years, recalls how, at the age of sixteen, when he and his friends stole pears, he does not feel the dubious joy he felt at that time, but shame (*conf.* 2.8.16).

---

[4] Cf. Plato's idea of anamnesis as a recollection of what has always been present in the soul (*Meno* 81c–d; 85d; 86b; see also *Phd.* 74e–75b; 75e; *Phdr.* 246a–249c; 275a3–5). I have dealt with this motif and its reception by Augustine in my study "Augustine on Recollection between Plato and Plotinus," *Studia Patristica* 75 (2017), 81–102.

[5] Similarly, Augustine, *ord.* 2.15.43. On the difference between the "number by which we count [*hō arithmoumen*]" and "numbers counted in things [*to arithmoumenon kai to arithmēton*]," see Aristotle, *Phys.* 219b6–9.

Memory is like the soul's stomach [*venter animi*], which digests sweet or bitter food. This food (joy or sorrow) is stored here, but it has lost its original taste (*conf.* 10.14.21). Therefore, one can recall these emotions from his/her memory and process them further without experiencing their original effect. And yet one retains a memory of joy, grief, fear, and desire. Not only do we keep the names of given emotions in our memory, but also certain notions [*notiones*] of things referred to by these names (*conf.* 10.14.22). These emotions, too, are present in their images (or notions) in our memory, similar to things that are no longer available to one's senses (*conf.* 10.15.23). Unlike images coming from the outside, these are experiences of the soul itself, although not current ones, but stored in its "stomach."

Finding Oneself in Memory?

But how is memory present within itself? When I pronounce its name, *memoria*, I know what I mean. Is it only its image that is present to me, or is it memory itself? Can I even remember my memory if it is immediately present (*conf.* 10.15.23-16.24)?

As for forgetting, it is even more paradoxical. If it is present, it means that memory is missing, but if forgetting is not present, it cannot be remembered. And yet Augustine is certain that he can remember what it is like when he forgets; that is, when a certain thing escapes his memory (*conf.* 10.16.24–25). Moreover, forgetting that compromises memory comes in various degrees. When we try to recall a person's name that has slipped from our memory, we can recognize it and will not mistake it for another. Where did it come from, though, if not from memory? And even if someone reminds us, it is still found in memory when we recall the name. If it disappeared completely, we would not be able to recall it. We would at least remember that we have forgotten it. What we have forgotten escapes our memory completely, together with the fact that it has been forgotten (*conf.* 10.19.28).

Such, then, is the paradoxical nature of memory: "This is a faculty of my mind, belonging to my nature, yet I cannot myself comprehend all that I am. Is the mind, then, too narrow to grasp itself [*animus ad habendum se ipsum angustus est*], forcing us to ask where that part of it is which it is incapable of grasping" (*conf.* 10.8.15)?

Augustine's self-knowledge, which he gains during his analysis of memory, is highly paradoxical. In the mind's self-comprehension, there is always some evasive latency that can be brought to light only to some extent, and with great pains. This faculty of latency, resistance, and evasion is memory, liable to forgetting and to the danger of losing itself.

And yet it is only due to memory that Augustine can give an account of himself as well as find himself (*conf.* 10.16.25).

Finding God in Memory?

Searching for God in memory is similarly paradoxical. On one hand, Augustine is aware of the fact that, in order to find God, he has to overcome the strength of memory, a faculty that, to some extent, we share with animals. If he is to find God, he must search outside his memory beyond it. On the other hand, how could he find God if he were not in his memory, if he could not remember him (*conf.* 10.17.26)?

Augustine is familiar with the Platonic paradox according to which we can only search for what we already partially know (*conf.* 10.18.27–19.28).[6] In the course of his narration, he mentions a "memory of God [*memoria tui*]" (*conf.* 7.17.23), which had accompanied him ever since his ascents toward the immutable light of eternity, truth, and love (*conf.* 7.10.16), inspired by the reading of the "books of the Platonists" (*conf.* 7.9.13). But he is convinced that the "memory of God" does not first arise from these experiences. By seeking a happy life, which is what everyone desires, we are actually seeking God. Where, however, did we learn about a life of happiness so that we started to seek it? "Evidently we possess it in some fashion," says Augustine in *conf.* 10.20.29. We must have known it once, and, if this knowledge is a recollection (Augustine is not quite certain here), we must have been happy once, either individually, or through our forefather. It is a similar case to that of the recollection of emotions: not only do we know the name "a life of happiness," but we also have a notion of the thing itself in our memory (*conf.* 10.20.29). It is neither a mere image of the thing that we possess, as is the case with corporeal objects, nor the thing itself, as is the case with mathematical entities. We have a certain knowledge of a happy life, and yet we still long for it – perhaps in the way in which we long for joy amid grief (*conf.* 10.21.30). A happy life is actually a certain kind of joy, according to Augustine: "joy directed to God, about God, and because of God [*gaudere ad te, de te, propter te*]" (*conf.* 10.22.32), or, in other words, "joy over the truth [*gaudium de veritate*]" (*conf.* 10.23.33). All human beings desire joy over the truth even though they might not know its true nature. Nobody wishes to be deceived, not even

---

[6] See the "eristic objection" regarding the pointlessness of searching in *Meno* 81e2–5, from where Plato develops his idea of *anamnēsis*.

those who wish to deceive others, and therefore everyone desires the truth as well as the joy of knowing the truth (*conf.* 10.23.33–34).

In this sense, Augustine also found God in his memory because he already knew enough truth to be able to desire it. And yet, when Augustine learnt about God [*ex quo te didici*] (*conf.* 10.24.35), he did not find him in his own memory, but above himself [*supra me*]. Similarly, the truth does not dwell in each individual mind, but above it, without being in a "place [*nusquam locus*]" (*conf.* 10.26.37).

Although searching for God, for the truth, and for the joy of knowing the truth presupposes a certain kind of knowledge that makes the search possible, the mind does not find it in itself like mathematical entities, but far above itself, as a permanent vanishing point of one's effort and desire, not as a stated goal. This search, according to Augustine's antiskeptical conviction, would not be genuine if there was nothing to be found, even though the accomplishment (i.e., a happy life as the attainment of joy from God and from the truth) is, in Augustine's view, an eschatological goal that cannot be achieved fully in this life (*c. Acad.* 3.9.20). In our present life, we cannot achieve happiness itself [*in re*], we can only "hope" for it [*in spe*]. Even that, however, is much more than the vague memory that motivates the search (*conf.* 10.20.29). The transition from the vague memory of truth and happiness to the possibility of "hoping" for them is what Augustine calls finding God. Finding God, however, does not mean one should stop longing for and searching for God.

As we can see, Augustine both has and has not found God in his memory, just as he has and has not found himself. He already knew his God as well as himself, and thus had both in his memory, and yet he was able to find out even more about both of them, although not enough to prevent them from escaping him again. The obstacle to the attainment of full knowledge – and, at the same time, the condition of the searching it – is memory in its ambivalence: a treasury of memories as well as impenetrable escaping latency.

ETERNITY

God, too, according to Augustine, "keeps us in his memory [*nostri sis memor*]" (*conf.* 9.3.6; cf. Ps 135[136]:23). However, God's "memory," unlike the human memory, is not a mysterious opaque abyss, but a permanent and simultaneous presence of all things. Together with his Platonic predecessors, this is how Augustine understands God's eternity.

Eternity as a "Simultaneous" and Immutable Presence of All Things

As Plato puts it in his *Tim.* 37d–38a, eternity "abides in unity," while time is its "movable image." In their interpretation of this idea, the Neoplatonic authors maintain that, in eternity, which pertains to the divine Intellect, all things are present "simultaneously" – they do not change or pass – while time, as a product of the soul, develops this eternal presence into a transition from the future into the past.[7]

According to Scripture, too, all our past and future days and years represent a single "day" for God (cf. Ps 89 [90]:4; 101[102]:27; Heb 1:12). That is why Augustine can state that in God "nothing dies," and "the causes of all unstable things" "stand firm" in him (*conf.* 1.6.9–10). If things only changed and retained nothing of their identity, they would not be changeable things, but a sequence of completely different things. If they have something that abides so that they can be changeable, it is because they are rooted in eternity, in God's "today," which includes all their temporal development simultaneously. "If I do not abide in him, I shall not be able to in myself," says Augustine (*conf.* 7.11.17).

Eternal Presence of Temporal Creation in the Word of God

It was on this Neoplatonic idea of time rooted and contracted in eternity that Augustine built his exposition of time and eternity in the eleventh book of his *Confessions*. However, the text to which he refers is neither Plotinus' treatise *On Eternity and Time*, nor Porphyry's *Sent.* 44 on the same topic (it is disputable whether or to what extent Augustine was familiar with these texts),[8] but the biblical verse in Gen 1:1: "In the

---

[7] On eternity, see Plotinus, *Enn.* 3.7(45).3.16–23; Porphyry, *Sent.* 44.17–31; on time, see Plotinus, *Enn.* 3.7(45).11; Porphyry, *Sent.* 44.32–36; cf. W. Beierwaltes, *Plotinus, Über Ewigkeit und Zeit. Enneade III,7*, third ed. (Frankfurt am Main: Klostermann, 1981); A. Smith, "Eternity and Time," in *The Cambridge Companion to Plotinus*, ed. L. P. Gerson (Cambridge: Cambridge University Press, 1996), 196–216; S. K. Strange, "Plotinus on the Nature of Eternity and Time," in *Aristotle in Late Antiquity*, ed. L. P. Schrenk, Studies in Philosophy and the History of Philosophy 27 (Washington, DC: Catholic University of America, 1994), 22–53.

[8] On Augustine's Neoplatonic inspiration, see, for example, R. J. Teske, *Paradoxes of Time in Saint Augustine*, Aquinas Lecture 1996 (Milwaukee, WI: Marquette University Press, 1998), 20–22 and 33. The discussion of Augustine's (not very probable) direct acquaintance with Plotinus' *Enn.* 3.7 and Porphyry's treatise on time in *Sent.* 44 is summarized by K. Flasch, *Was ist Zeit? Augustinus von Hippo, Das XI. Buch der Confessiones: historisch-philosophische Studie: Text-Übersetzung-Kommentar*, Klostermann Rote Reihe 13 (Frankfurt am Main: Klostermann, 1993), 130–150; and P. Hoffmann, "Temps et éternité dans le livre XI des Confessions: Augustin, Plotin, Porphyre et saint Paul," *Revue des Études Augustiniennes* 63 (2017), 31–79, esp. 35–46 and 52.

beginning God created the heavens and the earth" (*conf.* 11.3.5). The word with which God created is not a sound with temporal duration (*conf.* 11.6.8), but his eternal Word, God with God (John 1:1), one that is "uttered eternally [*sempiterne*], and through him are eternally [*sempiterne*] uttered all things ... simultaneously in one eternal speaking" (*conf.* 11.7.9).

All things are eternally pronounced in the Word of God, and thus all things are created, but they "do not all come to be simultaneously, nor are they eternal" (*conf.* 11.7.9). Each thing as eternally abiding in its "eternal reason [*ratio aeterna*]" is given the beginning and the end of its being (*conf.* 11.7.10). Therefore, although it is eternally included in eternity, it is temporal or "defined [*finita*]" in time and space (*conf.* 7.15.21). The Word of God, with which all things are created, delimits each thing "from here and thus far," thus assigning its beginning, duration, and end (*conf.* 4.10.15). This is the mode or measure [*modus*] (*conf.* 8.3.8) of being of all created things, which go through growth and decay, or fall and rise [*defectu et profectu*] (*conf.* 13.33.48).

Double Eternity

This paradoxical connection of eternity and temporality in created things is very difficult to conceive, and human reasoning can easily suppress one at the expense of the other. Augustine expresses this problem by raising two doubts: (1) If creation is temporal, what did God do "before" he created it? (2) And if creation was not produced by some kind of new will in God, how come it is not eternal?

Augustine addresses the first, a Manichaean issue,[9] by employing the Platonic notion of eternity, which "stands forever," unlike time, which will "never stand still." In eternity, nothing passes, and everything is present "simultaneously," while time is never present all at once (*conf.* 11.11.13). "Before" God created heaven and earth there was no time in which God could be doing anything. God does not precede time in a temporal way, but he includes all future and past things into his eternity and thus precedes time by being elevated above it (*conf.* 11.13.15–16).

---

[9] While referring to the question of what God did "before [*antequam*]" creating the world (*conf.* 11.10.12), Augustine probably has Manichaean questioners in mind. However, the same question also appears in the Epicurean polemic against the Stoics; see Cicero, *Nat. deor.* 1.9.21; Lucretius, *Rer. nat.* 5.168–169.

As to the second question, it is surely not the case that there was a new motion in God and a new will by means of which he created heaven and earth. God's will is eternal, and, as such, it does not involve any change. And yet creation is not eternal, although it is included in eternity (*conf.* 11.10.12; 12.15.18). Not even good angels are coeternal with God because they, too, have their beginning and were created (*conf.* 12.15.19–20). Since they have a beginning, they came to be through change and, therefore, they can be affected by change [*mutabilitas*], even if they do not succumb to it owing to the fact that they are turned toward God (*conf.* 12.15.21).

As one can see, Augustine makes a distinction between the eternity that pertains to God (i.e., a complete absence of mutation and passing), and eternity in the sense of abiding, which pertains to angels, who are forever turned toward God. These beings are not temporal in the proper sense, but eternity is not part of their nature either. Instead, it is a consequence of their persistent clinging to God.

In Augustine's view, it is the participation in this kind of eternity in the sense of persistence, not the eternity of uncreated God, that is the eschatological hope for human beings as well (*conf.* 12.15.21). Presumably by analogy with eternity in the sense of persistence, Augustine also speaks of eternal perdition in other places (e.g., *civ. Dei* 21.2, 7, 12).

TIME

As we know from his previous account of eternity, time, according to Augustine as well as the Neoplatonic authors, is rooted in eternity. This gives unity and thus continuity to temporal events. Without such continuity, there would be no time because it would disintegrate into discontinuous fragments without inner coherence and succession. On the other hand, there would be no time without the multitude of stages, without the "variation of movement" (*conf.* 12.11.14) – that is, without the "changes of things" in terms of their forms (*conf.* 12.8.8). This is the reason why neither angels, who are immutably turned toward God, nor the (presupposed) formless matter, in which there are no forms at all, are temporal (*conf.* 12.9.9, 12.15).

In Augustine's opinion, which already crystallized in his early works, time is unification of a multitude of stages or persistence in mutation (cf. *imm. an.* 3.4–4.5; *mus.* 6.8.21, 11.29, 13.37). When, in the eleventh book of his *Confessions*, following the account of eternity, he poses the question of what time is, he is actually asking what makes time different from eternity, which gives time its unity. His analysis, however, leaves the framework of Neoplatonic metaphysics behind and focuses on how time is known to human beings.[10]

The Time of Passing Things

We know well enough, says Augustine, what time is, and we especially know that as we speak (*conf.* 11.25.32). The certainty with which we speak of time, however, falls apart if we are supposed to define time as such (*conf.* 11.14.17).

Augustine supports his analysis with the grammatical classification of time into the past, the future, and the present [*praeteritum, futurum, praesens tempus*], and he is well aware of the fact that time can never be void: "If nothing passed away there would be no past time; if there was nothing still on its way there would be no future time; and if nothing existed, there would be no present time" (*conf.* 11.14.17, cf. also 4.8.13: *non vacant tempora*). Thus, the first thing mentioned in Augustine's analysis is the relationship between time and temporal things.

The next step is the tendency of time toward non-being. The past (i.e., what took place in the past) does not exist any more, and the future does not exist yet. The nature of the present is such that it is constantly transformed into the past – if it did not, it would not be time, but eternity. Augustine interprets this skeptical aporia[11] as a certain paradox relating to time: we "cannot really say that time exists, except because it tends to non-being [*tendit non esse*]" (*conf.* 11.14.17). Time, in fact, is the time of things that are about to reach the end of their being: without these things and their passing there would be no time at all.

The Threefold Present

Yet, there are different ways in which we speak of time (at this moment, Augustine is interested in how we actually *speak* of time): we can speak of a "short" or of a "long" time. This can only be concerned with the past or the future and, therefore, we should not say, "That is a long

---

[10] This is the reason why Augustine's analysis of time is often accused of "subjectivism." However, this might be a misunderstanding that neglects the argument in the *Confessions* as a whole (cf. Teske, *Paradoxes*, 40–46).

[11] The objection regarding the nonexistence of time (because neither the past nor the future exists) is one that Plotinus (*Enn.* 3.7[45].13) and Aristotle before him (*Phys.* 221b31) also had to face. An elaboration of this objection (including the issue of the ungraspable present) can be found in the writings of Sextus Empiricus (*Hypot.* 3.19.136–150; *Adv. mathem.* 10.169–247), whose ideas bear a resemblance to Augustine's account: time cannot have a beginning in time and it does not exist outside the soul (see Flasch, *Was ist Zeit?*, 125–130).

time", but only, "That was or will be a long time." When was it long
though? When did it not exist yet? Or, when was it still present (*conf.*
11.15.18)? Can a present time be "long" at all? If the present, through
which the future becomes the past, has no extension [*nullum habet
spatium*], then it really cannot be "long" (*conf.* 11.15.20). On the other
hand, we still have a notion of the length of time (*conf.* 11.16.21). In
order for us to be able to measure what is the longer and what the
shorter time, time has to have extension [*spatium*] (*conf.* 11.21.27).
This, too, is a "most intricate enigma [*implicatissimum aenigma*]"
(*conf.* 11.22.28) of time, namely the paradox related to its length.

Perhaps it is the case that we are conscious [*sentiri*] of time in its
transition from the future into the past; that is, when it passes by. Can
we also measure [*metiri*] it when it passes by though (*conf.* 11.16.21)?

This analysis reveals the nonhomogenous nature of the present, or
its threefold structure: "the present of past things, the present of present
things, and the present of future things [*praesens de praeteritis, praesens de praesentibus, praesens de futuris*]"; that is, "memory [*memoria*]," "attention [*contuitus*]," and "expectation [*expectatio*]" (*conf.*
11.20.26). This motif modifies Augustine's initial idea of a present that
has no extension.

Time and Movement

If we are aware of time as it passes by, and if we can measure its trace in
our mind, it follows that time cannot be identified with the movement
of celestial bodies, as Augustine heard from "a certain learned man"
(*conf.* 11.23.29). Even if they stopped moving (which, according to
Augustine, is a possibility, cf. Josh 10:12–13), it did not mean that time
as such stopped. Events, such as the battle of Joshua and uttering a
speech, but also rest as an absence of movement still had their temporal
duration (*conf.* 11.23.29). Time, then, is not movement, and we do not
measure time by movement: on the contrary, movement and rest are
measured by time (*conf.* 11.23.30–24.31). Time is a kind of distension
(*distentio*) in which movement (or rest) takes place (*conf.* 11.23.30). But
what is it that we measure? Do we measure time, or do we measure by
time? If we measure movement by time, how do we measure time (*conf.*
11.26.33)?

Time as Distension of the Soul

In order to solve the last paradox related to the measurement of time,
Augustine focuses on the notion of time as distension in which movement takes place or speech is pronounced (*conf.* 11.26.33). How is this

distension – or time – measured? "Long" and "short" time is long and short distension, respectively, which can be observed, and the length is determined by the length of the observation (*conf.* 11.24.31). In other words, time is measured by the observation, and its "length" is the length of the distension of the observing mind: "I have therefore come to the conclusion that time is nothing other than distension [*distentio*]: but distension of what, I do not know, and I would be very surprised if it is not distension of the soul itself [*ipsius anim*]" (*conf.* 11.26.33). What is measured by the observation is not, however, the future, which does not exist yet, or the past, which does not exist any more. We measure time as it passes by, not when it has passed by [*praetereuntia tempora, non praeterita*] (*conf.* 11.26.33).

By way of exemplification, Augustine refers to the sound of a voice. The interval given by the beginning and the end of the sound makes it possible to measure its length, but, once the sound has stopped, it means there is no voice to be measured (*conf.* 11.27.34). Thus, we do not measure short and long syllables, which do not exist any more, says Augustine, but "something in my memory, something fixed and permanent there [*aliquid in memoria mea metior quod infixum manet*]" (*conf.* 11.27.35). Time is measured in the soul because what is measured is its own distension, the "impression [*affectio*]" that the passing thing leaves in it and that abides as present (*conf.* 11.27.36). What is present, however, is not the things themselves, but certain "words [*verba*]" or meanings formed from their images that these things, while they were passing by, left through sensory perception as "traces [*vestigia*]" in our minds (*conf.* 11.18.22–23).

As for the impression of a future thing, however, that can only be measured on the basis of a past thing with which we are familiar and the impression that it left behind: for example, when one is reciting a hymn in his/her mind. The idea of future lines that, when recited, pass from the future into the past is used to explain how time itself passes: "Our present awareness drags what is future into the past [*praesens intentio futurum in praeteritum traicit*]. As the future dwindles the past grows, until the future is used up altogether and the whole thing is past" (*conf.* 11.27.36).

Future things, which are used up, as well as past things, which grow, do not exist on their own, but only in the mind, which "expects [*expectat*]," "pays attention [*adtendit*]," and "recalls [*meminit*]." As time passes by, what is expected by the mind turns into what it remembers through what it observes. The present moment as the transition of the future into the past has no extension [*carere spatio*] – it "passes in an instant" as an ungraspable point [*in puncto praeterit*]. And yet the attention through which the present passes into the past has duration [*perdurat attentio*]. The quality of being "long" thus does not pertain to future or past time, but to the expectation of future things [*longum futurum longa expectatio futuri*] and the memory of a past thing [*longum praeteritum longa memoria praeteriti*], respectively (*conf.* 11.28.37). A "long expectation" and a "long memory" refer to a long-lasting attention [*attentio*]. A memory, as well as its future projection in the form of an expectation, "strains [*tenditur*]" (*conf.* 11.28.38) in accordance with the thing that our attention transforms from the expectation into the memory.

Time, then, according to Augustine, is the time of the observed thing (there would be no time without passing things), but only in the form of an impression that a passing thing leaves in the soul. The impression is distension of the soul itself – that is, distension of its attention into a memory and an expectation.

Without the attention focused on the present, which transforms the future into the past, there would be no passing of time because there would be no extensionless moment in which the future changes into the past. Without the distension of the soul into a memory and an expectation, there would be no continuity, which the passing of time presupposes as well. In other words, time as continuity and transformation presupposes distension of the soul, as well as its attention focused on the present. The soul must include both the extentionless attention given to the present moment, and the memory and the expectation extended in accordance with the passing things – that is, retaining their traces. If these traces are in the soul as present, then the present cannot be entirely extentionless.

The World-Soul

Augustine is naturally aware of the fact that the distension of one's soul can measure a hymn during a recitation or, at most, one's own life. Nevertheless, human history as a whole [*saeculum*], constituted by individual human lives, has its own time (*conf.* 11.28.38). Does our own soul measure it, too, by some kind of memory passed on through humankind? Even though Augustine is familiar with the notion of the memory of Adam's race (*conf.* 10.20.29), he does not employ it here. Instead, he poses the question whether "there is a soul whose knowledge and foresight are so vast, that it knows all past and all future things in the same way that I know a song that is very familiar to me" (*conf.* 11.31.41)? Such a soul would have to be "wonderful, so amazing as to fill us with awe [*nimium mirabilis ... animus iste atque ad horrorem stupendus*]" (*conf.* 11.31.41).

This soul, however, cannot be God, as Augustine makes clear ("But far be it from us to suppose that you ... know all things future and past in this fashion! [*Sed absit ut tu ... ita noveris omnia futura et praeterita*]" [*conf.* 11.31.41]), because God's knowledge is not temporal. God does not expect the future or remember the past, but abides in unchangeable eternity [*inconmutabiliter aeternus*] (*conf.* 11.31.41), where all is present to him "simultaneously," as we have discussed. This soul would have to be created because there is no time without creation (*conf.* 11.13.15). On the other hand, it would probably not be angelic mind because such a spirit, although created, does not succumb to time (*conf.* 12.15.19–21). Some scholars are of the opinion – probably rightly so – that what Augustine is referring to is some kind of Platonic world-soul, an idea with which he was familiar and that he regarded as a legitimate (although arguable) hypothesis.[12]

Dispersion in Time and the "Stretching" for the Eschatological Future

The human soul, as Augustine puts it, distends in time without being always able to genuinely unite it: sometimes it is "eating up time" as it is "eaten by it" (*conf.* 9.4.10). Its temporal nature, however, can be realized not only as "dispersion" between the past and the future, which will also pass away [*distentus*], but also as "stretching [*extentus*]" to the eschatological future. In other words, it can be not only "distension [*secundum distentionem*]," but it may turn into "focused attention [*secundum intentionem*]" toward that which does not pass away. This unification is carried out by the soul, but soul's own unity is due to the mediator between the divine unity and created multitude [*inter te*

---

[12] See R. J. Teske, "The World-Soul and Time in St. Augustine," *Augustinian Studies* 14 (1983), 75–92; Teske, *Paradoxes*, 46–56 (the author, however, mistakenly identifies the world-soul with the soul as hypostasis – that is, the unity of all souls). In his other works from the same period as the *Confessions*, Augustine states explicitly that he cannot answer the question regarding the world-soul (see *cons. Ev.* 1.23.35); even though he is certain that God is not the world-soul (see *Gen. litt.* 7.4.6) because the world-soul would have to be created (*retr.* 1.11.4); cf. Flasch *Was ist Zeit?*, 404–415; A.-I. Bouton-Touboulic, *L'ordre caché. La notion d'ordre chez saint Augustin* (Paris: Institut d'études augustiniennes, 2004), 201–210; Hoffmann, "Temps et éternité," 54–59 (even though the author rightly points out inaccuracies in Teske's concept of the world-soul, his rejection of the existence of the world-soul as such in Augustine's thinking is not convincing).

unum et nos multos]; namely, the Word of God that not only created the world, but even entered time (*conf.* 11.29.39).[13]

Time and Speech

In Augustine's opinion, time does not originate in the soul and its curiosity, as Plotinus would have it (*Enn.* 3.7[45].11.15–20). Similarly to Plato's *Tim.* 38b, Augustine posits that time was created together with the world, and its creator is undisputedly God himself (*conf.* 11.13.16–14.17). On the other hand, even in Augustine's analysis, the soul is an executor of time because it retains passing things and establishes their intervals. However, it did not achieve unity, thanks to which it concentrates time, on its own, but owes it to its rootedness in eternity. It does not manage to concentrate time from the devastating dispersion on its own either, but thanks to the mediator between unity and plurality – namely, to the Word of God that entered time.

What stands out in Augustine's theory when compared with the Neoplatonic authors is, among others, the relationship between time and speech, where speech functions as a mediator between unity and multitude. God creates by means of the timeless Word/Speech, in which all is pronounced "simultaneously." Through speech, in which time is present, human beings connect passing things into a whole and transform past or expected things into present ones (e.g., when, like Augustine in the first part of the *Confessions*, people tell the stories of their lives), thus performing their task of unifying the passing plurality. In passing things, like in syllables pronounced one by one, they try to capture a whole that can be grasped simultaneously. They rejoice at the unity even though it is a mere shadow of the unity that things achieve in eternity with God (*conf.* 4.11.17). A prerequisite of this task is the human ability to observe how things pass and connect them in time intervals. The three-dimensionality of the mind (its orientation to the present, the past, and the future), united in the present, provides the basis for speech, which, although it unites passing things, is of a temporal nature. (In this respect, it is a certain counterpart of God's atemporal speech, which provided grounds for temporality [*conf.* 13.29.44]). Speech thus appears as the culmination of the temporal task that the mind carries out by means of its triple structure; at the same time,

---

[13] Cf. G. O'Daly, "Time as Distentio and St. Augustine's Exegesis of Philippians 3:12–14," *Revue des Études Augustiniennes* 23 (1977), 265–271. On the polarity of *distentio-intentio*, see also P. Ricoeur, *Temps et récit / T. 1, L'intrigue et le récit historique*, Éditions Points (Paris: Éditions du Seuil, 1983), 19–53.

however, speech is the location of time and it must be registered by the mind and grasped as a whole. Perhaps it is due to the inseparable link between speech and time that the time riddle cannot be fully solved in speech; even so, speech remains a privileged place where this riddle can be displayed and a place where we are familiar with time (*conf.* 11.14.17).

Just as Augustine has no other source of narration than the bottomless and treacherous memory, he has no other way of dealing with time than human speech. Both memory and speech attempt to concentrate time into a kind of unity, which is enabled by the unity of temporal sequences in eternity, but they can only imitate this latter unity very remotely. Even this fragment, though, will make it possible to put together a story from Augustine's memories and his narration, a story in which he as the narrator finds not only himself, but also his God. Both these achievements, however, are only preliminary and both will continue to escape him, for it cannot be otherwise during our temporal life.

Further Reading

Flasch, K. *Was ist Zeit? Augustinus von Hippo, Das XI. Buch der Confessiones: historisch-philosophische Studie: Text-Übersetzung-Kommentar.* Klostermann Rote Reihe 13. Frankfurt am Main: Klostermann, 1993.

Hoffmann, P. "Temps et éternité dans le livre XI des Confessions: Augustin, Plotin, Porphyre et saint Paul." *Revue des Études Augustiniennes* 63 (2017), 31–79.

Meijering, E. P. *Augustin über Schöpfung, Ewigkeit und Zeit: das elfte Buch der Bekenntnisse.* Philosophia Patrum 4. Leiden: Brill, 1979.

Mesch, W. *Reflektierte Gegenwart. Eine Studie über Zeit und Ewigkeit bei Platon, Aristoteles, Plotin und Augustinus.* Frankfurt am Main: Klostermann, 2003.

Mourant, J. A. *Saint Augustine on Memory.* Saint Augustine Lecture Series. Villanova: Villanova University Press, 1980.

O'Daly, G. *Augustine's Philosophy of Mind.* London: Duckworth, 1987.

Ricoeur, P. *Temps et récit / T. 1, L'intrigue et le récit historique.* Éditions Points. Paris: Éditions du Seuil, 1983.

Teske, R. J. "Augustine's Philosophy of Memory." *The Cambridge Companion to Augustine,* ed. E. Stump. Cambridge: Cambridge University Press, 2001, 148–158.

  Paradoxes of Time in Saint Augustine. Aquinas Lecture 1996. Milwaukee, WI: Marquette University Press, 1998.

Von Herrmann, F.-W. *Augustinus und die phänomenologische Frage nach der Zeit.* Frankfurt am Main: Klostermann, 1992 (English translation by F. Van Fleteren and J. Hackett [Lewiston, NY: Edwin Mellen, 2008]).

12 Philosophy

GIOVANNI CATAPANO

PHILOSOPHY AND METAPHILOSOPHY

We can look at philosophy in the *Confessions* from two different points of view. First of all, we can look at it as something that Augustine concretely *does* within this work – that is, as a specific form of reflection and reasoning. From this first point of view, what we can see in the *Confessions* is the discourse on themes proper to the philosophical tradition – that is, the *philosophical* contents of the *Confessions*. However, in the *Confessions*, philosophy is present and can be studied in another way, as something Augustine *speaks* of – that is, as the object of his narratives and evaluations. From this second point of view, what we can see in the *Confessions* is the discourse on philosophy itself – that is, the *metaphilosophical* contents of the *Confessions*. Some of the major philosophical themes of the work, such as memory and time, are specifically addressed elsewhere in this *Companion*.[1] For this reason, the present chapter leaves aside the philosophy of the *Confessions* and focuses exclusively on the metaphilosophy of this work. In the following pages, the places of the *Confessions* in which Augustine speaks explicitly of philosophy, of the philosophers, and of their writings will be taken into consideration. These textual places all belong to the part of the work in which Augustine recounts his past, from childhood to conversion (Books 1–9). Consequently, an analysis of these places will reveal the way in which Augustine, at the time he wrote his *Confessions*, recalled and judged the role played by philosophy until his baptism at the age of thirty-two.

The *Confessions* contain thirteen occurrences of lemmata belonging to the lexical family of *philosophia*. This is not a very high number – in fact, it represents just over 2 percent of the total

---

[1] Another important theme would be matter. Cf. E. Moro, *Il concetto di materia in Agostino*, Flumen sapientiae 3 (Canterano: Aracne, 2017), 149–282.

occurrences in Augustine's *opera omnia*. However, this is a larger number than other fundamental works, such as *De Genesi ad litteram* (seven occurrences) and *De doctrina Christiana* (two), and only slightly smaller than the occurrences in *De Trinitate* (twenty-one).[2] To these thirteen occurrences, moreover, we must add the fourteen occurrences of the names proper to philosophers and of the adjectives that designate their schools: the Academics (three) and the Platonists (*Platonici*; i.e., Neoplatonists) (three) *in primis*, but also Aristotle (one), Epicurus (two), Cicero (four), and Seneca (one). The twenty-seven total occurrences in the *Confessions* are concentrated in sixteen paragraphs: four in Book 3 (3.4.7–8, 5.9, 6.10), one in Book 4 (4.16.28), four in Book 5 (5.3.3, 6.11, 10.19, 14.25), three in Book 6 (6.5.7, 11.18, 16.26), two in Book 7 (7.9.13, 20.26), and two in Book 8 (8.2.3, 7.17).

Beyond this statistical aspect, the metaphilosophical occurrences of the *Confessions* are interesting for at least two reasons. First, they are located along the essential stages of the spiritual journey that Augustine remembers and "confesses" in the first nine books of the work, and so they constitute a lexical gauge of the philosophical element present in the history of his conversion. Second, the particular context in which the occurrences are inserted sheds light on Augustine's conception of philosophy and allows us to establish a confrontation with the metaphilosophy of his early writings. It may be said that, in a sort of hermeneutic circularity, Augustine's relationship with philosophy and the philosophers helps us focus on some points in the *Confessions* account and, conversely, the *Confessions* make us understand more clearly the conceptual contents of Augustine's metaphilosophy and the extent of its evolution over time.

CICERO'S *HORTENSIUS* AND AUGUSTINE'S CONVERSION TO WISDOM

In a very famous passage in Book 3, Augustine recalls an episode in his school career that, in his opinion, had a profound impact on his life. When he was eighteen years old, while he was in Carthage to complete his studies in rhetoric, following the traditional cycle of reading the classics, he came across a now-lost work of Cicero. Augustine was

---

[2] Cf. the table in G. Catapano, *Il concetto di filosofia nei primi scritti di Agostino. Analisi dei passi metafilosofici dal* Contra Academicos *al* De vera religione, Studia ephemeridis Augustinianum 77 (Rome: Institutum Patristicum Augustinianum, 2001), 309.

impressed not so much by the formal perfection of Cicero's work, which for this reason was proposed to the students as a model to be imitated, as by its contents.

This book contains Cicero's exhortation to philosophy and is called *Hortensius* (*conf.* 3.4.7).[3] Here, for the first time in the *Confessions*, the term *philosophia* appears. Besides paragraphs 7–8 in Book 3, only in a few other places in his mature production does Augustine devote so special an attention to the word "philosophy" and its implications. The value of the passages in the *Confessions*, compared with those of other works, is increased by the fact that Augustine is speaking here of himself and of the role that philosophy has played in his personal history of returning to God.

According to Augustine's own words, the *Hortensius* changed his mood, modifying his prayers and transforming his aspirations and desires (*conf.* 3.4.7). His hopes for worldly success were debased in his eyes before the immortality of wisdom, for which he now yearned with unspeakable ardor. It was in this way that he began to rise again and return to God.

Augustine therefore explicitly places the encounter with Cicero's *Hortensius*, and with the philosophy to which it invited, at the starting point of his conversion. Pierre Courcelle, among others, has termed this as "conversion to philosophy."[4] Courcelle in particular was relying on the research carried out by Arthur Darby Nock on the various types of conversion in the ancient world, including that to the philosophical way of life.[5] In fact, in a text chronologically preceding the *Confessions*, Augustine compares his spiritual journey to navigation toward the port of philosophy and makes it begin precisely with the reading of the *Hortensius* (*b. vita* 1.4).[6] However, while in *De beata vita* the focus is on the stages that led the young Augustine to embrace the philosophical life – and therefore it is legitimate to speak of "conversion to philosophy" – in the case of the *Confessions*, it would perhaps be preferable to

---

[3] All the translations are mine and are based on the Latin text critically revised by Simonetti (*Sant'Agostino: Confessioni*, five vols., ed. M. Simonetti, Scrittori greci e latini [Milan: Fondazione Lorenzo Valla, 1992–1997]).

[4] Cf. P. Courcelle, *Recherches sur les Confessions de saint Augustin*, second ed. (Paris: De Boccard, 1968), 49–60; L. C. Ferrari, *The Conversions of Saint Augustine*, The Saint Augustine Lecture Series (Villanova: Villanova University Press, 1984), 1–17; R. J. O'Connell, *Images of Conversion in St. Augustine's* Confessions (New York: Fordham University Press, 1996), 5–8.

[5] A. D. Nock, *Conversion: The Old and the New in Religion from Alexander the Great to Augustine of Hippo* (Oxford: Oxford University Press, 1933), 164–186.

[6] Catapano, *Il concetto di filosofia*, 183–188.

speak of "conversion to wisdom."[7] The object for which Augustine burns with love is not, as in *De beata vita*, the kind of ascetic and contemplative life, free from all impediments, to which the name "philosophy" was traditionally given.[8] Rather, it is a condition, or better a transcendent reality, that has its seat in the sphere of the divine, as can be well understood from the beginning of *conf.* 3.4.8: "How burning, my God, how burning I was with the desire to return to You flying away from earthly things ... Wisdom is in fact close to you."

The *Confessions*, therefore, lay stress not on the love of philosophy, but on the love of wisdom. This is, after all, the very meaning of the word *philo-sophia*, as Augustine takes care to specify: "The love of wisdom [*amor sapientiae*], instead, has a Greek name, 'philosophy,' by which that work inflamed me" (*conf.* 3.4.8). This etymological explanation, in itself, is not at all original. Cicero had made use of it in his *Hortensius*, according to a testimony by Boethius (*Top. diff.* 2 = *Hort.* fr. 93 [Grilli⁹]), as well as in his other works (Cicero, *Leg.* 1.22.58; *Off.* 2.2.5). Augustine had taken this explanation up and had used it several times in his early writings (*c. Acad.* 2.3.7; 3.9.20; *ord.* 1.11.32; *mor.* 1.21.38; *vera rel.* 5.8).[10]

The identification of wisdom with a divine entity is also nothing new. Since the time of Cassiciacum, Augustine has borne in mind the Pauline verse in which Christ is preached as "the power of God and the wisdom of God" (1 Cor 1:24),[11] and the equation between the wisdom of God and the Son of God has since been one of the fundamental pillars of his theology.[12] If we take this into account, we cannot be surprised at two statements in *conf.* 3.4.8. The first statement, already mentioned, is that wisdom is "close to God [*apud Deum*]" – perhaps an echo of the prologue of John.[13] The second statement is that the passion for wisdom, aroused by the *Hortensius*, was dampened only by the fact that the name of Christ was obviously absent in Cicero's work. The young student had drunk the name of Christ with his mother's milk, so that

---

7 Augustine liked precisely Cicero's invitation in the *Hortensius* to love and seek not this or that philosophical sect, but wisdom itself (*conf.* 3.4.8).

8 Cf. Augustine, *c. Acad.* 2.2.4–5.

9 *Marco Tullio Cicerone: Ortensio*, ed. A. Grilli, Testi e manuali per l'insegnamento universitario del latino, n.s. 112 (Bologna: Pàtron editore, 2010).

10 Cf. Catapano, *Il concetto di filosofia*, 93–95.

11 Cf. Augustine, *c. Acad.* 2.1.1 and the passages mentioned in Catapano, *Il concetto di filosofia*, 58, n. 142.

12 Ibid., 96–97.

13 As well as an allusion to Job 12:13 and 16.

nothing without it was capable of completely winning his persuasion. Augustine, in reality, is telling us nothing other than that he had immediately associated wisdom with Christ, even before knowingly possessing the conceptual tools necessary to justify their inseparability.

Those who tend to consider the *Confessions* account as a more or less deliberate distortion of Augustine's youth, which would be more directly and faithfully related by his early writings, might object that here we are dealing with a conception that belongs exclusively to Augustine the bishop, who reinterprets his past according to the theological scheme, only recently elaborated by himself, of sin and grace. In fact, it seems quite evident that the author of the *Confessions*, valuing the meaning of "philosophy" as the love of divine wisdom, wants to suggest that the *Hortensius* was a providential instrument of his return to God in Christ. However, this does not necessarily imply that Augustine has radically changed his concepts of philosophy and wisdom in comparison with his early dialogues.[14]

It is interesting, in this regard, to examine the quotation from Col 2:8–9 with which Augustine continues his narration in *conf.* 3.4.8. He reports that, at the time when he first read the *Hortensius*, he did not yet know the words with which Paul had warned the Christians of Colossae of those who could have deceived them by means of philosophy. However, Augustine now says retrospectively that in Cicero's book the authentic meaning of the Pauline warning is clearly manifested, which does not condemn philosophy in itself, but the use of its name by those who seduce souls by attracting them to the elements of this world.

> There are people who seduce by means of philosophy, dyeing and embellishing their errors with such a great, attractive, and respectable name, and almost all those who were such at that time and before then, are censored in that book and unmasked, and that salutary warning of your Spirit is manifested there through your good and pious servant: "Take care that no one deceives you by means of philosophy and empty seduction

---

[14] Cf. the remarks made in G. Catapano, "La *philosophia* e i *philosophi* nelle *Confessioni*," in *Le* Confessioni *di Agostino (402–2002): bilancio e prospettive. XXXI Incontro di studiosi dell'antichità cristiana. Roma, 2–4 maggio 2002*, Studia ephemeridis Augustinianum 85 (Rome: Institutum Patristicum Augustinianum, 2003), 89–100, at 99–100, with reference to G. Lettieri, *L'altro Agostino. Ermeneutica e retorica della grazia dalla crisi alla metamorfosi del* De doctrina christiana, Letteratura cristiana antica. Studi (Brescia: Morcelliana, 2001), 549–558.

according to the tradition of men, according to the elements of this
world and not according to Christ, because in him dwells every
fullness of the divinity corporally (Col 2:8–9)." (conf. 3.4.8)

The same exegesis of Col 2:8, aimed at safeguarding philosophy as love
of wisdom and limiting Paul's condemnation to the "philosophies of
this world," had already been enunciated in Augustine's *mor.* 1.21.38.
Similar interpretations are also implicit in two of his Cassiciacum
dialogues: in *ord.* 1.11.32 and in the famous passage on the "system
[*disciplina*] of very true philosophy" at the end of the *c. Acad.* 3.19.42.[15]

Therese Fuhrer has corroborated the hypothesis, put forward by
Ragnar Holte, according to which Augustine's interpretation of the
Pauline verse was influenced by the Milanese cultural milieu.[16] If this
hypothesis is true, then we have another reason not to underestimate
the importance of Col 2:8 (the only biblical text in which philosophy is
mentioned [*dia tēs philosophias*]) on the formation of Augustine's conception of the relationship between philosophy and Christianity. Courcelle has shown that the Johannine prologue was the touchstone for the
balance of concordances and discrepancies between the "books of the
Platonists" and Scripture.[17] However, it must also be recognized that,
alongside the theology of the Word [*Logos/Verbum*], the principle that
guided Augustine in discerning the difference in value between the
various philosophies was precisely the distinction between philosophy
itself – defined in Cicero's manner as love of wisdom – and the philosophies of this world, rejected by Paul in his letter to the Colossians.

This distinction represents, in my opinion, the best key to understanding not only the episode of the *Hortensius*, but also all the other

---

[15] On Augustine's exegesis of Col 2:8, see G. Catapano, "The Development of
Augustine's Metaphilosophy: *Col* 2:8 and the 'Philosophers of this World',"
Augustinian Studies 38 (2007), 233–254.
[16] In the Vulgate and other Old Latin translations of Col 2:8 the adjective "this [*huius*]"
is missing (it is also absent in Greek: *ta stoicheia tou kosmou*), which instead appears
in Augustine's early writings and the *Confessions* (but not in *civ. Dei* 8.10, *ep.*
149.2.25, and *s.* 160.1.3). This may suggest that Augustine was making use of a
translation utilized in the diocese of Milan (T. Fuhrer, *Augustin,* Contra
Academicos *[vel De Academicis], Bücher 2 und 3. Einleitung und Kommentar,*
Patristische Texte und Studien 46 [Berlin: De Gruyter, 1997], 453–444, n. 84–85).
According to Holte, Augustine followed the exegetical tradition of the School of
Alexandria (Clement in particular), which was transmitted to him by Simplicianus
(R. Holte, *Béatitude et sagesse: Saint Augustin et le problème de la fin de l'homme
dans la philosophie ancienne,* Collection des Études Augustiniennes. Série Antiquité
14 [Paris: études Augustiniennes, 1962], 146–147).
[17] Courcelle, *Recherches,* 168–174.

places of the *Confessions* in which Augustine speaks of the philosophers. The first of these place is found shortly afterward in Book 3,
where Augustine narrates the way in which he let himself be captured
by Manichaean preaching (*conf.* 3.6.10). The followers of Mani managed
to get a grip on Augustine's soul because they continually named both
the things that Augustine was seeking: Christ and the truth. To the
young Augustine it must have seemed that Manichaeism could offer the
superior wisdom, united to the name of Christ, of which the *Hortensius*
had kindled his desire and that he had not been able to find in his
personal reading of Scripture. In reality, the Manichaeans did not really
possess the truth that they were emphatically promising – neither the
truth about God nor the truth about the world. Actually, it was not the
latter truth that Augustine was longing to possess, but rather the former
one – the Truth that God himself immutably is. Therefore, for the sake
of that supreme and subsistent Truth, Augustine should have overcome
not only the Manichaeans, but also the philosophers who had formulated theories on the elements of the sensible world that were much
truer than those of Mani:

> And they used to say, "Truth and truth," and they talked a lot about
> it to me, and it was never in them, but they were saying false things
> not only about You, who are truly the Truth, but also about these
> elements of this world, your creature, about which, for your
> sake, my most good Father, the beauty of all beautiful things,
> I would have to overcome even the philosophers who said true
> things. (*conf.* 3.6.10)

In this passage, the expression "for your sake" means "for love of the
Truth" and, therefore, it should be taken in the sense of "in virtue of
philosophy itself," understood as love of divine wisdom.[18] On the one
hand, there is philosophy in its most authentic meaning and, on the
other, there are the philosophers, who must be overcome to the extent
that they have known only truths confined to the sensible world.

ARISTOTLE'S *CATEGORIES* AND GOD

In Book 4 of the *Confessions*, Augustine presents his years from the
nineteenth to the twenty-eighth as the period of his greatest

---

[18] As noted by G. Madec, "La notion augustinienne de *Philosophia*," *Revue de
l'Institut Catholique de Paris* 18 (1986), 39–43, at 39.

commitment both to the liberal arts and to the practice of Manichae-ism, "there superb, here superstitious, everywhere empty" (*conf.* 4.1.1). In this book, we find precious information on Augustine's readings in those years and on the *De pulchro et apto (The Beautiful and the Suitable)*, his first theoretical work, written in 380/381 and already lost at the time of writing the *Confessions*. For our purposes, it is particu-larly interesting what Augustine says about his reading of Aristotle's *Categories* at the age of twenty:

> And what was my advantage that, at about twenty years of age, having come into my hands a certain Aristotelian text that they call *Ten Categories* – to that name, when the rhetor of Carthage who was my professor mentioned it with his cheeks crackling with pride, and others who passed for learned people [talked about it], I stood gaping, as I if was tending towards something undefinably great and divine – I read it alone and understood it?
>
> (*conf.* 4.16.28)

It is not known in which version Augustine read the *Categories* in Carthage. Someone has supposed that it was a translation with a com-mentary in eight books by Marius Victorinus, of which Cassiodorus informs us (*inst.* 2.3.18). Lorenzo Minio-Paluello has put forward, with great caution, the hypothesis that Augustine had in his hands the *Categoriae decem*, a pseudo-Augustinian work written in Rome shortly after the middle of the fourth century, perhaps by a certain Albinus or by Marius Victorinus, as later suggested by Anthony Kenny.[19] In any case, Augustine recalls that he made a theological use of that text, arriving at the erroneous idea that God is the subject of his attributes, just as a body is the subject of its qualities. Actually, God as such *coincides* with his attributes, while a body as such does not coincide with its qualities (*conf.* 4.16.29). What Augustine lacked, and what the *Categories* could not give him, was the concept of God as an incorporeal being. It will be another philosophical reading that will open up to him access to the spiritual level of being: the reading of the "books of the Platonists," as we will see.

---

[19] L. Minio-Paluello, "The Text of the *Categoriae*: The Latin Tradition," *The Classical Quarterly* 39 (1945), 63–74, at 66; A. Kenny, "Les Catégories chez les Pères de l'église latins," in *Les* Catégories *et leur histoire*, eds. O. Bruun and L. Corti, Bibliotheque d'histoire de la philosophie, Nouvelle série (Paris: Vrin, 2005), 121–133, at 133.

MANICHAEISM, NATURAL PHILOSOPHY, AND
ACADEMIC SKEPTICISM

The distinction/opposition between philosophy, which is oriented to
the transcendent, and the philosophers, who are prisoners of the immanent, emerges in all its evidence in the context of the subsequent
occurrence of the term *philosophus*. We have reached Book 5. Ten years
have passed since the events narrated in Book 3. In the meantime,
Augustine, who is now in Carthage no longer as a student but as a
teacher, has read many philosophical writings and has confronted them
with the Manichaean myths:

> And because I had read many texts by philosophers and had learned
> them by heart, I compared some of their doctrines with those
> long myths of the Manichaeans, and such doctrines enunciated
> by the philosophers, who were so capable as to scrutinize the
> world of becoming [*saeculum*] even though they had not
> discovered its Lord at all, seemed to me more probable than
> those myths. (*conf.* 5.3.3)

I propose to leave aside the problem of identifying what were the
philosophical writings that Augustine read and memorized.[20] What is
important is that he found the theories contained in them to be much
more probable than the Manichaean stories. Helping him turn away
from Mani's errors, these writings thus performed a providential
function.

Nevertheless, the *Confessions* dwells for a long time on denouncing
the limits of the authors of these philosophical texts (*conf.* 5.3.3–5.9).
Alluding to Wis 13:9, Augustine says that these philosophers were able
to accurately predict sun and moon eclipses, but did not notice the
eclipse of their hearts, which were obscured because they were far from
the light of God. Philosophers say many true things about creation, but
do not investigate with devotion the Truth that is the Creator and,
therefore, do not discover God; or, even if they perceive God's existence,
they do not worship him in the proper way. Their books are full of
worldly wisdom, but their calculations do not reach the true Wisdom,

---

[20] On this question, see the article by A. Solignac, "Doxographies et manuels dans la
formation philosophique de saint Augustin," *Recherches Augustiniennes* 1 (1958),
113–148, which is still irreplaceable. The "philosophical" texts that contributed to
determining Augustine's detachment from Manichaeism must in any case have been
of an astronomical nature, because they highlighted, by contrast, the rational
unsustainability of Manichaean cosmology.

who, as the Psalm says (147:5), is incalculable.[21] This Wisdom is the Word through whom God created the universe – that is, the only-begotten Son of God who "became for us wisdom, justice, sanctification, and redemption" (1 Cor 1:30). The knowledge of physical realities that the books of these philosophers provide does not give happiness. On the contrary, the person who knows God is happy, even if he/she ignored the explanation of solstices, equinoxes, and eclipses.

Here, then, Augustine is clearly opposing, once again, the love of true Wisdom to the "philosophies of this world." Similarly, in *De moribus*, Augustine had built the antithesis between the love of wisdom, designated by the name "philosophy," and the curious investigation of the physical world *(mor.* 1.21.38).

Let's return to the story of the *Confessions*. Augustine has moved to Rome, hoping to find more disciplined students than the Carthaginian ones. Disappointed by the promises not kept by the Manicheans,[22] and still struck by their objections against the Catholic Church and Scripture, Augustine now despairs of finding the truth and, therefore, thinks that neo-Academic skepticism ultimately represents the most prudent position:

> In fact, the thought also occurred to me that the philosophers called "Academics" had been more prudent than all the others, for they had been of the opinion that they should doubt everything and had determined that nothing true can be understood by a human being.
> *(conf.* 5.10.19)

This (provisional) influence of the Academics[23] reinforces that of the aforementioned philosophers and prompts Augustine to abandon Manichaeism. Augustine now esteems the philosophers more than the Manichaeans; yet he refuses to entrust the philosophers with the care of the sickness of his soul, because they lack the name of Christ.[24]

---

[21] The opposition between the wisdom of the world and the wisdom of God derives from 1 Cor 1:17–3:4. For the patristic reworkings, see Holte, *Béatitude et sagesse*, 143–152; H. A. Wolfson, *The Philosophy of the Church Fathers* (Cambridge, MA: Harvard University Press, 1956), 1–23.

[22] He was struck, for example, by the scarce culture of the Manichaean bishop Faustus, who was incompetent in the liberal arts and had read only "some orations of Cicero, very few books of Seneca, and a few volumes of poets and of his own sect," written in Latin *(conf.* 5.6.11).

[23] Also recalled in *c. Acad.* 2.9.23, *b. vita* 1.4 (where it rather appears as an intermediate moment between the abandonment of Manichaeism and the achievement of spiritualism), and *util. cred.* 8.20.

[24] The same "defect" was found in Cicero's *Hortensius*.

Consequently, he decides to remain catechumen in the Catholic Church, until some certainty came to enlighten his path:

> But nevertheless, as I was pondering and comparing more and more, I judged that, with regard to the very body of this world and every nature that the sense of the flesh can touch, most philosophers had much more probable opinions. Therefore, in the manner of the Academics (just as they are esteemed), doubting everything and oscillating between everything, I determined at least to abandon the Manichaeans, not considering it my duty, at the time itself of my doubt, to remain in that sect, before which I was now placing more than one philosopher. To these philosophers, however, I completely refused to entrust the care of the languor of my soul, for they were without the salutary name of Christ. (*conf.* 5.14.25)

In the meantime, Augustine has learned an important lesson: human beings do not have sufficient strength to discover the truth (namely, the truth about God) with pure reason, so they need to rely on authority (*conf.* 6.5.8). Now, if there is an authority that has spread all over the world, why not believe that it was willed by God? This is precisely the case of Scripture – believing in its inspired nature is therefore more reasonable than not believing in it (*conf.* 6.5.8).

This was the most necessary and urgent faith for Augustine when, in Milan, he had already become accustomed to listening to Ambrose's sermons. As for the existence of God and his Providence, Augustine had always believed in them, despite the objections of which he had come to know through the many works of conflicting philosophers that he had read:

> Precisely this, in fact, had to be believed most of all, because no fighting of slanderous issues through so many writings that I had read of philosophers in conflict with each other managed to get that sometimes I did not believe that You exist, whatever You are (which I did not know), or that the administration of human affairs does not concern You. (*conf.* 6.5.7)

Augustine's philosophical readings were therefore not only of an astronomical nature, but they also touched on theological themes. Moreover, Augustine was aware of the doctrinal differences and debates among philosophers (a *topos* of very ancient origin). The philosophers, as we will soon see, were not only "philosophers of this world" in the materialistic sense of the term. There were also some among them who had opposed materialism and thus had come closer to the ideal of philosophy as the love of transcendent Wisdom. They were the Platonists, the encounter with whom Augustine will recount in Book 7.

CICERO AGAIN

Before coming to the crucial Book 7, let's recall the one that precedes it. Book 6 tells of how the second intellectual obstacle that had kept Augustine away from the Catholic faith came to an end. Thanks to the spiritual exegesis of the Old Testament practiced by Ambrose, he understood that the doctrine of the human being made in the image of God did not imply at all the absurd attribution to God of a human body, and in general that the apparently simple language of Scripture, accessible to all, was susceptible to a deeper interpretation and reserved for adequately prepared intellects. As a result, the Catholic precept of believing before understanding seemed reasonable to him, and the authority acquired by the sacred texts throughout the world seemed providential. After a skeptical parenthesis, the hope of finding the sapiential truth sought from the first reading of the *Hortensius* had been rekindled in him, but it was in conflict with worldly ambitions and passions.

> And above all I was amazed, giving myself a great deal to do and reflect, at how much time had passed since the nineteenth year of my life, when I had begun to burn with the study of wisdom, arranging, once I had found wisdom, to abandon all the empty hopes and the mendacious follies of vain desires. And behold, I was already thirty years old, hesitating in the same mud because of greed to enjoy the present things that fled and dissipated me, while I say: "Tomorrow I will find it; here it will be evident and I will keep it; here Faustus will come and explain everything. O great Academic men! Can nothing certain really be understood to lead one's own life? On the contrary, let us seek more carefully and not despair!" (*conf.* 6.11.18)

The reference to his reading of the *Hortensius* twelve years earlier characterizes Augustine's conversion in a philosophical sense, placing it under the banner of the *studium sapientiae*. Augustine's conversion begins when the loving desire for wisdom is kindled in him, and it continues until the desired wisdom is finally reached and the love for it prevails over any other love. Confirmation of this can be found in Book 8, when Augustine recalls for the third time the reading of the

Hortensius, precisely when he is telling his emotional reactions to Ponticianus' account of the conversion of two imperial officials.

> Then, with all the more ardor I loved those young men, whose healthy moods I was hearing of, for they had given themselves totally to You in order to be healed, with so much more execration I hated myself in comparison to them, because many of my years had passed away with me – about twelve years – since, having read Cicero's *Hortensius* at the age of eighteen, I had been excited by the study of wisdom and I was deferring the moment of being free to put myself in search of wisdom neglecting earthly success: Not only the discovery of wisdom, but also the search for it alone had to be placed before the treasures and kingdoms of the nations, even if I had found them, and before the pleasures of the body that surrounded me at my nod. (*conf.* 8.7.17)

Academic skepticism plays, in this process, a dual role. On the one hand, it contributes to detaching Augustine from the false wisdom of Manichaeism. On the other hand, it represents an obstacle to be overcome, insofar as it empties wisdom of every intellectual certainty and declares it unattainable on the cognitive level. The dialogue *Contra Academicos*, the first work Augustine wrote immediately after his conversion (*retr.* 1.1), both documents and justifies Augustine's judgment about the essentially antiphilosophical character of skepticism.[25]

Book 6 concludes with a reference to Epicurus. Augustine says that, at that time of his own life, he tended to put happiness in carnal pleasures, and the only thing that kept him from sinking even deeper into their vortex was the fear of death and of future divine judgment.

> And I used to discuss with my friends Alypius and Nebridius about the ends of good and evil [*de finibus bonorum et malorum*], claiming that Epicurus would have received in my soul the palm of victory, if I had not believed that after death remain the life of the soul and the extensions of merits, which Epicurus did not want to believe. (*conf.* 6.16.26)

These words clearly reveal an allusion to Cicero's *De finibus*, where, in the first two books, the Epicurean conception of the supreme good is examined and criticized. Implicitly, however, Augustine seems to denounce the limits of Cicero's position: without faith in the

---

[25] See G. Catapano, "Quale scetticismo viene criticato da Agostino nel *Contra Academicos?*" *Quaestio* 6 (2006), 1–13.

immortality of the soul and in divine judgment, the young Augustine would not have had compelling reasons to place another doctrine of the supreme good before that of Epicurus (or presumed so). What Augustine needed, as he explains shortly after the passage quoted, was to be able to think of the light of a beauty that the eye of the flesh does not see and that is seen instead in our inner self. It is, once again, the intelligible beauty, whose existence and knowability only genuine Platonism, among the ancient philosophies, has acknowledged.

THE "BOOKS OF THE PLATONISTS"

Finally, we have arrived at Book 7 of the *Confessions*. By now Augustine has finished his *adulescentia* (that is, he is thirty years old [cf. *conf.* 6.11.18]) and is at the beginning of his *iuventus*, "the older I was, the fouler was I in vanity, who could not think of any substance other than the kind that is usually seen through these eyes" (*conf.* 7.1.1). He conceived God himself as a body extended to infinity, however incorruptible, inviolable, and unalterable, and the relationship between the world and God appeared to him as the one between an enormous sponge and the sea in which it is immersed. Consequently, the presence of evil, in a world completely impregnated with a good God, was inexplicable to him. The solution of the problem of evil, and therefore the overcoming of the last intellectual obstacle on the way to full adhesion to the Catholic faith, were made possible thanks to the famous "books of the Platonists," about whose identity so much has been discussed.

> And first of all, wanting to show me how much You resist the proud and give grace to the humble instead, and with how much mercy You have shown to the human beings the way of humility, for your Word became flesh and dwelt among human beings, You procured for me by means of a man swollen with immense pride certain books of the Platonists translated from Greek into Latin, and there I read that is recommended with many and multiple reasons, certainly not with these words, but absolutely this same truth, that is, that *In the beginning was the Word.* (*conf.* 7.9.13)

The enigma of what these "books of the Platonists," translated by Marius Victorinus (*conf.* 8.2.3), were has fascinated scholars ever since.[26] Evidently, they coincide at least in part with the "very few

---

[26] Cf. M. Erler, "*Platonicorum libri*," in *Augustinus-Lexikon*, ed. C. Mayer (Basel: Schwabe, 2016), vol. 4, 762–764.

books of Plotinus" of *b. vita* 1.4. Various hypotheses have been put forward about the number and identity of these Plotinian books, but the absence both of literal citations in Augustine's earlier writings and of other information on the translation made by Victorinus poses a serious obstacle to the transformation of conjectures into certainties. In short, we do not know in what form Plotinus' texts were presented – that is, whether they were enneadic treatises such as we now read them, or they were accompanied by comments by Porphyry, or they were passages quoted by Porphyry himself in some of his lost works. In fact, there are various reasons to think that the "books of the Platonists" also (or exclusively, according to some) included texts of Porphyry. But exactly which texts is difficult to determine with precision, because of difficulties similar to those met with in the case of Plotinus. In addition, one must add the fate suffered by most of the writings of Porphyry, which are either completely lost, or only survived in a fragmentary state. The quotations of Plotinian and Porphyrian texts in later Augustine's works such as the *City of God*, finally, do not prove that those texts were part of the "books of the Platonists" that Augustine read in 386 – he could have learned about them later. It can however be considered out of the question that through the "books of the Platonists" Augustine directly met with the Neoplatonism both of Plotinus (with whose thought he may have unconsciously come into contact before, via certain homilies by Ambrose) and Porphyry, and that this encounter marked his thought more than any other on the philosophical level.

This decisive reading too is presented in the *Confessions* as the fruit of God's providential intervention. The "books of the Platonists" in fact contained a doctrine concerning the eternal Word of God and his relationship with the human souls that was substantially identical to the Christian one, but they completely lacked faith in the Incarnate Word and in his Paschal Mystery – a faith whose necessity Augustine discovered personally, by experiencing his own inability to remain in the ecstatic contemplation of God and by meditating again on Paul's letters (*conf.* 7.20.26–21.27). Nevertheless, the author of the *Confessions* expressly recognizes his debt to the texts of pagan Platonism: he was exhorted by them to return to himself and to enter his inner self, in order to see above himself the unalterable light of divine Truth, whose eternal being does not extend into space (here a spiritual substance!) and is the source both of the finite being of all other things and of their substantial goodness. The corruptibility of creatures is indicative of their goodness, because something that was not good could not suffer damage (that is, a diminution of good) by being corrupted. Evil is therefore not a substance, for, if it were, it would be either corruptible and therefore a good, or incorruptible and therefore an even greater good. Some parts of creation are considered bad because they do not suit others; in themselves and in relation to those which they suit, however, they are good, so it is wrong to wish that they do not exist. Not even iniquity is a substance, but it is the perversion of a will that distracts itself from God's supreme substance and turns to the lowest things. If we compare these statements, as well as the ascent to God through the analysis of the mind's capacity for judgment in *conf.* 7.17.23, with the basic theses of the *De libero arbitrio* (387–395), we will easily perceive the extent of the "Platonic" influence on the formation of Augustine's philosophy.

The last passage from the *Confessions* in which occurrences of the lemma *philosophus* appear is in Book 8, where Augustine reports on his conversation with Simplicianus, Ambrose's spiritual father:

> When, however, I mentioned that I had read certain books of the Platonists that Victorinus – once a rhetor of the city of Rome, about whom I had heard that he was dead as a Christian – had translated into Latin, he rejoiced with me for I had not stumbled upon the writings of other philosophers, full of fallacies and deceptions according to the elements of this world, while in these books God and his Word are insinuated in every way. (*conf.* 8.2.3)

Having known God and his eternal Word imperfectly, the Platonists represent not one of the "philosophies of this world," but a philosophy of the other, the intelligible world, as Augustine had specified in *c. Acad.* 3.19.42. Hence the consequence that Augustine will make explicit in the *City of God:* among the ancient philosophers, the Platonists are the most worthy of this name (*civ. Dei* 8.1).[27] Philosophies are not all of equal value, because not all are "philo-sophies" in the proper sense of the term.[28]

This criterion of discernment among philosophers, intrinsic to the very notion of *philosophia*, is eventually applied by Augustine, as is known, to the Platonists themselves of his time, who did not fully love

---

[27] G. Catapano, "L'uso del termine 'philosophus' nel *De civitate dei*," in *Conflict/Dialogue? Augustine's Engagement with Cultures in* De civitate dei. *International Symposium, Institutum Patristicum Augustinianum, Roma, 25–29. September 2012*, eds. C. Müller et al., Res et signa 11 (Würzburg: Augustinus bei Echter, 2015), 187–199.

[28] Not all philosophers "philosophize according to the elements of this world," as Paul attests in Rm 1:19–20 and Acts 17:28 (cf. Augustine, *civ. Dei* 8.10).

divine Wisdom, the Son of God, because they did not recognize his Incarnation in Christ.[29] The only true philosophy, then, is ultimately Christian philosophy, as Augustine will affirm in the course of his controversy with Julian (c. *Jul.* 4.14.72),[30] but as he had already suggested in his early writings.[31] It can therefore be concluded that the examination of the occurrences of *philosophia* and *philosophus* in the *Confessions* highlights the continuity, rather than the fracture, of Augustine's metaphilosophy with respect to the previous literary production of that great lover of Wisdom who the bishop of Hippo was.

Further Reading

Byers, S. "Augustine and the Philosophers." In *A Companion to Augustine*, ed. M. Vessey. Blackwell Companions to the Ancient World. Oxford: Wiley-Blackwell, 2012, 175–187.

Cary. P., J. Doody, and K. Paffenroth (eds.), *Augustine and Philosophy*. Lanham, MD: Lexington Books, 2010.

Catapano, G. *L'idea di filosofia in Agostino. Guida bibliografica*, Subsidia mediaevalia Patavina 1. Padova: Il Poligrafo, 2000.

"*Philosophia.*" In *Augustinus-Lexikon*, ed. C. Mayer. Basel: Schwabe, 2016, vol. 4, 719–742.

Domínguez, P. *Augustins Philosophiebegriff: Fides und Ratio im Hinblick auf die Glücksfrage*. Augustinus, Werk und Wirkung 4. Paderborn: Schöningh, 2016.

Madec, G. "*Philosophia: secundum Ambrosium - secundum Augustinum.*" *Medioevo* 28 (2003), 7–16.

Saint Augustin et la philosophie. Notes critiques. Collection des Études Augustiniennes. Série Antiquité 149. Paris: Institut d'Études Augustiniennes, 1996.

Mann, W. E. (ed.), *Augustine's Confessions: Philosophy in Autobiography*. Oxford: Oxford University Press, 2014.

Van Fleteren, F. "Augustine and Philosophy," *Augustinian Studies* 41 (2010), 255–274.

[29] Cf. *vera rel.* 4.6–7; *conf.* 7.9.14–15, 21.27; *s. Dolbeau* 26.59.61; *ep.* 118.3.17, 3.21, 5.33; *civ. Dei* 10.29.

[30] This point has been well highlighted by G. Madec, "*Philosophia christiana* (Augustin, *Contra Iulianum* 4.14.72)," in *L'art des confins. Mélanges offerts à Maurice de Gandillac*, eds. A. Cazenave and J. F. Lyotard (Paris: Les Presses universitaires de France, 1985), 585–597. A summary of Madec's studies on this subject can be found in G. Catapano, *L'idea di filosofia in Agostino. Guida bibliografica*, Subsidia mediaevalia Patavina 1 (Padova: Il Poligrafo, 2000), 233–253.

[31] Cf. Catapano, *Il concetto di filosofia*, 287–294.

13 Pride and Humility

NOTKER BAUMANN

The *Confessions* takes the form of a prayerful address to God and concerns itself with roughly the first thirty-three years of Augustine's life. According to O'Donnell, the main purpose for composing this work was theological rather than autobiographical.[1] Indeed, the *Confessions* can be seen as a *protreptikos* – a genre intended to encourage conversion.[2] In the *Confessions*, as well as among other things, Augustine speaks about the importance of pride and humility in his own life. Writing between 397 and 401, he reflected on his past life – a life that had been motivated by ambition and egoism – and realized that pride; that is, human reliance on self will and personal ability constituted the root of all evil.

Pride is designated by the Latin word *superbia*. A broad spectrum of other terms similar in meaning can be put together to express the various aspects of pride, such as *ambitio, audacia, cothurnus, elatio, exaltatio, fastus, iactantia, praesumptio, tumor*, and *typhus*, as well as *uana gloria*.[3] The Latin *humilitas*, in turn, can be translated as "humility." *Cognitio sui, confessio*, and *oboedientia* also have a role to play in this semantic field.

---

[1] J. J. O'Donnell, *Augustine: A New Biography* (New York: Harper Perennial, 2006), 65–86.

[2] On the *Confessions* as a *protreptikos*, as an "encouraging" or "hortatory" text, see E. Feldmann, "*Confessiones*," in *Augustinus-Lexikon*, ed. C. Mayer (Basel: Schwabe, 1986–1994), vol. 1, 1134–1193, at 1166.

[3] Cf. D. J. MacQueen, "Augustine on *Superbia*: The Historical Background and Sources of His Doctrine," *Mélanges de Science Religieuse* 34 (1977), 193–211, at 196–200; P. Courcelle, "Le Typhus, maladie de l'âme d'après Philon et d'après Saint Augustin," in *Corona gratiarum: miscellanea patristica, historica et liturgica Eligio Dekkers O.S.B. XII lustra complenti oblata*, Instrumenta patristica 10–11 (Brugge: S. Pieter-sabdij, 1975), 245–288, at 269–272; N. Baumann, "*Praesumptio*," in *Augustinus-Lexikon*, vol. 4, 884–887, at 886.

The themes of pride and humility run throughout the *Confessions*, offering important moments of reflection and contextual references. The conviction that God opposes the proud yet rewards the humble with his grace (e.g., Prov 3:34; Ps 137:6; Jas 4:6; 1 Pet 5:5) is one of the main themes in the *Confessions* and a dominant factor in the development of Augustine's theology.[4] Following the structure of the *Confessions*, this chapter brings to the fore the dialectic of humility and grace. In the conclusion, the results are summarized and systematically reviewed.

PUFFED UP WITH PRIDE

In a very prominent position – in the second sentence of the *Confessions* – Augustine wrote: "A human being longs to praise you, even as a part of your creation; a human being who carries his mortality about with him, the testimony of his sin and a testimony that you resist the proud [*quia superbis resistis*]" (*conf.* 1.1.1).[5] As Augustine demonstrated, God opposed the proud and eventually overcame the pride of those he wished to save. In the *Confessions*, Augustine took this idea up four more times to confirm that God would confer his grace to the humble (*conf.* 4.3.5, 15.26; 7.9.13; 10.36.59). All this underlines the significance of the connection between pride, humility, and grace. The narrative of the *Confessions* constantly employs the tension between *superbia* and *humilitas*.

God opposes the proud and lets the arrogant [*superbos*] grow old "without their knowledge" (Job 9:5 [Old Latin version]) [*conf.* 1.4.4]. Augustine writes that, as a child, he was disobedient [*inoboediens*] because he was "over-eager to win arrogant victories [*superbas uictorias*] in contests and to listen to false fables" (*conf.* 1.10.16). He had, nevertheless, already heard of the eternal life promised by the humility of Jesus [*per humilitatem domini dei nostri*], who had descended to the hubris of humanity [*ad superbiam nostram*] (*conf.* 1.11.17). Moreover, "It was the humility [*humilitatis*] of children, of which their bodies are a

---

[4] W. M. Green, "Initium omnis peccati superbia: Augustine on Pride as the First Sin," *Classical Philology* 13 (1949), 407–432, at 421.

[5] In consultation with M. Boulding, *Saint Augustine: The Confessions* (New York: New City Press, 1997); and P. Burton, *Augustine: The Confessions* (London: Everyman's Library, 2001), translation is mine.

symbol that you, our King, were commending when you said: theirs is the kingdom of heaven" (*conf.* 1.19.30).

Pride produces mortality:

> I was deafened by the clanking of the chains of my own mortality, the punishment for my soul's pride [*superbiae*] ... At that time you remained silent, and I removed myself ever further from you to sow ever more barren seeds of grief in arrogant [*superba*] depravity.
> (*conf.* 2.2.2)

In his arrogance, Augustine continued to distance himself from God. At the age of fifteen, he went to a pear-stealing "expedition." Looking back at this event, he realized, "Thus pride [*superbiae*] itself feigns sublimity; whereas you alone are God, supremely exalted [*excelsus*] above all things" (*conf.* 2.6.13).

Augustine contends that he began to swell with pride when, at the age of sixteen, he achieved a somewhat elevated rank in the school of rhetoric in Carthage. "I rejoiced in my own vanity and was puffed up with pride [*gaudebam superbe et tumebam typho*]" (*conf.* 3.3.6). Quick progress made Augustine proud. "At that time, during my capricious youth I discovered textbooks on eloquence and I desired to excel [*eminere*] in this discipline, motivated by the reprehensible and dubious objective of gratifying my human vanity" (*conf.* 3.4.7).

After Augustine had read Cicero's *Hortensius*, he was filled with a new longing for immortal wisdom and turned to God and to Christ, whose name he had learned to love in childhood. This also prompted him to examine the Holy Scripture.

> The result of my scrutiny was this: it is a thing not accessible to the proud and which remains hidden from the immature [*non compertam superbis neque nudatam pueris*]; it is lowly on entering but sublime as one advances [*incessu humilem, successu excelsam*] and it appears veiled in mystery. (*conf.* 3.5.9)

Augustine found himself unable to fathom the text of Scripture. "My puffed-up conceit [*tumor*] shunned its restrained style and my perspicacity failed to penetrate its depth of meaning" (*conf.* 3.5.9). He, Augustine, did not wish to be considered immature, but rather saw himself as a mature adult, puffed up by pride [*turgidus fastu*], and as having outgrown the Bible. However, he had yet to discover that the one who desired to comprehend Scripture, had "to bend his neck [*inclinare ceruicem*]."

FREE OF SIN?

Augustine thought of the Manicheans "whose pride [*superbe*] made them appear as idiots, displaying altogether too carnal an attitude and talking too much" (*conf.* 3.6.10).

He reflected on their erroneous understanding of God and creation, for example, in *conf.* 3.6.10. Manichees believed, for example, that not God but an evil being had created the living beings (e.g., *conf.* 13.30.45).

In contrast to prideful Manichees, Augustine emphasized that obedience was part of being human; it was a fundamental human disposition. A state, for example, functioned through compliance to the agreement made with its ruler. Therefore, how much more humankind had to obey [*oboediendum*] God, the Ruler and Lord of all creation (*conf.* 3.8.15)? Blame and sin were the consequences, if one forsook God, the source of all life, the one true Creator and controller of the universe and instead, through one's own pride (*priuata superbia*), worshipped a false god (*conf.* 3.8.16). Augustine used here an incisive expression, "private arrogance [*priuata superbia*]." A greedy and proud human being reduced the Truth to an object of private possession. By loving one's own, he/she sought to partially "privatize" the Creator, to reduce God to his/her possession, claiming to be the owner of the whole Truth. Yet Truth could not be monopolized in this way.[6]

Augustine concluded that whoever failed to acknowledge God as Creator and thereby him/herself as a creature was committing a sin. "Thus it is that through humble piety [*pietate humili*] the way leads back to you; you cleanse us from bad habits and are merciful regarding the sins that we confess" (*conf.* 3.8.16). An attitude of humility is linked to the confession of sin, which enables one to return to God, the Re-creator of humankind.

> During the nine years between my nineteenth and twenty-eighth years, I spent my time indulging in various cupidities [*in uariis cupiditatibus*] both as seduced and seducer, deceived and deceiver; both publicly as a teacher of the so-called liberal arts and privately under the pretext of religious practice. In the one with arrogance and in the other with superstition but in both full of empty vanity [*hic superbi, ibi superstitiosi, ubique uani*]. (*conf.* 4.1.1)

---

[6] Cf. B. Bruning, "Augustine's Concept of Pride: Ut cancer serpit (en. Ps. 1,1)," *Augustiniana* 63/1–4 (2013), 9–81, at 76.

So, Augustine too was motivated by arrogance. Therefore, it was good to make confession before God [*confiteri*] and to ask for God's mercy. Astrologers, on the contrary, suggested that the heavens were to blame for the urge to sin [*causa peccandi*]. Thus, a "spiritless being made up of flesh, blood and pride [*superba putredo*]" (*conf.* 4.3.4) might be free of blame, transferring it to the one who ordered the heavens and the celestial bodies.

While in Carthage, Augustine won a competition of rhetoric and the victory wreath was placed on his, as he put it, "sick head [*non sano capiti meo*]" by the proconsul, a distinguished doctor (*conf.* 4.3.5). "You alone can heal this sickness; you who resist the proud [*superbis*] and give grace to the humble [*humilibus*]" (*conf.* 4.3.5). In his lost treatise *De pulchro et de apto*, which Augustine dedicated to the Roman rhetorician Hierius, he is thought to have outlined his Manichaean-inspired aesthetic. Obviously, Augustine did not yet succeed in seeing God as the author of the beautiful. At that time, the highest and unchanging good for Augustine was the human mind, not God (cf. *conf.* 4.15.24). In retrospect, because he lacked humility, he experienced again and again the opposition of God to the proud (cf. *conf.* 4.15.26).

> I longed to stand there and listen to you, rejoicing in the voice of the bridegroom but I could not do so because the voices of my errors drove me out and the weight of my pride [*pondere superbiae meae*] dragged me into the depths. Because you did not yet permit me to hear the sounds of joy and delight and my bones did not yet exult as they had not yet been humbled [*humiliata*]. (*conf.* 4.15.27)

Augustine was burdened with pride and could not hear the voice of Christ among the many voices that he did hear. To hear the voice of Christ and to rejoice, he had to learn humility first.

GREED FOR FAME, WEALTH, AND MARITAL HAPPINESS

Book 5 encompasses three stages of Augustine's life that were connected with three different places: first Carthage, then Rome, and lastly Milan. In contrast to the "long-winded myths of the Manichees" (*conf.* 5.3.3), it appeared to Augustine that what the philosophers contended had a higher level of plausibility.

> For you are tremendous, Lord, and you look with concern on the lowly [*humilia*], while you regard the lofty [*excelsa*] searchingly from afar. You draw close only to those whose heart is

broken and the arrogant cannot approach you [*nec inueniris a superbis*]. (*conf.* 5.3.3)

While emphasizing the sublimity of God, Augustine stated that only the humble and reverential had access to God. "The learned rejoice and are boastful and in their impious pride [*per impiam superbiam*] draw back from your dazzling light and find themselves in darkness" (*conf.* 5.3.4), writes Augustine. The proud cut themselves off from the light of God. "They do not know the Way by which they can climb down from themselves to him and thus through him ascend to him. They do not know this Way and consider that they are exalted [*excelsos*] and as luminous as the stars" (*conf.* 5.3.5). Even if some writings refuted the assertions of Mani, his followers were still required to believe Mani. Augustine explained, "Clearly not only that of which he knew nothing but also that which was erroneous, and with the ludicrous and arrogant presumption [*superbiae uanitate*] ... to insist that his insights should be attributed to him as to those of a divine person" (*conf.* 5.5.8). Augustine's encounter with Faustus, a bishop of the Manichees, caused in him some fundamental doubts about Manichaeism. Their teaching on sin, however, seemed to have appealed to him:

> It still seemed to me that it was not we ourselves who sin but rather an unknown alien nature within us. It gratified my pride [*superbiam meam*] to be free of sin and if I committed a misdemeanour not to have to confess that I myself had committed it, so that you might heal my soul because it was my soul that had sinned against you. (*conf.* 5.10.18)

Evidently, humility also included perceiving one's sins as one's own, instead of taking no responsibility for them.

Augustine continued to search for certainty and was unable to believe unreservedly everything that he was taught. He described the Bible as a work that presented itself in a clear language and in a completely humble style [*humillimo genere loquendi*]. Scripture "gathers the crowds into the bosom of its holy humility [*gremio sanctae humilitatis*]" (*conf.* 6.5.8).

Augustine still eagerly sought fame, wealth, and marital happiness. However, these passionate desires were to bring him bitter hardships [*amarissimas difficultates*]. "The more you manifested your favour to me, the less you left me to wallow in something other than yourself" (*conf.* 6.6.9). In Bishop Augustine's eyes, God was assisting him with grace.

After he had delivered a *laudatio* to the Emperor Valentinian II, which was, as he put it, "spiked with lies" and insincere, he encountered a beggar. "He was, without doubt, the happier ... not least because he could obtain his wine through nothing more than wishing people well, whereas I sought fame [*typhum*] through lying" (*conf.* 6.6.10). Augustine was finding it increasingly difficult to seek happiness and respect, especially by dishonest means.

HUMILITY AS THE DISTINGUISHING MARK OF THE CHRISTIAN

From Book 7 onward, the midpoint of the thirteen books of the *Confessions*, Augustine's understanding of the substance of God and the nature of evil changed. He used Book 7 to investigate his inner intellectual transformation(s). He also addressed the question of self-knowledge in connection with humility and creatureliness.

> If I had subjected myself to you, my true joy would have been in you, as you have made everything subject to me that you had created to be below me. This is how the right ordering of things should be; my salvation lay in a central position ... But because I reared up arrogantly [*superbe*] against you and stubbornly assailed the Lord with my shield (Job 15:26), even those inferior things were elevated above me and pressed me down so that nowhere could I find respite or draw breath ... And all this resulted from my wounds because you humble the arrogant [*humiliasti superbum*] (Ps 88:11) like a wounded man, I was separated from you by my own pride [*tumore*] and my face was so swollen [*nimis inflata*] that my eyes were closed. (*conf.* 7.7.11)

According to Augustine, the created human being is superior to the objects in space, yet inferior and subordinate to God. If Augustine had only remained faithful to his true image of God, served God, had controlled his fleshly disordered desires (which were both a natural consequence and an appropriate punishment), and thus had retained his right place, it would have definitely contributed to his salvation. Naturally, the ultimate destiny of humankind was to regain to the likeness of God, its Creator. Such elevation, in turn, was dependent on humility – it was only when humans acknowledged their status and situation, they could attain the goal and fully realize their true God-like identity. "Under the inner nurture of your medicine my pride [*tumor meus*] subsided" (*conf.* 7.8.12). At the beginning of his inner salvific process, Augustine realized ever more clearly how strongly "God resists the proud [*superbis*] but gives grace to the humble [*humilibus*]" (1 Pet 5:5). In *conf.* 7.9.13, Augustine made a reference to this passage when he understood that there was a *lacuna* in Neoplatonic thought.[7] He described the moment with the following words: "With what great mercy you revealed to humankind the Way of humility [*uia humilitatis*] and that your Word became flesh and dwelt among humankind (Jn 1:14)" (*conf.* 7.9.13). Augustine read 1 Pet 5:5 Christologically: God's grace was made manifest in the incarnation, which was "the way of humility [*uia humilitatis*]."

Augustine added that God, by means of "a man grossly swollen with pride [*per quendam hominem immanissimo typho turgidum*]" (*conf.* 7.9.13), brought to his attention various Platonic writings. In these he discovered many topics that related to Christian teaching on the Word/ *Logos* of God. Nevertheless, he emphatically did not discover that the Word became flesh, or that the Son of God had "humbled himself [*humiliauit se*] and was obedient [*oboediens*] to the point of death (Phil 2:8)" (*conf.* 7.9.14). Neither did he read in these writings that Christ was "meek and humble in heart" (Mt 11:29). In other words, he did not discover the exemplary function of humility and, particularly, that humility was essential for the Incarnation.

In a visionary experience, Augustine attained a perception of "that which was," albeit in a flash of one tremulous glance (*conf.* 7.17.23). He still lacked the humility to continue to enjoy God's presence [*ad fruendum te*] (*conf.* 7.18.24); a humility that would move him to the acknowledgment that his very ability to confess his faults was entirely dependent on God. "I had not, in fact, grasped my God, the humble [*humilem*] Jesus, in a humble fashion [*non humilis*]; and I did not yet know what his weakness [*infirmitas*] was intended to teach us" (*conf.* 7.18.24).

The *Confessions* depicts clearly the vast significance of the humility of Christ to Augustine and his spiritual progress. That is, his conversion was halted because he had not yet acknowledged the *humilitas* of Christ. Augustine admitted that he did not know what the weakness of the humble Jesus was actually meant to reveal to humankind.

In the lower regions of creation he built himself a humble dwelling [*humilem domum*] from our clay in order to release from their

[7] Cf. V. H. Drecoll, "Gratia," in Augustinus-Lexikon, vol. 3, 182–242, at 232.

pretentious selves those intended to be subordinate to him and to draw them to himself. Thus he heals their pride [*tumorem*] and nourishes their love so that they do not stray further from him in their self-confidence [*fiducia sui*]. (*conf.* 7.18.24)

Because of false self-confidence, people removed themselves from God. However, as human beings lied exhausted on the ground before the humble God, this humble God raised them up to himself (cf. *conf.* 7.18.24). Augustine thus understood what humility entailed: one should acknowledge and confess one's own weaknesses. False self-confidence merely impeded true self-knowledge.

> For then, filled with my own torment, I began to desire recognition for wisdom and I shed no tears over this but rather puffed myself up with knowledge. Where, then, was that charity which is built upon the foundation of the humility [*a fundamento humilitatis*] which is Christ Jesus? (*conf.* 7.20.26)

Augustine clarified that Christ was the foundation of humility on which the true love stood. Knowledge puffed up, whereas love built up (1 Cor 8:1). Nevertheless, the fact that love was based on Christ, the foundation of humility, continued to evade Augustine for the time being.

In antiquity, there were no other examples of the divine humility that would match with the humility of Christ. Augustine could not find the humility of Christ in the Platonic books [*libri Platonicorum*]. Only his reading of Scripture against the background of Platonic writings revealed to him the difference between presumption [*praesumptio*] and confession [*confessio*]; between those who saw where the journey would lead, but who could not see the path that actually lead there (i.e., philosophers), and the Way itself, which lead to that blissful homecoming that humankind was intended to behold and enjoy (cf. *conf.* 7.20.26). *Confessio* before God meant an affirmation of Christ as Lord over one's own existence. This, in turn, meant an acknowledgement that God had become human for the sake of humankind and had made it possible for humans to love God. Love, then, was the core of the incarnation of Christ.

In retrospect, Augustine saw his stumbling upon Neoplatonic books before discovering the deeper meaning of Scripture as providential. The portions of Scripture that he read most zealously were the letters of Paul. These referred to God's grace much more clearly than the Platonic books did. "Those who gain insight should not boast as though everything they have were not a gift; both the insight and the power of insight. For what do we have that we have not been given? (1 Cor 4:7)" (*conf.* 7.21.27). The Platonic books "manifest neither [*non habent illae paginae*] the tears of confession [*lacrimas confessionis*], nor your sacrifice, nor the spirit of regret, nor a contrite and humbled heart [*cor contritum et humiliatum*]" (*conf.* 7.21.27). They neglected the concept of learning from him who was "gentle and humble in heart [*mitis et humilis corde*] (Mt 11:29)" (*conf.* 7.21.27). Here Augustine compared Neoplatonism to Christianity, just like pride compared to humility and grace. The human heart should put itself aside, forget and deny itself, in order to have a share in that which is "good." The general term for this movement peculiar to the heart is self-denial or humility. In this way, Christ shows the path to the homeland of peace.

EXAMPLES UNDER THE EASY YOKE OF HUMILITY

According to the *Confessions*, Augustine's intellectual conversion was, at this point, complete. But his self-will had not been overcome; he still had to wage war with pride and desire. Consequently, Augustine went with his questions to Simplicianus, the spiritual father of Ambrose (*conf.* 8.2.3). "He [i.e., Simplicianus] then told me about Victorinus, with the intention of exhorting me to emulate the humility of Christ [*ad humilitatem Christi*], which is hidden from the wise but revealed to the little ones (Mt 11:25)" (*conf.* 8.2.3). Marius Victorinus, the translator of Platonic books into Latin, had at first concealed his faith from his friends, ("these proud demon-worshippers [*superbos daemonicolas*]" [*conf.* 8.2.4]), but had later been publicly baptized to the acclaim of his fellow Christians. He was not ashamed "to become a slave of your anointed one; an infant of your font, after bending his head beneath the yoke of humility [*ad humilitatis iugum*] and lowering his brow before the ignominy of the cross" (*conf.* 8.2.3). Victorinus's example, especially his humility and courage to go public, deeply impressed Augustine.

> As study and longing brought him to solid ground, he began to fear that he might be disowned by Christ before his holy angels if he were afraid to confess him before his fellow human beings [*coram hominibus confiteri*]; he considered it a great offence to be ashamed of the mysteries of the humility of your Word [*de sacramentis humilitatis uerbi tui*] while being unashamed of the profane cults of proud demons [*superborum daemoniorum*] whose

adherent he had been in his proud imitation [*imitator superbus*] of them. (*conf.* 8.2.4)

Apparently, there was no lack of vehement reaction to Victorinus's baptism: "The proud [*superbi*] looked on and were furious" (*conf.* 8.2.4).

However, the example of Victorinus is not the only one mentioned. Christ had chosen others – the weakest in the eyes of the world – in order to shame the strong (cf. 1 Cor 1:27). Thus,

> the least of your apostles [i.e., Paul] ... brought the proconsul Paulus under Christ's gentle yoke [*sub lene iugum Christi*] and having used his weapons to conquer his pride [*per eius militiam debellata superbia*],[8] made him a subject of the great King ... He [i.e., the enemy] holds the proud [*superbos*] with their aristocratic titles in the firmest of grips, using their authority to work on many others.
> (*conf.* 8.4.9)

The conversion of the proconsul was a telling example for Augustine of one's subordination to the yoke of Christ: the governor had become subordinate to the King of Kings.[9] Augustine so wished to follow the example of Victorinus, but felt that he was still enchained by the Enemy. Lust [*libido*] arose from wrong desires [*ex uoluntate peruersa*] and those who succumbed to it forfeited habit [*consuetudo*] and compulsion [*necessitas*]. "Thus two wills fought it out in me; the new against the old, the carnal against the spiritual" (*conf.* 8.5.10). Before his conversion experience in Book 8, Ponticianus, an imperial official, visited him and told him about the Egyptian desert father Anthony, as well as about the communities of monks in the desert. Ponticianus also spoke about the city of Milan and about the conversion of two imperial officials in Trier, who stumbled on the biography of Anthony in a garden hut belonging to a Christian community. After reading it, they immediately decided to change their lives. During Ponticianus's narration, "you, Lord, made me look at myself. You brought me out from behind my own back ... You revealed to me my own face" (*conf.* 8.7.16). Augustine employed this garden scene to describe his own conversion experience. Anthony seemed to have been personally addressed by a

---

[8] Cf. Vergil, *Aen.* 6,853: "Nurture the one who acquiesces but break or subdue the defiance of the rebels [*parcere subiectis et debellare superbos*]" (my translation) (also cited three times in Augustine's *civ. Dei* 1 praef.; 1.6; 5.12).

[9] Cf. M. Testard, "La 'superbia' dans les Confessions de saint Augustin," in *Homo Spiritualis. Festgabe für Luc Verheijen OSA zu seinem 70. Geburtstag*, ed. C. Mayer, Cassiciacum 38 (Würzburg: Augustinus, 1987), 136–170, at 158.

passage from the gospels he heard inadvertently. And when the voice of a child caused Augustine to open the letters of Paul at Rm 13:13–14, the light of certainty streamed straight away into his heart (*conf.* 8.12.29).

Augustine, the successful rhetorician, had reached the limit of his lust [*cupiditas*] (*conf.* 9.2.4). But even after giving up his post as rhetorician, he had to admit while conversing with his friends in the country house:

> What I achieved there in literary terms was certainly devoted to your service but craved with its very breath the pretension of academia [*superbiae scholam*] ... How well I recall – and how eagerly I acknowledge before you – the incentives you used to tame me and how you took away the mountains and hills of my thinking by humbling [*humilitatis*] me. (*conf.* 9.4.7)

The arrogance continued to accompany Augustine, as he realized in retrospect. "How I cried out to you, my God, as I read the Psalms of David ... which left no room for any pride [*turgidum spiritum*]" (*conf.* 9.4.8). Augustine would "have most dearly loved to sing them throughout the whole world, against human pride [*adversus typhum generis humani*]" (*conf.* 9.4.8).

HUMILITY APPROPRIATE TO THE SACRAMENTS

Augustine, Alypius, and Adeodatus humbly received baptism at Easter in 387. Augustine reported: "Alypius also wished to join me in being reborn in you, and was already practising the humility [*humilitate*] that befits your mysteries. He subdued his body to the point of walking barefoot on the frozen soil of Italy" (*conf.* 9.6.14). Augustine seemed to perceive asceticism as the practice that enabled an individual to imitate Christ and to draw closer to him. Again, it was *humilitas* that connected ascetic practices to the humble Christ.

When Augustine's mother died in Ostia shortly afterward, he found it comforting that it was God who heard his weeping, and "not just anyone who would dismiss it from a lofty height [*superba*]" (*conf.* 9.12.33). Augustine was sure that his mother had praised God with her way of life, even if perhaps she had sometimes violated God's commandments. Moreover, Augustine was convinced that God was lenient in judging human transgressions. For this reason, he hoped to stand before God with confidence. Anyone who addresseed God and cataloged his/her own merits was actually cataloging the divine gifts. That's why Augustine implored: "that humans might acknowledge that they are human [*cognoscant se homines homines*], and anyone minded to boast would boast in the Lord (2 Cor 10:7)" (*conf.* 9.13.34).

THE CONCEPT OF *CONFESSIO*

In the *Confessions*, Augustine performed his own "confession of sins [*confessio peccatorum*]." God had had compassion on him even before he had acknowledged God [*me miseratus es et nondum confitentem*]. God's grace preceded any confession of faith. God was and is more deeply within him than his own inner being and higher than his highest self (*conf.* 3.6.11).

One of the keys for understanding the concept of *confessio* in the *Confessions* can be found in the first section of Book 10.[10] Augustine said that he wanted to know God just as he was fully known by God (cf. 1 Cor 13:12). So he wrote, programmatically for the whole *Confessions*:

> You love the truth because anyone who does so comes to the light (Jn 3:21). I want to act in truth in my heart through confession [*in confessione*] before you, and with my pen before many witnesses.
> (*conf.* 10.1.1)

The *confessio* first takes place silently in the heart, between God and the human being. In writing, merely the faintest echo of it can be captured. For Ratzinger, the "doing what is true" (Jn 3:21), required by the Lord, takes place precisely in the *confessio*.[11] By way of further explanation, Ratzinger cites a section from Augustine's *Jo. ev. tr.* 12.13, which likewise makes reference to Jn 3:21. In fact, works performed independently from Christ do not lead to the Light. Human beings should no longer consider themselves good, but should accept to their own nothingness, acknowledging and honoring God as the only "good." By the action of God, by God's grace, human beings are made aware of their sin; they must decide to confess this in order to "do what is true." "Whoever confesses [*confitetur*] and accuses his sins is already doing that with God. God accuses your sins; if you also accuse them you are connected to God" (*Jo. ev. tr.* 12.13). Human beings, and human

---

[10] G. Folliet, "L'explication par Augustin dans ses *Confessions* X,1,1 du mot *confessio*: 'Qui facit ueritatem uenit ad lucem' (Jean 3,21). Quelques parallèles complémentaires, voire contemporains," *Revista agustiniana* 44/134 (2003), 545–549, at 545.

[11] J. Ratzinger, "Originalität und Überlieferung in Augustins Begriff der 'confessio'," *Revue des Études Augustiniennes* 3 (1957), 375–392, at 385 and 388.

beings as sinners, are to a certain extent two different "things": human beings are created by God, but what is sinful is made by humans themselves. To confess one's sins and misdeeds is the very beginning of good works. This way, by "doing truth," humans come to Light. *Confessio* constitutes a key concept in Augustine's teaching on grace and saves the reality of grace, as Ratzinger puts it.[12] In this sense, *confessio* means doing what is True and coming to the Light.

Folliet adds three more texts of Augustine in consolidation of Ratzinger's examination, all of which cite Jn 3:21.[13] He lists three elements that can also be found in *conf.* 10.1.1: (1) all sinners must act in truth and in God; (2) a quest of this kind demands conversion through confession and penance; and (3) such conversion is only possible with God's help and the sinner must ask for it in humility.[14]

According to Augustine, there would be many people who would read the *Confessions* out of curiosity but who would not be interested in changing their lives because of it. Besides, who could guarantee that what he had written was true? In contrast, however, the Word of God could not be made out to be a lie (*conf.* 10.3.3). "How is hearing the truth about oneself from you [i.e., God] any different from knowing oneself [*cognoscere se*]? And is someone who has this self-knowledge and rejects it as false, not himself lying" (*conf.* 10.3.3)? Love (1 Cor 13:7) would tell people that Augustine was not lying; love within them would make them to believe him (*conf.* 10.3.3). Augustine professed: "Any goodness in me derives from you and is your gift; the evil in me is my fault and your punishment" (*conf.* 10.4.5).

EXAMINATION OF CONSCIENCE IN THE TENSION BETWEEN PRIDE AND HUMILITY

Based on the Johannine threefold concupiscence [*triplex concupiscentia*] (1 Jn 2:16), in Book 10, Augustine listed three types of temptation (*conf.* 10.30.41, 41.66), of which the last and the greatest was pride. Pride underlies the other two desires (lust of senses and lust of the eyes) and one could not be healed of it without humility. In this context, pride meant to be feared and loved by others for its own sake (i.e., *libido*

---

[12] Cf. Ibid., 386.
[13] Folliet, "L'explication par Augustin," 545–549.
[14] Cf. Ibid., 549.

dominandi) and for the sole purpose of obtaining the joy that was really no joy, but a loathsome arrogance [*foeda iactantia*] (*conf.* 10.36.59). Augustine examined his own perpetual susceptibility to pride:

> You satisfy my longing with good things. First you crushed my pride [*superbiam meam*] under the weight of awe of you and made my neck submissive to your yoke [*iugo tuo*]. Now I wear it and find it light, as you promised, and as you still made it.
> (*conf.* 10.36.58)

While God alone reigned without pride [*sine typho*], Augustine doubted that it was possible to escape pride in this life. "This is one of the chief reasons we fail to love you and revere you with chaste fear, and therefore you resist the proud [*superbis*] and bestow your grace on the humble [*humilibus*]" (*conf.* 10.36.59). Anyone who received praise, even on account of his/her own piety, could easily be overpowered by pride, begin to have confidence in oneself, imitate the devil, and, thus, become his prisoner. Augustine admitted that he took pleasure in praise and was hurt by defamatory speech, concluding from these feelings that his victory over pride had by no means been won yet (*conf.* 10.37.60–62). He made no claims anywhere that he had finally conquered his pride. It was also the case that "one often boasts with increasing vanity that one holds vainglory in contempt [*de ipso uanae gloriae contemptu uanius gloriatur*]" (*conf.* 10.38.63). The one who took pride in him/herself was just boastful. Concluding this train of thought, Augustine saw a similar temptation in pride. A smug person rejoiced over the good he/she had received from God as if it had been the good of his/her own making (*conf.* 10.39.64).

Shortly thereafter Augustine considered the question of whether practices such as magic (theurgy) might mediate between humankind and God. He denied such mediation, noting that these practices depended on the wrong mediator. "They summoned the satanic powers of the air as their accomplices and they were of the same mind; allies of their pride [*socias superbiae suae*] ... it appealed to their proud flesh [*superbam carnem*] as he himself had no physical body" (*conf.* 10.42.67). The true Mediator [*uerax mediator*] stood between God and humankind (1 Tim 2:5), "your hidden mercy revealed and sent [him] to the humble [*humilibus*]. From your example [*exemplo*] they might learn humility [*humilitatem*]" (*conf.* 10.43.68). The true Mediator was mortal like a human being, yet also righteous like God. Through his divine righteousness, he annihilated the death of the godless.

SYSTEMATIC REVIEW

If a human being sets themselves above their Creator, they offend against the order of the existing reality and is guilty of pride. The same happens if a human being enjoys something created [*frui*] rather than uses it [*uti*] – if they therefore bestow on something lowly more worth than is permitted and fitting. For Augustine, pride explains the irrationality of the world. Some things in the universe are incomplete because the divine order has been brought into disorder by presumptuous pride. Furthermore, pride is also the failure to acknowledge one's own sins (*conf.* 5.10.18) and to consider oneself free of sin.

The starting and central point of pride is excessive and arrogant complacency.[15] In *conf.* 10.39.64, Augustine distinguished between four reasons for, or types of, complacency:[16] First, complacency boasts about something that is not good as though it were good. Augustine has done this himself while he adhered to the teaching of the Manichees (*conf.* 5.10.18). A second expression of complacency is when one congratulates oneself on one's own virtue while ignoring the fact that it is God who has bestowed it in the first place. A third expression is to consider that one has earned the grace of God. And a fourth expression of arrogant complacency is to acknowledge receiving the grace of God but to be envious if others receive it too.

It is clear from the *Confessions* that Augustine views *superbia* as the root of sin and evil. Nevertheless, his goal is not some kind of total, negative self-denial. There is evidence of positive self-assertion in his references to 1 Cor 1:31 (*conf.* 10.31.45) and 2 Cor 10:17 (*conf.* 9.13.34) as well. The main idea is "boasting in the Lord," because humankind has been called by God to follow and imitate Christ in a humble life. Arrogant behavior in the sense of self-aggrandisement is caused by *superbia*, but boasting in Christ is engendered by humility.

The *Confessions* clearly shows that, for Augustine, humility is closely allied to self-knowledge. The reminder that humans are not God is inherent in both the Delphic maxim [*gnōthi seauton*] and Augustine's *cognitio sui*. Humility as self-knowledge in Augustine includes four principles: creatureliness, sinfulness, confession, and grace.[17]

[15] J. F. Procopé, "Hochmut," in *Reallexikon für Antike und Christentum*, eds. E. Dassmann et al. (Stuttgart: Hiersemann 1991), vol. 15, 795–858, at 850.
[16] Ibid., 850–853, which gives a detailed breakdown of these four types.
[17] N. Baumann, *Die Demut als Grundlage aller Tugenden bei Augustinus*, Patrologia 21 (Frankfurt am Main: Peter Lang, 2009), 75–132.

The first principle: in Christianity and thus in Augustine's *Confessions*, the creatureliness of humankind is a central theme. In antiquity, the creation of human beings in the likeness of God was not how it way typically understood. Creation in the Christian sense stands in opposition to the dualism of the Manichees and the Neoplatonic concept of emanation. Fallen humankind tends to belong to itself and to be its own creator; autocratic, and without control by someone else. Yet, only in humility can one acknowledge and accept God as their Creator. It is to comply with one's position in the hierarchy of the *ordo rerum*. Taking this into consideration, the person who does not accept God as Creator and oneself as a creature must turn back to oneself, recollect oneself in heart, and acknowledge that they are a sinner.

The second principle: the first human being was given free will, which also meant that he should have used it for obeying God and God's commandments. However, being proud and disobedient, Adam failed the test of temptation. Every human being is mortal as a result of original sin. Ignorance and ineptitude are consequences of the fall. Desires and longings attract human beings and drive them to self-abandonment. Anyone who prefers created things to the Creator and enjoys them instead of simply using them must come to a realization that they are a sinner. The humility of Christ is the basis for and an aid to acknowledging one's sinfulness.

The third principle: confession and self-knowledge are interrelated. On one hand, "confessing of sins [*confessio peccatorum*]" is a means of self-knowledge. One has to see the truth about oneself. Only by disclosing and confessing faults and sins to Christ, salvation becomes possible. On the other hand, confession presupposes a humble demeanor and can only be undertaken with humility. Human beings must be aware of and understand their position in the *ordo rerum* and realize that they are not God but creatures. Moreover, the *confessio* always commends one in front of whom it has to be made, because it shows evidence of trust. Both "the confession of praise [*confessio laudis*]" and "the confession of sins [*confessio peccatorum*]" acknowledge the difference between the Creator and the creation. Above all, a successful confession is an act of grace.

The fourth principle: in his *Confessions*, Augustine confirms that humility predisposes the receiving of grace [*humilibus autem dat gratiam*]. Moreover, humility can be received only if bestowed by grace. The fact that the Holy Spirit enables one to be humble is a most explicit expression of grace. Because it is grace alone that makes acts of humility possible, adequate self-knowledge is also a divine gift. "What do you have that you did not receive?" (1 Cor 4:7).

Humilitas stands in direct opposition to *amour propre*. In humility, Augustine sees the hallmark of the new Christian life. Christ gives the example of divine *humilitas* – something that the Platonists lacked. God himself abases himself in Christ: "How exalted you are and yet you make your home among the humble-hearted [*o quam excelsus es, et humiles corde sunt domus tua*]!" (*conf.* 11.31.41). The Augustinian concept of humility is based on Christology. Christ – God and human being in one – abases himself to save humankind and becomes the Mediator. The salvation of humankind is only possible through the intervention of a Mediator between God and fallen humanity; and this Mediator saves humanity solely and exclusively because of his humility.

The humble Christ demands humble followers, because only humility enables his followers to reach the Truth. In this sense, humility becomes the hub and foundation of the Christian life. "The humble Christ [*Christus humilis*]" is, however, not merely a model. Christ's self-abasement has a sacramental effect as it delivers humankind from sin. It is precisely as the humble Savior that Christ becomes a Sacrament for humankind. The four outlined principles – which act as mysteries and effect adequate self-knowledge – are the sacramental presence of Christ in humankind. At the same time, Christ is, no doubt, also the model. He is the example of humility *par excellence* for the wicked, arrogance, and envious human beings.

Humility is also crucial to Augustinian anthropology. Original sin militates against humility and, thus, humankind is at the mercy of arrogance and egoism. Human pride prevents us from loving our Creator (i.e., God) and our neighbor. A human being as a creature and a sinner is in no position to discern one's lostness and return to "order of things [*ordo rerum*]"; the humility of Christ can make this possible. A humble person is able to acknowledge that one is created by God and responsible for one's sin.

In short, Christ enables a human being to possess self-knowledge and salvation. This is the form of a "double grace." Whereas the responsibility for *superbia* lies with humankind, *humilitas*, as defined by Augustine, does not come from humankind, but from God. This is the very core of Augustine's theology of grace. In his *Confessions* as well, Augustine makes it very clear that *humilitas* is interrelated with *gratia*. With his grace, God helps those whom he wishes to save to overcome their pride.

Further Reading

Baumann, N. *Die Demut als Grundlage aller Tugenden bei Augustinus*. Patrologia 21. Frankfurt am Main: Peter Lang, 2009.

Bruning, B. "Augustine's Concept of Pride: *Ut cancer serpit* (*en. Ps.* 1,1)." *Augustiniana* 63/1–4 (2013), 9–81.

Courcelle, P. "Le Typhus, maladie de l'âme d'après Philon et d'après Saint Augustin." In *Corona gratiarum: miscellanea patristica, historica et liturgica Eligio Dekkers O.S.B. XII lustra complenti oblata*. Instrumenta patristica 10–11. Brugge: S. Pieter-sabdij, 1975, 245–288.

Hombert, P.-M. *Gloria Gratiae. Se glorifier en Dieu, principe et fin de la théologie augustinienne de la grâce*. Collection des Études Augustiniennes, Série Antiquité 148. Paris: Études Augustiniennes, 1996.

Jamieson, I. W. A., "Augustine's Confessions: The Structure of Humility." *Augustiniana* 24 (1974), 234–246.

Mayer, C. "*Humiliatio, humilitas*." In *Augustinus-Lexikon*, ed. C. Mayer. Basel: Schwabe, 2004–2010, vol. 3, 443–456.

Procopé, J. F. "Hochmut." In *Reallexikon für Antike und Christentum*, eds. E. Dassmann, et al. Stuttgart: Hiersemann 1991, vol. 15, 795–858.

Schaffner, O. *Christliche Demut. Des hl. Augustinus Lehre von der Humilitas*. Cassiciacum 17. Würzburg: Augustinus, 1959.

Testard, M. "La 'superbia' dans les Confessions de saint Augustin." In *Homo Spiritualis. Festgabe für Luc Verheijen OSA zu seinem 70. Geburtstag*, ed. C. Mayer. Cassiciacum 38. Würzburg: Augustinus, 1987, 136–170.

14 Soul, Self, and Interiority

PHILLIP CARY

One of the things Augustine clearly wants to accomplish in the *Confessions* is to direct his readers' attention in an unfamiliar way.

> And people go marveling at the height of mountains, the vast waves of the sea, the wide course of rivers, the extent of the ocean and the cycles of the stars, and leave themselves behind, not marveling that when I spoke of all these things I didn't see them with my eyes, but I couldn't have spoken of them unless the mountains and waves and rivers and stars I have seen, and the ocean I believe in, were something I inwardly saw in my memory, in a space as vast as I outwardly saw them.
>
> (*conf.* 10.8.15, all translations mine)

Augustine wants us to marvel at the vast inner space of the self, a dimension not of the body, but of the soul. Of course it is not literally a space, as if it could be measured in feet or miles, but rather "a more inward place that is not a place [*interiore loco, non loco*]" (*conf.* 10.9.16). It is like a space in that it contains things; it is a dimension in which things have room to exist. It is in fact ourselves, our mind and memory, that Augustine pictures as a kind of inner world containing mountains, seas, and stars – not the things themselves, of course, but only images of them – and not just images of what we have seen, but also of things we can only imagine, like the ocean that Augustine believes in because he has heard about it but not seen it for himself. Without these images inside us, he is convinced, none of us would be able to speak of the things we have seen and believe. Yet, astonishingly, we fail to be astonished. We pay no attention to what is in us, more impressed by the external mountains we can see with our physical eyes than the marvelous capacity to contain the mental images of mountains in our souls.

FINDING GOD INSIDE

Why do we hardly notice the greatness of the vast world within us? For Augustine this is a serious problem, because it is within this inner space that God must be found – and not just an image of what we believe about God, but God himself. Augustine leads up to this crucial point by indicating something else we can find in the inner space of memory: not just images of the sort of things we can perceive with the senses, like mountains and oceans, but also the things we learn in the liberal arts and sciences, which are unchanging intelligible truths, perceived by the intellect alone and not by the senses (*conf.* 10.9.16–11.19). The important thing about the latter is that they are present in memory not as images, but as the things themselves [*res ipsas*] (*conf.* 10.9.16). When we remember that two plus two equals four, we are not considering an image of this truth but the truth itself, which we see in our minds, not in the external world.

Following a long tradition that goes back to Plato, Augustine suggests that such truths have always been in our memory, because otherwise we could not recognize them when we find them.[1] We find what we forget, after all, by looking for it in memory (*conf.* 10.19.28), and unless we could find things in memory we could not find anything. As Augustine argues, the woman in the Bible could not rejoice at finding a lost coin (Lk 15:8) unless she remembered and recognized it when she saw it (*conf.* 10.18.27). And when what we recognize is an unchanging truth, we do not find it like a coin outside us, but by seeing it in our memory, with an inward vision of the eye of the mind.

All this is important to understand, Augustine thinks, because God also is present as unchanging Truth. God is "the unchanging Truth containing all that is unchangingly true," as he puts it in his most important previous exploration of the inner world (*lib. arb.* 2.12.33). To see any unchanging truth, even something as trivial as two plus two equals four, is to see something that belongs properly to the mind of

---

[1] This famous Platonic doctrine of recollection is an answer to the so-called Meno problem, formulated by young Meno asking Socrates: "How can you seek what you don't know? Even if you came across it, how would you know that this is the thing you don't know" (Plato, *Meno* 80d)? Augustine uses the parable of the woman finding her lost coin to give a version of Socrates' answer to the Meno problem, viz., that we recognize what we are looking for by recollecting it: "if she had no memory of it, she would not have found it" (*conf.* 10.18.27). Augustine explicitly affirms Socrates' answer in *ep.* 7.2, but strips away Plato's recourse to the myth of reincarnation in *Trin.* 12.15.24.

God, which is not different from God himself.[2] Even when we do not know or see the unchanging Truth, we cannot say that it is distant from us in space, as if we had to go to some place far away in order to see it like the mountains or the ocean. Hence Augustine can say, at the culmination of his long exploration of the inner space of memory: "Look how much space I have covered in my memory searching for You, O Lord, and I have not found You outside it" (*conf.* 10.24.35).

And it is not as if the unchanging Truth had at some in time in the past migrated into our inner selves from outside. Augustine makes this point at the beginning of the *Confessions*, where his opening prayer asks questions that hint at the solution to many philosophical problems he raises later in the text. "How can I invoke my God?" he asks at the beginning of Chapter 2, using a Latin verb that literally means "to call in." Augustine infers that "when I invoke him, I call him into myself [*in me ipsum eum vocabo, cum invocabo eum*]," and this generates a problem: "what place [*locus*] is there in me, that I can call him into me" (*conf.* 1.2.2)? The solution he hints at is that God needs no place, for he is omnipresent, present in all places precisely because he made them and they are dependent on him for their existence, not *vice versa*. "Since without You, whatever exists could not exist, does whatever exists contain You" (*conf.* 1.2.2)? The suggestion is clear: I contain God, simply because I exist and could not exist if he were absent from me and not in me. But that only raises a new and deeper question: "Since I also exist, why do I ask You to come into me – I who would not exist if You were not in me" (*conf.* 1.2.2)? It is not as if God needs to travel some distance in space in order to be with me and come into my soul. Rather, it is I who need to move and change – to alter the direction of my love and attention in order to see the God who is already present in my inmost self. For, if God is within, then my failure to know what is in me is a failure to know God.

OUTSIDE OURSELVES

Augustine wants his readers to see this for themselves. Like everything that exists, I have always had God in me, but, unlike the mountains and the seas, I can know I have God within me. I have a mind capable of understanding and seeing the Truth, and therefore I can also be culpably ignorant of the God within me. This is the deeper marvel that Augustine

---

[2] Augustine makes a similar argument to establish the existence of Platonic Ideas in the mind of God in *div. qu.* 46.

wants us to be astonished at, a greater marvel than the mountains and seas in our inner world: God is within us, and yet we don't know God. The light of Truth shines in the inner space of the self, and we don't see it. The whole of the *Confessions* narrates a long, agonizing search for God – but why is finding God so hard if God has always been within? Augustine has a long answer to this question, but he can sum it up in a brief, startling picture: "And look! You were within, and I outside" (*conf.* 10.27.38). Explaining this picture is a good way to see what Augustine wants us to see about soul, self, and interiority.

God is found within me, yet I do not find God because I am outside myself. I am where my mind is, and my mind is where its attention is, and my attention is inveterately, sinfully turned outward, away from both self and God. This explains why it took Augustine so long to find what he was looking for – why he must confess, in the famous words at the beginning of the same chapter: "Late have I loved You, O Beauty so ancient and so new, late have I love You" (*conf.* 10.27.38). He came late to the Beauty of God because he spent years looking in all the wrong places, paying attention to outward things. He was fascinated and enamored with everything but God, clinging to external things as if they could make him happy. Thus he proceeds to explain the picture: "You were within, and I outside; and I sought You there and rushed, deformed, upon the well-formed things that You have made" (*conf.* 10.27.38). The problem is not with God's creation, which is good and beautiful, but with our perverted attention, longing more for the beautiful form of things outside us than for the eternal Beauty that formed them. Beauty, new to us whenever we find it but more ancient than anything in creation, is a name for God, like the names Truth and Goodness. The Beauty and Truth and Goodness of God are omnipresent and inescapable, always within us, yet we rush away from them toward the lure of external things. That is why Augustine goes on to say: "You were with me, but I was not with You. For these things kept me far from You" (*conf.* 10.27.38). He is blaming himself, not the things outside him.

We come late to the God in our inner self because our attention is persistently turned outward, so that we know neither God nor self. This is a moral failing reinforced by bad habits of thought, as Augustine explains at the beginning of Book 7 when he describes his efforts to overcome the materialist thinking he had developed when he was a Manichean. He was stuck imagining only physical things. He knew well enough that he had images of mountains and oceans inside him, but he did not really see their source, which was deeper and greater than any mountain or ocean that he could behold with his physical eyes.

"My heart went through such images as the forms my eyes were used to, and I did not see that the attention [*intentionem*] by which I formed these images was not something of that sort – yet it could not form them unless it was itself some great thing" (*conf.* 7.1.2). Our mental images of bodily things are not themselves bodily things, but formed by the attention of the heart or mind (as usual, Augustine does not see a difference between heart and mind, both of which are terms referring to what is highest in the soul). What is within us is not physical, bodily, corporeal, material, or external (for purposes of understanding Augustine, these are equivalent terms). What we need is a clear view of a different dimension of being, one not extended in space yet containing things that are high and great. If only we could see our own heart – not the organ in our chest, but the attention that forms mental images within us – we would have a clue to the nonmaterial being of God.

PLATONIST ADMONITIONS

What Augustine wants us to see is not obvious, and his view of the mind was not uncontroversial even in his own day. In addition to the Manicheans, many schools of philosophy, including Stoics and Epicureans, were also materialists, thinking of the human mind or soul and everything within it as a bodily thing. Like today, it was not at all obvious to intellectuals in the ancient world that we can look at our own attention and see something that has an utterly different kind of being from things that take up space in the external world. Augustine himself needed help seeing this, and he explains how that help came to him later in Book 7, when he describes what his mind did when he came upon "some books of the Platonists" (*conf.* 7.9.13). Augustine never tells us exactly which books these were, but the broad consensus of scholars is that they were mainly writings by Plotinus and his student Porphyry, pagans who lived in the third century CE and founded a school of philosophy that we now call "Neoplatonism." They were the most important representatives of a nonmaterialist philosophy available to Augustine. Although few of Porphyry's writings now survive, we have a large collection of Plotinus's essays called the *Enneads*. Evidently a Latin translation of some of these essays and perhaps some of Porphyry's writings as well came into Augustine's hands in the year 386.

Augustine himself describes what happened then. The books did not provide knowledge or revelation. Human words are not able to do that, Augustine believes, but can at best serve as admonitions or reminders [*admonitiones* or *commemorationes*] to look and see for ourselves (*mag.* 10.33–11.36). So the Platonist writings admonished him to turn his attention in a new and more inward direction. "Admonished from this to return to my own self," he writes, "I entered into what is inmost in me" (*conf.* 7.10.16). The "self" here is the reflexive pronoun, *memetipsum* in Latin, and "what is inmost" is *intima,* the superlative form of the Latin adjective *intus,* meaning "inner"; we have already encountered the comparative form, the Latin adjective *interior,* meaning "more inward." This turn to the inmost self is only the first step, but even the first step requires more than books and outward words; it is possible only by the inward leading of God. "I entered," Augustine says, "led by You, and I was able to do it, for You had become my helper" (*conf.* 7.10.16). So it was by the help of God's grace that Augustine turned inward and entered the inner space of his own soul, but it was pagan philosophy books that God used to admonish Augustine and tell him this is what he had to do. Faith and reason come together in a distinctive way here, because Augustine believes that the Platonists have beheld the inner Truth that is God, and therefore can tell us where to look to find it.

Another step is necessary after entering the inmost self, however. It is not enough to marvel at inner images of mountains and rivers and seas; to see God we must look higher. So, after turning inward, Augustine looks upward. "I entered, and with the eye of my soul, such as it was, I saw Your unchangeable Light shining above the eye of my soul, over my mind" (*conf.* 7.10.16). The Light of God is "other, wholly other" than any physical light, being above the soul not like oil on top of water or the sun above the earth, but as the Creator is above all things that he has made: "it was above because it made me" (*conf.* 7.10.16). As he later explains, he comes to see this light by reflecting on how it is possible to stand in judgment over the beauty of external things, saying, "This ought to be just so, but that shouldn't" (*conf.* 7.17.23). By turning his attention from the beautiful things to the Light by which he judges them, he finds "the unchanging and true eternity of Truth above my changing mind" (*conf.* 7.17.23). And, having seen this, Augustine at last can say, "I marveled that now I loved You, and not some mental image instead of You" (*conf.* 7.17.23).

THREE LEVELS OF BEING

The movement of Augustine's attention, in then up, can be tracked on the map of a metaphysical landscape that is broadly Platonist. It is a three-tiered ontological hierarchy, a scale of being rising from bodily, external things at the lowest level to God at the highest and inmost level, with the soul in the middle. This explains why Augustine can say in *conf.* 3.6.11 that God is "more inward than what is inmost in me [*interior intimo meo*]" as well as "higher than what is highest in me [*superior summo meo*]." When Augustine first presents this hierarchy of being in *ep.* 18.2, about a decade before the *Confessions*, he distinguishes the three levels in terms of their mutability or changeability: bodies change in space and time, literally taking up space and moving about; souls do not change in space, as they have no spatial dimensions like inches or feet but do change in time, learning and growing in wisdom (or not); and God is utterly unchangeable, which is why Augustine describes God as unchanging Light, eternal Truth, the highest Good, Beauty ancient and new, and so on. This threefold hierarchy forms the background of every description of the soul's movements in the *Confessions*. When the soul turns its attention inward it is moving in a higher direction, but when it pursues what is external, it is falling among lower things. The whole hierarchy is by nature good, from top to bottom, but everything in the external world is an inferior good that cannot ultimately make us happy.

It is the soul alone that can be morally good or evil, and the soul's inner moving and turning always has an ethical value in the *Confessions*, for better or worse. Augustine agrees with the ancient philosophers that the whole aim of ethics is happiness, so it is significant that he identifies God as "Happiness itself," whereas at the lowest level of the hierarchy is "that which can be neither happy nor unhappy" and the soul in the middle is what can become happy or unhappy, because it "lives in unhappiness when turned toward what is lowest but in happiness when turned toward what is highest" (*ep.* 18.2). To live in happiness is *beata vita*, happy life, which was the standard Latin translation (put into circulation by Cicero) of the Greek philosophical term *eudaimonia*, commonly translated into English as "happiness," but perhaps better rendered "human flourishing." It means the fulfillment of human nature, true and ultimate success in life, whatever that might be – with heavy emphasis on *true*. Since a true happiness must be a lasting happiness, Augustine argues, the true *beata vita* must be *aeterna vita*, eternal life, which is course the consummation of what the New Testament promises to those who believe and follow Christ.[3]

---

[3] The identification of classical *beata vita* with biblical *aeterna vita* is an important point for Augustine, to which he frequently returns, e.g., *Trin.* 14.1.3, 15.4.6; *s.* 150.10; *civ. Dei* 11.11, 14.25; *ep.* 130.18, 155.16; *div. qu.* 35.2, and *ench.* 7.20.

This argument is Augustine's way of giving a biblical answer to the fundamental question of ancient ethics, which is "what is happiness?" It also gives an ethical meaning to his persistent emphasis on the unchanging nature of God, for to find unchanging Happiness is to rest in a happy life that is eternal and cannot be lost.

THE LONG INWARD JOURNEY

The soul's attention is driven by what it loves and seeks, so rightly ordered love is at the heart of Augustine's ethics. The loving and seeking in *Confessions* can be notoriously dramatic, even when the drama is inward. We seek to understand the truth by asking questions, for example, but the seeking can become a silent inner anguish of soul, as Augustine portrays it in a passage leading up to his discovery of the books of the Platonists. He was tormented by the question, "Where does evil come from?" God heard his inward sighing and groaning as he suffered this question, although Augustine was unaware of this at the time. Quoting Ps 38:10, he says, "The light of my eyes was not with me." His point here is the same as in the previous passage with the startling picture, where he says "You were with me but I was not with You" (*conf.* 10.27.38). For the inner Light of Truth never left him – it cannot ever be absent – but he didn't see it because "it was inward, but I was outside" (*conf.* 7.7.11). It is as if he had his back turned to the inner Light with his attention turned outward: "It was not in space, but I was paying attention [*intendebam*] to things contained in space, and I found no place there to rest" (*conf.* 7.7.11). Our hearts are restless because the perishable things of the external world are not lasting enough to give us rest when we cling to them, and they make us miserable with grief when we lose them (*conf.* 4.10.15). Our clinging to them is in fact a disordered love that captivates us, defies the ontological order of things, subjects us to what is beneath us, and makes us incapable of true happiness.

> I was above these things and below You – You who are true joy to me when subjected to You – and You subjected to me the things that You created beneath me. This was the proper balance and healthy placement of me in the middle, so that I would remain Your image, serving You and ruling over the body. But when I rose up against You in pride ... even these lower things came to be above me and pressed me down, so that I could not get loose and breathe.
>
> (*conf.* 4.10.15)

Pride for Augustine is always the name of a sin, a turning to the self that is not a turning to God, but a turning against him, putting self above God in disordered love. Thus, it earns an inevitable punishment, as the disordered soul cannot govern itself in the light of Truth, but is mastered by desire for lower things. It is unwilling to give up clinging to what is outside it, the mortal and perishable things it will inevitably lose, because in its pride and foolishness it thinks that by possessing such things it can be happy. So we turn to wealth, sex, power, friends, even ourselves, and find nothing that gives rest to our souls.

Augustine's turning in then up to see God is only the start of a long process of correcting this disordered love. As the second half of Book 10 will make clear, with its extensive analysis of the temptations of desire that a Christian faces every day, none of us in this mortal life has yet arrived at the happiness that will give us eternal rest. The great discovery in Book 7 is only a brief glimpse of the goal, after which Augustine falls back into his old, darkened self, dazzled by the inner Light that he is not yet strong and pure enough to hold steadfast in his gaze. Getting back to that inner vision in a stable and lasting way is a long journey. Of course it is not a literal journey – not a journey for the feet, as Augustine explains in a striking passage that combines the biblical parable of the Prodigal Son (Lk 15:11–21) with Plotinus's language for the inward turn:

> For it is not by feet or spatial distance that we go from You or come back to You, nor did that younger son of Yours take horses or chariots or ships, or fly with visible wings or need to travel by moving his legs, in order to go live in a far country as a prodigal wasting what You gave him ... for it is in the darkened affection of lust that there is distance from Your face.
>
> (*conf.* 1.18.28)

It is a recurrent theme of the *Confessions*: we flee the omnipresent God. We do so not by traveling from one place to another, but by turning our back on the inner Light because of our lustful love of external things ("lust" here means any greedy desire), with the result that our heart is darkened by ignorance of the Truth. The language of feet, chariots, and ships comes from Plotinus's essay "On Beauty," where it describes the kind of movement that does not help us to find the ultimate Beauty, which we will see only if we "turn into the inside [*eis to eiso*]" and awaken an unfamiliar kind of vision that has always been in us (*Enn.* 1.6.8).

GOD BECOMES EXTERNAL

Christ himself admonishes us in the same way, Augustine thinks. As true God and true man, Christ is both the eternal Truth teaching us inwardly (*mag.* 11.38) and a human teacher using external words to admonish us to turn inward. In the incarnation, Augustine says, he "became external so as to call us away from external things to inner things" (*c. ep. Man.* 36.41). When God takes on external form, in other words, it is to reinforce rather than disrupt the journey in and up. This is why Christ's life on earth was so short, as Augustine puts it in an evocative passage in *Confessions*: he ran through his life quickly to show that we too should not be detained by the transitory things of this mortal life. "He did not delay but ran on, calling out by word and deed, death and life, descent and ascent – calling out that we should return to him. And he withdrew from our eyes so that we might return to the heart and find him" (*conf.* 4.12.19). He departed from our outward sight so that we would look inward to find him, turning our attention from his humanity to his divinity – from his temporary, external presence at particular places long ago to his abiding divine presence in the heart.

Yet for us it is a long journey, taking the whole of our mortal lives. Ever since Adam we are all inveterately turned outward, and the work of purifying our hearts from sinful external attachments cannot be short circuited. This is why we have a lifelong need for the external authority of Christ incarnate.[4] In his divine nature he is the Truth that is goal of our journey, but in his human nature he is the Way that we travel, the example we follow, the external teacher whose authority we must always believe. For, as Augustine explains, we are not yet ready for the food of eternal life. After finding himself unable to gaze steadily at the Truth within, he hears, as it were, the divine voice still high above him saying "I am food for grown-ups; grow and you shall feed on me. And you shall not change me into you like the food of your flesh, but you shall be changed into me" (*conf.* 7.10.16). To be united with God by

---

[4] In insisting on the need for purification in order to see God, Augustine combines biblical language (e.g., Mt 5:8 and Acts 15:9) with Platonist conceptuality (e.g., Plato, *Phaedo* 64a–84b, where the task of philosophical ethics is to purify the soul, and Plotinus's essay, "On Virtues," *Enn.* 1.2, in which the virtues that lead to happiness are purifications of the soul). For how Augustine combines these see P. Cary, *Inner Grace: Augustine in the Traditions of Plato and Paul* (New York: Oxford University Press, 2008), 10–14. The lifelong need to have faith in external authority is the crucial new development in Augustine's mature theology, as argued in P. Cary, *Outward Signs: The Powerlessness of External Things in Augustine's Thought* (New York: Oxford University Press, 2008), 116–120.

the love that intellectual vision makes possible changes us into what he is: wise, incorruptible, and happy. But at present the best we can do is long for what we do not have, drawn upward in a love that is like fire in ancient physics, whose weight pulls it up to the distant heavens where it ultimately finds rest (*conf.* 13.9.10).

In the meantime, since we cannot steadily see the Truth for ourselves, we need to hear it in the authority of outward teaching by a God who has become external for our sake. We are like little children who cannot take solid food and therefore need the milk of authority. This is a recurrent theme in Augustine's preaching. As he puts it in one sermon:

> Was there no food on the table? Yet the infant is not capable of eating the food on the table. What does the mother do? She incarnates the food and makes milk from it. She produces something we are able to have. That's the way the Word became flesh, so that we little ones could be nourished by milk. (*s.* 117.16)

Here God is our mother, and Christ incarnate is the milk containing the nourishment of eternal life in an external form that we little ones can take. We are far from grown up, and even the bishop Augustine acknowledges, "I am a little one" (*conf.* 10.4.6). So the first thing he had to learn after his mind was dazzled by the inner Light of Truth is that Jesus Christ is not only the inner Truth (Jn 14:6), the eternal Word of God (Jn 1:1), and the unchanging Wisdom of God (1 Cor 1:24) by which all things were created (Prov 8:27–31), but also the Mediator, the one person who in his incarnation "combined the food I was incapable of with his flesh, for the Word was made flesh so that Your Wisdom, by which You created all things, might become milk for our infancy" (*conf.* 7.18.24).

Augustine repeatedly presses this point because it is humiliating for a grown man to admit he is a little one needing milk, but this humiliation is good for him. In Latin there is no difference between humiliation and humility [*humilitas*]. The point is that both are difficult for us, and the Christian virtue of humility often seems to pagans like an unacceptable form of humiliation. In Augustine's view, this is what kept proud pagan philosophers such as Porphyry, who wrote a famous tract *Against the Christians*, from accepting the Christian faith.[5]

---

[5] The critique of philosophical pride in *conf.* 7.20.26–27 draws from a polemic against pagan Platonists that Augustine typically directs at Porphyry; cf. *civ. Dei* 10.23–32 and the discussion in J. O'Meara, *Young Augustine: The Growth of St. Augustine's Mind up to His Conversion* (London: Longman, 1980), chapter 10.

They had seen the unchanging Beauty of the one true God, "the Beauty of all things beautiful" (*conf.* 3.6.10), which Plato himself had recognized as "the Beauty by which all beautiful things are beautiful" (*Phaedo* 100d). But they could not humble themselves to accept an incarnate, mortal, crucified God.

This same difficulty, Augustine confesses, initially prevented him from being "humble enough to hold on to my humble God Jesus" (*conf.* 7.18.24). The humbleness, humility, or humiliation of God, which is often translated also, quite aptly, as his "lowliness," is essential to the incarnation. As we could put it nowadays, it is a real "come down" for God to take up our flesh and make it his own, which means taking up our mortality and suffering as his own. Of course Augustine does not think Christ ceased to be the unchanging Truth of God when he took up our human lowliness. Rather, as the Church Father Gregory of Nazianzus put it, "He remained what he was and took up what he was not."[6] He remained the eternal God even as he took up our mortal humanity. That is why he can be the mediator between God and man: he is in one person both the immortal, unchanging God and the man on the cross who suffers death as truly as we do (*conf.* 10.43.68). It is precisely as mediator that his lowly, suffering, mortal humanity can be our road to his immortal, blessed, supreme divinity. And that is why Augustine's interiority cannot do without the externality of God in flesh.

THE SPACE OF INTELLECTUAL VISION

Still, the goal of Augustine's journey is to return to God as the Truth shining in the inner space of the self, heeding Christ's call to "return to the heart and find him" (*conf.* 4.12.19). So, what is this inner space, really? What is it, in other words, that Augustine wants us to understand when he speaks this way? It is not an easy question to answer, as Augustine himself has taken pains to show us. It requires awakening a new kind of vision, or rather becoming aware of a kind of vision that has always been ours, going on within us unnoticed when, for example, we make judgments about what is beautiful (*conf.* 7.17.23). Even the term "vision" is of course a metaphor, just like the language of an

---

[6] Gregory of Nazianzus, *Or.* 29.19 (the third "Theological Oration"). This formula echoes throughout Augustine's writings on Christ; for examples and discussion, see Cary, *Outward Signs*, 145–146.

inner "space," which Augustine has reminded us is not literally a space, but rather "a more inward place that is not a place" (*conf.* 10.9.16). This is a pervasive feature of Platonism, which persistently uses metaphors and allegories derived from sensible experiences like space and vision to describe what is literally beyond imagination. The problem Augustine was facing at the beginning of Book 7 was precisely that all imagination (in his view) is based on the senses, and it runs over images of the same kind of forms that the physical eye sees. So, when we imagine our own inner space and the vision that takes place in it, we are not yet understanding it as it is, using the true eye of the mind, which is the intellect not imagination. We literally cannot imagine the inner space.

Plato gave us the metaphor of the vision of the mind's eye in the allegory of the cave (*Rep.* 7.514a–519b) and it has come down through Plotinus and Porphyry to Augustine. We can call it *intellectual* vision, because the mind that sees is *nous* in Greek, translated as *intellectus* in Latin, best rendered "understanding" in English. Augustine wants us to realize that our capacity for such vision is both ordinary and exalted, as familiar as understanding that two plus two equals four, and as sublime as recognizing the unchanging Light of Truth by which we judge with certainty that this is true. I suggest the best modern term to describe the experience he has in mind is "insight." Think of the moment when you say, "Aha! now I see it!" as you have the insight that gives you full understanding of a mathematical idea. In that moment you have the joy of seeing an unchanging truth, the very same truth that is in the mind of God. It is a kind of insight you can also have while thinking critically about the beauty of external things, as Augustine suggests in *conf.* 7.17.23, for example when you judge that this building is well-designed and that one isn't (cf. *ord.* 2.11.34).

We have an inner space because we have the capacity for such vision. Or, to put it more skeptically – for it is worth thinking critically about this – Augustine's metaphors of inner space and inner vision derive from a nonmaterialist interpretation of such experiences. If his interpretation is correct, then when we find the truth about our own minds and their attention, their ability to form images of mountains and oceans, and their power to understand unchanging truth, we are coming closer to understanding the Truth that is God. For Augustinian theology, a great deal rides on this interpretation, for the ultimate happiness of eternal life is nothing other than "joy in the Truth" (*conf.* 10.23.22) and it is in the inner space of memory that we must seek this long-lost happiness, as if we were the woman in the Bible seeking not just a coin, but the pearl of great price, which it is worth selling everything in order to acquire (Mt 13:46).

VARIETIES OF INTERIORITY

Augustine's innovative conception of interiority stands or falls with the Christian Platonist notion of intellectual vision as the natural capacity of the mind to understand the same unchanging truths or ideas that are eternally present in the mind of God. Later forms of interiority in the West owe much to Augustine, but often depart from his Platonism. In the mystical tradition, for example, the vision of God is regarded as a supernatural gift rather than a natural capacity. (That Augustine regards it as natural is implied by his insistence on purification and his pervasive use of metaphors of healing: to heal and purify the heart is to restore it to its natural condition, not to elevate it in a supernatural fashion). In modernity, by contrast, the possibility of intellectual vision tends to be denied altogether, and the inner self is regarded as inherently private and alone. Whereas in Augustine the inner self is like the inner courtyard of a great palace open to the sun above (cf. *conf.* 10.8.14), modernity puts a roof on the inner self, as it were, so that the inner ideas we see are only images of things outside us, which we never directly behold. Hence the great problem for a long line of modern thinkers is not that "You were within, and I outside" (*conf.* 10.27.34), but rather that I may be forever trapped inside my inner self with my own private ideas and no reliable knowledge of the external world. A third version of Western interiority emerges when the Romantic tradition turns intellectual vision into artistic or poetic insight, and the inner space becomes a place of powerful emotional experience rather than the clarity of intellectual understanding. A variant of this Romantic inner self becomes important in the turn to experience in liberal Protestant theology.

Any one of these later forms of interiority can turn into an alternative to Augustine's long inward journey, which requires the humility to be subject to the external teaching of the humble God Jesus, as carried forward in history by Scripture and the teaching of the Church. Augustine teaches us to long for the day when faith in the authority of external teachers gives way to seeing for ourselves in pure intellectual vision, but he does not think that day will come while we are still sinners amid the temptations of this mortal life. Hence, for those who follow Augustine, the life of reason and the life of authority, the one based on the understanding of inner vision and and the other on faith in external teaching, make for one life – a social life shared in the body of Christ – and no inward flight takes us outside the authority of the Church.

What Augustine intended is perhaps best illustrated by the vision at Ostia, which he shares with his unlearned but devout mother (*conf.* 9.10.23–25). It is a foretaste of the eschatological unity of the Church, when all shall enjoy the vision of God together, and it is also a picture of the true meaning of the life of the Church on earth, where the words of Christ admonish us all to turn inward and look upward, so that we may all enjoy the same Truth and Wisdom, joined to one another by a love and unity that lasts forever. The same shared vision is what Augustine is admonishing us to seek in *Confessions*, hoping his book will do for us what the books of the Platonists did for him, but more reliably, because it also admonishes us to remain in the way of the humble God Jesus, which is the surest road to the divine goal (cf. *civ. Dei* 11.2). For Christ himself is both road and goal, both external Way and inner Truth, both the human Mediator and the divine Wisdom that Augustine and Monica, the brilliant philosopher and the faithful believer in the authority of the Church, briefly touch together as they speak.

Further Reading

Bourke, V. *Augustine's Love of Wisdom: An Introspective Philosophy.* West Lafayette, IN: Purdue University Press, 1992.

Cary, P. *Augustine's Invention of the Inner Self: The Legacy of a Christian Platonist.* New York: Oxford University Press, 2000.

Inner Grace: Augustine in the Traditions of Plato and Paul. New York: Oxford University Press, 2008.

Outward Signs: The Powerlessness of External Things in Augustine's Thought. New York: Oxford University Press, 2008.

Kenney, J. P. *The Mysticism of Saint Augustine: Rereading the* Confessions. New York: Routledge, 2005.

Menn, S. *Descartes and Augustine.* New York: Cambridge University Press, 1998.

O'Connell, R. J. *St. Augustine's* Confessions: *The Odyssey of Soul.* Cambridge, MA: Harvard University Press, 1969.

O'Meara, J. J. *Young Augustine: The Growth of St. Augustine's Mind up to His Conversion.* London: Longman, 1980.

Plotinus. *The Enneads,* trans. Stephen McKenna. New York: Penguin, 1991.

Pseudo-Dionysius. "Mystical Theology." In *Pseudo-Dionysius: The Complete Works,* trans. C. Luibheid. *Classics of Western Spirituality.* New York: Paulist, 1987.

Part III

Reception and Reading Strategies

15 Manuscript Transmission, Critical Editions, and English Translations

GERT PARTOENS

For cultured readers of today, the *Confessions* definitely is the best known and most appreciated work in the large Augustinian text corpus; for many, it might even be one of the few Latin texts of which they are acquainted with or even know. The work clearly appeals to modern sensibilities, as is shown in the continuous publication of new translations and reprint of older ones. Since these translations were/are produced for different audiences and according to divergent translation principles, the *Confessions* presents itself today in many different forms. What the average reader of the translations is less aware of, however, is that the Latin text on which they are based has an equally unstable character, albeit for different reasons. Scribal errors, material accidents, and various intentional interventions have affected the work's extensive medieval manuscript transmission in such a way that no two manuscripts offer an identical Latin text. Moreover, the modern critical editions, which are the direct basis for most translations, present reconstructions of the hypothetical common ancestor of all manuscripts (the archetype) that often contradict one another, mainly because they are not based on identical manuscript selections and/or presuppose divergent reconstructions [*stemmata*] of the genealogical relationships between the selected manuscripts.

The present contribution offers an overview of the main English translations that have appeared since 1620 (the section titled "English Translations") and of the most important text editions, starting with the *editio princeps* of ca 1470 (the section titled "Critical Editions"). The first paragraph will present the most important surviving manuscripts as well as the different hypotheses that have been proposed with regard to their genealogical relationships. This means that the manuscript transmission will be discussed uniquely from a stemmatical point of view. Studies dealing with manuscripts as witnesses of the way

Confessions was read, interpreted, or used by certain persons or specific communities have not been considered.[1]

MANUSCRIPT TRANSMISSION

The Oldest Direct and Indirect Witnesses (6th–11th Centuries)

"*Quid autem meorum opusculorum frequentius et delectabilius inno-tescere potuit quam libri Confessionum mearum* [Which work of mine has been able to become more widely and more agreeably known than the books of my *Confessions*]?" (translations are the author's own). This rhetorical question, which Augustine poses toward the end of his life in *De dono perseuerantiae* (20.53; 428/429 CE), implies that some two and a half decades after its publication the *Confessions* belonged to the bishop's most successful and widely available works. The success of the "autobiography" is also testified to in *Retractationes* (426/427 CE), where it is said that "these books have given much pleasure to many brothers and still do so [*multis tamen fratribus eos multum placuisse et placere scio*]" (2.6.1). Both remarks suggest that, apart from the copy kept in the library of Hippo Regius and mentioned in Possidius' *Indiculus* as item X³.6, several copies of the *Confessions* were circulating already during Augustine's lifetime. This impression is further confirmed by allusions to and quotations from the *Confessions* in several other Christian works of the early fifth century, which testify to its early presence in several of the most important cultural regions of the Western Empire (Africa, Italy, and Spain).[2] Moreover, at the beginning of Book 10 of the *Confessions*, Augustine himself states that the previous nine books – that is, those offering an account of his past life – are being read and listened to by different kinds of people (*conf.* 10.3.4). This remark has been interpreted as implying that the autobiographical part of the *Confessions* was already circulating – at a probably limited scale – before the completion of the entire work. Finally, in the decades and

---

[1] See, e.g., L. Olson, "Reading Augustine's *Confessiones* in Fourteenth-Century England: John de Grandisson's Fashioning of Text and Self," *Traditio* 52 (1997), 201–257; L. Mancia, "Reading Augustine's Confessions in Normandy in the 11th and 12th Centuries," *Tabularia. Études* 14 (2014), 195–233.

[2] P. Courcelle, *Les Confessions de saint Augustin dans la tradition littéraire. Antécédents et postérité* (Paris: Études Augustiniennes, 1963), 201–205; M. Veronese, "Antichi lettori delle Confessioni: maldicenti, subdoli, critici," in *Le Confessioni di Agostino (402–2002): Bilancio e prospettive: XXXI Incontro di studiosi dell'antichità cristiana, Roma, 2–4 maggio 2002*, Studia Ephemeridis Augustinianum 85 (Rome: Institutum Patristicum Augustinianum, 2003), 569–587; D. Weber, "Confessiones," in OGHRA, vol. 1, 167–174, esp. 167.

centuries immediately following the bishop's death (430), the work was frequently used, quoted, or referenced.[3]

In light of its popularity in Late Antiquity and the Early Middle Ages, it might be somewhat surprising that only a few of the ca. 425 preserved manuscript witnesses were produced before the year 800.[4] The oldest preserved complete witness is a parchment codex in half-uncial script consisting of two codicological units that are commonly dated to the first half of the sixth century. The manuscript ended up in the Roman National Library via the Abbey of San Silvestro in Nonantola and the Roman Santa Croce in Gerusalemme (Rome, Biblioteca Nazionale Centrale, Sessorianus 55 [2099]; *CLA* 4, 420a; *LDAB* 7772). Apart from the *Confessions* (fol. 1^v–79^v), this manuscript of 200 folia mainly contains a series of patristic sermons.[5] A second sixth-century witness, that might have been slightly older than the *Sessorianus*, but today consists of only one folium (*conf.* 9.13.1–10.3.4), was discovered during the Spanish Civil War in Madrid (Convento de la Encarnación, s. n.). This witness in uncial script, which was probably also produced in Italy (although Spain cannot be excluded), unfortunately disappeared shortly after its discovery and is presently known uniquely through a photograph preserved among the Lowe papers in the Pierpont Morgan Library in New York (*CLA* 11, 1640; *LDAB* 9077).[6] Apart from these two codices and an eighth-/ninth-century fragment (*conf.* 1.15.24–16.25) in Würzburg (Universitätsbibliothek, M.p.misc.f.5a, orig. [south]west Germany, fol. 40v; *CLA* 9, 1402; *LDAB* 8810), we dispose of only a limited number of manuscripts up until the end of the eleventh century, while the bulk of the preserved witnesses was produced in the twelfth to the fifteen centuries.[7]

Although several studies have been dedicated to the subject since the late nineteenth century, the transmission of the *Confessions* remains to a certain degree a *terra incognita* calling for further inquiry. Thanks to the publication of the series *Die handschriftliche Überlieferung der Werke des heiligen Augustinus*, the inventory of preserved

---

[3] Courcelle, *Les Confessions*, 205–264; Weber, "*Confessiones*," 167–168.

[4] M. M. Gorman, "The Early Manuscript Tradition of St. Augustine's *Confessiones*," *Journal of Theological Studies* 34 (1983), 114–145, esp. 115 = M. M. Gorman, *The Manuscript Traditions of the Works of St Augustine*, Millennio Medievale 27 (Firenze: SISMEL, Edizioni del Galluzzo, 2001), 216–247, esp. 217.

[5] For a detailed description, see Manus OnLine (https://manus.iccu.sbn.it//).

[6] L. Verheijen, "Contributions à une édition critique améliorée des Confessions de saint Augustin," *Augustiniana* 28 (1978), 13–17, esp. 13–15.

[7] Compare the numbers given in footnote 10.

witnesses was greatly enlarged over the past decades: whereas André Wilmart's inventories published in 1929/1931 contained respectively 204 and 258 (complete and partial) witnesses,[8] the collaborators of the Austrian series have presently identified no less than 299 manuscripts.[9] Their inventory does not yet comprise, however, the important number of manuscripts that have been preserved in French libraries; for these, we are still depending on the information offered by Wilmart and some supplementary lists that have been published since.[10] Luc Verheijen, the most recent critical editor of the *Confessions*, estimates that the total number of preserved witnesses has to be situated around 425.[11]

A second major lacuna concerns the stemmatical relationships between the manuscripts: these have been studied only for part of the oldest manuscripts, whose number – as indicated earlier – is already rather limited. The direct witnesses that have been at the center of stemmatical research are presented in the following list (more or less in chronological order)[12] together with the *sigla* they have been attributed in the studies that will be discussed further on. A striking feature of this list is that most ninth-century witnesses were produced in France.[13]

[8] A. Wilmart, "Les manuscrits des Confessions de S. Augustin. Répertoire méthodique," *Revue bénédictine* 41 (1929), 325–332; A. Wilmart, "La tradition des grands ouvrages de saint Augustin," in *Studi Agostiniani*, Miscellanea Agostiniana 2 (Rome: Tipografia Poliglotta Vaticana, 1931), 257–315, esp. 259–266.

[9] The first eleven volumes of *Die handschriftliche Überlieferung der Werke des heiligen Augustinus* (Vienna: Verlag der Österreichischen Akademie der Wissenschaften, 1969–2010) cover the following countries: Italy (1), Great Britain and Ireland (2), Poland and Scandinavia (3), Spain and Portugal (4), Germany (5/10), Austria (6), Czech and Slovak Republics (7), Benelux (8), Switzerland (9), and Russia, Slovenia, and Hungary (11).

[10] M. Skutella, "Der Handschriftenbestand der Confessiones S. Augustini," *Revue bénédictine* 42 (1930), 205–209; *Sancti Augustini Confessionum libri XIII*, ed. L. Verheijen, CCL 27 (Turnhout: Brepols, 1981), lix–lxxi; Gorman, "The Early Manuscript Tradition," 115 and 144–145. The eleven volumes of *Die handschriftliche Überlieferung* list 299 witnesses, 262 of which postdate the year 1100. For the preceding centuries, the numbers are as follows: sixth century (2); eighth and ninth centuries (1); ninth century (8); tenth century (8); tenth and eleventh centuries (1); eleventh centuries (14); and eleventh and twelfth centuries (3).

[11] *Sancti Augustini Confessionum libri XIII*, lx.

[12] The dates and places of origin of the ninth-century manuscripts are those proposed in B. Bischoff, *Katalog der festländischen Handschriften des neunten Jahrhunderts (mit Ausnahme der wisigotischen)*, three vols. (Wiesbaden: Harrassowitz, 1998–2014). For the tenth- and eleventh-century manuscripts, see Gorman, "The Early Manuscript Tradition," 144–145.

[13] This list comprises all preserved witnesses from the sixth to the ninth centuries, with the exception of the manuscripts mentioned in n. 31–33, the Madrid and Würzburg fragments, Trier, Stadtbibliothek-Stadtarchiv, 144/1188, s. $IX^{3/4}$, orig. East France (?) (abbreviation), and Sankt Gallen, Stiftsbibliothek, 156, s. IX med. (fragment).

S   Rome, Biblioteca Nazionale Centrale, Sessorianus 55 (2099), s. VI$^{1/2}$

J   Fulda, Hessische Landesbibliothek, Aa.9, s. IX in., orig. southwest Germany? Alsace? (Books 11–12)

P   Paris, Bibliothèque Nationale, Latin 1912, s. IX$^{2/4}$, orig. north France

D   Paris, Bibliothèque Nationale, Latin 1913A, s. IX$^{2/3}$, orig. region of Ghent?

C   Paris, Bibliothèque Nationale, Latin 1913, s. IX med., orig. central France?

O   Paris, Bibliothèque Nationale, Latin 1911, s. IX$^{3/3}$, orig. north Italy (region of Milan)?

F   Paris, Bibliothèque Nationale, Latin 10862, s. IX$^{3/4}$, orig. east France

H   Paris, Bibliothèque Nationale, Latin 12224, s. IX$^{3/4}$, orig. France

E   Paris, Bibliothèque Nationale, Latin 12191, s. IX$^{2/2}$ and X$^{1/2}$, orig. central France (Tours?)

A   Stuttgart, Württembergische Landesbibliothek, HB.VII.15, s. IX$^{4/4}$, orig. east France?

V   Biblioteca Apostolica Vaticana, Vat. lat. 5756, s. IX$^{4/4}$, orig. north Italy

G   Paris, Bibliothèque Nationale, Latin 12193, s. IX–X, orig. Loire Valley (Fleury?)

B   Bamberg, Staatsbibliothek, B.III.23 (Patr. 33), s. X in.

M   Munich, Bayerische Staatsbibliothek, Clm 14350, s. X$^{2/2}$, orig. south Germany

W   Vienna, Österreichische Nationalbibliothek, lat. 712, s. X–XI

Z   Tours, Bibliothèque Municipale, 283, s. XI in.

Q   Berlin, Deutsche Staatsbibliothek, Phillipps 1678 (Rose 19), s. XI

In addition to these direct sources, part of the *Confessions* has also been transmitted through indirect witnesses. The oldest of these are a letter of Augustine's companion Evodius of Uzalis (d. ca. 425), the *Vita sancti Augustini* by Possidius of Calama (ca. 370–ca. 440), and the *Liber sententiarum* compiled by Prosper of Aquitaine (ca. 390–455), which contain some loose quotations from the *Confessions* that are of little importance from a text critical point of view.[14] More important in this respect are three anthologies that contain substantial and faithful extracts from Augustine's text.

The most important of these anthologies was compiled at the beginning of the sixth century by Eugippius of Lucullanum (ca. 455–

---

[14] *Sancti Augustini Confessionum libri XIII*, lxxii–iv and lxxviii.

ca. 535), the *Excerpta ex operibus sancti Augustini*. This anthology originally contained five extensive extracts, which cover 6 percent of the complete text of the *Confessions*, but in a few manuscripts this number was expanded to 8 percent. The three additional extracts, which may depend on a different source text than the five original ones, were inserted very early on, since we encounter them already in the sixth-century codex Biblioteca Apostolica Vaticana, Vat. lat. 3375, orig. south Italy (*CLA* 1, 16; *LDAB* 7361).[15]

A second early medieval florilegium that extensively quotes the *Confessions* is the *Collectio ex opusculis sancti Augustini in epistulas Pauli apostoli*, a line-by-line commentary on the Pauline Epistles compiled by the Venerable Bede (672–735) and consisting exclusively of quotations from the works of the African Church Father.[16] Although Bede borrowed many extracts of this commentary from Eugippius' *Excerpta*,[17] this does not seem to be the case for his nine quotations from the *Confessions*.[18] A second but more extensive Pauline commentary composed of Augustinian quotations was produced around the middle of the ninth century by Florus of Lyons. This monumental compilation, which not only depends on direct witnesses of Augustine's works, but possibly also on Eugippius and certainly on Bede,[19] contains no less than twenty-two extracts from the *Confessions*.[20]

The genealogical relationships between the oldest manuscript witnesses of the *Confessions* have been represented in various and even contradicting ways. The remaining part of this paragraph will offer an overview of the different hypotheses that have been proposed.

---

[15] Ibid., x–xii and lxxiv–v. Original extracts: V.5/5a, VI.6, X.25, and XI.26 in Pius Knöll's edition of the *Excerpta* (*CSEL* 9.1); additional extracts: VIII.8 and VIIII.9 (combining two extracts).

[16] *Sancti Augustini Confessionum libri XIII*, lxxvi–vii. The extracts are numbers 113, 127, 146, 164, 198, 326, 362, 396, and 437 in P.-I. Fransen, "Description de la Collection de Bède le Vénérable sur l'Apôtre," *Revue bénédictine* 71 (1961), 22–70.

[17] P.-I. Fransen, "D'Eugippius à Bède le Vénérable. À propos de leurs florilèges augustiniens," *Revue bénédictine* 97 (1987), 187–194.

[18] I owe this information to Nicolas De Maeyer, who presently prepares the *editio princeps* (*CCL*) of Bede's still unedited commentary.

[19] For a general presentation of Florus' commentary (and its sources), see S. Boodts, "Florus of Lyon's Expositio epistolarum beati Pauli apostoli and the transmission of Augustine's Sermones ad populum," in *On Good Authority: Tradition, Compilation and the Construction of Authority in Literature from Antiquity to the Renaissance*, ed. R. Ceulemans et al., Lectio: Studies in the Transmission of Texts and Ideas 3 (Turnhout: Brepols, 2015), 141–156.

[20] *Sancti Augustini Confessionum libri XIII*, lxxvii–viii.

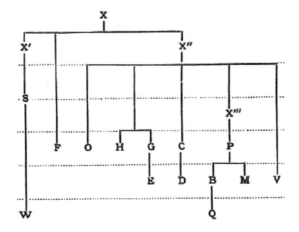

Fig. 1

Pius Knöll, who was the first to use the testimony of the *Sessorianus*, claimed that the latter codex was very close to the archetype of the entire transmission. His *CSEL* edition of 1896 followed, by consequence, closely the text of *S*,[21] although the latter's influence was lessened in Knöll's *editio minor* in the *Bibliotheca Teubneriana* (1898).[22] Knöll did not propose, however, a real *stemma codicum*. The first to do this was Felice Ramorino in the *Prolegomena* to his Roman edition of 1909. Using Knöll's collations, the Italian scholar proposed the above-mentioned *stemma* of the manuscripts used by his predecessor (see Fig. 1).[23]

A second *stemma* was proposed by Martin Skutella in his Teubner edition of 1934. This *stemma* did not mention *W* because Skutella also considered it a descendant (or even a "mere copy") of *S*. There are, however, several significant divergences from Ramorino's *stemma*, the most important of which regards the status of manuscript *F*. Together with all other *codices* (*W* excepted), this manuscript now forms a family that stands opposite *S* (and *W*). The *Sessorianus* has thus become the hyparchetype of one of the two families into which the entire transmission has been divided (see Fig. 2).

[21] *Sancti Aureli Augustini Confessionum libri tredecim*, ed. P. Knöll, *CSEL* 33 (Prague: F. Tempsky/G. Freytag, 1896).

[22] *Sancti Aureli Augustini Confessionum libri tredecim*, ed. P. Knöll, Bibliotheca Scriptorum Graecorum et Romanorum Teubneriana (Leipzig: Teubner, 1898), v–x.

[23] *Aurelii Augustini Confessiones*, curante Felici Ramorino, Bibliotheca Sanctorum Patrum et Scriptorum Ecclesiasticorum 6.2.1 (Rome: Ex Officina Typographica Forzani et Socii, 1909), xxxi–v.

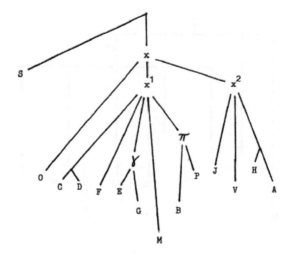

Fig. 2

In reconstructing the transmission's archetype, Skutella also attached great value to the testimony of Eugippius' *Excerpta*. In this, he was following a suggestion by Bernard Capelle (1927), according to whom Eugippius's source manuscript – probably datable to the fifth century – must have closely resembled that of the transmission's archetype.[24] Skutella remained, however, somewhat vague with regard to the exact stemmatical position of Eugippius's excerpts.[25]

The old *Sessorianus* was attributed a much less important position in Gorman's correction of Skutella's *stemma* (1983). According to Gorman, the manuscript constituted a branch together with *O* against all other direct witnesses. He also claimed that Eugippius's five original extracts constituted a third independent branch. For the three additional extracts, Gorman suggested a dependence on a source close to *S* (see Fig. 3).[26]

In the *stemma* proposed by Luc Verheijen in his *CCL* edition of 1981,[27] the *Sessorianus* was attributed an even less important

[24] B. Capelle, "Bulletin d'ancienne littérature chrétienne latine," *Revue bénédictine* 39 (1927), 245–252, esp. 248–251.
[25] *S. Aureli Augustini Confessionum libri tredecim*, ed. M. Skutella, Bibliotheca Scriptorum Graecorum et Romanorum Teubneriana (Leipzig: Teubner, 1934), ix, xx–xxiii.
[26] Gorman, "The Early Manuscript Tradition," 119–138.
[27] *Sancti Augustini Confessionum libri XIII*, v–lviii. Before 1981, Verheijen proposed two different *stemmata*: "Contributions à une édition critique améliorée," *Augustiniana* 20 (1970), 35–53, esp. 52; *Augustiniana* 22 (1972), 35–52, esp. 43. Both *stemmata* are discussed in Gorman, "The Early Manuscript Tradition," 139–142.

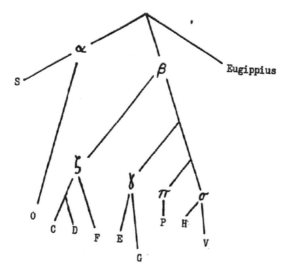

Fig. 3

position: manuscript *S* is now thought to have formed a family together with all other codices and Eugippius's five original extracts. This family as a whole stands opposite manuscript *O* alone.[28] From a stemmatical point of view, the latter has thus become as important as *S* was in the initial *stemmata* of Ramorino and Skutella. We are far removed here from Knöll's high appreciation of the critical value of *S* (see Fig. 4).

In spite of their differences, the conclusions of Ramorino, Skutella, Gorman, and Verheijen rest on the common presupposition that the transmission of the text of the *Confessions* was not strongly contaminated. This presupposition, however, was recently challenged by Bengt Alexanderson, who claimed that the entire transmission is heavily contaminated, to the exception of manuscript *S*, which according to him was too strongly depreciated by Gorman and Verheijen. Convinced that the contamination made it completely impossible to construct a global *stemma*, Alexanderson limited his positive conclusions merely to the identification of some groups of related manuscripts. These groups correspond with some of the subfamilies in the *stemmata* proposed by Alexanderson's predecessors: probably linked are *SO* (compare Gorman), while *DC*, *HAV*, *PBZ*, and *EGM* are groups of

[28] For the additional extracts, see *Sancti Augustini Confessionum libri XIII*, lxxiv–v.

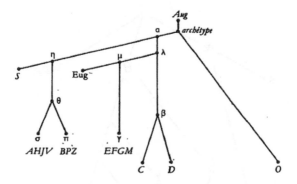

Fig. 4

certainly related manuscripts (compare Skutella, Gorman, and Verheijen). With regard to *W*, Alexanderson recognizes the close links with *S*, although he attributes them to contamination and not to a dependence of *W* on *S*. Finally, Alexanderson refrains from definitive conclusions with regard to the stemmatical position of Eugippius and manuscripts *J* and *F*.[29]

Apart from the old manuscripts listed, there exist a few ninth-century and a series of tenth-/eleventh-century witnesses that have played only a marginal or even no role in stemmatical studies. Most of these are listed in Verheijen's *CCL* edition, if possible with an indication of their affiliation with one of the accepted families.[30] A few of them have a kinship with *DC*,[31] *HAV*,[32] or *EGM*,[33] but the large majority of the tenth-/eleventh-century codices have a connection with *PBZ*.

Finally, no clear conclusions could be drawn concerning the stemmatical position of the extracts in Bede's *Collectio*, while traces of the influential *PBZ* family have been detected in some, but not all, extracts in Florus' *Expositio*. There is, however, reason to believe that

[29] B. Alexanderson, *Le texte des* Confessions *de saint Augustin. Manuscrits et stemma*, Acta Regiae Societatis Scientiarum Litterarum Gothoburgiensis 42 (Göteborg: Kungl. Vetenskaps- och Vitterhets-Samhället, 2003); B. Alexanderson, "Les Confessions de saint Augustin: manuscrits et stemma," in *Le Confessioni di Agostino (402–2002)*, 31–34.

[30] *Sancti Augustini Confessionum libri XIII*, lx–xiv.

[31] E.g., Rome, Biblioteca Casanatense, 641, s. IX in., orig. south Italy (fragment).

[32] E.g., Rome, Biblioteca Angelica, 162 (B.6.15), s. IX$^{3/4}$, orig. north Italy? (partial witness).

[33] E.g., Wolfenbüttel, Herzog-August-Bibliothek, Weiss. 57, s. IX$^{3/4}$, orig. Weissenburg (fragment).

the latter also borrowed material from Bede's commentary,[34] which implies that the Carolingian scholar depended on both direct and indirect sources.

The Circulation of the *Confessions* in Post-Conquest England

The later manuscript transmission of the *Confessions* has not yet received the attention it deserves. An interesting exception, however, is the study Teresa Webber dedicated to the work's diffusion in England in the eleventh/twelfth centuries.[35] According to the English scholar, the first traces of the circulation of the *Confessions* (direct witnesses, quotations, and book lists) date from after the Norman invasion (1066) – apart from some much earlier quotations in the work of Bede and Alcuin as well as in the Royal Prayer Book (London, British Library, Royal 2.A. xx, s. VIII$^{2/2}$).[36] Since the oldest preserved English manuscripts of the *Confessions* date from after the Conquest and can be divided, according to Webber, into two separate families that each depend on an imported codex of continental origin, she suggests that the *Confessions* circulated in England in the eighth and early ninth century, but that the text was subsequently lost, possibly through "the devastation of book collections wrought by the Vikings, or through lack of interest, or both."[37] The dissemination of the *Confessions* in England from the second half of the eleventh century onward thus seems to depend on the reintroduction of the work after an absence of some 200 years.[38]

Although neither of the two continental codices on which the aforementioned two families of English witnesses depend has been preserved, we do still dispose of their continental models, viz. the Carolingian manuscript *D*, which from at least the middle of the eleventh until the late twelfth century belonged to St. Peter's in Ghent, and

---

[34] I owe this information to N. De Maeyer (footnote 18).

[35] T. Webber, "The Diffusion of Augustine's *Confessions* in England during the Eleventh and Twelfth Centuries," in *The Cloister and the World: Essays in Medieval History in Honour of Barbara Harvey*, eds. J. Blair, et al. (Oxford: Clarendon, 1996), 29–45.

[36] According to Webber, "There is some evidence that the *Confessions* had been known in England in the eighth and early ninth centuries, if only through extracts . . . even though no copies of the complete text nor *florilegia* containing extracts have survived from that date" ("The Diffusion," 31). This remark is partially incorrect, since Bede's Pauline commentary, which Webber does not mention, contains nine extracts from the *Confessions*. This correction, however, does not affect her general argument.

[37] Webber, "The Diffusion," 31.

[38] Ibid., 30–33.

Boulogne-sur-Mer, Bibliothèque Municipale, 46, s. XI mid., which may
have been produced at/for Saint-Bertin and is acquainted with the *PBZ*
family. The preserved direct witnesses of English origin thus seem to
depend on two Flemish ancestors. According to Webber, this dependence was probably not mediated by models from Normandy; both the
Norman and English transmissions of the *Confessions*, she believes,
started more or less simultaneously and should be set within the
broader context of a general renewed interest in the Fathers throughout
Western Europe during the eleventh century.[39]

The oldest English descendants of *D* date from around 1100 and
were produced in southwest England (Oxford, Bodleian Library, Bodley
815; Salisbury, Cathedral Library, 6; London, British Library, Harley
3080; Royal 5.B.XIV); from the twelfth century onward the family
became widely diffused in England as a whole (Webber gives examples
of copies at Hereford, Lanthony, and Lincoln).[40] The most important
descendants of the manuscript of Boulogne-sur-Mer are a late eleventh-
century codex from Christ Church, Canterbury (Cambridge, Trinity
College, B.3.25 [104]) and a twelfth-century manuscript from Durham
(Cathedral Library, B.IV.6). Other representatives of the family depend
on the Canterbury manuscript and were produced in southeast England
(Webber offers examples from Canterbury and Rochester).[41]

CRITICAL EDITIONS[42]

The *editio princeps* of the *Confessions* was published by printer and
bookseller Johann Mentelin in Strasbourg around 1470.[43] The text of
this edition is linked with the influential family *PBZ*. Subsequently, the

---

[39] Webber, "The Diffusion," 39–43. For the renewed interest in the Fathers, see also T.
Webber, "Monastic and Cathedral Book Collections in the Late Eleventh and
Twelfth Centuries," in *The Cambridge History of Libraries in Britain and Ireland*,
eds. E. Leedham-Green, et al. (Cambridge: Cambridge University Press, 2006), vol. 1,
109–125.

[40] Webber, "The Diffusion," 34–36.

[41] Ibid., 36–39.

[42] The editions mentioned in this section are generally considered milestones in the
editorial history of the *Confessions*. For minor editions, see the list of the fifteenth-
to eighteenth-century editions (and translations) offered in C. T. G. Schönemann,
Bibliotheca historico-literaria Patrum Latinorum (Leipzig: In libraria Weidmannia,
1794), vol. 2, 235–250 (= *PL* 47:134–141), synthesized in B. Warfield, "The
Confessions of St. Augustine," *The American Journal of Theology* 7 (1903),
500–514, esp. 506–507 (with additions for the nineteenth century).

[43] *Augustinus: Confessiones* (Strasbourg: Johann Mentelin, ca. 1470) (GKW 2893;
USTC 743106).

work appeared as part of the Church Father's *Opera omnia*[44] issued in Basel by Amerbach and Froben in, respectively, 1505–1506 (vol. 4) and 1528–1529 (vol. 1), Erasmus being the editor of the latter.[45] It was in these editions – again connected with *PBZ*[46] – that the work, which in the manuscripts and the *editio princeps* had been divided only into thirteen books, was subdivided into chapters. In the *Opera omnia* produced by the theologians of Leuven and published by Christoffel Plantijn in Antwerp (1576–1577), the *Confessions* was also included in volume 1.[47] Its text relied on the previous editions and five manuscripts from four Belgian monasteries (Gembloux, Saint-Martin [Tournai], Parc, and Bethlehem [Leuven]).[48]

In 1649, Robert Arnauld d'Andilly published an important French translation that has been reprinted many times. In the preface, Robert claimed that his translation was based on a (then still unpublished) Latin text that had been purified through collation with nine manuscripts *fort bons & fort anciens*.[49] In 1659, at the latest, the same translation was published together with the Latin text, which, meanwhile, had been perfected through collation with three further manuscripts.[50] In a critical appendix written by Robert's brother, Antoine Arnauld, the twelve manuscripts in question are identified: *CHG* and nine twelfth- to fourteenth-century codices, eleven of which are still

---

[44] For the publication of Augustine's *Opera omnia* in early modern times (overview of different editions and reprints), see P. Petitmengin, "Éditions princeps et *Opera omnia de saint Augustin*," in *Augustinus in der Neuzeit*, eds. D. de Courcelles, et al. (Turnhout: Brepols, 1998), 33–51, esp. 43.

[45] *Prima [-Undecima] pars librorum diui Aurelii Augustini* (Basel: Johann Amerbach, 1505–1506) (USTC 686497); *D. Aurelii Augustini Hipponensis episcopi omnium operum primus [-decimus] tomus, summa uigilantia repurgatorum à mendis innumeris, per Des. Erasmum Roterodamum* (Basel: Johann Froben, 1528–1529) (USTC 625902).

[46] For the impact of *PBZ* on the first editions, see *Sancti Augustini Confessionum libri XIII*, vi–vii.

[47] *Opera D. Aurelii Augustini ... tomis decem comprehensa: per Theologos Louanienses ex manuscriptis codicibus multo labore emendata* (Antwerp: Christoffel Plantijn, 1576–1577) (USTC 406342).

[48] Ibid., vol. 1, 376.

[49] *Les Confessions de S. Augustin. Traduites en François par Monsieur Arnauld d'Andilly* (Paris: widow Jean Camusat, 1649), fol. aVII[r/v].

[50] For the year 1659, see Schönemann, *Bibliotheca*, 247. I have consulted *Les Confessions de S. Augustin. Traduites en François par Monsieur Arnauld d'Andilly. Nouvelle edition. Avec le Latin à costé, reveu & corrigé ... Par Monsieur Arnauld, son frere* (Paris: Pierre le Petit, 1676).

preserved in Parisian libraries.[51] Two decades later, the Benedictine monks of the Congregation of Saint-Maur published a new edition of the *Confessions* in volume 1 of their influential *Opera omnia* edition.[52] It was based on all of the mentioned editions as well as on twenty-seven manuscripts, including the old Parisian *codices DE* and those used by Arnauld (including *CHG*). Other manuscripts were consulted in French libraries (mainly Parisian), the Vatican, and Oxford.[53] This new edition, which was reprinted in the nineteenth century in Migne's *Patrologia Latina* (vol. 32), retained the chapter division of the Basel editions (Roman numbering), but supplemented it with an alternative division in paragraphs (Arabic numbering). This double numbering system is still in use today.

Later modern editions based on original manuscript research were published independently from *Opera omnia* projects. The most important of these editions are those of Laurent-Étienne Rondet (1776; using fifteen manuscripts from the Royal Library in Paris, including *DC* and – for the first time – *PO*),[54] Edward Bouverie Pusey (1838; correcting the Maurist text on the basis of several Oxford manuscripts),[55] Pius Knöll (1896 [*CSEL* 33]; using for the first time and heavily relying on *S* [*editio minor* in the *Bibliotheca Teubneriana* in 1898]), Felice Ramorino (1909), Martin Skutella (1934 [*Bibliotheca Teubneriana*]),[56] and Luc Verheijen (1981 [*CCL* 27]). The last three editions are each based on a different *stemma codicum*, but all take a critical stance toward the value of the old *Sessorianus*.

Other modern editions of the *Confessions* are not based on original manuscript research, but depend more or less on one of the already

---

[51] For the appendix, see fol. fffVI^r–gggVII^v. For the eleven preserved witnesses, see Gorman, "The Early Manuscript Tradition," 116–117.

[52] *Sancti Aurelii Augustini Hipponensis episcopi Operum tomus primus [-undecimus]. Post Louaniensium theologorum recensionem castigatus ... Opera et studio Monachorum Ordinis S. Benedicti è Congregatione S. Mauri* (Paris: Franciscus Muguet, 1679-1700).

[53] M. M. Gorman, "The Maurists' Manuscripts of Four Major Works of Saint Augustine. With Some Remarks on Their Editorial Techniques," *Revue bénédictine* 91 (1981), 238–279, esp. 245–246 = id., *The Manuscript Traditions,* 62–103, esp. 69–70.

[54] *Diui Aurelii Augustini, Hipponensis episcopi, Confessionum libri tredecim. Ad calcem additae sunt uariae lectiones,* ed. L.-É. Rondet (Paris: Typis Philippi Dionysii Pierres, 1776) (list of manuscripts: i–iv). With regard to *C*, I am following Gorman, "The Early Manuscript Tradition," 116 and 118.

[55] *S. Aurelii Augustini Confessiones. Post editionem Parisiensem nouissimam ad fidem codicum Oxoniensium recognitae,* ed. E. B. Pusey (Oxford: Parker, 1838).

[56] A revised edition was published by H. Jürgens and W. Schaub in 1969.

mentioned editions. The edition of John Gibb and William Montgomery (Cambridge Patristic Texts [1908]) depended heavily on Knöll's *CSEL* edition,[57] while Pierre De Labriolle produced an edition in which the choices between variant readings were based on an "intuition formée en contact prolongé avec le texte" (1925–1926; Collection des Universités de France).[58] Skutella's text was reproduced in the Bibliothèque Augustinienne (1962) and – with some corrections by Michele Pellegrino – in the Nuova Biblioteca Agostiniana (1965).[59] The text offered by James O'Donnell (1992) is mainly based on the editions of the Maurists, Knöll, Skutella, and Verheijen as well as on the information offered in their critical apparatuses.[60] Although these "derived" editions do not contain a critical apparatus, most of them – especially that of O'Donnell – do offer critical notes.

ENGLISH TRANSLATIONS[61]

The first complete English translation of the *Confessions* was published by the Catholic convert Tobie Matthew at the English College of St. Omer in 1620 (republished both in full and in the form of extracts at Paris in 1638).[62] A Protestant "counter-translation" of the entire work, which nevertheless strongly depended on Matthew, appeared in London in 1631, authored by William Watts (republished in 1650; several later reprints).[63] Translations

---

[57] *The Confessions of Augustine*, eds. J. Gibb and W. Montgomery, Cambridge Patristic Texts (Cambridge: Cambridge University Press, 1908).

[58] *Saint Augustin:* Confessions, two vols., ed. and trans. P. de Labriolle, Collection des Universités de France (Paris: Les Belles lettres, 1925–1926).

[59] *Augustin: Les* Confessions, Bibliothèque Augustinienne 13–14 (Paris: Desclée de Brouwer, 1962); *Le confessioni [di] Sant'Agostino*, Nuova Biblioteca Agostiniana 1 (Rome: Città nuova, 1965).

[60] J. J. O'Donnell, *Augustine:* Confessions, three vols. (Oxford: Oxford University Press, 1992), esp. vol. 1, lx.

[61] For the translations up until that of Chadwick (1991), this selective overview owes much to Warfield, "The *Confessions*," 512–514; and M. Vessey, "Saint Augustine: *Confessions*," *Augustinian Studies* 24 (1993), 163–181, esp. 164–170 and 180.

[62] *The Confessions of the Incomparable Doctour S. Augustine*, translated into English [by Sir Tobie Matthew] ([St. Omer: English College, 1620]) (USTC 3009277/1436865); *The Confessions of S. Augustine Bishope of Hippon. and D. of the Church*, translated into English by S. T. M, second ed. (Paris: for widow Blageart, 1638) (USTC 6004193/ 6004269/3020126); *The Kernell or Extract of the Historicall Part, of S. Augustins Confessions; Together with All the Most Affectuous Passages Thereof; Taken Out of That Whole Booke, & Severed from Such Parts, as Are Obscure* (Paris: for widow Blageart, 1638) (USTC 6004272/3019612).

[63] *St. Augustines Confessions Translated: and with Some Marginall Notes Illustrated* by *William Watts* (London: for John Partridge, 1631) (USTC 3015445); same title

of the first ten books were subsequently produced by the Catholic translators Abraham Woodhead (London, 1660 [with an expanded edition in 1679])[64] and Richard Challoner (London, 1739 [several reprints until 1904]).[65]

In 1838, a full translation of the *Confessions* was published by Edward Bouverie Pusey as the first volume of *A Library of Fathers of the Holy Catholic Church* (several reprints within and outside the series). This translation, which was partly based on that of Watts and was to become the most widely read of English translations until the early twentieth century, appeared in abbreviated form (Books 1–10) from 1848 onward.[66] Comparable abbreviations were produced during the second half of the nineteenth century by W. H. Hutchings (Books 1–10)[67] and Charles Bigg (Books 1–9).[68] A second full translation of the work produced in the nineteenth century was that by J. G. Pilkington.[69] This translation, which was influenced by those of Watts and Pusey, became a text of reference until the second half of the twentieth century thanks to its reprints in NPNF (from 1886 onward) and *Basic Writings of Saint Augustine* (from 1948 onward).[70]

(London: for Abel Roper, 1650) (USTC 3040999). For the polemical religious context of Matthew's and Watts' translations, see Vessey, "Saint Augustine: *Confessions*," 164–166; K. Curtin, "Augustine in the Lady's "Closet": Gender, Conversion, and Polemic in Seventeenth-Century English Translations of the *Confessions*," *Studies in Philology* 115 (2018), 524–543.

[64] *The Life of S. Augustine. The First Part. Written by Himself in the First Ten Books of His Confessions Faithfully Translated* [by Abraham Woodhead] (London: for John Crook, 1660); *S. Augustine's Confessions. With the Continuation of His Life to the End Thereof, Extracted Out of Possidius, and the Father's Own Unquestioned Works*, translated into English [by Abraham Woodhead] (s.l.: s.n., 1679).

[65] *St. Augustine's Confessions; or, Praises of God*, in ten books, newly translated into English from the original Latin by Richard Challoner (London: for T. Meighan, 1739). For the reprints, see Vessey, "Saint Augustine: *Confessions*," 167 and 180.

[66] *The Confessions of S. Augustine*, trans. E. B. Pusey, A Library of Fathers of the Holy Catholic Church Anterior to the Division of the East and West 1 (Oxford/London: John Henry Parker, 1838). About reprints, see Vessey, "Saint Augustine: *Confessions*," 167–169.

[67] *The Confessions of S. Augustine, Ten Books*, trans. W. H. Hutchings, Library of Spiritual Works for English Catholics (London: Longmans, Green and Co., 1878) (with reprints).

[68] *The Confessions of Saint Augustine*, trans. C. Bigg, The Library of Devotion (London: Methuen & Co., 1898) (with reprints).

[69] *The Confessions of St. Augustine, Bishop of Hippo*, trans. J. G. Pilkington (Edinburgh: T. & T. Clark, 1876) (with reprints).

[70] NPNF 1 (Buffalo: Christian Literature Co., 1886) and *Basic Writings* (New York: Random House, 1948).

The twentieth and twenty-first centuries saw the publication of several new translations, of which only a selection can be presented here (most of these have had several reprints). In 1912, a two-volume edition of the *Confessions* was included in the *Loeb Classical Library*; its accompanying translation was a reprint of Watts' translation (1631), which was corrected by William Henry Denham Rouse on the basis of the then recent *CSEL* edition of Knöll (1896) and the nineteenth-century translations of Pusey and Bigg.[71] This old *Loeb* translation was recently replaced by that of Carolyn J.-B. Hammond (2014 and 2016).[72] Other influential translations were those of Frank J. Sheed (1942 [Books 1–10]; 1943 [Books 1–13 in Catholic Masterpiece Tutorial Series 1/7]), Vernon J. Bourke (FC 21 [1953]), Albert Cook Outler (LCC 7 [1955]), John Kenneth Ryan (1960), R. S. Pine-Coffin (Penguin Classics [1961]), Henry Chadwick (Oxford World Classics [1991]), and Maria Boulding (WSA I/1 [1997]). The most recent translations – together with the already mentioned *Loeb* volumes of Hammond – are those of Sarah Ruden (2017)[73] and Peter Constantine (2018).[74]

Further Reading

Alexanderson, B. *Le texte des* Confessions *de saint Augustin. Manuscrits et stemma*. Acta Regiae Societatis Scientiarum Litterarum Gothoburgiensis 42. Göteborg: Kungl. Vetenskaps- och Vitterhets-Samhället, 2003.

Gorman, M. M. "The Early Manuscript Tradition of St. Augustine's *Confessiones*." *Journal of Theological Studies* 34 (1983), 114–145 = M. M. Gorman, *The Manuscript Traditions of the Works of St Augustine*. Millennio Medievale 27. Firenze: SISMEL, Edizioni del Galluzzo, 2001, 216–247.

Petitmengin, P. "Éditions princeps et Opera omnia de saint Augustin." In *Augustinus in der Neuzeit*, eds. D. de Courcelles et al. Turnhout: Brepols, 1998, 33–51.

Sancti Augustini Confessionum libri XIII, ed. L. Verheijen, *CCL* 27 (Turnhout: Brepols, 1981), v–xci.

---

[71] *Saint Augustine's* Confessions, trans. W. Watts and W. H. D. Rouse, Loeb Classical Library 26–27 (Cambridge, MA: Harvard University Press, 1912).

[72] *Augustine:* Confessions, trans. C. J.-B. Hammond, LCL 26–7 (Cambridge, MA: Harvard University Press, 2014 and 2016).

[73] *Augustine:* Confessions, trans. S. Ruden (New York: The Modern Library, 2017).

[74] *Saint Augustine:* Confessions: *A New Translation*, trans. P. Constantine (New York: Liveright, 2018).

Vessey, M. "Saint Augustine: *Confessions.*" *Augustinian Studies* 24 (1993), 163–181.

Webber, T. "The Diffusion of Augustine's Confessions in England during the Eleventh and Twelfth Centuries." In *The Cloister and the World: Essays in Medieval History in Honour of Barbara Harvey,* eds. J. Blair, et al. Oxford: Clarendon, 1996, 29–45.

Weber, D. "Confessiones." In OGHRA, vol. 1, 167–174.

16 Reception in the Middle Ages

ERIC LELAND SAAK

It should come as no surprise that Augustine's *Confessions* was one of his most widespread and best-known works in the Middle Ages. The extant manuscripts, which exceed 300, peaked in the ninth, twelfth, and fifteenth centuries, with the earliest extant copy dating to the sixth century.[1] In many ways, the reception of Augustine's *Confessions* in the Middle Ages parallels the reception of Augustine himself; namely, as an unwieldy, overly complex, impossible task to chart and trace with any precision.[2] Augustine was, as Douglas Gray put it, omnipresent, even if not always seen or recognized.[3] Gray thus spoke of the "diffused Augustinian Tradition," whereby Augustine was simply in the air, so to speak. Does, for example, Paulinus of Pella's *Eucharisticus* evidence early medieval reception of Augustine's *Confessions* simply because Paulinus wrote a poem that seems, somehow, to parallel Augustine's biographical treatment of himself?[4] Aside from the autobiographical treatment, and the fact that Paulinus addressed his poem to God, there is very little resemblance to the *Confessions*, and Paulinus nowhere mentioned Augustine or the *Confessions*. Did Paulinus know, or know of, the *Confessions*? Perhaps. Could he have written his *Eucharisticus*

---

[1] See D. Weber, "Confessiones," in *OGHRA*, vol. 1, 167a–174a; at 167a; Chapter 15 in this volume.

[2] The point of departure for treating the reception of the *Confessions* in the Middle Ages is P. Courcelle, *Les Confessions de Saint Augustin dans la Tradition Littéraire. Antécédents et Postérité* (Paris: Études Augustiniennes, 1963), 201–351. Courcelle recognized as well the magnitude of his undertaking, even limiting it as he did to the literary tradition (Ibid., 12–13). More recently, see *Le Confessioni di Agostino (402–2002): Bilancio e Prospettive. XXXI Incongro di studiosi dell'antichità cristiana, Roma, 2–4 maggio 2002* (Rome: Institutum patristicum Augustinianum, 2003), which focuses primarily on the *Confessions* themselves, but does have some insightful articles on the reception.

[3] D. Gray, "Saint Augustine and Medieval Literature I–II," in *Saint Augustine and His Influence in the Middle Ages*, eds. E. King and J. T. Schaefer (Sewanee, TN: The Press of the University of the South, 1988), 19–58, at 20.

[4] A. Söltenfuß, "Paulinus of Pella," in *OGHRA*, vol. 3, 1506a–1508a.

without knowing or knowing of the *Confessions*? Certainly. If Paulinus did know the *Confessions*, how are we to measure its impact on him aside from the paltry literary parallels? The same problem faces us with Anselm, whom we know knew Augustine and knew Augustine well, although Anselm only cites Augustine once in the prologue of his *Monologion* and not at all in his *Proslogion*. Augustine's influence on Anselm though seems to be clear, yet how to describe it in any concrete way is rather elusive at best.[5] Literary parallels prove neither influence nor causation, even as tempting as it can be to have them do so. Thus we can speculate that Guibert of Nogent, for example, modeled his *Monodiae* on the *Confessions*, or Aelred of Rievaulx his *De spirituali amicitia*, although there is no conclusive evidence that either author actually did so.[6] Peter Abelard knew the *Confessions*, but the *Confessions* had no role in his autobiographical *Historia Calamitatum* or his *Soliloquium*, even as Augustine was a major influence for his work.[7] The late twelfth–early thirteenth-century Cistercian Helinand de Froidmont knew Augustine well, at least *De civitate Dei*,[8] but he based his *De cognitione sui* on the Delphic Oracle's *cognosce te ipsum* ["Know Thyself"] and classical sources, not on the *Confessions*.[9] Scholars used the *Confessions* for purposes not based on a direct interpretation of or engagement with the text itself. Augustine was a universal authority, yet the text of the *Confessions* was most often simply a vehicle of that authority, offering Augustinian material that could likewise be found in other works of the Church Father as a means of corroboration. There is no clear evidence that any medieval author took the *Confessions* as the model for his or her own introspective self-analysis as a creature standing in the presence of its creator seeking in wonder.

---

[5] D. S. Hogg and H. C. Thompson, "Anselm of Canterbury," in *OGHRA*, vol. 2, 531a–533b.

[6] P. Turner, K. Enenkel, and P. Liebregts, "Autobiography and Autobiographical Writing," in OGHRA, vol. 2, 603a–610b.

[7] S. Lake and W. Otten, "Peter Abelard," in OGHRA, vol. 3, 1519a–1523a.

[8] E. L. Saak, "In the Wake of Lombard: The Reception of Augustine in the Early Thirteenth Century," *Augustinian Studies* 46/1 (2015), 71–104.

[9] Helinand's *De cognitione sui* was the title given to an excerpt from book eight of Helinand's *Chronicon* by Vincent of Beauvais, who made a number of such extracts under the title *Flores Helinandi*; see E. L. Saak, "The Limits of Knowledge: Hélinand de Froidmont's *Chronicon*," in *Pre-modern Encyclopedic Texts. Proceedings of the Second COMERS Congress, Groningen, 1–4 July 1996*, ed. Peter Binkley, BSIH 79 (Leiden: Brill, 1997), 289–302; for the text of Helinand's *De congnitione sui*, see *PL* 212, 721–734.

Yet what modern scholars have termed autobiography was by no means the only genre of the medieval reception of the *Confessions*, and the extent to which the *Confessions* can be categorized as such is itself a matter of scholarly debate. Indeed, the reception of Augustine cannot be limited to any particular genre of medieval literature, and elsewhere I have pointed to the literary, philosophical, theological, legal, political, religious, and iconographic avenues of Augustine's medieval reception.[10] The same applies, for the most part, for the *Confessions*; it was omnipresent in the Middle Ages, beyond its use for treatments of the philosophical issues of time, evil, and creation.[11] Thus, the earliest manuscript of the *Confessions*, the sixth-century *Codex Sessorianus* from northern Italy, includes marginalia on Books 1–6, highlighting issues of Neoplatonism.[12] Yet, to my knowledge, there is no study that has analyzed the marginalia on the manuscripts in general of the *Confessions*, a work that would reveal, at least potentially, vast insight into how the *Confessions* were read. With such a study lacking, we can only base our evaluation on how scholars cited the *Confessions* and the source(s) for their having done so.

In addition to the direct reception of the *Confessions* by means of copies of the text, medieval scholars also received Augustine indirectly either via florilegia, handbooks, and textbooks, or simply as cited by other scholars. The earliest florilegium of Augustine, that of the early sixth-century Eugippius, extracted material from Book 1 of the *Confessions*, and then from Books 10 through 13, dealing with time, memory, and creation,[13] which did not give later scholars a comprehensive selection representing the work's scope. While Charlemagne's favorite book was *De civitate Dei*, there is no indication that the Carolingian Renaissance spawned a new interest in the *Confessions*. Indeed, Hrabanus Maurus cited the *Confessions* only once, in his *De clericorum institutione*, and this one citation was to *conf.* 10.33.49, which did not come from Eugippius;[14] Hrabanus simply used his citation to prove the value of singing in church and does not exhibit a thorough knowledge of the

---

[10] E. L. Saak, "Augustine and his Late Medieval Appropriations," in OGHRA, vol. 1, 39a–50b.

[11] For Augustine's influence on these issues, see, for example, R. Sorabji, *Time, Creation and the Continuum. Theories in Antiquity and the Early Middle Ages* (Ithaca, NY: Cornell University Press, 1983).

[12] Weber, "*Confessiones*," 167a.

[13] A. Fürst, "Eugippius," in *OGHRA*, vol. 2, 954a–959a.

[14] Hrabanus Maurus, *De clericorum institutione* 2.48 (*PL* 107, 362A). For a listing of Augustine's works excerpted by Eugippius, see Fürst, "Eugippius," 955–957.

text, even though the *Confessions* was present in the library at Fulda.[15] The *Confessions* did, however, have a major role in the predestinarian controversy of the ninth century, and Gottschalk of Orbais knew the *Confessions* well.[16] Yet Florus of Lyon, "the greatest contemporary authority on Augustine,"[17] cited Augustine 2,107 times in his *Expositio in Epistolas Beati Pauli ex Operibus S. Augustini Collecta*, composed in the 840s, but of those citations only sixteen are to the *Confessions*, and, here, Florus cited only Books 7, 9, 10, 12, and 13.[18] While Peter Lombard, perhaps the greatest source for late medieval theological citation of Augustine, composed his *Sentences* as a compendium of sorts of Augustine, the *Confessions* are not prominent. Furthermore, there is only one citation of the *Confessions* in the *Glossa Ordinaria*,[19] and only one citation in Gratian's *Decretum*.[20] Peter Cantor, in his *Distinctiones Abel*, cited Augustine fifty-six times, although repeating the same citation eight times, leaving forty-eight distinct citations. However, none of these are to the *Confessions*, and they all can be traced to intermediary sources.[21] Such transmission allowed for the continued importance of the *Confessions*, but did not include a reception of the work itself as such. Despite its apparent popularity based on extant manuscripts, the *Confessions* was not received much at all in the Middle Ages, even as it was used for a variety of purposes.[22]

Yet, if it was not in the realm of the autobiographical that we find evidence of the *Confessions'* reception, we do find it in the realm of the biographical and/or hagiographical, where scholars turned to the *Confessions* to represent the life of Augustine, an endeavor that was far more than a pious attempt to depict one of the Church's great saints. Yet, even here, the role of the *Confessions* was limited. The *Confessions* include biographical material up to Augustine's return to Africa, or, in other words, they cover the period of Augustine's life only through the death of his mother, Monica, in 387, and do not include Augustine's return to Thagaste, his ordination as priest or his life as bishop of Hippo. The first biography was composed by Possidius, who had lived with

---

[15] S. C. Berarducci, "Hrabanus Maurus," in *OGHRA*, vol. 2, 1158b–1161a, at 1160b.

[16] D. Ganz, "Gottschalk of Orbais," in *OGHRA*, vol. 2, 1059a–1061b.

[17] C. Herbers, "Florus of Lyon," in *OGHRA*, vol. 2, 1000a–1002b, at 1001a.

[18] Florus of Lyon, *Expositio in Epistolas Beati Pauli ex Operibus Sancti Augustini Collecta*, PL 119, 279–420.

[19] A. Andrée, "Glossa Ordinaria," in *OGHRA*, vol. 2, 1055–1057.

[20] B. C. Brasington, "Decretum of Gratian," in *OGHRA*, vol. 2, 861–863.

[21] R. Quinto, "Peter Cantor," in *OGHRA*, vol. 3, 1523–1526, at 1524.

[22] Cf. Courcelle, *Les Confessions*, 301–305.

Augustine and knew him well.[23] Possidius explicitly avoided by and large the material in the *Confessions* (v. *Aug.*, Praef. 4–7) and already in chapter 3 of his *Vita* progressed to the post-*Confessions* period of Augustine's life, for which Possidius offers invaluable insights having been an eyewitness (v. *Aug.* 3.1–5). Biographers after Possidius used the *Confessions* more thoroughly, although still were faced with how to portray Augustine's life after it had become, in the words of James O'Donnell, boring.[24] It was precisely the "boring" portion of August-ine's life that was the most interesting for medieval authors for it was after the emplotment of the *Confessions* that Augustine returned to Hippo, became first a priest and then a bishop, battled heretics, founded monasteries, and composed his major works.

In the mid-twelfth century, the Premonstratensian Philip of Har-vengt (d. c. 1183) composed the most extensive life of Augustine that had been written to that time, consisting of thirty-three chapters.[25] Philip went far beyond Possidius in the attention he gave to Augustine's early life, drawing heavily from the *Confessions*. The first fourteen chapters of Philip's *Vita* trace Augustine's life from his birth to his baptism, a progression Possidius treated altogether in his first two chapters, before moving on to Augustine's ordination. Possidius had already left the *Confessions* behind in chapter 3 of his *Vita*, whereas Philip devoted over a third of his biography to Augustine's early years; namely, to the period Augustine himself presented in his *Confessions*. Yet, Philip's treatment was focused on the details of Augustine's biog-raphy and did not, as such, engage with the text itself. There is no real reflection in Philip's *Vita* of Augustine's anguish, of Augustine seeking happiness, or the origin of evil. Philip does, though, present Augustine's errors and his soul's disturbances, before he found resolution in the grace of his conversion. In many ways, Philip "de-personalizes" the text, presenting his account as a de-existentualized narrative of the course of events, adhering to what in medieval history writing was termed the *series temporum*. Philip though did include Augustine's own struggles and the conflicts of his soul at least in passing, but without the adornment of digressions of personal, philosophical, or

[23] *Possidius, Vita Augustini: zweisprachige Ausgabe*, ed. W. Geerlings, Augustinus Opera/Werke (Paderbor: Schöningh, 2005).

[24] J. J. O'Donnell, *Augustine: A New Biography* (New York: Harper, 2005), 70; see also E. L. Saak, "Lives of Augustine," in OGHRA, vol. 3, 1314b–1323b.

[25] E. L. Saak, *High Way to Heaven. The Augustinian Platform between Reform and Reformation, 1292–1524*, SMRT 89 (Leiden: Brill, 2002), 179–183; C. Neel, "Philip of Harvengt," in OGHRA, vol. 3, 1539b–1541a.

theological speculation, which Augustine himself had made central to his own biographical emplotment. Philip was telling a story, the story of Augustine's conversion and his founding of the Order of Augustinian Canons; he was not engaging with the text as the account of all of God's creatures, whereby Augustine was, in so many ways, Everyman who seeks happiness and seeks God in a fallen world, Augustine's *regio dissimilitudinis*. The *Confessions* offered the plot; otherwise, they were of little use to his purpose. Philip used the text of the *Confessions* for his biography of Augustine. He did not as such enter the "world of the text" in an attempt to represent the work as such. That was beyond Philip, as he acknowledged in his prologue. Even with the help of the Holy Spirit, it was impossible to present the life of Augustine. Philip was aware of what he was doing. He was textualizing the life of Augustine, not the text of the *Confessions*.[26]

A similar humility of awareness of the impossibility of the endeavor was recognized by Jordan of Quedlinburg, who composed his own *Vita Sancti Augustini* in the early fourteenth century, and who drew on Philip's biography to do so, a biography Jordan referred to as the *Legenda famosa*.[27] Times had changed and Jordan saw the need for a new biography of Augustine based on his order's ongoing conflict with the Augustinian Canons, a group to which Philip had belonged as a Premonstratensian, over which order, the Canons or the Augustinian Hermits, was the original and true order of St. Augustine. The conflict broke out in 1327 in the midst of imperial–papal conflict. Politically, the Augustinian Hermits were the architects of papal hierocratic theory and they received privileges in return from popes beginning with Boniface VIII and extending to John XXII, whose bull *Veneranda sanctorum* acknowledged the Hermits as the true sons of their father, leader, teacher, and head, Augustine.[28] The question concerned the historical evidence for whether Augustine first founded his Hermits, or his Canons. Philip's *Vita* portrayed Augustine as the father of the Canons. The Hermits needed a competing account to make their case. In addition to the *Confessions*, Jordan drew on a source now lost, the *Chronica*

---

[26] Philip of Harvengt, *Vita Sancti Augustini*, Prol., PL 203, 1205.

[27] For the text of Jordan's *Vita*, see Saak, *High Way to Heaven*, appendix D, 774–810. Jordan explicitly referenced the *Legenda famosa* throughout, and acknowledges Philip as author in *Vita* 13.9 (Ibid., 810.1210–1218). Regarding Jordan's realization of the magnitude of his task, see his *Vita*, prol. (Ibid. 781.2–18).

[28] E. L. Saak, *Creating Augustine. Interpreting Augustine and Augustinianism in the Later Middle Ages* (Oxford: Oxford University Press, 2012), 57–79; Saak, *High Way to Heaven*, 160–175.

of Datius, although fragments have been preserved in the *Historia Mediolanensis* of Landulfus.[29] In addition, Jordan had at his disposal a newly discovered source that gave explicit evidence of the Hermits' position, namely, Augustine's own sermons to his Hermits, the *Sermones ad fratres suos in eremo*.[30] Yet, reconstructing Augustine's early biography was also essential, as even the basic chronology was not at times clear, or was simply forged, as can be seen in the Augustinian Hermit Nicholas of Alessandria's *Sermo de beato Augustino*, given in Paris in 1332, when Nicholas, a fervent supporter of the Hermits' position, explicitly argued that Augustine had written his rule for his Hermits in the year 392, without realizing that Augustine, according to modern chronology, had been ordained in 391. Moreover, Nicholas, as did previous Hermits treating the matter, claimed that Augustine first established his order in Italy.[31] Jordan apparently felt a more erudite treatment was needed. Thus, he returned to the sources to establish Augustine's *curriculum vitae*, and he started with the *Confessions*.

Jordan's *Vita Sancti Augustini* was included, along with the *Sermones ad fratres suos in eremo*, in Jordan's *Collectanea Sancti Augustini*, a miscellany of Augustinian material that Jordan presented to his order's cloister in Paris in 1343. In his *Collectanea*, the autograph of which is extant,[32] Jordan also included what seems to have been preparatory notes for his *Vita*; namely, his *Annotatio Temporum beati Augustini*. Here Jordan went through the *Confessions* to determine the dates of the events in Augustine's early life, drawing from other works, particularly Augustine's *De beata vita*, for supplementary information, citing the *Confessions* by book and chapter to determine as precisely as he could the historical chronology. The *Annotatio* does not make for exciting reading. It does, though, demonstrate Jordan's efforts to ensure as accurate a chronology as possible for his *Vita*, and to do so based on Augustine's own testimony. The last reference to the *Confessions* in the *Annotatio* is the date for Monica's death, which Jordan used to determine that Augustine was baptized at Easter when he was thirty-three, arguing against claims that Augustine had been baptized when he was thirty, or, only at the end of his thirty-third year,[33] which is

---

[29] Ibid., appendix D, 778.
[30] See Saak, *Creating Augustine*, 81–137.
[31] See Saak, *High Way to Heaven*, 201–208.
[32] Paris, Bibliothèque de l'Arsenal MS 251.
[33] *Ex quo manifeste conuincitur eum non prius anno xxxiii(mo) fuisse baptizatum. Et transierat iam de illo anno quantum est ab ydibus nouembris usque ad pascha. Quod autem tempore paschali baptizatus fuerit hoc expresse dicit Possidonius et*

essentially the general position of scholars today; namely, that Augustine was baptized in Easter of 387. In his *Vita*, Jordan followed his reconstruction as in his *Annotatio* through the first eight chapters, extending to the death of Monica, which served for Jordan as a transition, since Augustine dealt with the death of his mother in Book 9 of the *Confessions*, as they had begun their journey back to Africa. Augustine never arrived in Africa in the *Confessions*, whereas, for Jordan, the return to his homeland was the most important element of his biography, for it was there, not in Italy, according to Jordan, that Augustine had established his first monastic foundation, having brought with him twelve Hermits from the monastery of Simplicianus to establish the order in Africa.[34] Thus the birth of the Order of Hermits of St. Augustine (*Ordo Eremitarum Sancti Augustini* [*OESA*]) clearly had historical primacy with respect to Augustine's establishing his Canons after he had been ordained bishop. Yet for this part of Augustine's life Jordan drew primarily from his new source, the *Sermones ad fratres suos in eremo*, for the *Confessions* were no longer of use. Jordan's *Vita*, and indeed his *Collectanea* as such, represents a genuine, historical return *ad fontes*, and Jordan had painstakingly gone through the first nine books of the *Confessions* for his reconstruction, but there he left it. He had other concerns. Augustine's life, and most of all his life after the *Confessions*,

potest haberi ex illo quod dicit nono libro confessionum capitulo sexto. Inde ubi tempus aduenit, quo me nomen dare oportuit. Tempus enim quo cathecumini in ecclesia nomen dare solebant et baptizari erat tempus paschale. Anno eodem etatis sue xxxiii(mo) mater sua apud Hostia Tybernia defuncta est, ut ipse dicit nono libro confessionum, capitulo undecimo in fine. Ex quibus patet quod dictum illorum stare non potest qui dicunt eum in tricesimo suo anno fuisse baptizatum, nec aliorum qui dicunt eum tempore baptismi fuisse trigenta trium annorum complete predicta ergo omnia absque scrupulo certissima sunt ex dictis suis propriis [From which is it clearly shown that he was not was baptized prior to his thirty-third year, for he had already lived through that year from the the ides of November (November 13) until Easter. Possidius said explicitly that he was baptized at Easter, and this is able to be had as well from what he said in the *Confessions*, book nine, chapter six: *wherefore the time had come to give me a name.* Easter was the time when it was customary that catechumens in the church were given a name and baptized. In that same thirty-third year of his, his mother died at Ostia on the Tiber, as he said in book nine of the *Confessions*, towards the end of chapter eleven. From these considerations it is clear that the position of those who claim that he was baptized when he was thirty is not able to be maintained, neither is that of those who say that he was baptized at the end of his thirty-third year. Therefore it is most certain that both positions have no basis at all based on his own words]" (Jordanus de Quedlinburg, *Annotatio Temporum Sancti Augustini*, Paris, Bibliotheque de l'Arsenal MS 251, fol. 72rb).

[34] Jordanus de Quedlinburg, *Vita* 7 (Saak, *High Way to Heaven*, 228–229, appendix D, 791.428–792.483).

was the most important factor for Jordan, for which the *Confessions* essentially offered background detail. It was for Jordan a central text, an essentially vital text to his endeavor, but his point, his purpose, far transcended his use of the *Confessions*, which could only go so far. In the late medieval debates over Augustine's heritage, the *Confessions* were conscripted for the background of a larger plot. The *Confessions* served a purpose; the text was not itself the focus, but simply a means to an end. Perhaps we can say that for the later Middle Ages, the *Confessions* were received, but never really appropriated.

There was, however, one possible exception to the rule. As the Augustinian Hermits were continuing their battles for their authenticity and originality, one of the order's masters of theology at the *studium* in Avignon, Dionysius de Burgo, served as the confessor for a young scholar, and in 1333 had given his charge a copy of the *Confessions*. Father Dionysius perhaps had no idea what his student would make of it, but make something of it he did. His name was Petrarch.

Petrarch's relationship to Augustine, and to the Augustinian Hermits, is rather complex.[35] He had a copy of Augustine's *De civitate Dei* already in 1325, his first acquisition of Augustine's works, and then added the *Confessions* in 1333. Both of these, together with the *Soliloquium*, *De vera religione*, and the pseudo-Augustinian *De orando deo*, Petrarch included in his list of his favorite books.[36] The *Confessions* have often been seen as a model for Petrarch, serving not only as the inspiration at least of his infamous ascent of Mount Ventoux, but also as the model for his *De vita solitaria* and his most famous work, his *Secretum*. Yet Petrarch explicitly claimed St. Basil as the model for *De vita solitaria*,[37] and although the *Secretum* is a dialogue with Augustine, the work itself is modeled far more on Boethius's *Consolation of*

---

[35] See E. L. Saak, "Augustine and Augustinianisms in the Fourteenth Century: Petrarch and Robert de Bardis," in *Augustine, Augustinians, and Augustinianisms in the Italian Trecento*, eds. J. Bartuschat, et al. (Ravenna: Longa, forthcoming); G. Mazzotta, "Petrarca, Francesco," in OGHRA, vol. 3, 1533b–1536a; É. Luciani, *Les Confessions de Saint Augustin dans les Lettres de Pétrarque, Collection des études augustiniennes. Série Antiquité* (Paris: Études Augustiniennes, 1982), 49–54.

[36] B. L. Ullman, "Petrarch's Favorite Books," in *Studies in the Italian Renaissance*, Storia e Letteratura 51 (Rome: Edizioni di storia e letteratura, 1973), 113–133, at 118–119 and 132.

[37] Petrarca, *De vita solitaria* 1.1.4 (Francesco Petrarca, *De vita solitaria, Buch I*, ed. K. A. E. Enenkel, Leidse romanistische Reeks van de Rijksuniversiteit te Leiden 24 [Leiden: Brill, 1990], 62.30–34).

Philosophy than it is on the *Confessions*.[38] Nevertheless, in his *De otio religioso* Petrarch testified to the importance the *Confessions* had for him. He returned to himself, as he put it, and claimed that by God's guidance, in his later years, he began to hesitate and to step back from his previous attachments, and in this context became confronted with Augustine's *Confessions*.[39] Petrarch then gave the *Confessions* the importance to himself that Augustine had given to Cicero's *Hortensius* (*Otio rel.* 2), claiming that the *Confessions*

> was the first to bring me to the love of the true, it was the first to teach me to breathe healthfully, while I had for so long previously only breathed morbidly. May he rest happily in the age without end by whose hand that book was first offered to me, which gave a bridle to my wild soul [*Ille me primum ad amorem veri erexit, ille me primum docuit suspirare salubriter, qui tam diu ante letaliter suspirassem. Quiescat in secula sine fine felix, cuius manu ille michi primum liber oblatus est, qui vago animo frenum dedit*].
>
> (Otio rel. 2)

Petrarch continued to explain that he was reluctant to follow Augustine's counsel at first, afraid of losing his lifelong ambitions for Augustine was calling him away from his studies of the classics; but in time, although at first slowly, he began following Augustine more and more so that he became happier than he had hoped. Petrarch had changed paths.

Yet, in the *Secretum*, Petrarch viscerally expressed his ongoing struggle with the advice a literary character "Augustinus" offered.[40] Although Petrarch remained devoted to Augustine, he could not follow in his footsteps. The *Secretum* ends with "Franciscus" knowingly and willingly not accepting "Augustinus's" counsel. While he admitted to the truth thereof, he returned to his writing: "But I am not strong enough to rein in my desire [*Sed desiderium frenare non valeo*]" (*Secr.*

---

[38] Turner, Enenkel, and Liebregts, "Autobiography and Autobiographical Writing," 606a.

[39] Francesco Petrarca *De otio religioso*, 2, in *Il "De Otio Religioso" di Francesco Petrarca*, ed. Guiseppe Rotondi, Studi et Testi 195 (Vatican City: Biblioteca Apostolica Vaticana, 1958), 104.5–10; all further citations to *De otio religoiso* are to this edition.

[40] I have associated *Franciscus* here with Petrarca and *Augustinus* with Petrarca's understanding of Augustine. The extent to which the characters in the *Secretum* correspond to their historical namesakes is debated. For my argument that they do indeed represent Petrarca and Petrarca's understanding of Augustine, respectively, see Saak, "Augustine and Augustinianisms in the Fourteenth Century."

3.18.7) The verb he used was *frenare*, echoing his use of the noun *frenum* to refer to what the *Confessions* had given his wandering soul in *Otio rel.* 2. Petrarch never reached Augustine's *conf.* 8.12.[41] While the *Confessions* had provided a rein to his wandering soul, it did not bring him to the state that Augustine had achieved. And neither could "Augustinus." This is then confirmed when the *Confessions* enters the *Secretum*. "Augustinus" recounts his own story, and how he was "transformed into another Augustine," which he knows "Franciscus" knows from the *Confessions*.[42] "Franciscus" responds that he knows it well and cannot forget the miracle (*Secr.* 1.5.5). Then, "Augustinus" asserts that "Franciscus" should remember the miracle under the fig tree, and should hold that memory as more important than the hope for the laurel tree, which "Franciscus" considers more dear (*Secr.* 1.6.1). "Franciscus" does not object. Although "Franciscus" knows the story, he has not achieved it himself, having substituted for Augustine's fig tree the laurel tree of fame. "Franciscus" then admits that he reads the *Confessions* as recounting his own story, but he does not include the conversion; he reads it as a story "caught between two contrary feelings, namely hope and fear" (*Secr.* 1.6.3)." While Petrarch's devotion to Augustine, his estimation of Augustine, did not waver, his judgment and will could not follow. "Franciscus" remained a conflicted soul, imploring "Augustinus" not to abandon him regardless of how distant he was, "for without you, dearest father, my life is bleak [*Sine te enim, pater optime, vita mea inamena*]" (*Secr.* 3.18.4).

It was not his appropriation of Augustine that reveals Petrarch's reception of the *Confessions*, but his disappropriation, signified at the end of his life when he returned his copy of the *Confessions* to the Augustinian Hermits, its proper home.[43] Yet Petrarch had engaged with the text in ways previous scholars never had, at least that we can discern based on how the *Confessions* was used. The *Confessions*, for Petrarch, was not a text to be cited as an authority to prove a point, nor as offering details on Augustine's life. It was a text to be wrestled with. As such, Petrarch offers essential insight into the reception of the *Confessions* in the Middle Ages. How many of his medieval forebears

---

[41] Saak, "Augustine and Augustinianism in the Fourteenth Century."

[42] Francesco Petrarca, *Secr.* 1.5.5 (Francesco Petrarca, *Secretum*, ed. U. Dotti, *Opere latine: testo traduzione commento* [Rome: Archivio Guido Izzi, 1993], 20); all further references will be to this edition.

[43] Saak, "Augustine and Augustinianisms in the Fourteenth Century."

likewise wrestled with the text in their own lives we cannot know, for they do not tell us.

The history of the reception of the *Confessions* in the Middle Ages, however, still remains to be written, which is not meant as any slight to the magisterial work of Pierre Courcelle.[44] Such an undertaking, overwhelmingly vast and complex, would also need to be based on what is meant by "reception" in the first place.[45] The *Confessions*, as Augustine's works in general, were indeed "in the air," the "diffused Augustinian tradition" that defies concrete analysis. John Flemming argued that the *Confessions* was the intertext behind the *Romance of the Rose*, although Jean de Meun, if he received the *Confessions* at all, did so to refute its basic tenet of chastity being the entryway for the path leading to the return to God.[46] We can chart the extant manuscripts, although the marginalia thereof, which surely would shed important light on the text's reception, are still unstudied; we can chart the citations to the work, but that does so little to reveal the real impact of the text itself. Philosophers, theologians, preachers, and literary authors knew the text and used the text, but what do such citations actually tell us of the text's reception? No one in the Middle Ages really dealt with Adeodatus and Augustine's explicit admiration and love for his son (*conf.* 9.6.14), even if artistic representations included Adeodatus in scenes depicting Augustine's baptism, together with his son.[47] No one dealt with Monica as such, although *Vitae Sanctae Monicae* were around, including in Jordan's *Collectanea*.[48] Either philosophical and/or theological themes were extracted from the *Confessions*, or, the *Confessions* were used for representations of Augustine's biography for hagiographical and/or religiopolitical purposes.

---

[44] See footnote 2.

[45] K. Pollmann, "The Proteanism of Authority. The Reception of Augustine in Cultural History from his Death to the Present: Mapping an International and Interdisciplinary Investigation," in OGHRA, vol. 1, 3a–14b; Saak, *Creating Augustine*, 222–228.

[46] J. Flemming, *Reason and the Lover* (Princeton, NJ: Princeton University Press, 1984), 83; Saak, "Augustine and His Later Medieval Appropriations," 39b–40a.

[47] K. A. Zins, "St. Augustine among the Mendicants: The Order of Augustinian Hermits and Early Renaissance Art in Italy," PhD Dissertation, The Pennsylvania State University, ProQuest Dissertations Publishing, 2016, 42–51.

[48] Jordan of Quedlinburg, *Collectanea Sancti Augustini*, *Vita Sancte Monice*, Paris, Bibliotheque de l'Arsenal MS 251, fol. 82va–85ra. Jordan's *Vita Sancte Monice* was not his original composition, but a twelfth-century *Vita* composed by a Regular Canon Walter, included as well in the *Acta Sanctorum*, May 4, BHL Number: 6000.

While it is legitimate to speak of a renaissance of Augustine in the later Middle Ages,[49] there was no renaissance of the *Confessions* as such. Jordan's return *ad fontes* was inspired by the political necessity to defend his order as the original Order of St. Augustine more than it represents a new reception. Perhaps all such reception of classical texts was and still is similar. Petrarch wrestled with the text, and while Petrarch's love of the classics for their own sake was perhaps genuine, can it be distinguished from his own desire for fame and his conscious rejection of Augustine's expressions of humility and utter dependency on God and God's grace, which is itself a mystery, as the closing of the *Confessions* so eloquently expresses? Is scholarship ever pure? Is not all reception, one way or another, political? This recognition by no means delegitimates the reception, or the authority of the text itself, or the impressive scholarly achievement. What the reception of the *Confessions* in the Middle Ages reveals perhaps most of all is that scholars of all sorts, and for various purposes and various agendas, in their reception made Augustine something he wasn't. In so many ways, our own reception of Augustine and his *Confessions* still does the same thing. The text remains. Augustine we still do not know, and the Augustine that Augustine himself presented in the *Confessions* is an artificial, highly skilled work of art, which is an object terribly complex to unravel. The Augustine behind the text we can only recreate in our own image, as did those scholars in the Middle Ages who, one way or another, did indeed receive, in one way or another, the *Confessions*.[50] Can we ever really grasp the reception of the *Confessions* in the Middle Ages? That too remains a question, the answer to which we can only seek, for which we can only beg, knocking on the door to gain some understanding, as it, no less than we ourselves, remains a problem.

Further Reading

Courcelle, P. *Les Confessions de Saint Augustin dans la Tradition Littéraire. Antécédents et Postérité*. Paris: Études Augustiniennes, 1963.

Luciani, É. *Les Confessions de Saint Augustin dans les Lettres de Pétrarque, Collection des études augustiniennes. Série Antiquité*. Paris: Études Augustiniennes, 1982.

Pollmann, K. and W. Otten (eds.), *The Oxford Guide to the Historical Reception of Augustine*, three vols. Oxford: Oxford University Press, 2013.

---

[49] E. L. Saak, "The Augustinian Renaissance: Textual Scholarship and Religious Identity in the Later Middle Ages," in OGHRA, vol. 1, 58a–68b.

[50] Cf. Courcelle, *Les Confessions*, 547.

Saak, E. L. *High Way to Heaven. The Augustinian Platform between Reform and Reformation, 1292–1524*, SMRT 89. Leiden: Brill, 2002.

Creating Augustine. The Interpretation of Augustine and Augustinianism in the Later Middle Ages. Oxford: Oxford University Press, 2012.

"In the Wake of Lombard: The Reception of Augustine in the Early Thirteenth Century." *Augustinian Studies* 46/1 (2015), 71–104.

"Augustine and Augustinianisms in the Fourteenth Century: The Cases of Petrarch and Robert de Bardis." In *Augustine, Augustinians, and Augustinianisms in the Italian Trecento*, eds. J. Bartuschat, et al. (Ravenna: Longa, forthcoming).

Schaefer, J. T. (ed.), *Saint Augustine and His Influence in the Middle Ages.* Sewanee, TN: The Press of the University of the South, 1988.

17 Reception in the Period of Reformations: The *Confessions*, 1500–1650

KATRIN ETTENHUBER

The period between 1500 and 1650 saw an unprecedented rise in the literature of interiority, as processes of introspection and spiritual self-scrutiny were explored in autobiographies, diaries, and essays. But it was also a time of radical religious division when, in the wake of the Reformation, confessions of faith became the subject of local, national, and international conflict, culminating in the Thirty Years' War (1618–1648). During the sixteenth and seventeenth centuries, the *Confessions* were also made available to a much wider range of audiences: in addition to printed editions in Latin, Augustine's text was opened up to vernacular readers through translations, most notably in English- and Spanish-speaking territories. Thanks to increasing diversification in the marketplace of print, the *Confessions* also appeared, piecemeal, in hugely popular compilations of Augustinian devotions designed to aid private prayer and meditation. Set pieces from Augustine's *Confessions* (such as the vision at Ostia or the conversion in the garden at Milan), now familiar to ever-greater numbers of churchgoers, were used by preachers to exhort their congregations to a life of virtue and spirituality. And, lastly, the story of Augustine's conversion became the subject of many plays in Jesuit theater and illustrated, in vividly embodied form, the importance of loyalty to the Church.

Tracking Augustine's *Confessions* in the period 1500–1650, then, demands attention to the techniques and conventions of different media: comparing printed texts and dramatic performances, for instance, invites us to consider not only which version of Augustine is being presented to us, but how this presentation is shaped and framed. Even if we focus on the printed text of the *Confessions*, however, we will rarely find Augustine alone. Editions and translations of the *Confessions* are, in fact, full of other voices: editors and publishers write prefaces that frame and explain what we are about to encounter; translators engage in acts of interpretation as they usher the text from Latin into the vernacular, even though their decisions are all but invisible to the average reader. The Augustine we meet in the early modern period is not a solitary writer in his study, but a cultural icon surrounded and mediated by other presences. The religious literature of inwardness, and especially autobiographical writing based on the *Confessions*, is not primarily designed to be an expression of individual subjectivity. Autobiography in the Augustinian mode is engaged in two types of dialogue: with Augustine as spiritual and literary exemplar; and with God, the ultimate source of meaning and the object of praise. In this sense, the interiority of the autobiographical subject is always already relational. In times of crisis and conflict, these relations extend more deeply into the institutional and social dimensions of religious identity: in the examples that follow, the act of confessing one's sins is inseparable from assertions of confessional allegiance to the Catholic or Protestant faiths; at moments of existential threat, the fate of the individual soul becomes fundamentally enmeshed with the fate of his or her church.

TRANSLATING THE *CONFESSIONS*

In a work entitled *Paratexts*, the French literary theorist Gerard Genette examines the techniques used by authors and editors to manage the relationship between a text and its readers. Perhaps the most prominent of these strategies is the preface, described evocatively by Genette as a "threshold," or a "vestibule," an "undefined zone between the inside and outside [of a text]," "always a conveyor of commentary, a zone not only of transition, but also of transaction."[1] There are few better examples of this phenomenon than the first English translation of the *Confessions* by the Catholic convert Sir Tobie Matthew, published in exile at St. Omer in 1620. Prefaces frame and guide the reader's experience, and Matthew's title page is unapologetically directive, presenting the *Confessions* "Togeather with a large Preface, which it will much import to be read ouer first; that so the Book it selfe may both profit, and please, the Reader, more." Matthew's prefatory material weighs in at a hefty 108 pages and wastes no time in claiming Augustine for the Catholic Church. While Protestants distort and manipulate Augustine's text for polemical ends, Matthew argues, his own work demonstrates beyond doubt that "the beliefe and practise of S. *Augustine*, and the church of his tyme, were fully agreeable to that of the Catholike *Roman*

---

[1] G. Genette, *Paratexts: Thresholds of Interpretation*, trans. J. E. Lewin (Cambridge: Cambridge University Press, 1997), 2.

Church at this day."[2] In the middle section of the preface, Matthew presents extracts from a range of Augustine's texts to demonstrate agreement between the beliefs of the early church and contemporary Catholic practice. His translation of the *Confessions* thus becomes an opportunity to survey the doctrinal differences between the Catholic and Protestant churches more broadly: unsurprisingly, it turns out that Augustine's loyalty lies firmly with the Catholic side, and Matthew concludes that, if Augustine were alive at the present moment, he would readily join Matthew's battle against the "hereticall Spirit" of the Reformation.[3] This first English translation of the *Confessions*, then, draws on the early history of Christianity to imagine a Catholic future for a country that had been institutionally Protestant since the Elizabethan Settlement of 1559. Writing in exile, Matthew also builds textual alliances that are symbolic of a common political purpose. His prefatory remarks refer at length to the 1598 Spanish translation of the *Confessions* by the prominent Jesuit Pedro de Ribadeneyra (1526–1611), whose memoirs traveled under the title *Confessions* and who had published, in 1588, an account of England's break from the Church of Rome. Matthew's work thus moves within an international network of Augustinian texts, and it is no accident that he invokes the support of the Jesuits – the religious order most notable for its scholarly pursuits and its militant evangelizing – to complete his vision of England's return to the mother church.[4]

LIFE-WRITING AFTER AUGUSTINE

The *Confessions* are a touchstone for writers of religious autobiography in the period. And, although, on the whole, these texts eschew the openly polemical tone of Matthew's preface, they are often examples of what Hilmar Pabel terms "confessional self-fashioning": the presentation of the autobiographical subject is framed by his or her allegiance to a (broadly) Catholic or Protestant system of beliefs.[5] This idea of

[2] Tobie Matthew, *The Confessions of the Incomparable Doctour St Augustine* (St. Omer, 1620), 7.
[3] Ibid., 89.
[4] Unsurprisingly, Matthew's project met with fierce criticism in England, and in 1626 the dean of Exeter, Matthew Sutcliffe, published a formal refutation entitled *The Unmasking of a Masse-Monger, Who in the Counterfeit Habit of Augustine Hath Cunningly Crept into the Closets of Many English Ladies.*
[5] H. M. Pabel, "Augustine's *Confessions* and the Autobiographies of Petrus Canisius, SJ," *Church History and Religious Culture* 87 (2007), 453–476, at 464.

confessionalized self-presentation is exemplified most clearly in the life-writing of two prominent sixteenth-century churchmen: the French scholar and Reformed theologian Franciscus Junius (1545–1602) and the Dutch Jesuit priest Petrus Canisius (1521–1592).

Junius, who studied theology in Geneva under Calvin and Beza, spent most of his professional life in teaching, scholarship, and ministry in the Palatinate. From 1573 until his death in 1602 he was affiliated with the University of Heidelberg, first to collaborate with Emmanuel Tremellius on a Reformed Latin translation of the Bible (later known as the Tremellius–Junius version) and, from 1583, as professor of theology. Junius's *Vita*, or *Life*, was published at Leiden in 1595, but probably composed significantly earlier, between 1575 and 1578.[6] In its early Christian context, the term *confessio* had three distinct meanings, all of which are present in Augustine's *Confessions*. The first of these is the admission of sins, inspired by penitential practice, and Augustine's text abounds with examples of self-accusation and repentance, from the early theft of the pears to his sexual adventures in Carthage. The second meaning is an offering of praise derived from the Psalms, and we need look no further than the first line of Augustine's text to illustrate this: "You are great, Lord, and highly to be praised," he says, quoting Ps 47:2. The third meaning is an affirmation of faith in response to persecution or attack; the *Confessions* contain many such defenses of "the Catholic faith," against the Manichees and other "heretics" (see, e.g., *conf.* 5.14.24, 7.19.25).[7]

The first line of Junius's *Vita* combines the first two meanings of *confessio* through a play on the Latin words for mercy [*misericordia*] and misery [*miseria*]: "I will proclaim the Lords' mercies by giving account of my miserable existence so that my life will glorify the Lord who created it."[8] Misery is the dominant note in Junius's early years: he almost perishes at birth and suffers frequent bouts of ill health thereafter; he is an overly ambitious child, prone to fits of anger, incapable of showing affection, and afflicted with a crippling shyness and, most troublingly, with a lack of faith. At the age of thirteen, Junius arrives

---

[6] K. A. E. Enenkel, "Autobiographie als kalvinistische Erbauungsschrift: François du Jons (Junius') *Vita* (1575–78; 1595)," in *Die Erfindung des Menschen. Die Autobiographik des frühneuzeitlichen Humanismus von Petrarca bis Lipsius* (Berlin: De Gruyter, 2008), 670–727, at 688.

[7] For the three meanings of the term *confessio*, see Pabel, "Augustine's *Confessions*," 463.

[8] Franciscus Junius, *Vita Nobilis et eruditi viri Francisci Junii* (1595), sig. A1r (translations from Junius are my own).

in Lyon, and his experiences there are modeled closely along Augustinian lines. Much like the Carthage of the *Confessions*, Junius's Lyon is full of carnal temptations, and he finds himself set upon by whole groups of predatory women at a time. During one of these onslaughts, young Junius is confronted by "three or four who pressed in on me together;" his revulsion is such that he responds to one attempted embrace by "slapping her hard across the face in full view of everyone in the room."[9]

It is at this point of crisis in Junius's *Life* that the workings of God's providence begin to manifest themselves more fully and explicitly. In terms of narrative structure, this means that the reader feels more keenly the difference between the narrated and the narrating self: events and experiences that seemed accidental or fortuitous to young Junius are given order and meaning by Junius the autobiographer, who presents the vagaries of life as parts of a larger design – God's providential plan for his chosen people.[10] Junius relays three key events in quick succession to confirm this interpretation. First, he recounts how God miraculously saved his younger self from the women of Lyon. This escape is accomplished through highly dramatic means, however; Junius and his friends are attacked by murderous Catholics during the festival of Corpus Christi and are forced to leave the city in some haste, thus cutting off the possibility of further sexual temptations. Having fled, somewhat implausibly (at least to a doubting mind), through the front door of their house, Junius and his friends move around the countryside without any food or much of a plan. They are eventually taken in by a kindly farmer, who not only feeds them, but, in response to their story of hardship, invites them to explain the principal points of difference between the Catholic and Protestant faiths. Shortly thereafter, Junius experiences a moment of divine illumination that is clearly derived from the *Confessions*. Again, seemingly by accident, Junius walks into a church one day and hears a sermon; not, as he says, "with any particular devotion, but not completely without profit either." He walks home, "not really sure what to do, read, or learn next," and happens upon his father's Bible. The New Testament falls open to reveal Jn 1:1, "In the beginning was the Word."[11]

The parallels with Augustine's experience at the garden in Milan (Book 8 of the *Confessions*) are obvious, but they are also – and

---

[9] Junius, sig. C1r.
[10] See Enenkel, "Autobiographie als kalvinistische Erbauungsschrift," 718–726.
[11] Junius, sig. C4v–D1r.

crucially – reshaped to speak more directly to Junius's confessional
context. Where Augustine hears the voice of a child and discovers Rm
13:13, Junius's encounter with Scripture is dominated by the living,
spoken word: he discovers the Bible immediately after hearing a
sermon, the book falls open at Jn 1:1, and this moment of revelation
will inspire Junius's own career as a preacher and pastor to the Protestant minorities in the Palatinate. After this crucial turning point, the
narrative style of the *Vita* changes again to reflect the change in Junius's
internal disposition. In describing the three incidents I have just discussed – the escape from Lyon, the encounter with the farmer, the
discovery of Scripture – the *Vita* draws a clear distinction between the
immersive narration of young Junius, who seems to relay events directly, and the framing interpretation of Junius the autobiographer, who
(literally) tops and tails this section of the narrative with prayerful
tributes to God's mercies: "[Y]ou, my Lord and God, remembered your
servant, who was lost through his own wretched action ... You remembered me, Lord my God, and out of your infinite mercy accepted me into
your flock".[12] But following this moment of scriptural conversion, and
as Junius begins to choose a life devoted to Christian service, the two
perspectives merge: faith has now been internalized, so editorial interventions become unnecessary. From now on, every moment of danger
or crisis becomes an opportunity to demonstrate God's love for his
chosen servants; when Junius is on the point of getting arrested in
Ghent, for instance, his friends fear for their safety, but Junius calmly
reassures them in the midst of chaos and confusion: "I, by contrast, had
complete faith that God would help me, and told them to be of good
cheer ... Trust in the Lord's providence, you who serve him, rest in the
certainty of his truth and fidelity, for he is a faithful Lord, the protector
of Israel."[13]

Junius defines his autobiographical project above all as an act of
bearing witness [*testari*]: his life testifies to God's loving mercy, which
emerges most clearly and movingly at times of crisis and doubt, such as
the periods of religious persecution endured by Junius's Protestant readership. The *Vita* is designed to shore up faith in a larger providential
design that will eventually see the Protestants triumph; it seeks to
inspire courage in the present moment precisely by taking a longer
view.[14]

---

[12] Junius, sigs C2r, D1r.
[13] Junius, sig. G2r–v.
[14] Enenkel, "Autobiographie als kalvinistische Erbauungsschrift," 708 and 724.

The Jesuit Petrus Canisius also uses Augustine's *Confessions* to bear witness to God's mercy, but from a radically different perspective. Canisius composed two autobiographies during his life: an account of his early years now known as the *Confessions* (c. 1570), and his *Testament*, dictated to an amanuensis shortly before Canisius's death in 1597. The *Testament* was described by the head of the Jesuit Province of Upper Germany as written after "the manner of the *Confessions*," and the text certainly bears the marks of the threefold definition of *confessio* already discussed.[15] Canisius is unsparing in his self-accusation, especially in relation to a sinful and godless youth, full of idleness and anger; he reports that he wasted "hours, days, nights, weeks, months, and years" on immoral pursuits.[16] As in Junius's *Vita*, this confession of sin is accompanied by a proclamation of praise, and Canisius invites his readers, "with me and on my behalf," to "love, acclaim, and worship" God.[17] This act of thanksgiving is, however, inseparable from Canisius's confession of faith in the Catholic Church, the sustaining external force in a life dedicated to the evangelizing work of the Jesuits. Canisius was raised on "the milk of the Catholic church" from an early age, by parents who remained "Catholic and orthodox to the end of their lives," when "the deadly doctrine of the Lutheran plague, not without the destruction of many people, had begun to break out in both parts of Germany and to seduce even the hearts of the innocent with sweet words."[18] Like Junius's *Vita*, then, Canisius's *Testament* is a response to the deep religious divisions of the sixteenth century, but, where Junius's version of the *Confessions* stresses the importance of internal resolve to encourage his Protestant coreligionists, Canisius's seeks to combat the onslaught of heresy by appeals to the institutional authority of the Catholic Church.

Despite their differences in confessional outlook, Junius and Canisius could be confident that their autobiographical accounts would be taken seriously: both men write from a position of institutional security (Junius as a university professor and preacher; Canisius as a senior member of the Jesuit order) and likely took their moral and intellectual authority for granted. None of this was the case for Teresa of Avila (1515–1582), the Spanish nun who encountered Augustine's *Confessions* at the age of thirty-nine and used the text not only as

---

[15] Pabel, "Augustine's *Confessions*," 462.
[16] Ibid., 472.
[17] Ibid., 471.
[18] Ibid., 467.

inspiration for her own autobiography (Teresa's *Vida* was composed in
1562 and revised in 1564), but as a way of justifying her sense of
apostolic vocation to her male superiors. In Teresa's *Vida*, the connections between gender and textual authority become a major concern.
Unlike Junius and Canisius, Teresa had been a member of a religious
order for almost twenty years when she read the *Confessions*, although
her life as a Carmelite nun had been far from happy. She suffered from a
number of chronic illnesses and experienced a profound sense of spiritual emptiness. As a result, she became the object of intense scrutiny by
her confessors, who prescribed a tightly supervised regimen of spiritual
exercises; these included the practice of writing a series of autobiographical reports for her confessors, which eventually led to the composition
of the *Vida*.

In line with previous examples of spiritual autobiography, Teresa's
Vida is not a simple construction of the past, but involves a providential
reinterpretation of the events that have shaped her existence. Her crucial encounter with Augustine's *Confessions* is a prime example of this
process. Teresa is at pains to stress that her discovery of Augustine is
unsought for, but far from accidental: "It seems the Lord ordained this,
because I had not tried to procure a copy, nor had I ever seen one. I am
very fond of St Augustine, because the convent where I stayed as a lay
person belonged to this order."[19] In view of this doubly providential
setup, it is unsurprising that Teresa forms an immediate and strong
attachment to the text:

> As I began to read the *Confessions*, it seemed to me I saw myself in
> them. I began to commend myself very much to this glorious saint.
> When I came to the passage where he speaks about his conversion
> and read how he heard that voice in the garden, it only seemed to
> me ... that it was I the Lord called.[20]

Teresa probably read the *Confessions* in the Spanish translation of
Sebastián Toscano. Her own autobiography closely follows the three
central requirements of confessional life-writing in the Augustinian
mode: an acknowledgment of sin, an offering of praise, and a defense
of faith. In Teresa's case, however, these requirements intersect with a
second triad of confessions, which arise from the specific conditions of

[19] Teresa of Avila, *The Book of Her Life, in The Collected Works of St. Teresa of Avila*,
eds. K. Kavanaugh and O. Rodriguez (Washington, DC: ICS Publications, 1976),
vol. 1, 72.
[20] Teresa of Avila, *The Book of Her Life*, 73.

female autobiography. This involves a confession of obedience (she notes that "my confessors commanded me" to write the *Vida*); a confession of abject humility (unlike Augustine and other saints, she will "turn back and become worse" even after God has begun to show his favor), and a confession of vocation, as she asks for help "in my weakness to give the Lord something of the service I owe him."[21] As Elena Carrera has argued, this second triad is in part strategic: aligning herself with Augustine shores up Teresa's credibility and authority as a writer, while her avowal of obedience guards against accusations of vanity.[22] But in stressing her repeated backsliding – a sin that is identified as an explicit contrast with Augustine's more committed and durable conversion – Teresa also makes herself a more accessible and human example than the male saints whose stories form the substance of medieval life-writing.[23] She also advertises the distinctive qualities of female autobiography in other ways: by writing in the vernacular and foregrounding an affective form of piety that fuses understanding and love, intellect and will, she creates a space for devotion that is distinct from the religious practices of the male clerical elite. This space is spiritual and metaphysical, in that it inscribes a particular approach to prayer and contemplation. But the composition of Teresa's autobiography is also inseparable from the more material and pragmatic aspects of religious service. In 1562, the year in which the first version of the *Vida* was completed, Teresa founded the convent of St. Joseph in Avila, the first of seventeen religious houses whose institution she oversaw during her lifetime. Her project was triggered, at least in part, by recent religiopolitical events, such as the desecration of local churches by the Huguenots (i.e., French Protestants). Teresa's *Vida* stresses the importance of self-knowledge and introspection in the development of confessional identity; her convents created the physical space in which such devotions could take place. These religious houses became known as "Discalced" convents, from the Latin *discalceatus*, "barefooted" or "unshod." Teresa's reforms sought to restore monastic institutions to the austere discipline of their first founders; this, too, was in reaction to a post-Reformation climate in which many religious foundations had relaxed their rules in order to retain their members. It is tempting to see this as a reactionary move that restricted women's agency, but an

---

[21] Ibid., 32.

[22] E. Carrera, *Teresa of Avila's Autobiography: Authority, Power and the Self in Mid-Sixteenth-Century Spain* (London: Legenda, 2005), 163–164.

[23] Carrera, *Teresa of Avila's Autobiography*, 163.

alternative reading emerges from the powerful connection between textual and material spaces. Genette's description of the paratext as a vestibule suggests that a book can be imagined as a kind of building; Teresa's *Vida*, in its careful negotiation of gendered power relations, creates – to adapt a famous phrase – a room of her own. In a similar way, the foundation of a convent carves out a space where female leadership and initiative can flourish. The structural inequalities of Catholicism may impose limits on Teresa's story: unlike Augustine's, her conversion will not place her in a position of authority in the Church during her lifetime. Nevertheless, her reading of the *Confessions* underwrites a strong sense of apostolic vocation and Catholic identity that left a lasting physical and spiritual legacy.

THE *CONFESSIONS* ON STAGE

Teresa's *Vida* got off to a slow start: it initially circulated among local readers in the 1560s, only to be denounced by the Inquisition in 1575. But the text's reputation grew steadily after her canonization by Pope Gregory XV in 1622, and Teresa's status as one of the foremost devotional writers of the Counter-Reformation is established and secure. The devotional plays composed by Jesuit priests in the sixteenth and seventeenth centuries followed the opposite trajectory: they were enormously popular and influential at the time of their performance, but are almost completely forgotten today. According to one (conservative) estimate, 7,650 plays were staged in the German-speaking province between 1555 and 1773 alone; these performances were usually produced by Jesuit schools, but were attended with equal enthusiasm by the local citizenry.[24] Jesuit pedagogues were in no doubt as to the plays' emotive power and spiritual efficacy: the preface to Jakob Bidermann's 1666 play *Cenodoxus* proclaimed that the work "led to such a move towards great piety in the souls of the audience that these few hours of the play brought about an effect a hundred sermons could hardly have had."[25] Dorothea Weber estimates that, between the end of the sixteenth and the middle of the eighteenth century, there were almost

[24] *Augustinus Conversus: Ein Drama von Jakob Gretser. Einleitung, Text, Übersetzung und Kommentar*, ed. D. Weber (Vienna: Verlag der österreichischen Akademie der Wissenschaften, 2000), 11–12.
[25] Jakob Bidermann, "Cenodoxus," in *Ludi Theatrales sacri* (Munich, 1666), 16; cited in D. Weber, "Augustine and Drama," in *Augustine beyond the Book: Intermediality, Transmediality, and Reception*, eds. K. Pollmann and M. J. Gill (Leiden: Brill, 2012), 97–109, at 108.

sixty plays that based their plots on Augustine's *Confessions*; at least twenty-five of these are now lost.[26] The majority of these plays seem to have focused on Books 6–9 of Augustine's narrative – that is, the time spent in Milan leading up to his baptism (384–386 CE) – and therefore tend to have a happy ending.[27] The title page of Jacob Gretser's *Augustinus Conversus*, first performed at Ingolstadt (Bavaria) in 1592, clearly illustrates this textual focus by specifying that the play's plot derives from "Books 6, 7, 8, and 9 of the *Confessions*;" any spectator with training in Latin would have been able to read the relevant sections of Augustine's text before or after the performance.

The Jesuit plays of the sixteenth and seventeenth centuries present the *Confessions* in a different medium, but they also mobilize Augustine's text in different ways and offer different forms of engagement for the audience. Gretser's play concentrates on the events of 384–386 and brings his source text to life through a range of intertextual gestures: from near-literal quotation to looser forms of allusion, and from thematic adaptation to the transposition of concepts and characters into the specific context of Jesuit devotion. In dramatic performance, the opposing forces that lay claim to Augustine's soul can appear before the spectators with embodied immediacy; in plays like Gretser's, Augustine's role is not as saint or bishop, but as a young man plagued by doubt and seeking enlightenment. In this respect, he offers a ready point of identification for the student members of the audience, but also for more mature spectators who may have been unsettled by the religious strife that afflicted the German-speaking provinces in the wake of the Reformation.

Augustine himself was, of course, deeply skeptical about the moral effects of the theater. Book 3 of the *Confessions* opens with a searingly self-accusing account of lust and misdirected love: for the women of Carthage and "the filth of concupiscence" (*conf.* 3.1.1), but also for the perverse pleasures experienced by watching the performance of tragic suffering on stage. "Why is it," an older and wiser Augustine asks, "that a person should wish to experience suffering by watching grievous and tragic events which he himself would not wish to endure? Nevertheless he wants to suffer the pain given by being a spectator of these sufferings, and the pain itself is his pleasure" (*conf.* 3.2.2). This statement goes some way toward explaining why plays based on the *Confessions* tend to have a happy outcome, and why catharsis – the purgative effect attributed by Aristotle to watching suffering on stage – is eschewed in

---

[26] See, for a brief survey, Weber, *Augustinus Conversus*, 53–54.
[27] D. Weber, "Drama," in OGHRA, vol. 2, 906–907.

favor of redemption. It may also account for the dramaturgical expression of Augustine's struggles: in Gretser's play, we never find Augustine alone on stage – left exposed, as it were, to feelings of doubt and despair without help. Nor does he ever appear in the sole company of his principal adversary, the personified Evil Spirit, whose arguments are always countered by Augustine's Guardian Angel. In performance, the Evil Spirit and the Guardian Angel give physical form to the internal conflict related at *conf.* 8.11.27: "This debate in my heart was a struggle of myself against myself." At the same time, however, the on-stage confrontations of Angel and Spirit also replicate, in an intensely vivid mode, the fundamental conditions of all Jesuit spiritual exercises. The practice of spiritual discernment [*discretio spirituum*] was based on the assumption that each individual could be ruled either by evil forces or by good; that life involved a daily choice between the two, and that rigorous religious discipline would enable one to recognize the former and follow the latter.[28] *Augustinus Conversus* performs this battle on stage.

But if Gretser's play translated Augustine's internal battles into the language of Jesuit devotion, he was equally attuned to the contemporary political resonances of Augustine's narrative. As Weber has shown, Gretser contracts the complex and gradual conversion story of his source text into a clear-cut confrontation between Christianity and Manichaeism, which are in turn equated with Catholicism and heresy. As Monica's soliloquy in Act I, Scene 5 makes clear, these competing factions are also associated with contrasting states of sexual morality: she longingly anticipates the day when her son will "leave behind the shameless Manichaean sect and the filth of their shameful lust," and instead "seek to be united with the chaste Catholic throng".[29] At a time when monks and nuns left religious houses and gave up their vows of celibacy, the present-day applications of this argument are not difficult to discern: the choice is between a chaste life of true Christianity – that is, Catholicism, or the dissolute heretical practices of the new Manichees, the Protestant Reformers. Gretser's play provided powerful incentives for affirming one's allegiance to the Catholic faith at a moment in history where such appeals to the Church's base were most desperately needed. The immersive experiences of theater enabled audiences to live through Augustine's drama of doubt, crisis, and enlightenment, even if they did not require conversion in the more literal sense; as the Guardian Angel advises in his opening address,

---

[28] Weber, *Augustinus Conversus*, 44.

[29] Ibid, 224–227; I have translated from the Latin text provided in Weber's edition.

"Pay attention, observe him [Augustine], and imitate him. This is what Augustine desires for you, this is his fondest wish for those who have been deceived by the flowering of youth and by heresy."[30]

In 1642, another play that took its cue from Books 6–9 of the *Confessions* was performed in the Bavarian town of Eichstätt, also under the title *Augustinus Conversus*. Weber argues that the author may have been Willibald Starck, a teacher at Eichstätt's Jesuit gymnasium.[31] Like Gretser's *Augustinus*, the 1642 play concludes with Augustine's decision to be baptized. But Starck's version departs from the conversion narrative early on to incorporate a glance at *conf.* 1, where Augustine reviews the classical education he received as a boy. His account of Virgil and Terence is dismissive: they merely sanction immorality through rhetorical skill (*conf.* 1.13.20, 1.16.25–26). The 1642 *Augustinus* seeks to respond directly to these concerns: in a set piece that takes up more than one-fifth of the play (verses 69–214), the classical poets Ovid, Catullus, Plautus, Tibullus, Propertius, and Statius appear on stage and attempt to make amends with Augustine.[32] Ovid and Catullus in particular, as authors of sexually allusive poetry, seek forgiveness from Augustine, pleading their moral integrity and promising to mend their ways. The value of classical literature is examined again in the epilogue, when the Liberal Arts enter the stage to give thanks for Augustine's conversion. In pledging his allegiance to God, Augustine has given new meaning to the arts of discourse especially: stripped of their unwholesome associations with romantic love, rhetoric and eloquence can now be put in the service of religion.[33]

AUGUSTINE AND THE POETICS OF HUMILITY

The transformative repurposing of the language arts from secular to divine literature was also a major preoccupation for religious poets in the sixteenth and seventeenth century. In England, the clergyman – and former Cambridge University orator – George Herbert (1593–1633) put the case succinctly in a sonnet addressed to his mother:

> My God, where is that ancient heat towards thee,
>   Wherewith whole showls of *Martyrs* once did burn,
>   Besides their other flames? Doth Poetry

---

[30] Ibid., 48–50 (and 46–47).
[31] Ibid., 107.
[32] Weber, "Augustine and Drama," 107.
[33] Weber, "Augustine and Drama," 107–108.

Wear *Venus* Livery? only serve her turn?
Why are not *Sonnets* made of thee? and layes
   Upon thine Altar burnt? Cannot thy love
   Heighten a spirit to sound out thy praise
As well as any she? Cannot thy *Dove*
Out-strip their *Cupid* easily in flight?
   Or, since thy wayes are deep, and still the same,
   Will not a verse run smooth that bears thy name!
Why doth that fire, which by thy power and might
   Each breast does feel, no braver fuel choose
   Than that, which one day, Worms, may chance refuse.[34]

Herbert's tone reminds us of the slightly hysterical contempt voiced by young Junius when he first encountered the female sex in the streets of Lyon. The argument is clear, and unmistakably Augustinian: the desire for women – and, more specifically, a poet's desire to commemorate it in verse – is a fundamental misdirection of emotional, moral, and intellectual energy; love should be focused on a higher and more noble power, God. That the question "Why are nor sonnets made of thee?" is a purely rhetorical one emerges in the final lines of the poem, where the low worth of women is confirmed in the cruel image of the grave. Instead of soaring toward divine love, poets who worship women are crawling around in graves feasting on bits of rotten flesh that even "Worms ... refuse." Herbert himself sought to provide some redress for this deplorable state of affairs in the shape of *The Temple* (published posthumously in 1633), a collection of poems of astonishing formal virtuosity devoted entirely to religious subjects. In the preface to *The Temple*, Herbert's friend Nicholas Ferrar describes Herbert's trajectory in suitably Augustinian terms: despite notable success in the academic and political sphere, Herbert "betook himself to the Sanctuarie and Temple of God, choosing rather to serve at Gods Altar, then to seek the honour of State-employments."[35] In 1646, another preface to a prominent collection of religious verse stressed the Augustinian roots of Herbert's poetics. Joseph Beaumont, a Fellow of Peterhouse, Cambridge, introduced his former colleague Richard Crashaw as

Herbert's second, but equall, who hath retri'vd Poetry of late, and return'd it up to its Primitive use; Let it bound back to heaven gates,

---

[34] *The English Poems of George Herbert*, ed. H. Wilcox (Cambridge: Cambridge University Press, 2007), 4.
[35] Ibid., 42.

whence it came. Thinke yee, St. *Augustine* would have steyned his graver learning with a booke of Poetry, had he fancied their dearest end to be the vanity of Love-Sonnets ... ? No, no, he thought with this, our Poet, that every foot in a high-borne verse, might helpe to measure the soule into that better world: *Divine Poetry*.[36]

Beaumont's reference to the "vanity of Love-Sonnets" – referring both to the futility of the genre and the love poets' prideful conceit – draws a direct line from Herbert's programmatic sonnet to Crashaw's own writing. Not that this link was really in need of strengthening: the very title of Crashaw's collection, *Steps to the Temple*, acknowledged his debt to Herbert. To write poetry in the tradition of Augustine is to direct it to a higher end; and, rather than being a vanity project designed to showcase the writer's art, religious poetry merely seeks to return its gifts to the creator: "Let it bound back to heaven gates, whence it came." Or, as Herbert's "Dedication" to *The Temple* put it: "Lord, my first fruits present themselves to thee;/Yet not mine neither: for from thee they came,/And must return" (lines 1–3). However, as with the generic conventions of Augustinian life-writing, the same gestures can encode radically different ideological convictions and stylistic choices. Herbert and Crashaw both stress the importance of poetic humility, but, while in Herbert this produces poems of deliberate linguistic simplicity and purity, Crashaw's devaluation of human ability leads him to praise and celebrate God's love in exuberantly elaborate images and conceits. Doctrinally, Herbert's allegiance is to the English Church, which he sees as a moderately Protestant institution bound together by the liturgical patterns of communal worship. Crashaw, on the other hand, felt a far greater affinity with the Church of Rome (he converted to Catholicism in the mid-1640s), and emphasizes its distinctive rituals – including the worship of saints and meditations on the crucified body of Christ – in his poetry.

An even more radical transformation was wrought by the *Confessions* in the life of the English poet and preacher John Donne (1572–1631). The prime evidence for Donne's profound debt to this text are his *Essayes in Divinity*, a series of prose meditations on the Scriptures. Probably composed in 1614, the year before Donne entered into holy orders, they are also a kind of dry run for a career in the Church: the *Essayes* are both demonstrations of scriptural knowledge and practice sermons without an audience (Donne refers to them as examples of

---

[36] *Crashaw's Poetical Works*, ed. L. C. Martin (Oxford: Clarendon, 1927), 75.

"Unvocall preaching").[37] Donne's *Essayes* are also a liminal text in Genette's sense: Donne positions himself "upon the *threshold*" of the English Church, about to enter into the company of "professed divines."[38] The figure who ushers him across that threshold is Augustine, and the *Confessions* will come to define Donne's identity as a reader of Scripture and as a future servant of God's Church. The *Essayes* draw on the *Confessions* more than a dozen times, in passages of doctrinal argument, moral exhortation, and – most crucially – to articulate a sense of religious vocation. This vocation is built, above all, on Donne's relationship with the Bible, and he uses a passage from *conf.* 7.9.14 to insist (like Herbert and Crashaw) that God's Word must be approached with a stance of humility:

> *Discite à me*, sayes our blessed Saviour, *Learn of me*, as Saint Augustine enlarges it well … *quia mitis sum*; learn to be humble. His humility, to be like us, was a Dejection; but ours, to be like him, is our chiefest exaltation … Where this humility is, *ibi Sapientia*.[39]

The flipside of this argument is a condemnation of prideful curiosity on the reader's part, and Donne duly draws on *conf.* 11.12.14 to demarcate the limits of licit inquiry and human knowledge:

> And therefore Saint Augustin says religiously and exemplarily, *If one ask me what God did before this beginning, I will not answer, as another did merrily, He made Hell for such busie inquirers: But I will sooner say, I know not, when I know not, then answer that, by which he shal be deluded which asked too high a Mystery, and he be praysed, which answered a lie.*[40]

Looming over these experiments in Scripture interpretation, however, is the larger issue of Christian identity. Donne constructs the trajectory of his own life in parallel with Augustine's, and, as he contemplates the transition from a secular to a religious career, he looks to the *Confessions* for answers. In the most moving section of the *Essayes*, Donne's quest for faith triggers a moment of intimate textual communion with

---

[37] John Donne, *Essayes in Divinity*, ed. A. Raspa (Montreal: McGill-Queen's University Press, 2001), 47. The *Essayes* were not published until 1651, two decades after Donne's death.

[38] Donne, *Essayes in Divinity*, 15; and see K. Ettenhuber, *Donne's Augustine: Renaissance Cultures of Interpretation* (Oxford: Oxford University Press, 2011), chapter 3.

[39] Donne, *Essayes in Divinity*, 7–8.

[40] Ibid., 23.

Augustine, as Donne repeats, almost word for word, Augustine's appeal to God for understanding at *conf.* 11.3.5:

> Let me in thy beloved Servant *Augustine's* own words, when with an humble boldnesse he begg'd the understanding of this passage, say, *Moses writ this, but is gon from me to thee; if he were here, I would hold him, and beseech him for thy sake, to tell me what he meant. If he spake Hebrew, he would frustrate my hope; but if Latine, I should comprehend him. But from whence should I know that he said true? Or when I knew it, came that knowledge from him? No, for within me, there is a truth, not Hebrew, nor Greek, nor Latin, nor barbarous; which without organs, without noyse of Syllables, tels me true, and would enable me to say confidently to Moses, Thou say'st true.*[41]

Augustine is the patron saint of the *Essayes*, and Donne's invocation of the *Confessions* has a distinctly prayerful dimension. He cannot, of course, overcome the historical distance that separates him from Augustine, nor can he deny the doctrinal differences that make complete identification impossible. And he insists that truth does not belong to any human intermediary – not Moses, not Augustine – but is only God's to convey. At the same time, however, it is clear that Donne's recourse to the *Confessions* goes beyond simple strategies of self-authorization. Like all the authors discussed in this chapter, he recognizes Augustine's qualities as both timeless and acutely relevant to contemporary concerns. And he shares with them a profound conviction that, in order to give meaning and purpose to his own life story, he must revive and retell Augustine's first.

Further Reading

Conybeare, C. *The Routledge Guidebook to Augustine's Confessions.* London: Routledge, 2016.

Courcelle, P. *Les Confessions de Saint Augustin dans la Tradition Littéraire. Antécédents et Postérité.* Paris: Études Augustiniennes, 1963.

DiBattista, M. and E. Wittman (eds.), *The Cambridge Companion to Autobiography.* Cambridge: Cambridge University Press, 2014.

McCabe, W. J. *An Introduction to Jesuit Theatre.* St. Louis, MI: Institute of Jesuit Sources, 1983.

Pollmann, K. and W. Otten (eds.), *The Oxford Guide to the Historical Reception of Augustine,* three vols. Oxford: Oxford University Press, 2013.

[41] Ibid., 19.

Saak, E. L. "Augustine in the Western Middle Ages to the Reformation." In *A Companion to Augustine*, ed. M. Vessey. Blackwell Companions to the Ancient World. Chichester: Wiley-Blackwell, 2012, 465–477.

Vessey, M. "Classicism and Christianity." In *The Oxford History of Classical Reception in English Literature*, eds. P. Cheney and P. Hardie. Oxford: Oxford University Press, 2015, vol. 2, 103–128.

Visser, A. "Reading Augustine through Erasmus' Eyes: Humanist Scholarship and Paratextual Guidance in the Wake of the Reformation." *Erasmus of Rotterdam Society Yearbook* 28 (2008), 67–90.

18 Reception during the Enlightenment: A for Anti-Augustine

PATRICK RILEY

Philippe Sellier begins his *Pascal et Saint Augustin* with the declaration: "The seventeenth century is the century of Saint Augustine."[1] Although Augustine's influence is clearest in the Jansenism of Port-Royal, it extends from the philosophy of Descartes, to the tragedies of Racine, and to the internecine conflicts between Jesuits, Jansenists, Calvinists, Quietists, and others. Such theological antagonism pervades France until at least the expulsion of the Jesuits in 1764, fueled by virulent critique from both the Jansenists and the *philosophes* of the Enlightenment.[2]

On the other hand, the Enlightenment is perhaps the most anti-Augustinian of all epochs in European history.[3] The rejection of Augustine in the eighteenth century is partly the result of the Enlightenment's worldview. Its philosophy, and that philosophy's reflection in literary

---

[1] P. Sellier, *Pascal et Saint Augustine* (Paris: Armand Colin, 1970), 11 (translation is mine). Sellier is not the first to make such a claim on behalf of the French seventeenth century. As early as 1951, Jean Dagens delivered a lecture entitled: "Le XVIIe siècle, siècle de Saint Augustin" ("The Seventeenth Century, Century of Saint Augustine"), *Cahiers de l'Association internationale des études francaises* 3–5 (1953), 31–38.

[2] There will not be enough space in this chapter to discuss the demise of the Jesuits, who, in Bayle's day, must have seemed like an unassailable institution. Although there was little love lost between the Jansenists and the *philosophes*, their mutual efforts did coalesce somewhat to hasten the Jesuits' expulsion. For a thorough account, see D. Van Kley, *The Jansenists and the Expulsion of the Jesuits from France, 1757–1765* (New Haven, CT: Yale University Press), 1975.

[3] Indeed, in the *Cambridge Companion to Augustine*, eds. E. Stump and N. Kretzmann, (Cambridge: Cambridge University Press, 2001), 267–279, Gareth B. Matthews' chapter (which closes the volume), "Post-medieval Augustinianism," skips from Descartes, Grotius, Malebranche, and Leibniz (i.e., all essentially seventeenth-century figures) to John Stewart Mill (nineteenth century) and Wittgenstein (twentieth century). It might be almost as accurate to say that the Enlightenment is "non-Augustinian" as to say that it is anti-Augustinian. Little has been written about the reception of Augustine in general, and the *Confessions* in particular, in the Enlightenment. Much of the existing literature compares the two *Confessions* of Augustine and Rousseau.

production, is staunchly rooted in the primacy of reason, the "New Science" of English empiricism and its culmination in Newtonian mechanics, its anticlericalism, its inclination toward deism, its low regard for metaphysics, and in its broad denigration of theology.[4] But it would be a mistake to view the anti-Augustinianism of the eighteenth century as only an effect of ideological forces inimical to Augustine's writings. At least in France, eighteenth-century attacks on Augustine also constitute a proxy war against many of the religious, philosophical, and political developments of the prior century. A critique of Augustine is also a way to disavow Cartesianism, the Jansenist view of grace and freewill, and religious intolerance of nonorthodox sects in the wake of Louis XIV's Revocation of the Edict of Nantes.

The Enlightenment is perhaps best symbolized by the immense project of Diderot's and D'Alembert's *Encyclopédie*, whose first volume was published in 1751.

The eighteenth century is very much an age of dictionaries and encyclopedias. The Chevalier de Jaucourt's entry, "Père de l'église" ("Church Father"), in volume 12 of the *Encyclopedia*, contains an unflattering treatment of Augustine that combines his theological doctrine with an *ad hominem* argument clearly based on the *Confessions*. It is that nexus of theology and biography that seems most to distress the encyclopedist. A half-century before the *Encyclopedia*, one finds a similar procedure in Pierre Bayle's sprawling *Dictionnaire historique et critique* (*Critical and Historical Dictionary*) of 1697. Nominally responding to the *Encyclopedia*, Voltaire's *Questions sur l'Encyclopédie* of 1770–1774 (itself structured like an encyclopedia) presents a similarly uncharitable characterization of Augustine. As much as Bayle, Jaucourt, and Voltaire seem to enjoy lampooning St. Augustine in his own right, each of them also has an ulterior motive: to heap ridicule on

---

[4] For the reader interested in classic studies of the Enlightenment, see P. Gay, *The Party of Humanity: Essays in the French Enlightenment* (New York: Knopf, 1964), as well as *The Enlightenment, an Interpretation* (New York: Knopf, 1969). See also E. Bréhier, *The History of Philosophy*, trans. W. Baskin (Chicago: The University of Chicago Press, 1967), vol. 5. For a reading of the Enlightenment from a Marxist perspective, see L. Goldmann, *The Philosophy of the Enlightenment: The Christian Burgess and the Enlightenment*, trans. H. Mass (Cambridge, MA: MIT Press, 1973). For more recent studies of the Enlightenment, see D. Outram, *The Enlightenment* (Cambridge: Cambridge University Press, 2013); D. Edelstein, *The Enlightenment: A Genealogy* (Chicago: University of Chicago Press, 2010); and J. I. Israel, *A Revolution of the Mind: Radical Enlightenment and the Intellectual Origins of Modern Democracy* (Princeton, NJ: Princeton University Press, 2010).

theological controversies rooted in the seventeenth century and extending into the Age of Enlightenment.

In this chapter, I want to show how the Enlightenment reception of Augustine looks backward toward the "century of Saint Augustine." I also want to suggest that this retrospective denigration of the Augustinianism that arose in the wake of the Reformation and (especially) the Counter-Reformation, in the quintessentially Enlightenment forms of the dictionary and the encyclopedia, is also a kind of propaganda for the triumph of the Enlightenment mainstream.

BAYLE

Ruth Wheelan writes: "The challenge to ecclesiastical tradition, the derision visited on the church Fathers in the Age of Reason – as the case of Saint Augustine illustrates – owe much of their power to that Arsenal of the Enlightenment, Pierre Bayle."[5] "Arsenal" is certainly an apt term, in that it suggests that Bayle is himself a storehouse of critical arms that he deploys in his own writings, and in the sense that Bayle served as an inexhaustible source of inspiration for the *philosophes* a half-century later.

Because Louis XIV's Revocation of the Edict of Nantes was an open invitation to persecute French Protestants, Bayle's Calvinist faith made of him an exile, who spent most of his mature years in Rotterdam. He publishes his *De la tolérance: Commentaire philosophique* between 1686 and 1688, and the two editions of the *Dictionnaire historique et critique* to appear during his lifetime between 1697 and 1702.[6]

In his virulent pamphlet, "Ce que c'est que la France toute catholique sous le règne de Louis-le-Grand" ("What all-Catholic France Is under the Reign of Louis the Great" [1686]), Bayle already makes clear that the intolerance and injustice of the Catholic Church following the Revocation is inextricably linked to the vindictive fanaticism of the person of Louis XIV.[7] The *Commentaire* is, in a similar vein, a plea for tolerance and a denunciation of obligatory adherence to a hegemonic and orthodox religion. Here, however, Bayle frames intolerance

---

[5] R. Wheelan, "The Wage of Sin is Orthodoxy: The *Confessions* of Saint Augustine in Bayle's *Dictionnaire*," *Journal of the History of Philosophy* 26/2 (April 1988), 195–206.

[6] For the most recent edition of the *Commentaire philosophique*, see *De la tolérance. Commentaire philosophique*, ed. J.-M. Gros (Paris: Champion, 2006).

[7] *Ce que c'est que la France toute Catholique, sous le règne de Louis le Grand*, ed. E. Labrousse, Bibliothèque des textes philosophiques (Paris: Vrin, 1973).

historically by analyzing defenses of forced orthodoxy in the patristic tradition, in particular Augustine's interpretation and endorsement of the scriptural passage commonly known as the Parable of the Great Banquet (Lk 14:15–24), often invoked in Catholicism to validate persecution. Although Bayle is aware of the chaos and sectarianism and of the real threats to Catholicism in Augustine's lifetime, he nevertheless argues that there is no way to justify forced conversion, and that the particular circumstances of the Church in Augustine's day explain (at least in part) but do not justify persecution. He reminds the reader that tolerance – the single most important thread running through all of Bayle's work – is by definition accepting coexistence with those with whom one disagrees.

Bayle's focus in the *Commentaire* is far more on Augustine's theology than on his person. His approach in the *Dictionnaire historique et critique* is just the opposite: drawing from Augustine's self-portrait in the *Confessions*, Bayle constructs a caricature of the younger Augustine that hammers obsessively on his sexual incontinence and mercurial religious experience.[8] The "biographical" portion of Bayle's entry extends beyond the years covered in the *Confessions* to describe Augustine's ecclesiastical career in North Africa, but, throughout the text, Bayle's account of Augustine's life seems perfunctory, if not entirely dismissive, of the Church Father's accomplishments. And, while it is clear that the bulk of the biographical section of the entry draws heavily from Augustine's autobiography, Bayle only cites the *Confessions* in the footnotes and their marginalia, not in the body of the entry (Jaucourt fails to mention the *Confessions* entirely, and Voltaire mentions it only once).

The reader will also note that Bayle's description of Augustine's conversion consists of one anodyne sentence, while the entry goes on to ridicule the new convert's inability to wait two years to consummate an arranged marriage. Bayle writes: "He could not resist his natural impulses so long: he once again took up his impure practices" (*Dictionnaire*, 392).[9] Since most of the *Commentaire philosophique* consists of an attack on Augustine's defense of forced conversion, it should perhaps

---

[8] In this chapter, for the *Dictionnaire historique et critique*, I am relying on the online ARTFL (American and French Research on the Treasury of the French Language) Project reproduction of the fifth edition (1740) of the work: http://artfl-project.uchicago.edu/content/dictionnaire-de-bayle.

[9] This and all subsequent translations from the *Dictionnaire* are mine.

not come as a surprise that Bayle does not wish to recognize the significance of Augustine's own conversion, voluntary though it was.

Just when one begins to wonder why Bayle bothered to write about Augustine's life at all, Bayle explains himself:

> The details of his episcopal life & writings would be superfluous here; one can find them in Moréri's Dictionary & in Du Pin's Library; & if those gentlemen had not passed too lightly over St. Augustine's disordered life, I could have entirely dispensed with this article. But, for the better instruction of the public, it is best to show both the good and the bad sides of great men.
> (Dictionnaire, 393)

It is difficult to take Bayle entirely seriously here. To begin with, his entry on Augustine skews much more toward the bad than the good. Furthermore, the "instruction of the public" concerning Augustine's sins has already existed in book form since the fifth century; namely, the *Confessions* itself. And, if the late seventeenth-century reader's Latin were not up to the task of reading the autobiography in the original, the poet and Jansenist *solitaire* of Port-Royal, Arnauld D'Andilly's 1649 translation into French would have been readily available. Bayle is of course aware that Augustine spares himself very little criticism in the *Confessions*, taking on the task of *confessio peccati* as rigorously as anyone in the history of autobiography. Perhaps that is why Bayle never mentions the book in the body text of his entry.

Most importantly, it seems as if Bayle is deliberately missing the point. Failing to name the *Confessions* as the primary source of the entry; nearly passing over Augustine's conversion entirely; dwelling on Augustine's sins and indeed exaggerating them: in other words, Bayle refuses to recognize that one of the most important functions of Augustine's confession of sins is to underscore how completely the sinner is transformed through the gift of grace and how earnestly he repents of his former life. For Augustine, authentic being is exclusively the result of proximity to God, which presupposes a rejection of worldliness (*conf.* 7.11.17). And yet Bayle concerns himself inordinately with Augustine's worldliness.

Bayle's entry concludes with an extraordinary pivot toward recent theological controversies within Christianity. The last two paragraphs would seem to reveal Bayle's purpose in criticizing Augustine and in failing to refer directly to the *Confessions*. As in the *Commentaire philosophique*, it is once again Augustine's understanding of grace that is at issue, but, in the *Dictionnaire*, the question is reduced to two paragraphs that question why the Catholic Church would condemn contemporary views of grace in various Christian sects that resemble Augustinian doctrine as heretical, while continuing to enshrine Augustine himself.

Bayle first targets the Jesuits: "The approbation which Councils & Popes have given Saint Augustine on his doctrine of grace, have done a great service to his glory; for, failing that, the Molinists [Jesuits], in these recent times, would have raised their banner against him & reduced his authority to nothing" (*Dictionnaire*, 393). But the Jesuits had a more pressing concern at the time: destroying their far less powerful Jansenist adversaries. Since the Rosetta Stone of Jansenism is Jansen's *Augustinus*, and since the Jansenists claimed to be following only an ascetic strain of Augustinianism, to condemn the Jansenists without condemning St. Augustine himself is hypocritical and "ridiculous":

> The Church of Rome's commitment to respect St. Augustine's system puts it into a most ridiculous predicament. It is so obvious to anyone who examines things without prejudice, & with sufficient lights, that the doctrine of St. Augustine & that of Jansenius, Bishop of Ypres, are one and the same doctrine, that no one can see without indignation that the Court of Rome boasted of having condemned Jansenius, & nonetheless of having preserved all of Saint Augustine's glory. These are two entirely incompatible things. (Dictionnaire, 395)

Augustine's "system" referenced in this passage is his understanding of grace, freewill, and predetermination. A rather tedious debate between Jesuits and Jansenists over sufficient grace and efficacious grace was nevertheless sufficiently efficacious to inspire Blaise Pascal's brilliant satirical polemic, the *Provincial Letters* of 1656–1657. In that work, Pascal also sought to ridicule the moral laxity of Jesuitical casuistry. It would be more than a century until the expulsion of the Jesuits from France in 1764 (the year before the publication of Jaucourt's "père de l'église" in volume 12 of the *Encyclopédie*).

In a stunning conflation, Bayle goes on to claim that the Council of Trent, in condemning Calvin's doctrine of freewill and predetermination, is also (at least logically) a condemnation of Augustine's views on the same matter, as if the Counter-Reformation theologically annulled both Protestantism and Catholicism at the same time. Furthermore, says Bayle, Thomism at base has the same view as well. With one strike, he asserts that what was considered Catholic orthodoxy at the time (i.e., the combined doctrines of the Jesuits and of Aquinas), the breakaway asceticism of the Jansenists (i.e., the barely Catholic and almost Calvinist adversaries of the Jesuits), and the predestination of the Calvinists (i.e., the only sect more persecuted in France than the Jansenists, and Bayle's own nominal faith) are effectively identical:

> The physical predetermination of the Thomists, the necessity of St. Augustine, that of the Jansenists, and that of Calvin, are at base one and the same thing; & yet the Thomists renounce the Jansenists, & both claim they are being slandered when they are accused of teaching the same doctrine as Calvin. If people were allowed to judge their neighbors' thoughts, it would be very tempting to say here that Doctors are great Actors [*Comédiens*], & that they are not unaware that the Council of Trent condemned an illusion that had never entered the Calvinists' mind, or else that it condemned Saint Augustine & physical predetermination. (Dictionnaire, 393)

This kind of relativistic *reductio* concerning factions within Christianity will become a favored approach during the Enlightenment, and will be radicalized by writers like Voltaire and Lessing, who argue that all Abrahamic religions are essentially "one and the same thing."

Viewing the questions macroscopically, one can understand why Bayle might equate these various strains of Christianity. They are all, after all, Christocentric, they all hold a belief in divine grace, they all embrace conversion, and so on. But in a more important sense, Bayle's conflation is a *reductio ad absurdum* designed to ridicule theologians ("it would be very tempting to say here that Doctors are great Actors" [*Dictionnaire*, 393]).

Is Bayle's intent in mocking theological disputes just what it appears to be – a satirical attack on religious hypocrisy – or is it a critique of Augustine intended to defend Bayle's own Calvinist faith (as if he were imagining himself telling papal authority: "What we think is at least not any sillier than what Augustine thinks, so condemn or accept both"?). Or is it a suggestion that perhaps Bayle does not take any sectarian doctrine very seriously, his own included? For over 300 years, readers have been puzzled by the *Dictionnaire* for just this reason: here the lines between relativism, skepticism, tolerance, and (possibly) agnosticism are blurred, and the work's sometimes tortured logic and frequent self-contradiction make the issue impossible to resolve.[10]

---

[10] On Bayle's skepticism, see W. E. Rex's classic study, *Essays on Pierre Bayle and Religious Controversy* (Hague: M. Nijhoff, 1965). Also see R. H. Popkin, "Pierre Bayle: Superscepticism and the Beginning of Enlightenment Dogmatism," in *The*

The pyrotechnics of the entry's conclusion might allow something very important to pass unnoticed, which is that Bayle has shifted his focus from Augustine's personal shortcomings revealed in the *Confessions* to the same kind of doctrinal issues he had already pilloried at length in the *Commentaire philosophique*. One is left wondering if Bayle's attack on Augustine via the *Confessions* is merely a vehicle to attack well-worn Augustinian positions on grace and salvation, if the saint is being used simply as a proxy to ridicule Jansenism (or other variants of neo-Augustinianism), or whether the real target is sectarianism as such.

Yet we know that Jesuitism, Jansenism, Thomism, and Calvinism are, in a nontrivial way, *not* "one and the same thing." And the dictionary entry's inexorable suggestion – that we should not give credence to the theology of a man as concupiscent as Augustine (never mind his conversion and repentance) – if taken seriously, logically also implies that if the Jesuits, the Jansenists, the Thomists, the Calvinists (and maybe the Arminians too?) have all arrived at the same theological positions, we have to conclude that Loyola, Jansen, Aquinas, and Calvin were just as concupiscent, and therefore just as unreliable, as the bishop of Hippo himself.

What is the relationship between one's personal life and one's religious convictions? On the one hand, Bayle is arguing that a flawed person will generate flawed theology. But if the Augustinian position is really flawed, and all the other sectarian positions that he rehearses in the dictionary are essentially identical to Augustine's, are they also wrong? And let us not forget that Bayle is only able to assail Augustine's theology by ignoring everything after Book 8 of the *Confessions*. Would a less polemical and more balanced portrait of Augustine as an individual, taking into account his reform and his rejection of worldliness, come to the opposite conclusion about his theology? Could one not successfully question Augustine's theology without a prior, deliberately distorted attack on his character? In sum, Bayle, for all his satirical eloquence, has painted himself into a corner.

JAUCOURT

The Chevalier de Jaucourt, in the long entry in the *Encyclopédie*, "père de l'église" ("Church Father"), has done something interesting. Jaucourt

History of Scepticism: From Savonarola to Bayle (Oxford: Oxford University Press, 2003), chapter 18, 283–302.

covers the Church Fathers in chronological order, and some are treated at length, while others are discussed only very briefly. The section on Augustine is one of the longer ones, as one would expect. Most of what Jaucourt has to say about Augustine is lifted from Bayle, sometimes in paraphrase, sometimes in précis, sometimes taken practically verbatim. However, Jaucourt does not name Bayle as a source; instead, he mentions Dupin and Moréri. Recall that in a sentence from the *Dictionnaire critique et historique* quoted earlier Bayle says that he might have dispensed entirely with his entry on Augustine, since "the details of his episcopal life and writings" are already thoroughly covered by Dupin and Moréri, and that he is only writing on Augustine because his two predecessors had "passed too lightly over St. Augustine's disordered life." The relevant works of the authors that both Bayle and Jaucourt mention are Moréri's 1674 *Le Grand Dictionaire historique, ou le mélange curieux de l'histoire sacrée et profane* (*Great Historical Dictionary, or Curious Anthology of Sacred and Secular History*), and Dupin's 1686 *Nouvelle bibliothèque des auteurs ecclésiastiques* (*New Library of Ecclesiastical Authors*).[11]

It seems as if Jaucourt has reverted to Moréri and Dupin's "passing too lightly over St. Augustine's disordered life." Gone is Bayle's repetitive carping about Augustine's libertine character. What remains is a combination of anodyne biography and criticism of Augustine's theology. But very little, if any of it, appears to be drawn from Dupin or Moréri. The parts of Jaucourt's section on Augustine that are not closely modeled on Bayle's *Dictionnaire* are something like an extremely abbreviated summary of Bayle's argument in the *Commentaire philosophique*. Jaucourt takes Augustine to task on the issue of religious persecution. The critique follows another Baylesque passage that accuses Augustine of being mercurial, if not downright hypocritical in his theological views, and also calls out his shift from liberality to unnecessary rigor concerning persecution of nonorthodoxy.

The modern reader might be surprised by Jaucourt's entry. It is true that the section on Augustine is only part of a much larger text that tries to have something pertinent to say about all the Church Fathers, so it is understandable that Jaucourt, even as he borrows so heavily from Bayle, would not repeat certain sections of the *Dictionnaire* entry. Oddly,

---

[11] The ARTFL Project website includes a copy of the twentieth edition of Moréri's dictionary (Paris: Les libraires associés, 1759): https://artfl-project.uchicago.edu/content/dictionnaire-de-moréri. Several facsimiles of Dupin's *Nouvelle bibliothèque* are also available online.

however, Jaucourt cites Bayle in other parts of the entry, but fails to mention him in the Augustine section, even though that section is closer to the *Dictionnaire* (and seemingly the *Commentaire*) than sections on any other Church Father. Why would he name Bayle in parts of the text where he leans less heavily on him, but not in the Augustine section? It is tempting to imagine that Jaucourt has a reason for doing that, but what might it be? Did he think, as the modern reader might very well also do, that Bayle's *ad hominem* distortion of the Augustine presented in the *Confessions* fails to bolster the subsequent theological critique?

It is not clear whether Jaucourt's elision of Bayle's attack on Augustine's concupiscence strengthens or weakens the theological critique in the *Encyclopédie* entry. It is equally unclear whether Jaucourt's decision to add a précis of Bayle's condemnation of Augustine's views on forced conversion from the *Commentaire philosophique* is strategically successful. But, as for Jaucourt's liberal borrowing from Bayle, that should only be surprising to the reader who does not know much about Jaucourt's broader role in the project of the *Encyclopedia*. He was the single most prolific contributor to the text, writing some 18,000 entries. He had on occasion four or five secretaries simultaneously assisting him in that enterprise. And while Diderot and d'Alembert (coeditors of the *Encyclopedia* until d'Alembert dropped out in 1759) both ridiculed Jaucourt as something of a hack, a "compiler," there is no question that Diderot came to rely on him as a dependable and conscientious collaborator.[12] In more recent times, some critics have tried to show that Jaucourt was far more than a "compiler," and that, in fact, he represents the critical spirit of the *Encyclopedia* more than any other correspondent.[13]

That critical spirit is evident in Jaucourt's conclusion to the "Church Father" article. It is largely based on false encomium. He hails (several times in the concluding paragraphs) the accomplishments and intelligence of Church Fathers who were writing in centuries marked by prejudice and persecution. But the bulk of the conclusion is a laundry list of the errors and shortcomings in the Church Fathers' writings.

---

[12] For a biographical sketch of Jaucourt that describes the sometimes unflattering impressions his contemporaries held of him, see F. A. Kafker and S. L. Kafker, *The Encyclopedists as Individuals: A Biographical Dictionary of the Authors of the Encyclopédie* (Oxford: Voltaire Foundation, 1988), 175–180.

[13] See G. A. Perla, "La philosophie de Jaucourt dans l' 'Encyclopédie'," *Revue de l'histoire des religions* 197/1 (1980), 59–78. Also see M. F. Morris, *Le Chevalier de Jaucourt: un ami de la terre* (Geneva: Droz, 1979).

These include an excessive fondness for flashy rhetoric (a claim Jaucourt as well as Bayle also make about Augustine in particular), an overreliance on figural or allegorical reading of Scripture, an unhealthy insistence upon celibacy (and a condemnation of second marriages among widowers), an excessive endorsement of martyrdom, and more.[14] Some of those passages are boilerplate. But the very first sentence of the conclusion already states Jaucourt's view that the writings of the Church Fathers are obsolete: "Finally, enlightened centuries learned the correct way of explaining Scripture and of approaching morality seriously; they enlightened the world about the errors into which the *Church Fathers* had fallen" (12:348). Despite the praise, Jaucourt goes on to argue that the Church Fathers articulated nothing about morality that cannot be deduced by even the most rudimentary lights of reason. One may assume that, by the "enlightened centuries" that developed correct scriptural interpretation, Jaucourt means especially the French eighteenth century and the small chunk of the seventeenth century in which Bayle was writing.

Jaucourt's conclusion is typical of the self-propagandizing of the *parti philosophique* in general, and the encyclopedists in particular. An abiding belief in progress and human perfectibility; the privileging of reason over faith and superstition; the triumph of "philosophy" over "rhetoric": these are all characteristics that one encounters almost everywhere in Enlightenment discourse, and throughout the *Encyclopedia* (one need only read d'Alembert's *Discours préliminaire de l'Encyclopédie* to see them deployed).

Jaucourt's final sentence is particularly telling. The *Encyclopedia of Diderot & d'Alembert Collaborative Translation Project* gives the sentence as: "The faith they professed and the religion they spread everywhere in the face of obstacles and persecutions more than excuse their failings."[15] Jaucourt's original sentence, however, reads: "Enfin, la foi

---

[14] As with Bayle's *Dictionnaire*, I am using the ARTFL Project's online edition of the *Encyclopédie*: *Encyclopédie, ou dictionnaire raisonné des sciences, des arts et des métiers, etc.*, eds. D. Diderot and J. le Rond d'Alembert. Chicago: University of Chicago, ARTFL Encyclopédie Project (Autumn 2017 Edition), eds. R. Morrissey and G. Roe, http://encyclopedie.uchicago.edu, vol. 12, 339–350. This and all subsequent translations of Jaucourt's article are mine.

[15] "Church Father," in *The Encyclopedia of Diderot & d'Alembert Collaborative Translation Project*, trans. E. Jane Cohen. Ann Arbor: Michigan Publishing, University of Michigan Library, 2002, http://hdl.handle.net.exlibris.colgate.edu: 2048/2027/spo.did2222.0000.336, translation of "Père de l'église," *Encyclopédie ou Dictionnaire raisonné des sciences, des arts et des métiers*. Paris, 1765, vol. 12.

qu'ils ont professée, la religion qu'ils ont étendue de toutes parts malgré les obstacles & les persecutions, n'ont pu donner à personne le droit de faillir comme eux" (12:350). A more literal translation would be: "Finally, their profession of faith, the religion they spread everywhere despite obstacles and persecutions, were not able to give anyone the right to fail as they did." Surely this must be the most left-handed compliment in the entire entry. And it exemplifies the way criticism was accomplished in the *Encyclopedia*.

D'Alembert left the encyclopedia when the royal censor revoked the *privilège du roi*, threatening to derail the entire project. In order to ensure the publication of the remaining volumes, critique was moved, as it were, to the margins of the work. Historian Robert Darnton and others have written about how some of the more subversive elements of the *Encyclopédie* can be found, for instance, in Diderot's and d'Alembert's "figurative system of human knowledge," a kind of genealogical tree diagram representing epistemological categories (in which theology sits just above divination and black magic, and in which religion, "when abused," lapses into superstition, the two therefore residing on the same branch of the tree), and in entries' cross-references, the critique consisting in juxtaposition and insinuation.[16]

In "père de l'église," Jaucort uses a similar technique. One might have expected his entry to be in the plural ("Church Fathers"), especially since Jaucourt makes a point of having something to say about each and every patristic figure. But, once he has gone through the list of the individuals, the conclusion of the entry speaks about the shortcomings of *all* the Church Fathers as if they were one, enabling him to draw a distinction between the ignorance of "then" and the enlightenment of "now." If that is true, it might help to explain why Jaucourt, even as he borrows so liberally from Bayle, leaves out the latter's *ad hominem* caricature based on the *Confessions*, and perhaps explains why Jaucourt does not even mention Bayle in the section on Augustine, for fear it might send the reader back to the very particular portrait of Augustine in Bayle's *Dictionnaire* – his goal seems to be more to generalize than to particularize.

---

[16] See "Philosophers Trim the Tree of Knowledge: The Epistemological Strategy of the *Encyclopédie*," in *The Great Cat Massacre: and Other Episodes in French Cultural History*, ed. R. Darnton (New York: Basic Books, 2004), 191–209.

VOLTAIRE

Let us turn to Voltaire's treatment of Augustine in the *Questions sur l'Encyclopédie, par des amateurs* (1770–1774). Like his *Dictionnaire philosophique* (1764), Voltaire's *Questions sur l'Encyclopédie* is in the form of a dictionary or encyclopedia; in fact, articles from this work have sometimes been subsumed into later editions of the *Dictionnaire philosophique*, creating a certain amount of confusion for readers.[17] The *Questions* is Voltaire's longest and one of his last works. Many see it as reflecting his definitive views on issues that had concerned him for decades, particularly theological and philosophical questions that he had written about over a thirty- or fourty-year period.[18]

The title of the book is both descriptive and slightly misleading. In 1769, a Parisian printer had proposed a new, expanded version of the Diderot/d'Alembert *Encyclopédie*, and Voltaire had agreed to contribute articles to it. When the project fell through, Voltaire took the material he had already prepared and added greatly to it to form the *Questions*. What might confound the reader is the fact that the work does not consist primarily of "questions" that "*amateurs*" of the original *Encyclopédie* might have. There is really just one lover of the *Encyclopédie* here, Voltaire, and, rather than questions, he has written a large number of articles (420 between 1770 and 1772 and 460 in 1774, to be precise), organized alphabetically, that one could easily mistake for a vastly expanded edition of the *Dictionnaire philosophique*, as it repeats many of that work's subjects, sometimes containing language

[17] The confusion begins at least as early as the publication of the posthumous 1784 Kehl edition, edited and financed by Beaumarchais and Condorcet. In that edition, some 2,000 pages are included under the title *Dictionnaire philosophique*, when, in reality, the majority belongs to the *Questions sur l'Encyclopédie*, and some belong to neither. On this question, see L. Gil, *L'Edition Kehl de Voltaire: une aventure éditoriale et littéraire au tournant des Lumières* (Paris: Champion, 2018).

[18] In an invaluable service to Voltaire scholars, editors Christiane Mervaud and Nicholas Cronk have completed the task, more than ten years in the making, of establishing an eight-volume edition of the *Questions sur l'Encyclopédie*, published as volumes 37–43 of the *Oeuvres complètes de Voltaire* (completed 2018; the numbering is this way because there is a volume 42A and a volume 42B). The article "Augustin" discussed later is from this edition. See *Questions sur l'Encyclopédie, par des amateurs, Volume III (Aristote-Certain)*, eds. C. Mervaud and N. Cronk (Oxford: Voltaire Foundation, 2008). All subsequent references are to this edition, and all translations are my own.

identical to that in the *Dictionnaire* (hence the aforementioned confusing publishing history).[19]

It is in the *Questions* that we find the article, "Augustin." No such entry appears in the *Dictionnaire philosophique*. I noted earlier how great Voltaire's debt to Bayle is, and Voltaire's article on Augustine indeed draws from Bayle's *Dictionnaire*, but in a rather odd way. Voltaire repeats an anecdote that Bayle relates about the young Augustine's precocious virility in one of the many footnotes to his entry. The story, from *conf.* 2.3.6, is about Augustine's father noticing his son's sexual maturity while the two are in a public bathhouse. Voltaire acknowledges Bayle here, explaining that Bayle commented that a father and son bathing together publicly would have been against the rules of decorum in Augustine's time.[20] Voltaire goes on to say that such decorum would have applied to patricians in the Roman Empire, but not to the poor.

In an unusual but beautifully crafted paragraph, Voltaire speaks of the "opulent man" (*Questions*, 224) sleeping with his concubine in a bed of ivory and silver, with his wife sleeping with her lover in another room, while the family's children, teachers, and servants each slept in their own rooms. The common people, on the other hand, slept "in a jumble, in their hovel" (*Questions*, 224). Besides, Voltaire quips, "people did not much stand on ceremony in the city of Thagaste in Africa" (*Questions*, 224). He ends the paragraph with the provocative sentence: "Augustine's father took him to the baths of the poor" (*Questions*, 224).

The passage is a microsociology of the provincial and the cosmopolitan empire, and it does not exist in Bayle's dictionary. I am talking about it here because I think it is emblematic not only of Voltaire's markedly literary approach to "encyclopedic" discourse, but also of his fabled irony, which often renders interpreting his ideas difficult. As Voltaire presents a portrait of patrician excess in the Roman Empire, and contrasts it with the plebeian squalor of a provincial backwater such as North Africa, it is difficult to assess whether Voltaire meant to elevate or to denigrate Augustine and his father by stating that they

---

[19] On this question, see *Copier/Coller. Écriture et réécriture chez Voltaire*, eds. O. Ferret, et al. (Pisa: PLUS-Pisa University Press, 2007).

[20] Bayle's comment is in a marginal note (numbered 6) to footnote B. The immense network of additions, footnotes, and marginalia in Bayle's *Dictionnaire* can be overwhelming. The ARTFL Project online facsimile of the 1740 Amsterdam fifth edition (four in-folio volumes) shows the reader precisely what this textual mare's nest looks like on the page.

would have frequented the "baths of the poor." Most likely, in the context of the entire article, Voltaire wanted to suggest that the later apotheosis of Augustine is all the more remarkable considering his humble beginnings; but Voltaire also aims to show that such an apotheosis was probably unjust.

Voltaire goes on to propose that, just as nature authored Augustine's premature sexual development, it also brought out in him a precocious intellect. In a way that would seem to parody Montesquieu's often-ridiculed theories in *The Spirit of the Laws* about the relationship between climate, character, and politics, Voltaire portrays the young Augustine as a prodigy of nature, prematurely baked by the African sun into a sexual and intellectual *Wunderkind*. Augustine was able to father a child at fourteen; by twenty, Voltaire says, he was able to teach himself geometry, arithmetic, and music (*Questions*, 224–225). Voltaire uses this example to suggest that the part of the world we now call Barbary was a seat of culture and learning, while the lands comprising contemporary Europe were themselves "barbaric" and uncultured (225–226). Indeed, it was the Moors of North Africa having successfully "cultivated the sciences," who "instructed" Spain and Italy "for more than five centuries" (225).

Now the situation is reversed, and Europe has gone on to eclipse the greatest achievements of North Africa in the days of the Roman Empire. Augustine's country is today "nothing but a den of pirates" (225), while the England, Italy, Germany, and France have "cultivated the arts better than the Arabs ever had" (225–226). Voltaire claims that he hopes principally to show the ironies and the reversals of history: "Thus we wish, in this article, only to show how much this world is a picture of change" (226), he writes.

But his real purpose is revealed at the end of this most laconic, three-page entry on Augustine. The final paragraph is a head-spinning *tour de force*. Voltaire writes:

> Augustine the debauchee becomes an orator and philosopher. He strikes out in the world, he is a teacher of rhetoric; he becomes a Manichean; from Manicheanism he moves on to Christianity. He has himself baptized along with one of his bastard children named Deodatus: he becomes a bishop; he becomes a Church Father. His *system of grace* is respected for eleven hundred years as an article of faith. After eleven hundred years, some Jesuits find the means to anathematize Saint Augustine's system word for word, under the name of Jansenius, of Saint-Cyran, of Arnauld, of Quesnel. (See

'Grace'.) We ask if this revolution in its own domain is not as great as that of Africa, and if there is anything permanent on earth.

(Questions, 356; original italics)

While Bayle's entry in the *Historical and Critical Dictionary* is a verbose and unruly disquisition, and Jaucourt's article in the *Encyclopedia* is a similarly verbose, unruly (and largely plagiarized) cut-and-paste hodgepodge, Voltaire's entry is a compact and beautifully symmetrical rhetorical gem. And, yet, like Bayle, and like Jaucourt following Bayle, Voltaire arrives at the same basic point: while Augustine's doctrine of grace remains largely unscathed, its nearly identical recapitulation in Jansenism is condemned by the Jesuits and ultimately by papal authority.

Let us be a bit more precise. In Bayle's and Jaucourt's articles, we saw that Jaucourt simply follows Bayle in contending that, in relatively contemporary times, Augustinian theology escaped censure while the doctrines of Jansenism and Calvinism, even though they take positions on grace and predestination that are practically identical to St. Augustine's, have been roundly condemned; Thomism, on the other hand, managed to avoid condemnation despite holding an Augustinian view of freewill, and Arminianism steered clear of censure by throwing Augustinian theology to the wolves.

Bayle and Jaucourt are considering, then, anti-Calvinist church positions dating from the Council of Trent (1545–1563) and anti-Jansenist positions dating from Pope Innocent X's *Cum occasione* in 1653 (condemning five propositions of Jansen as heresy). Bayle died in 1706, before the bull *Unigenitus* was promulgated by Pope Clement XI in 1713 (condemning 101 propositions of Quesnel), so it could not be mentioned in the *Dictionnaire*. Nor are *Unigenitus* or Quesnel mentioned in Jaucourt's article, even though the bull was issued forty years before the encyclopedia entry was written. That omission is curious, given the fact that it was the most significant anti-Jansenist document of the eighteenth century. It reinforces the sense that Jaucourt did not bother to go much beyond what Bayle had already said in the *Dictionnaire* and the *Commentaire*.

In both Bayle and Jaucourt, one finds a kitchen-sink approach to everything resembling Augustinian theology that the Catholic Church condemned. Voltaire does something different: all the figures he mentions at the end of his Augustine entry are Jansenists. In including Quesnel, he must certainly have *Unigenitus* in mind. In naming Arnauld, he could plausibly be thinking of either of the two abbesses of Port-Royal, or of Arnauld d'Andilly (the aforementioned translator of Augustine's *Confessions*), but it is much more likely that he is thinking of Antoine Arnauld the younger, known as "Arnauld le grand" to distinguish him from his father. In a way, it doesn't matter: the mere name Arnauld is a synecdoche for Port-Royal, which itself is a synecdoche for all of Jansenism in France.

Voltaire had already targeted Jansenism decades earlier, close to the beginning of his very long career, in the *Lettres philosophiques* (1734). In that book, Voltaire presents an extended encomium of England – especially its political institutions, its empiricist philosophers, its tolerance, and its pluralism – only to conclude the work with a very long "Twenty-Fifth Letter" on Pascal. While most in France still showed a great deal of respect both for Pascal's literary genius and for his sincere piety, Voltaire lavishes withering criticism on a man he referred to as a "sublime misanthrope."[21] The encomium of England is also a polemic against France, and the final letter serves as a coda highlighting what is most wrong with religion in France during the age of Louis XIV (even if, in 1753, Voltaire wrote a book with precisely that title, and which suggested that the latter half of the seventeenth century was France's literary apogee).

Finally, Bayle and Jaucourt engage in an extended personal attack on Augustine's character. Most of their material is clearly drawn from the *Confessions*, but neither cites the work in the body of their texts, and, significantly, neither of them explicitly acknowledges that he is arguing *ad hominem*. Voltaire does not cite the *Confessions* either, but he *does* state in the first paragraph that he is writing *ad hominem* about Augustine: "It is not as a bishop, as a doctor, as a Church Father that I am here considering St. Augustine, native of Thagaste; it is as a man. It concerns a question of physics regarding the climate of Africa" (*Questions*, 223). The last sentence, as I suggested earlier, sounds as if it could have been culled from Montesquieu's 1748 *Spirit of the Laws*, but is deployed here ironically. What is most remarkable, though, is that Voltaire *specifically announces* his intention to argue *ad hominem* against Augustine, a fact made even more astonishing when the reader discovers that Augustine is not his real target.

The "question of physics" is really only a framing device that lends unity to the article and also imparts a kind of extended literary smirk to the entire text. It is true that the article begins and ends with an

[21] See A. Tichoux, "Sur les origines de l'Anti–Pascal de Voltaire," *Studies on Voltaire and the Eighteenth Century* 256 (1988), 21–47.

evocation of Africa. But, while Voltaire may have been discussing its "climate" literally at the beginning of the article (i.e., the African sun fueled Augustine's early sexual and intellectual development), by the end, Voltaire is thinking only of the *cultural* climate of North Africa, rich in Augustine's day, but now impoverished and entirely eclipsed by Europe.

Voltaire is scarcely "considering Augustine as a man." He uses the words "libertine" and "debauchee" to describe him, and, in the last paragraph (cited earlier), he summarizes his entire career in three sentences. Apart from that, Voltaire's portrait of Augustine "as a man" hinges almost entirely on the bathhouse episode recounted in *conf.* 2.3.6. Crucially, Voltaire appears to misremember an important detail: while Bayle correctly recalls that Augustine says he was sixteen when his father noticed his sexual maturity, Voltaire says he was only fourteen. Certainly Voltaire did not consult his copy of the *Confessions* to verify the details of the episode, and it appears that he did not consult Bayle's *Dictionnaire* entry either. But whether Voltaire simply misremembers what he read in Bayle, or deliberately makes Augustine two years younger, one of the guiding metaphors of his entry hinges on Augustine's "precociousness," both sexual and intellectual. A sixteen-year-old Augustine torpedoes the entire argument; Voltaire *needs* him to be fourteen!

In comparing Jaucourt's and Voltaire's treatment of Augustine's biography, it is clear that Jaucourt felt no compunction in appropriating large portions of Bayle's entry; Voltaire borrowed comparatively little, but his major appropriation from the *Dictionnaire* is inaccurate. Of the myriad authors who influenced Voltaire, Bayle is arguably the most important, and it is tempting to think that Voltaire intentionally changed Augustine's age to suit his argument.[22] On the other hand, it is easy to see how one could get lost in the endless footnotes, marginalia, and addenda in Bayle. Moreover, Voltaire is better known for "self-plagiarism" than for borrowing from others, and, unlike Jaucourt, whose section of his "Church Father" entry on Augustine makes no mention of Bayle, Voltaire does acknowledge Bayle as the source for this episode from *conf.* 2.3.6.

[22] For a discussion of Bayle's influence on the early works of Voltaire, see H. E. Haxo, "Pierre Bayle et Voltaire avant les *Lettres philosophiques*," *PMLA* 46/2 (1931), 461–497.

CONCLUSION

Taking a broader view of these three dictionary/encyclopedia articles on Augustine and the Patristic tradition, one is at first struck by how Jaucourt and Voltaire follow Bayle in using Augustine to examine non-orthodox Christian sects in more contemporary times. In hewing very closely to Bayle, Jaucourt evokes Calvinism, Thomism, Jansenism, and Arminianism, while Voltaire, in a much more compact entry, restricts his reflections to Jansenism.

In Bayle's case, it is easy to see why he would go back as far as the Council of Trent in his parallel with Augustine. Despite a skepticism bordering on agnosticism, Bayle is a nominal Calvinist who was forced to flee France in the years of persecution of the Huguenots leading up to the Revocation of the Edict of Nantes, following which a return to France would have been impossible. With an abiding focus on tolerance in his writings, and a penchant for full-bore relativism, Bayle's purpose in his lambasting of Augustine's moral character is really less about Augustine's shortcomings and more about the hypocrisy of Catholicism in persecuting nonorthodox Christian sects in the Early Modern period (with, perhaps, the exception of his denunciation in the *Commentaire* of Augustine's endorsement of forced conversion – but even that could be seen as most important for fueling Catholic intolerance in Bayle's own times).

Jaucourt's discussion of Early Modern Christianity is practically a replica of Bayle's. As we saw, Jaucourt chose to retain Bayle's criticism of the hypocrisy of the Catholic Church in condemning Protestant and Catholic sects other than Jesuits, while leaving Augustinian theology unscathed. But Jaucourt decided to omit most of Bayle's scathing personal attack on Augustine. It is up to the reader to decide whether Jaucourt's article is strengthened or weakened for that omission. But what it clear is that Jaucourt is writing a half-century after Bayle, long after the death of Louis XIV and the Revocation, and not as an exile in Rotterdam, but as the most prolific contributor to the *Encyclopédie* in mid-eighteenth-century Paris. The issues that most urgently concerned Bayle at the end of the seventeenth century are not dead letter by Jaucourt's time, but they are less pressing. One might suggest that, with 17,999 other encyclopedia articles to write, Jaucourt did not stop to consider whether Bayle's theological critique was still entirely relevant. But we should also remember that Jaucourt's section on Augustine in "Church Father" is only a part of a much larger analysis of *all* the Church Fathers, and, most importantly, that, at the end of the article,

Jaucourt essentially conflates them all in order to underscore their obsolescence in the Age of Reason. Perhaps Jaucourt thought that a general attack on all obviated the need for a particular attack on one.

Of the three, Voltaire alone claims to be considering Augustine not as an historical figure, but "as a man." Yet there is far less personal attack in Voltaire's article than in Bayle's, and less even than in Jaucourt's. Voltaire's account of Augustine "as a man," hinging almost entirely on the episode from *conf.* 2.3.6, is really an account of Augustine *becoming* a man, in a literal, physical sense. If his early puberty led to precocious "debauchery," Augustine's precocious sexual development itself obviously cannot be seen as a personal shortcoming, but only, in Voltaire's ironic rendering, as an effect of the African climate on both the body and the mind. And the winds of fortune have shifted. Enlightenment Europe has eclipsed the cultural significance of North Africa at the end of the Roman Empire, and after 1,100 years, Europe has rejected Augustinian doctrine in the form of Jansenism.

In Bayle's time, it appeared that the Jesuits had triumphed over the Jansenists; and the victory of the Jesuits over the Jansenists would appear to have been cemented some seven years after Bayle's death with the promulgation of *Unigenitus*. However, at the time Jaucourt was plundering Bayle for his *Encyclopédie* entry, the Jesuits were being expelled from France, due in no small part to what remained of the by-now factionalized Jansenist sect. By the time Voltaire writes his entry on Augustine, the Jesuits had been gone for some time, but the remnants of Jansenism were waning as well. It is not entirely clear whether Voltaire had greater contempt for the Jansenists or the Jesuits, but either could be subsumed under Voltaire's motto, *écrasez l'infâme*, and he would not have been unhappy to see either order eliminated. He had little use for the ascetic Augustinianism of the Jansenists and just as little for the corrupt worldliness of the Jesuits.

EPILOGUE: THE *CONFESSIONS* OF AUGUSTINE AND ROUSSEAU

In beginning this chapter, I had originally envisaged devoting much if not most of it to Rousseau's relation to Augustine in their respective *Confessions*. Although Rousseau almost entirely hides the influence and importance of Augustine in his own autobiography, the structural and thematic parallels between the two *Confessions* can hardly be overlooked. My own work on Augustine and Rousseau has focused primarily on those connections, as has that of other scholars.[23]

In the Enlightenment-era lexicographical treatment of Augustine we have investigated, his *Confessions* are turned against him to call into question the validity of his theology, and to distance the French Enlightenment from the "age of Augustine" in the latter half of the seventeenth century. Rousseau, on the other hand, takes the interiority and the imperative for complete and sincere self-disclosure of Augustine's *Confessions* and presses it into the service of founding modern autobiography.[24]

In my own work, I have tried to bring out the structural and thematic parallels between the two autobiographies, and, in particular, how Rousseau takes Augustine's conversion as a model for radical subjective change as he presents it in his *Confessions*. And one can argue that Rousseau has taken the two major confessional threads in Augustine's autobiography – *confessio peccati* ["confession of sins"] and *confessio laudis* ["praise of God"], and, while he largely retains *confessio peccati* as a major focus of his narrative, he has transformed the convert's praise of God into a kind of cult of the self.[25]

In the terms of St. Gregory's seven deadly sins, Rousseau's tactic would constitute the worst of all – pride, the usurpation of God's place by the ego; in secular terms, it would constitute the ascendancy of the

[23] In P. Riley, *Character and Conversion in Autobiography: Augustine, Montaigne, Descartes, Rousseau, and Sartre* (Charlottesville: University of Virginia Press, 2004), the chapter on Rousseau (88–137) takes as a point of departure the laconic and suggestive assertion of the great Augustinian scholar, Pierre Courcelle: "Rousseau ... presents his own *Confessions* as 'an undertaking which has no precedent.' However, they are the precise antithesis of Augustine's" (*Les "Confessions" de Saint Augustin dans la tradition littéraire: Antécédents et postérité* [Paris: Etudes augustiniennes, 1963], 459; translation mine). For a condensed version of the Augustine and Rousseau chapters in *Character and Conversion*, see my article, "The Inversion of Conversion: Rousseau's Rewriting of Augustinian Autobiography," *Studies in Eighteenth Century Culture* 28 (1999), 229–255. See also A. Hartle, *The Modern Self in Rousseau's "Confessions": A Reply to Saint Augustine*, Revisions 4 (Notre Dame, IN: University of Notre Dame Press, 1983).

[24] See Riley, *Character and Conversion*, 89–90, and review the relevant critical literature on autobiography, 193–194, n. 6.

[25] For a description of these confessional terms and Augustine's use of them, see K. J. Weintraub, *The Value of the Individual: Self and Circumstance in Autobiography* (Chicago: University of Chicago Press, 1978), 18–48; R. McMahon, *Augustine's Prayerful Ascent: An Essay on the Literary Form of the "Confessions"* (Athens: University of Georgia Press, 1989), 4, 10; and Riley, *Character and Conversion*, 27, 92–95, 106, and 108.

modern self. And yet, Rousseau mentions Augustine only once in his own *Confessions,* and in a trivial way. In other words, however significant Augustine's work may have been for Rousseau, its influence is almost entirely subterranean.[26]

Moreover, as important as Rousseau's *Confessions* are for autobiography, almost all of Rousseau's work goes against the grain of mainstream Enlightenment philosophy and, thus, the works of Bayle, Jaucourt, and Voltaire are more representative of the spirit of the era. On the other hand, Rousseau appears to have grasped and to have exploited what is most profound in Augustine's *Confessions;* namely the structure of conversion and the power of confession. Bayle, Jaucourt, and Voltaire have more or less deliberately ignored the most significant aspects of the *Confessions,* and Bayle seems to have set off a chain reaction in which all three attack a caricature of Augustine as a man in order to indict Augustine as a theologian. If one wishes to have a balanced view of the reception of the *Confessions* in Enlightenment France, it would be useful to consider both the stealth appropriation of Augustine in Rousseau, and the thinly disguised *misappropriation* of Augustine in the lexicographical works of Bayle, Jaucourt, and Voltaire.

Further Reading

Archambault, P. J. "Rousseau's Tactical (Mis)reading of Augustine," *Symposium* 41/1 (Spring 1987), 6–14.

Bost, H. "Bayle, Pierre." In *OGHRA,* vol. 2, 634a–636a.

Courcelle, P. *Les "Confessions" de Saint Augustin dans la tradition littéraire: Antécédents et postérité.* Paris: Etudes augustiniennes, 1963.

Hartle, A. *The Modern Self in Rousseau's "Confessions": A Reply to Saint Augustine,* Revisions 4. Notre Dame, IN: University of Notre Dame Press, 1983.

Qvortup, M. "Rousseau, Jean-Jaques." In *OGHRA,* vol. 3, 1657a–1677a.

Riley, P. *Character and Conversion in Autobiography: Augustine, Montaigne, Descartes, Rousseau, and Sartre.* Charlottesville: University of Virginia Press, 2004.

  "The Inversion of Conversion: Rousseau's Rewriting of Augustinian Autobiography." *Studies in Eighteenth Century Culture* 28 (1999), 229–255.

Weintraub, K. J. *The Value of the Individual: Self and Circumstance in Autobiography.* Chicago: University of Chicago Press, 1978.

Wheelan, R. "The Wage of Sin is Orthodoxy: The *Confessions* of Saint Augustine in Bayle's *Dictionnaire.*" *Journal of the History of Philosophy* 26/2 (April 1988), 195–206.

---

[26] On this question, see P. J. Archambault, "Rousseau's Tactical (Mis)reading of Augustine," *Symposium* 41/1 (Spring 1987), 6–14.

19 Reading (in) Augustine's *Confessions*

MARK VESSEY

READING TOGETHER

Talking, laughing, reading books together, agreeing and disagreeing, teaching and learning; as likeminded individuals respond to each other's cues, they become as one (*conf.* 4.8.13). So Augustine explains how groups of friends form. Scaled up in the *City of God*, the same psychology underpins his description of the two societies into which all human beings are sorted. In Book 4 of the *Confessions*, this modeling of community rehearses familiar Augustinian themes with a crispness owed to the narrative and scenographic techniques there in play. Augustine's confidence in the ability of human beings to learn from each other was unshakeable; it informs his dialogues, letters, sermons, and controversial writings from first to last and is the mainspring of his handbook on Christian teaching and learning, the *De doctrina Christiana*, a work in progress when he composed the *Confessions*. No less constant was his desire for social solidarity. As pastor in a divided church, director of a clerical household, monastic legislator, and embattled upholder of divine grace, he let pass no chance to proclaim an ideal harmony of hearts and minds. The chance that he created in the *Confessions* was to explore the linked processes of learning and association in a controled experiment with human subjects at once inside and outside the text.

   In the cluster of social pursuits named by Augustine as the pleasures and fomenters of friendship is one with a special salience for the *Confessions*: "reading books together [*simul legere libros*]." In Latin the books are called *dulciloquos* ("sweetly speaking") and the activity of shared reading is joined through repetition of the adverb *simul* with those of "joking around together and getting serious together [*simul nugari et simul honestari*]." A few lines earlier, the author listed the delights of "books and poetry" alongside those of pleasant scenery, gastronomy, and sex (*conf.* 4.7.12). Given the emphasis at this point on the transitoriness of all that is "sweet [*dulcis* or *suavis*]" in life, we may be tempted to write off the entire class of "sweet-talking books" as another snare to be avoided. Yet that would be a false inference, since in the second passage Augustine makes a point of *not* discrediting any of the social reflexes that he lists. And we know that he had identified another source of sweetness in the books of God's Scripture. Wherever Augustine left his readers at the end of the *Confessions*, he meant there still to be room there for games and laughter, differences of opinion, and sweetness of many kinds, including the sweetness that books can bring when read in the right company.

According to an influential, late-twentieth-century strain of thought, the right company for an "Augustinian" reader would be of one – oneself. That assumption fits neatly with a tendency to take Augustine as an early master of practices of self-analysis, self-knowing, self-care, and self-writing for which long genealogies can now be projected, converging on the present. Such interpretations are as settled in scholarship on Augustine as they are in general opinion. Augustine's self-questioning and self-fashioning have become inalienable factors of our own, whether we read Augustine closely, remotely, or not at all. Why is that? The *Confessions* should contain at least part of an answer.

A modern successor to Possidius (author of the first "Life of Augustine") has testified to how desolate every biographer of Augustine must feel "in that empty room," surrounded by Augustine's books, (long) after his death.[1] The reflex is modeled by Augustine in Book 4 of the *Confessions*, as he recalls how he felt upon the death of his friend, and draws up the checklist of activities by which friendships are made and kept. It is in the nature of such things that they pass, he writes:

> This is their limitation. This much you [God] gave to them, because they are parts of the universe; not all parts are there at once [*non sunt omnes simul*], but in ceding and succeeding to each other, they carry out the whole, of which they are separate parts.

Then he reaches for one of his favorite analogies for the order of existence:

> And, you see, this is the way that our speech is carried out from beginning to end, through vocal signals [*signa sonantia*]. It would not be complete speech if one word didn't cede, once the parts of it

---

[1] P. Brown, *Augustine of Hippo: A Biography*, second ed. (Berkeley: University of California Press, 2000), 437.

had made their sounds, so that another word could succeed it. Let my soul praise you for these things, *God, creator of all things.*
(conf. 4.10.15)[2]

Parsing life's fleeting pleasures as elements in the syntax of a divine universal statement true and complete for all times and beyond time, Augustine intones for the first time in this text the first phrase of one of the hymns composed for congregational singing at Milan in the late 380s by Bishop Ambrose: *Deus, creator omnium* (see *conf.* 9.7.15). The line will sound again, followed by the other seven lines that make up the first two stanzas of the hymn, at the place in Book 9 where Augustine recalls how he came to terms with the death of his mother, Monnica (*conf.* 9.12.32). It is the only transcription of nonbiblical, Christian poetry in the *Confessions*, and unique for the interruption that it makes of the confessional discourse, as if counting time in textual space. Coincidentally or (more probably) not, the cited passage is followed by the first explicit reference to the work in hand as a *written* text, which is also the first explicit evocation of the reader implied by that text:

> But now, Master, I testify to you in writing [*confiteor tibi in litteris*]: whoever wants to can read it, and let him put whatever meaning he wants on it. (conf. 9.12.33, trans. Ruden)

A few pages after that, Augustine's readers – his "brothers," he calls them – are gathered in remembrance of his parents, Monnica and Patricius, at the altar of the *Confessions*, in a unison prayer for which the *Confessions* is becoming the script (*conf.* 9.13.37).

Prayer, hymn, confession – Augustine's discourse in this text, on the page as writing and off it as audible signs, assumes the character of liturgical performance, communal and transtemporal at once. "At once," *simul.* Together, at the same time. Augustine's text or written discourse is of course still discourse, something that runs on and runs out. Its *simul* is nothing like God's *simul*, the *simul* [so to speak] of eternity in which "all things *are* [*sunt omnia*]" and to which Augustine in due course, meditating how "in the beginning, God created heaven and earth," momentarily assimilates an individual's experience of holding in mind the entire text of a hymn such as Ambrose's *Deus, creator omnium* – only to disclaim the analogy as soon as he makes it (*conf.* 11.26.33–31.41). With such a disclaimer, a person in the middle of reciting, chanting, or singing a poetic text could be thought to know

---

[2] *Augustine:* Confessions, trans. S. Ruden (New York: Modern Library, 2017).

that text as God knows creation. Pursuing the disclaimed analogy even further, we could say that, if God's creation were a text, then the Trinity would be its sole performer, in the signless silence of eternity. Augustine's God is not, however, the model for any textual experience or performance commended to his "brothers" in the *Confessions*.

READING (IN) THE ROMAN WORLD

Those "brothers," standing for all readers who could ever be brought by the *Confessions* into likemindedness with Augustine, are joined together in the first place by what makes them like Augustine's parents and the biblical parents of humankind, their mortality. To pick up the terms of Book 4 again: death is the limit behind all the limitations on human life. All things that we may love, apart from God, pass away: *omnia intereunt* (*conf.* 4.10.15). The passing of human beings from life to death is naturally comparable to the passage of meaningful sounds in speech, since articulate speech and other forms of communication by conventional signs are attributes specific to humans within a universal ecology of "things" that, under certain conditions, may also be "signs." This is the point from which Augustine's *De doctrina Christiana* begins its approach to the category of "signs divinely given and pointed out by human beings" in the medium of Scripture (*doc. Chr.* 2.1.1–3). When Augustine turns at length to the beginning of Genesis in the *Confessions* and prays to "hear and understand," his next move is to acknowledge that "Moses wrote this, wrote it and departed, went away from here ... and is not now before me" (*conf.* 11.3.5).

While it may have taken until the twentieth century for philosophers and theorists of textuality to deduce the inexorably posthumous quality of all inscriptions in all media, the association of writing with death had been lively in Mediterranean cultures for centuries by Augustine's time. A funerary inscription in the form of an elegiac couplet, cited near the end of Possidius's *Life of Augustine*, resumed a millennial tradition: "Didn't you know, traveller, that poets live on after death?/I speak what you read. That's right, your voice is mine!"[3] Even when not written in the first person, the street-level poetry incised in stone and on view to be read aloud by literate travelers in the Roman world spoke clamorously for the departed, voicing them by proxy, helping to sustain a multigenerational community of the living and

---

[3] *Sancta Augustini vita scripta a Possidio episcopo*, ed. and trans. H. T. Weiskotten (Princeton, NJ: Princeton University Press, 1919), chapter 31, 142, retranslated.

the dead that was consecrated by sundry rites (such as the tombside picnics evoked in *conf.* 6.2.2) and by monuments great and small, inscribed and named, lying thick across the urban and suburban landscapes.

Other species mark their habitats. Only humans carve out and pile up visible signs on this scale to customize a "meaningful environment."[4] No Mediterranean polity before the Roman Empire of the late fourth century had been more heavily or extensively endowed with signifying and symbolic displays in fixed (as well as mobile) media. The expanses of that built, sculpted, painted, inscribed, and impressed social environment, rich in memorable objects and places of memory, can be glimpsed at the edges of Augustine's inventory of his culture in *doc. Chr.* 2.19.29–42.62. Glimpses of it are all that we catch in the *Confessions*: a shrine outside Carthage named for the martyr Cyprian [*memoria beati Cypriani*], where Monnica stayed on the night Augustine took ship for Italy (*conf.* 5.8.15); the (Flavian) amphitheater in Rome, to which Alypius went with his friends (*conf.* 6.8.13); the forum (of Trajan) in Rome, where a statue to Marius Victorinus stood among others (*conf.* 8.2.3). So many speaking monuments of the dead, frequented daily by the living. The modern sightseer of the Roman Empire does not take the *Confessions* for a guidebook, even though the narrative takes in four capital cities (Carthage, Rome, Milan, Trier). The nearest Augustine comes in this work to conceptualizing the human artifact of "place" is in a passage of Book 10 when he puzzles over how he can remember forgetting. Somehow, he supposes, an image of forgetting must be copied in the memory, or a sign made of it there, as in the ordinary cognitive process that enables him to remember "Carthage or other places where I have been, and the faces of people whom I have seen" (*conf.* 10.16.25; see also 10.21.30). The verbs he uses in this case for the imprinting of memory are *conscribere*, meaning "to write" or "copy out," and *notare*, "to mark (down)" or, often in this period, "to take down by shorthand."

For a unit of living, neural memory, modern science has coined the term "engram," and, for an external marker or aid to individual and collective human consciousness – such as an inscription, icon, or statue – "exogram." In Augustine's society, as in others, the meaningfulness of a physical landscape covered with named and nameable *things* more and less readily taken for *signs* was underwritten by a set

---

[4] J. J. Gibson, *The Ecological Approach to Visual Perception* (Hillsdale, NJ: Lawrence Erlbaum Associates, 1986), 33–42.

of normative documents, which were subject in turn to real time, "live" updating by qualified interpreters and performers. Did Aeneas (in Virgil's *Aeneid*, a school text) ever really come to Carthage? Why would it matter? By raising those issues as sharply as he does in Book 1 of the *Confessions*, Augustine puts in question by synecdoche a vast apparatus for the discursive affirmation of ideally consensual understandings of Roman history, culture, empire, and social identity. As a teacher of grammar and rhetoric, and an orator retained by the court to ensure that the policies and exploits of the boy-emperor Valentinian II got good public spin, Augustine knew that system from the inside (see, e.g., *conf.* 6.6.9). The *Confessions* has enough "Roman world" color – places and inferrable dates, notable individuals, details of procedure and protocol – for it to be readable much of the way as an eyewitness document of the western empire c. 400. Yet, by Book 10, almost the only lingering reminiscence of that sign-laden, eventful, Roman environment is a reference to "Carthage" as placeholder for a certain kind of memory, and not the most valuable kind. It is as if, in flight from "lust of the eyes" and other hazards listed in 1 Jn 2:16, Augustine in the *Confessions* perambulated the landscape of his mind (in Book 10) and decoded the allegorical cosmology of Gen 1 (in Book 12) after completing a pilgrim's regress from the phenomenal world of his own times and places.

READING APART

If we sought an authorizing exemplar for such resort to seclusion, introspection, and allegorical hermeneutics, we might find it in the figure of Ambrose, depicted in the *Confessions* reading apart (*conf.* 6.3.3). The classic modern commentary on that scene is an aside by C. S. Lewis:

> You could see [Ambrose's] eyes moving, but you could hear nothing. In such a passage one has the solemn privilege of being present at the birth of a new world. Behind us is that almost unimaginable period, so relentlessly objective that in it even "reading" (in our sense) did not yet exist. The book was still a *lógos*, a speech; thinking was still *dialégesthai*, talking. Before us is our own world, the world of the printed or written page, and of the solitary reader who is accustomed to pass hours in the silent society of mental images evoked by written characters. This is a new light, and a better one than we have yet had, on that turning inward which I have tried to describe. It is the very moment of a

transition more important, I would suggest, than any that is commonly recorded in our works of "history." But it is seldom that Augustine is so unconscious as in this statement.[5]

Lewis' commentary, which can represent a thousand others like or launched by it, makes Augustine the inadvertent witness to an epoch-making shift in human cognitive history: the shift from an oral, dialogic, public community of discourse, taken to be normal for ancient "classical" and other "traditional" societies, to an experience of silent and solitary reading considered characteristic of Western modernity. The power of this testimony is enhanced by its presumed unconsciousness; as Lewis puts it, the "fact" that Ambrose, "when reading to himself, read silently" was "apparently remarkable" to Augustine – *apparently* so, because whatever reasons Augustine may be seen or thought to have had for remarking upon it, we do not imagine that he had any premonition of the historical importance that Lewis and other mid- and later-twentieth-century commentators would attribute to it. This line of inference splits the "fact" of Ambrose's silent reading into two facts, each with a signifying power of its own. There is a fact that signifies within the textual universe of signs constituted for us by Augustine's *Confessions.* And there is a fact, reported in the *Confessions,* that we are free to interpret in relation to the rest of our data for the practical, cognitive, and cultural history of reading over the *longue durée.* The historical meaning of the *Confessions* has never been confined by its text, nor will any long history of reading ever be assured or undone by a single Augustinian anecdote. The distinction of facts and meanings – Augustine might have said: of "things" interpretable as "signs" – nonetheless serves a purpose. It clarifies our option to read the *Confessions* for the presentation of readers and reading *in* the *Confessions.*

READING OTHER READERS

Every well-wrought, well-read text alters the cognitive and affective states of its readers by changing their environment. When inset scenes of reading occur in later works of the Western literary canon – think of Paolo and Francesca with the *Romance of Lancelot* in Dante's *Commedia,* Maggie Tulliver with the *Imitation of Christ* in George Eliot's *The Mill on the Floss,* or the antihero of Flaubert's *La Tentation de saint*

[5] C. S. Lewis, *The Allegory of Love: A Study in Medieval Tradition* (Oxford: Oxford University Press, 1936), 64–65.

Antoine with his bible – there is usually a lot at stake both in the fictional lives of the reading characters and for an external reader's developing sense of the action. What might such novelistic scenarios of life-altering reading owe to late antique precedent? Is there a conversional or confessional narrative type at work? Identifying the "confession" as a "distinct prose form" that Augustine "appears to have invented," a younger contemporary of C. S. Lewis, Canadian critic and literary theorist Northrop Frye, sought to distinguish it from the novel on the grounds that "[n]early always some theoretical and intellectual interest in religion, politics, or art plays a leading role in the confession." It is the author's "success in integrating his mind on such subjects," Frye suggested, that makes him "feel that his life is worth writing about." Despite the short circuit between those definitions of a literary genre and the original Augustinian instance, it may still be instructive to underline the degree to which the integration of Augustine's thinking about "religion" and "politics" (in the broadest senses) depends in the *Confessions* upon his representation of certain "arts" of the book. In this respect, the *Confessions* is distinctly of its own time and milieu.

There are scenes of books and readers in earlier Greek and Latin poetry and prose fiction, and in the visual arts of the classical period. An advanced agrarian society that relies on a cadre of super-literate individuals to manage large tracts of its common cognitive environment will produce stylized images of those technocrats as part of the intelligible landscape. Conversely, modifications to the public styling of expert literate actors can be an indicator of substantive revisions to a society's ruling ideology. Our documents reveal the extent to which bishops and other members of the clergy in the Roman, officially Christian empire of the 380s and 390s felt called to fix the minds of their readers and congregations on questions about the selection of socially normative texts and the forms of interpretative attention to be given to them. Three other prolific publishing Latin Christian intellectuals of those decades were known to Augustine either from face-to-face encounters (Ambrose) or by correspondence (Paulinus of Nola, Jerome). With their peers in a Mediterranean network of Christian book-users, these individuals created what we could now think of as a new movement of "literary criticism and theory" in Latin.

The competitive conditions under which sons of the minor Roman gentry like Augustine worked their way to positions of provincial and imperial influence guaranteed a high level of self-consciousness on their part with respect to the language and book arts that were the usual means to preferment. When their *arriviste* class-consciousness crossed with curiosity or concern about the intellectual equipment of an empire-wide Christian community of belief and ritual, as happened with some frequency in the last quarter of the fourth century, a new edge was given to issues of expressive and interpretative practice that had by then been under discussion for over 200 years but respecting which nothing like a definitive set of statements or examples yet existed in Latin (or Greek). The *Confessions* is our best single source for this unstable state of affairs, an outstanding document of an individual experience that in many of its details can be corroborated from other sources. For all that, no Greek or Latin writer before or contemporary with Augustine, and no other ancient Christian text except the *De doctrina Christiana*, evinces so urgent a concern for the social dynamics and consequences of reading. If our conception of "literary criticism and theory" as a field now includes an expectation that reading techniques will be a substantial part of its subject matter, then the *Confessions* has a claim to be counted among the formative experiments of a modern discipline.

READING CRITICALLY

Announcing in *De doctrina Christiana* a theoretical approach to the same set of critical problems that he would handle in the *Confessions*, Augustine compared his role as instructor to that of a person pointing out an old moon, a new star, or another barely visible heavenly body to a would-be fellow observer (*doc. Chr.* Prol. 3). The analogy has three components: there is the night sky peppered with discernible objects of God's creation, signifying the meaningful, intelligible, explicable text of the Bible, there is Augustine's pointing finger [*intento digito*], and there is the other person's power of sight [*lumen oculorum*], representing a gift of understanding that God will either grant or withhold. The verb used for Augustine's act of making visible the created (textual) order to other sky-gazers (readers) is *demonstrare*, a choice consistent with his later classing of astronomy, which he calls *demonstratio siderum* or "demonstration of the stars," among the kinds of disciplinary knowledge in which "present things" are "pointed out [*indicata*]" by demonstration, as distinguished from the one kind of knowledge in which "past things" are pointed out by narration, which is history (*doc. Chr.* 2.27.41–29.46). (Fictional narrative is ruled out as not worth the attention of Christian readers. Biblical allegory will be let back in later by a side door.)

As Augustine is quick to concede, however, this distinction between the one historical art of narration and the many arts of demonstration is not watertight, since some of the demonstrative arts, including astronomy, also depend partly on observation of past events or things. At the core of Augustine's mature treatment of the kinds of "knowledge [*cognitio*]" befitting a Christian learner is a recognition of the routine intertwining of narrative and demonstrative discourses – of showing and telling. Unsurprisingly, the Bible turns out to be an instance of such a mixed discursive type, at once a supremely nonfictional narrative of past events and a supremely reliable figuring forth of present and future realities. Hence, when, as quoted earlier, Augustine summarizes the purpose of the middle books of *De doctrina Christiana* as to "consider" (*considerare*, originally meaning "to observe the stars [*sidera*]") the "signs contained in the holy scriptures" – signs that, "divinely given," "have been pointed out [*indicata*] to us by the men who wrote them down [*qui ea conscripserunt*]" – we should see and hear in the allusion to human pointing in writing not only an affirmation of the combined divine and human authorship of Scripture, but also a further, deliberate approximation of the art of the biblical expositor (*tractator*) to that of an astronomer making "legible" the heavens (*doc. Chr.* 2.1.1–3).

Augustine had left astronomy out of the plan of his handbook of liberal disciplines, a work conceived in Milan in the late 380s and then abandoned. The exclusion may reflect his unease about astrological divination, which, we know from the *Confessions*, had long fascinated him. Questions of astronomy and cosmology also always had the potential to thrust him back into arguments with the Manicheans about theodicy and the order of the universe. Looming behind the *Confessions* and inseparable from Augustine's persistent attempt to make sense of St. Paul's Letter to the Romans was his project for a "literal" or "historical" commentary on the narrative of creation and the fall of humankind at the beginning of Genesis. In a tradition of Greek Christian thought launched by Origen and partly available to Augustine through the hexaemeral exegesis of Basil of Caesarea and Ambrose, study of the order of creation, or "natural contemplation," offered a way of understanding God's purposes complementary to the study of Scripture. An instinct for natural theology pervades the *Confessions*. Yet, when Augustine reads chapter 1 of Genesis straight through in Book 13, he does so only intermittently for any natural-theological insight the text might yield, and mainly for the sake of an allegory of love with the Church for its subject.

No moment in that exegesis is more striking than when he comes to the first clearly cosmographical details in the creation account, at Gen 1:7. Who but this creator, he asks, could make division of human beings – of the blessed and the damned – as if dividing day from night?

> Or did anyone but you, our God, make a supporting vault of authority for us through your holy scripture ... Your holy scripture in fact has more authority now that the mortals through whom you provided it have met their death ... But you know, Master, you know how you clothed humankind in animal skins when through sin they became mortal. Accordingly, you stretched like a tanned hide the vault of your book – your by all means harmonious discourse – that you placed over us by means of mortals' service ... Let's look, Master, at the heavens, the works of your fingers. Brush aside from our eyes the clouds with which you've covered the heavens underneath. (conf. 13.15.16–17, trans. Ruden)

"When I look up at the heavens, the work of your fingers" (Ps 8:4). The "heavens" of the Psalmist now become the parchment of a book written or composed, as if by the hand of God, by biblical authors long dead.

The words of dead writers on the skins of dead animals: that is the near horizon of interpretation for Augustine and his fellow readers, men and women who – as the second sentence of the *Confessions* reminds us – "carry their mortality around with them" as they carry their books. The exegesis of Scripture is like astronomy, a second-order demonstrative and narrative discourse in speech and gesture or in writing, with for its object a prior demonstrative and narrative discourse – the scriptural text – that not only relates the past and shows the present, but also predicts the future, as may be verified from the fulfillment of prophecies made by authors living generations before the events prefigured. From the immanent natural theology of the Psalms and other Old Testament writings, Augustine has moved in a few bold steps to a distinctively Latin, Western anatomy of the divinely programed and humanly inscribed book-mind.

READING WITH A SWEET VOICE

It is because of the freedom that the *Confessions* allows him, in contrast to the handbook format of *De doctrina Christiana*, that Augustine's experiment in criticism is so productive of theory and so compelling in practice. The compulsion is immediate and thirteen-books long.

Those compelled are Augustine's God and his readers – who are, whatever else they may be, characters in the *Confessions*.

Here is how Augustine will end things:

> But who among humankind can offer another human being a way to
> understand this? What angel could offer it to another angel? What
> angel could offer it to a human being? We must ask you for it, and
> look for it from you; we must knock at your door: in this way, *we*
> will receive it, *we* will find it, and *you* will open the door to *us*.
>
> (conf. 13.38.53, trans. Ruden, emphasis added)

As often with this author, fullness of the English version betrays sleight
of hand in Latin. After "in this way," the translation introduces three
second-person pronouns and one first-person pronoun to accompany
three verbs in the active voice. The original has only passive impersonal
constructions: "it will be received, it will be found, it will be opened."
There is no "door" in Augustine's text, and the translator's inference
from Mt 7:7–8 risks blocking others equally plausible. In this book
full of book openings, might not the last, book *closing* opening also be
of a book – God's book, repeatedly opened and bookmarked by Augustine but still full of mysteries that God could yet reveal to a prayerful
reader?

The verb translated earlier as "find [*invenire*]" appears in a technical
sense in *De doctrina Christiana* for the process of interpreting biblical
signs. The one translated "open [*aperire*]" is used twice in the first
sentence of that work for the act of interpreting Scripture in the presence and for the benefit of others as well as for oneself. The angels,
jostling in the *Confessions* for a chance to explain things that in *De
doctrina Christiana* Augustine insisted human beings were called by
God to explain to each other, came on the scene just a few pages earlier,
metaphorically "reading" God's eternal purposes without need of any
book that can be opened or shut, "reading" without syllables of recorded
sound or time (*conf.* 13.15.18). In the heaven above the heavens, there
are no readers in the literal sense, no letters, no writing. The eternal rest
of the seventh day of creation, allegorically interpreted in Book 13 of the
Confessions, is bookless. Meanwhile, the *Confessions* ends here below,
with a forward glance to a future time in this world, when "it *will* be
received," and so on. That triple passive construction is the last trick in
the book, a trick of written language. Whatever "it" may be – a book,
truth, life, grace, faith, understanding – the parties to the receiving,
finding and opening will be God and individuals like Augustine's
readers, parties that, without being indicated in the Latin at this point,

are directly implicated in an action reprophesied on the strength of a biblical promise claimed already at the outset of Book 12.

As a scriptural exegete, Augustine points things out (*indicare*). As the narrator-dramatist of the *Confessions*, he compels others actors to enter his scenes, starting with the very first words of the text, *Magnus es, domine, et laudabilis valde* ["You are great, Lord, and certainly deserving praise"]. The second-person verb and vocative case put spin on a characterization made repeatedly of God in God-facing contexts in the Psalms but not usually part of the address to him there. It is a tiny but consequential change that creates a "live" and present role for God in the *Confessions* similar to the on-stage roles that Roman orators routinely created for emperors in panegyrics spoken to their faces.

And where now, as it all begins, are Augustine's readers? Here is one speaking recently for them:

> This opening can give rise to the disconcerting feeling of coming into a room and chancing upon a man speaking to someone who isn't there? He gestures in our direction and mentions us from time to time, but he never addresses his readers. As literary text, [the *Confessions*] resembles a one-sided, non-fiction epistolary novel, enacted in the presence of the silence (and darkness) of God.[6]

If such readers feel as if they are "coming into a room," it may be not merely because they are used to reading epistolary novels. Unlike the Book of Psalms with its wide-skied, pastoral setting, the *Confessions* has a way of ushering its characters into domestic interiors and of architecting enclosed spaces out of doors. That is notably the case with its reading scenes. But *must* the incoming reader – one like ourselves, as yet without a place in this text – feel left out, shunned almost, from the outset? Only, surely, if we insist on reading the *Confessions* as C. S. Lewis and others have supposed that we moderns habitually read to ourselves – that is, without moving our lips or even so much as sub-vocalizing the words on the page with our mind's tongue to our mind's ear. To make such an assumption about modern reading is to forget how we still sometimes read poetry aloud, and how quickly, given the right cue, we break into a kind of song.

To an ear trained in the rhythms and rhyme-forbidding euphony of classical Latin prose, the found couplet *Mágnus és, dominé,/ét laudábilis valdé* must have sounded with a sickening jingle. As Augustine

---

[6] J. J. O'Donnell, *Augustine: Confessions* (Oxford: Clarendon, 1992), vol. 2, 8–9.

tells us, however, the sounds of the Psalms of David in the current Latin version, whether sung to a melody or chanted on a monotone, had such sweetness for him that at times he felt he should deny himself the pleasure of them (*conf.* 10.33.50; see also 9.4.8–11, 12.31). Take the cue from his opening here, murmur the lines that he puts in our mouths, and *we* are *in* the *Confessions* from page one, with a voice and dramatic character that we could mistake or even recognize for our own. The quasi-liturgical performance of the text begins with its first syllable, scripted from the songbook of the Hebrew Bible for the sake of a living performance by men and women "carrying their mortality around with them" (*conf.* 1.1.1). For the *I speak what you read* of the dead poet's epitaph, Augustine has in effect substituted: *You* (in the plural) *read and speak after me what I write in the words of praise long ago put into the mouth of the Psalmist.* The initially disconcerting quality of the *Confessions* is strategic. This is a text that would compel its human subjects as quickly as it can into *concerted* reading.

READING TOGETHER (IN THE BOOK)

The original vehicle or support of that reading was a book in some ways quite unlike those whose pages we now turn, if we are still reading "real" books, yet in one essential way just like them. Handwritten on animal skin, in Latin, without word division, scarcely if at all punctuated within sentences, and with few other reader-friendly features beyond the signaling of where one "book" (in the sense of "chapter") ended and another began, an early fifth-century copy of the *Confessions* presumed a reader with habits and skills that most of us would now have to acquire by special training in Latin and paleography. In another, mechanically and optically prior respect, however, early fifth-century book-in-hand readers of the *Confessions* found themselves situated exactly as we are: with a window of two pages facing them at a time, the twin columns of words parted by the vertical cleft made by the fold of the supporting material at the hinge-like spine of the text-container.

The Latin word for the kind of book that, upon opening, and then afresh at the turn of every page, puts a reader in that cognitive situation, is *codex*, a term formerly used by the Romans for two or more wooden tablets inlaid with wax, suitable for writing on, when fastened together so that they could be opened and shut "like a book." That "tablet" or "notebook" technology was the precursor of the spine-hinged parchment or papyrus book that came into general use in the Roman Empire between the second and fourth centuries CE. In earlier periods of Greek and Roman culture, the works of poets, philosophers, historians, and other writers had (literally) passed from hand to hand in the form of rolls or scrolls (*volumina*). Representations of traditional book-rolls still appeared in the visual and plastic art of the later Roman Empire, in both explicitly Christian and ostensibly non-Christian contexts, sometimes interchangeably with representations of the newly mainstreamed codex form of book. Modern scholarship has been entranced by the phenomenon of a large-scale shift "from roll to codex" in late antiquity and there is still debate about how and why the change occurred and what its immediate and longer-term consequences might have been. The *Confessions* is important for that discussion because it is one of the very few later Latin texts so visibly invested in the cognitive and cultural implications of reading as to offer us the prospect of further historical insights.

As a witness to material practices of the book in antiquity, the *Confessions* is unequivocal. It is an expression – and an enactment – of the technology of the codex. Every time the text specifies the format of a book in the hands of a human reader, and once when it metaphorically alludes to "reading" done by angels, the word used is *codex*. (Otherwise, "books" are simply *libri*, a word normally without distinct connotation of format at this date.) The books that Alypius might illicitly have obtained for his private use at government rates were codexes (*conf.* 6.10.6). When Ponticianus visits Alypius and Augustine at the house they shared in Milan and flips open [*aperire*] a book lying on the table, expecting it to be a rhetorical textbook, it turns out be a codex of St. Paul (*conf.* 8.6.14). When the same visitor tells the tale of two government agents chancing upon a copy of the *Life of Antony* at Trier, the text again specifies a codex (*conf.* 8.6.15). Finally, it is explicitly a codex of St. Paul – not just a "book" containing text, but a particular kind of text-containing object – that Augustine, in the garden of the same Milanese house, lays aside in despair, then picks up again at the sing-song urging of a voice from next-door [*Tolle, lege*, "Pick up and read!"].

The camerawork of the *Confessions* is nowhere tighter than for that nearly timeless moment:

> Excited, I returned to the spot where Alypius was sitting: I'd put down a book of the apostle Paul's letters there when I got up. I grabbed it and opened it [*arripui et aperui*], and I read in silence the passage on which my eyes first fell ... I didn't want to read further, and there was no need ... Then I put my finger or some

other placeholder in the book [*interiecto aut digito aut nescio quo alio signo*], closed it, and with a calm expression on my face told Alypius [*indicavi Alypio*] what had happened. And he, for his part, told me [*sic indicavit*] what was happening in himself ... He asked to see what I had read. I showed him, but he looked beyond the sentence I had read. (conf. 8.12.29–30, trans. Ruden)

If earlier book openings help set up this shot, none matches it for visual and dramatic power. Despite focusing on biblical text and quotation, and despite its best translators (including the one quoted), the narrative climax of the *Tolle, lege* scene is a tour de force of telling about acts of seeing and showing that are performed *without* telling or any other kind of speaking. Reading the Latin strictly as written, we watch Augustine's hands take hold of the codex and open it, we track his gaze as he scans the biblical text, and we see him mark the place with his finger or in some other way as he closes the book. We catch a look on his face that signals to Alypius what has happened, a look on the face of Alypius that answers it, and the latter's gesture or motion to see the passage of text from which his friend has just looked away. And then, as Augustine reopens the book, we read over their shoulders as one of them, putting his finger down next to the other's, glances from the end of that chapter to the beginning of the following one. Alypius, we are told, understood the next of St. Paul's injunctions to apply to himself and conveyed his understanding to Augustine: literally, he "opened" that application of the passage to his coreader (*aperire* again). A moment later, the two of them are disclosing a twofold life-changing event to Monnica (*indicare* again). Only then, after a string of verbs of showing, seeking, and seeing that do not require any words to be spoken at all, does the narrator introduce an unmistakeable verb of telling [*narrare*] into his tale: "We *relate* how it happened." By now, the characters in the scene have moved out of shot, like couples or survivors at the end of a play by Shakespeare, exiting the stage to begin making fuller, shared sense of the action.

Reading books together, *simul legere libros*. Nowadays the *Confessions* is often read in groups or classes, just as Virgil's *Aeneid* was by Augustine's students and contemporaries. Any society with means to multiply accurate copies of a single text can create conditions under which two or more readers will be able to follow along word-by-word together. Any single text can easily be shared when recited aloud, its "readership" expanding to include persons who might not be able to read it for themselves even if they had a copy in their hands.

Such routines of socially *coordinated* reading, applied to more or less stable and authoritative texts ("literary," legal, religious, etc.), were fundamental to the working of Roman government and society in Augustine's day. They were part of a larger collective and continuous improvisation of the "Roman world" as a cognitive ecology. As noted earlier, the later decades of the fourth century CE brought forth some especially creative interventions in this area of cultural activity, not the least of them by Latin intellectuals interested in extending the written apparatus of a distinctively Christian (Roman) worldview. The *Confessions* fits that general picture. It stands out, however, for the emphasis that it places on the social and cognitive implications of a practice of *concerted* reading that appears, on the evidence of this text, to have arisen in response to the material and mechanical possibilities, or "affordances" of the codex-style, spine-hinged book.[7]

A book opening makes the narrow aperture in which the pivotal scene of the *Confessions* is windowed. While at a pinch one could imagine the climactic action being restaged with two actors who juggle a partly unrolled *volumen* between them, it is hard to see how any author would ever have been led to script it like that in the first place. Augustine's silent, freeze-frame scenography creates a moment that is almost outside time, and that took some doing. Only if the visual impact of the instant of embodied reading seems to stop the flow of narrative, linear, syllabic discourse will other readers, such as ourselves, be held – *simul*, together and at once – with Augustine and Alypius, in their microenvironment of a garden. The arresting moment is produced by an optical trick for which the codex, unlike the book-roll, was naturally adapted.

Such a multibodied act of seeing oneselves/ourselves at once in a book-borne text bears no obvious relation to Ambrose's steady, repeated reading for himself apart. The closer analog would be Alypius's sudden sight of the carnage of gladiatorial combat, making him instantly one with the crowd and less than human (*conf.* 6.8.13). Against that echoing public spectacle of beastly socialization, set at the monumental center of the Roman world, the domestic scene that turns on a parchment page of St. Paul at the turn of Romans 13/14 models an intimate experience of shared reading with power to suspend all worlds.

---

[7] "Affordances": Gibson, *The Ecological Approach to Visual Perception*, 127–143.

Further Reading

Augustine: Confessions, trans. S. Ruden. New York: Modern Library, 2017.

Brown, P. *Power and Persuasion: Towards a Christian Empire*. The Curti Lectures. Madison: University of Wisconsin Press, 1992.

Cameron, A. *Christianity and the Rhetoric of Empire: The Development of Christian Discourse*. Berkeley: University of California Press, 1991.

Conybeare, C. *The Routledge Guidebook to Augustine's Confessions*. London and New York: Routledge, 2016.

Conybeare, C. "Reading the *Confessions*." In *A Companion to Augustine*, ed. M. Vessey. Blackwell Companions to the Ancient World. Chichester: Wiley-Blackwell, 2012, 99–110.

Grafton, A. and M. Williams, *Christianity and the Transformation of the Book: Origen, Eusebius, and the Library of Caesarea*. Cambridge, MA: Harvard University Press, 2006.

Jager, E. *The Book of the Heart*. Chicago: University of Chicago Press, 2000.

Johnson, W. A. *Readers and Reading Culture in the High Roman Empire: A Study of Elite Communities*. Classical Culture and Society. Oxford: Oxford University Press, 2010.

Kaster, R. A. *Guardians of Language: The Grammarian and Society in Late Antiquity*. Transformation of the Classical Heritage 11. Berkeley: University of California Press, 1988.

Markus, R. A. *Signs and Meanings: World and Text in Ancient Christianity*. Liverpool: Liverpool University Press, 1996.

O'Donnell, J. J. *Augustine:* Confessions, three vols. Oxford: Clarendon, 1992.

Avatars of the Word: From Papyrus to Cyberspace. Cambridge, MA: Harvard University Press, 1998.

Piper, A. *Book Was There: Reading in Electronic Times*. Chicago: University of Chicago Press, 2012.

Stock, B. *Augustine the Reader: Meditation, Self-Knowledge, and the Ethics of Interpretation*. Cambridge, MA: Harvard University Press, 1996.

Vessey, M. "The History of the Book: Augustine's *City of God* and Post-Roman Cultural Memory." In *Augustine's City of God: A Critical Guide*, ed. J. Wetzel. Cambridge: Cambridge University Press, 2012, 14–32.

Zanker, P. *The Mask of Socrates: The Image of the Intellectual in Antiquity*, trans. P. Shapiro. Sather Classical Lectures 59. Berkeley: University of California Press, 1995.

A Bibliographical Note

For a comprehensive bibliography for Augustine, including that for the "Confessions," see:

Literaturdatenbank, Corpus Augustinianum Giessene CD-ROM accompanying *Augustinus-Lexikon*, www.augustinus.konkordanz.de/.

In addition to the items mentioned in Further Readings at the end of each chapter, please see:

Andersen, C. (ed.). *Bibliographia Augustiniana*. Darmstadt: Wissenschaftliche Buchgesellschaft, 1972.

van Bavel, T. *Répertoire Bibliographique de Saint Augustin 1950–1960*. Instrumenta patristica 3. Hague: Maritinus Nijhoff, 1963, especially 296–315.

Severson, R. J. *The Confessions of Saint Augustine: An Annotated Bibliography of Modern Criticism, 1888–1995*. Westport, CT: Greenwood, 1996, especially 44–52.

For particular words and terms, see:

Catalogus verborum VI: Confessionum Libri XIII. Thesaurus linguae Augustinianae. Eindhoven: PaysPas, 1989.

Cooper, R. H., L. C. Ferrari, P. M. Ruddock, and J. Robert Smith (eds.). *Concordantia in libros XIII confessionum S. Aurelii Augustini*, two vols. Hildesheim: Olms/Weidmann, 1991.

Index